WAL

KEYGUIDE

MALLORCA

49

CONTENTS

KEY TO SYMBOLS

✚ Map reference
✉ Address
☎ Telephone number
◷ Opening times
💵 Admission prices
Ⓜ Underground station
🚌 Bus number
🚆 Train station
⛴ Ferry/boat
🚗 Driving directions
ℹ Tourist office
🎫 Tours
📖 Guidebook
🍽 Restaurant
☕ Cafe
🍷 Bar
🏬 Shop
🛏 Number of rooms
❄ Air conditioning
🏊 Swimming pool
🏋 Gym
❓ Other useful information
▷ Cross reference
★ Walk/drive start point

Understanding Mallorca	**4**
Living Mallorca	13
The Story of Mallorca	25
On the Move	**37**
Arriving	38
Getting Around	40
Visitors with a Disability	48
Regions	**49**
Palma	**50**
Sights	57
Walks	74
What to Do	78
Eating	86
Staying	90
Serra de Tramuntana	**94**
Sights	97
Drives	114
Walk	118
What to Do	120
Eating	124
Staying	127
The Northeast	**130**
Sights	133
Drive	144
Walk	146
What to Do	148

Eating   152
Staying   155

The South   **158**
Sights   161
Drive   170
Walk   172
Bicycle Ride   174
What to Do   176
Eating   180
Staying   184

Practicalities   **187**

Maps   **218**

Index   **229**

94

140

172

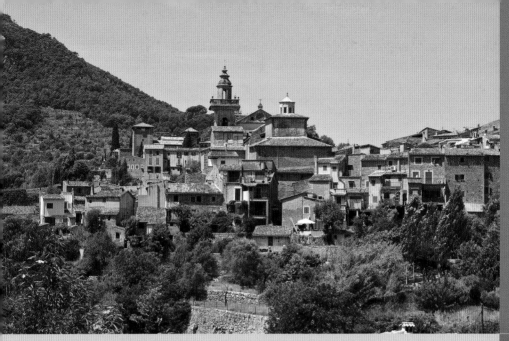

UNDERSTANDING

Understanding Mallorca is an introduction to the island, the geography, economy, history and its people. Living Mallorca gets under the skin of Mallorca today, while The Story of Mallorca takes you through the island's past.

Understanding Mallorca   6
    The Best of Mallorca   10

Living Mallorca   13

The Story of Mallorca   25

Mallorca is an extraordinarily diverse island with a landscape, history and culture that extends way beyond its primary reputation as a 'sunbed on the sand' holiday resort. Innovative architecture, sophisticated leisure and business facilities and an upsurge of picturesque rural accommodation have also helped to boost the island's reputation as a quality upmarket holiday destination. The island's diverse appeal encompasses spectacular scenery for outdoor enthusiasts, mild winter weather for golfers, gourmet restaurants for foodies, superb museums and galleries for culture enthusiasts and, of course, fabulous beaches and activities for children and families. Mallorca has a fascinating history with countless civilizations, from Roman to Moorish and Catalan to Spanish, leaving their mark here. Today, the island continues to absorb outside influences and maintain its position as one of Europe's most popular destinations, as well as a foreign resident haven, particularly among northern Europeans.

GEOGRAPHY

Mallorca (sometimes still known as Majorca) is the largest of the Balearic Islands (Illes Balears), which are situated off the east coast of Spain around 200km (124 miles) south of Barcelona. The other islands are Menorca, Ibiza and Formentera. Since 1983, the Balearics have been an autonomous region of Spain, with their capital in Palma.

Mallorca measures approximately 100km (62 miles) from east to west and 75km (47 miles) from north to south. The two main mountain ranges, the Serra de Tramuntana and Serra de Llevant, are divided by a fertile plain known as Es Pla. The Serra de Tramuntana runs along the north coast from Andratx to Pollença and includes the island's highest peak, Puig Major (1,447m/4,746ft).

The offshore islets of Cabrera (▷ 161) and Sa Dragonera (▷ 106–107) are nature reserves, which can be visited by boat. There are no rivers in Mallorca, though there are several torrents that rise in the mountains and swell after heavy rain.

PEOPLE

Mallorca has a population of around 767,000, of whom half live in the capital, Palma. The next largest towns are the industrial centres of Manacor (36,000) and Inca (25,000). Their populations increase significantly in summer, not just because of the number of visitors but also because of the many Spaniards and others who have second homes on the island. It is estimated that around 16 per cent of the permanent population of Mallorca are foreigners, including large numbers of British and German expatriates as well as migrant workers from Ecuador, Morocco and elsewhere.

There are churches, synagogues and mosques serving the various immigrant communities on the island, but the vast majority of the local population is Roman Catholic. However, as elsewhere in Spain, church attendance is in decline and Mallorca is now a largely secular and tolerant society. Although the many fiestas held in Mallorca's villages are religious in origin, they are now predominantly secular celebrations.

LANGUAGE

The official languages of Mallorca are Catalan and Castilian (Spanish). Most people actually speak Mallorquí, a local dialect of the Catalan language introduced by the Aragonese invaders in the 13th century. Since the death of General Franco in 1975 and the introduction of democracy to Spain, there has been a revival of regional languages and Mallorquí is once again the main language heard on the streets.

Most signposts and official notices are in Catalan, though you may see signs for both the *playa* (Spanish) and *platja* (Catalan), or for Puerto Pollensa (Spanish) and Port de Pollença (Catalan). The majority of place names in this book are given in Catalan, except where Spanish is in common use.

POLITICS

In political terms, Mallorca has been consistently out of step with mainland Spain. Shortly before José Luis Zapatero's Socialist party ousted the right-wing Partit Popular (PP) in the national elections of 2004, Mallorca's local government swung back to the PP, only to be overthrown in regional elections in 2007 by Socialist Francesc Antich, who formed a coalition government known as Mallorca's Bloc (Bloc per Mallorca).

ECONOMY

Tourism is the biggest industry on Mallorca, accounting for over two-thirds of jobs and around 72 per cent of the GDP (Gross Domestic Product). Over the past 40 years, Mallorca has become a byword for mass package holidays, and emerging leisure destinations often look to the island for guidance on how to create a successful tourism infrastructure. In recent years, Mallorca has also led the way in developing alternative forms of tourism.

As the holiday industry has grown in importance, agriculture has declined, though there are still significant crops of potatoes, vegetables and strawberries around Sa Pobla and oranges in the Sóller Valley. Other produce includes almonds, olives, olive oil and wine. There is little heavy industry, though tourism does support a substantial construction sector. Small-scale industries and crafts include the manufacture of leather goods, footwear, pottery, glassware and artificial pearls, much of which is sold at souvenir shops across the island.

MALLORCA TODAY

Mallorca in the 21st century is in a state of flux, with two apparently contrasting trends happening at the same time. On the one hand, the island is being steadily absorbed into the European mainstream, with the development of a multiracial society and the gradual erosion of the siesta in favour of more conventional business hours. The tourism industry is being driven upmarket, and the new hotels, congress centres, golf courses and marinas which have opened in recent years are virtually indistinguishable from their counterparts elsewhere. Alongside this, however, is a revival of island culture, seen in everything from art and music to language and cuisine, but most vividly in the traditional fiestas with their horned devils and giant carnival figures. Although these festivals attract huge numbers of visitors, they remain authentic village events at which everyone—

Opposite *The islet of Sa Dragonera, now a nature reserve, was used as a base by the pirate Redbeard in the 15th century*

COMMON TERMS

English	Catalan	Spanish
avenue	avinguda	avenida
beach	platja	playa
castle	castell	castillo
cave	cova	cueva
church	església	iglesia
market	mercat	mercado
monastery	monestir	monasterio
museum	museu	museo
palace	palau	palacio
square	plaça	plaza
street	carrer	calle

Mallorquíns, foreign residents and tourists—comes together to enjoy the fiesta spirit.

It is often said that the Mallorquíns share the Catalan capacity for exhibiting two conflicting sides to their character known as *seny* (common sense) and *rauxa* (emotion). Perhaps this helps to explain how they can party all night and still go to work in the morning, or how they manage to combine long working hours and one of the highest GDPs in Europe with an ability to find time for the important things in life, such as family, friends and long lunches by the sea. Today's Mallorquí entrepreneurs know how to get things done when they need to, but they are just as likely to shrug you off with a reply of *tanmateix*, an expression best translated as 'oh well' or 'all the same'.

HOW TO ENJOY MALLORCA

Many people spend their entire holiday in a self-contained beach resort, rarely venturing beyond the hotel pool except perhaps on an organized coach excursion to discover 'the real Mallorca' in the company of a guide. This is fine, but you will get much more out of the island if you explore it by yourself, either by hire car, bicycle or public transport (▷ 40–47). Mallorca is easy to get around and its small size means that even on a short visit it is possible to get to know each of its regions, spending your mornings visiting museums and markets or walking in the mountains and your afternoons on the beach. It obviously helps if you can speak some Catalan or Spanish, but most people are happy to help visitors and even in the smallest villages you will usually find someone who speaks English.

The other way to get the most out of your stay is to adopt the local attitude to time. Don't try to cram too much into the day; instead, relax, take things slowly and be spontaneous. You will always find a restaurant willing to serve you at northern European hours, but remember that few locals eat lunch before 1.30pm or dinner before 9pm. The early evening is for strolling, for putting on your smartest casuals and indulging in that delightful Spanish ritual called the *paseo* (*passeig* in Mallorquí). If you want to meet the locals, there's no better way.

MALLORCA'S REGIONS

The sights in this book are divided into four geographical regions, though these do not correspond to the island's administrative districts.

Palma encompasses the capital city, plus some of Mallorca's best known and busiest beach resorts. Palma is a truly lovely city, exuding sophistication and a vibrant street life against a backdrop of gracious ochre buildings, picturesque plazas and striking modern architecture. Home to the classiest nightlife and shopping on the

island, plus superb hotels and restaurants, Palma is also a city that is sufficiently compact for strolling. The resorts on either side of the bay, from S'Arenal to the east and Magaluf to the west, were some of the earliest in Mallorca and they are still crowded out with visitors in summer. Alongside these popular resorts are some of Mallorca's most exclusive communities, largely populated by a yachting crowd.

The Serra de Tramuntana is Mallorca's highest mountain range, running the length of the northwest coast. In many people's opinion this is the most enchanting part of the island. It is a region of stark, dramatic landscapes, and a vast outdoor playground offering superb opportunities for walking and rock-climbing. It contains Mallorca's most sacred site at Lluc (▷ 102–105), one of its prettiest villages, Deià (▷ 98), and a charming town, Sóller (▷ 108–109), nestling in a valley of orange trees. Small, luxurious hotels and excellent restaurants are scattered conveniently throughout the Serra de Tramuntana, making a driving tour of the mountains one of the joys of a Mallorcan holiday. Tourism is the Serra de Tramuntana's principal

Top *A monk parakeet at Santa Ponça*
Left *Windmills near Sa Pobla, north of Muro*
Opposite *The family-friendly resort of Porto Cristo*

source of income and its narrow, twisting roads become very busy in summer; the best times to explore are late spring and early autumn.

The Northeast has some of Mallorca's best beaches, along with a trio of historic towns—Alcúdia (▷ 133–134), Artà (▷ 135) and Pollença (▷ 140–143). The coastline is dominated by the great bay of Alcúdia, where, to the east, long beaches back onto dunes and marshland, favoured by birdwatchers from across Europe for the variety of birdlife. Among the other attractions of this region are the rugged peninsula of Formentor (▷ 138) and the cave systems at Artà and Campanet (▷ 137). The west of this region, Pollença especially, is popular with British holidaymakers and expatriates, while the east of the region, southward from Cala Ratjada, has a high proportion of German businesses.

The South is the rural heartland of Mallorca. The fertile plain at the centre of the island produces most of Mallorca's crops, sold in traditional country markets such as Sineu (▷ 167). Almond orchards blossoming in February are always an impressive sight. Creeks and coves indent the southeast coast, while the south coast is relatively undeveloped, especially around the magnificent dune-backed beach of Es Trenc (▷ 166). The small towns of the south receive few visitors and are ideal for soaking up the atmosphere of everyday Mallorca. Key attractions are the historic town of Petra (▷ 168) and the east coast's caves (▷ 164–165).

SERRA DE TRAMUNTANA

NORTHEAST

PALMA

SOUTH

Cabrera

PALMA

Abaco, Palma (▷ 79) Forget the prices, you'll gasp at Abaco's surreal opulence.

Abraxas, Palma (▷ 80) Clubbers dress up for the most stylish nightclub on the island.

La Bodeguilla, Palma (▷ 87) Spanish cuisine is skilfully prepared at this restaurant which has its own wine merchant.

La Bóveda, Palma (▷ 87) Queues form outside Mallorca's best tapas bar on weekend evenings, but it's worth the wait.

Dalt Murada, Palma (▷ 91) You'll get gorgeous, faded splendour for a bargain price at this town-house hotel behind Palma's cathedral.

Frasquet, Palma (▷ 78–79) Enter an ornate world of chocolate and temptation at Palma's top sweet shop.

Fundació Joan Miró, Palma (▷ 62) This modern museum is dedicated to Mallorca's favourite adopted artist.

Illetes (▷ 58) Locals prefer this small beach in the Bay of Palma to its commercialized neighbours.

Jazz Voyeur Club, Palma (▷ 81) It's small, dark and high-spirited—as a good jazz club should be.

Museu Es Baluard, Palma (▷ 63) Modern art is juxtaposed with solid military architecture at this new museum, with the cathedral looming in the background.

Palacio Ca Sa Galesa, Palma (▷ 92–93). This palatial town-house hotel has its own art collection.

Pirates Adventure (▷ 81) Acrobatic pirates host this bawdy show in Magaluf.

Santa Catalina market, Palma (▷ 75) Browse the stalls at this fascinating covered market in a lively district of Palma.

Simply Fosh, Palma (▷ 89) Run by Marc Fosh, the island's most celebrated Michelin chef (ex-Read's Hotel), this special-occasion restaurant won't disappoint.

Summer concerts at Castell de Bellver (▷ 85) Classical music is showcased at the Castell in this annual summer festival.

SERRA DE TRAMUNTANA

Café Sóller, Sóller (▷ 122) Enjoy tapas and drinks at the hub of Sóller's nightlife.

Ca's Xorc, Sóller (▷ 129) Make the effort to reach this luxurious celeb hang-out at the top of a mountain.

Ca N'Alluny (▷ 98) Robert Graves' home in Deià has been opened as a delightful museum.

Deià (▷ 98) Robert Graves put Deià's golden buildings on the tourist trail.

Finca Gourmet, Sóller (▷ 122–123) Souvenir hunting? Try some of Mallorca's seasonal specialities at this delightful delicatessen.

Fornalutx (▷ 109) Regularly voted Spain's prettiest village, Fornalutx doesn't disappoint.

Hiking Complete a section of the Dry Stone Route (▷ 21) on foot in the Serra de Tramuntana.

Orient (▷ 101) Orient is a picturesque place for a pit stop on a tour of the Serra de Tramuntana.

Read's Hotel, Santa Maria del Camí (▷ 129) The British chef at this exclusive hotel creates dishes that live up to the fabulously decorated dining room.

THE NORTHEAST

Can Planes, Sa Pobla (▷ 139) Toys are the highlight of this quirky museum in an otherwise unassuming rural town.

Cas Ferrer Nou Hotelet, Alcúdia (▷ 155) This small converted blacksmith's is a quiet and elegant hotel.

Formentor (▷ 138) Once the preserve of a local hotel, this narrow, idyllic stretch of pine-backed sand is open to all now.

Golf Play a round at one of Mallorca's toughest and prettiest courses, Canyamel Golf (▷ 149–150).

Hotel Juma, Pollença (▷ 157) Overlooking the town's main plaza, this historic hotel is great for people watching.

Illa d'Or, Port de Pollença (▷ 157) Call it old-fashioned, but this hotel still sets high standards and is perfectly placed.

Museu de Pollença, Pollença (▷ 142) An eclectic account of Pollença's history and residents can be found in this former convent.

Pollença and Alcúdia bays There's plenty of space and lots of watersports on some of Mallorca's best long beaches.

Sailing Hire a dinghy and learn a new skill with friends or family in Port de Pollença's sheltered bay (▷ 150).

Satyricon, Alcúdia (▷ 153) Wonder at the stunning faux Roman decor at this exciting new restaurant in a former art deco cinema.

Ses Rotges, Cala Ratjada (▷ 156) This French-owned restaurant is a fine-dining favourite with Cala Ratjada's German expats and holidaymakers.

THE SOUTH

Cala Mondragó (▷ 162) A pair of pretty coves are found in a protected natural reserve on the otherwise heavily developed east coast.

Camper Factory Shop, Inca (▷ 177) Camper's trendy shoes for men and women can be bought at bargain prices at this factory outlet.

Es Celler, Petra (▷ 181–182) Watch your meal being barbecued at this traditional *celler* restaurant. Don't miss the almond cake for dessert.

Es 4 Vents, Algaida (▷ 180) Mallorcan families congregate at this roadside restaurant on Sundays for outstanding cooking.

Es Trenc (▷ 166) Chill out on Mallorca's most bohemian beach; clothes are optional.

Sa Plaça, Petra (▷ 182) This modest hotel is situated on the pretty main square and exudes an atmospheric old-fashioned charm.

Vidrerías Gordiola, Algaida (▷ 176) Watch artisans create Mallorca's famous glassware, then buy it at a discount.

Opposite *Platja de Mura, Alcúdia Bay*
Below left *The arcaded courtyard of Castell de Bellver*
Below right *Fornalutx calls itself the prettiest village in Spain*

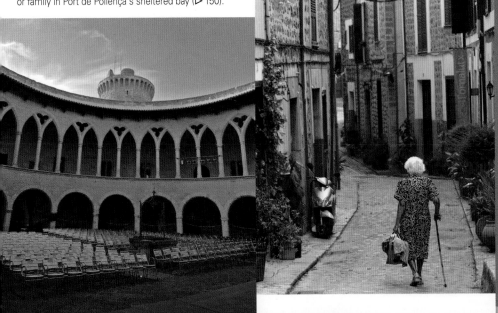

TOP EXPERIENCES

Marvel at the underwater magic of Palma's magnificent new aquarium, one of the best in Europe (▷ 68).

Watch a demonstration of traditional dancing and crafts at La Granja, a converted farmstead in the mountains that children will love (▷ 99).

Savour a Mallorcan speciality—*pa amb oli* for a snack, *tumbet* for vegetarians, baked sea bass in rock salt for fish-lovers and almond cake for all (▷ 210).

Sample the latest Mallorcan wines at a new-wave *bodega* in Binissalem (▷ 161), where some of Mallorca's best wines are produced.

Go caving, but there's no need to get cold and wet in Mallorca's famous limestone caves, which have sound and light shows in their enormous caverns (▷ 164–165).

Worship the sun on one of Mallorca's many dazzling beaches. You can still find remote, undeveloped stretches of sand.

Take a trip back in time and ride the vintage train from Palma to Sóller (▷ 42) through fruit tree plantations, then hop on a tram to Port de Sóller for an afternoon on the beach.

Spot black vultures at the Cúber reservoir (▷ 117), where the rare birds soar on thermals of rising air and scour the mountains for food.

Explore Palma's Modernist buildings (▷ 74–75), stopping for a pastry from the art deco-fronted Forn des Teatre shop.

Find Robert Graves' grave, which bears the simple epitaph 'Poet', in Deià's churchyard (▷ 98).

Spend a night in a hilltop monastery; the monks at Lluc monastery (▷ 213), and others, welcome respectful overnight guests.

Nose around some of the spectacular hidden courtyards in the back streets of Palma; not all are open to the public but you can peer through the wrought-iron gates.

People-watch on the Passeig Marítim on Saturday night when Palma's party crowd show off on the seafront (▷ 69).

Explore the villages of the Tramuntana foothills on a bicycle (▷ 46): a tour of Bunyola, Alaró, Biniamar, Moscari and Campanet makes a challenging day out.

Eat a first-rate meal with an unbeatable view: Ca's Xorc (▷ 129), Es Faro (▷ 125) and Bens d'Avall (▷ 126) all have absolutely stunning vistas.

Follow the twisting road out to the lighthouse at Cap de Formentor (▷ 138), where the Serra de Tramuntana finally drops into the sea.

Go hiking (▷ 21, 203 and 214) in the craggy mountains of the Serra de Tramuntana and breathe in the aroma of pine woods and wild herbs.

Spend Sunday morning in the market at Pollença (▷ 140–143), then climb the long, cypress-lined staircase to the Calvari chapel above the town.

Combine luxury with rural tranquillity by spending a night at one of the new breed of upmarket country hotels (▷ 212–213) springing up across the island.

Soak up the vibe of modern Palma with a visit to the Museu Es Baluard (▷ 63), then have a drink on the sculpture terrace overlooking the bay.

Left *A potter demonstrating his art at La Granja*
Below *Sailing is a popular pastime on Mallorca*

LIVING MALLORCA

Surviving Tourism	14
Arts and Architecture	16
Celebrity Island	18
The Great Outdoors	20
Living Traditions	22
Balearic Renaissance	24

Since the 1960s, the population has doubled in Mallorca; a statistic closely tied to the fact that this was also the decade that marked the onset of package tourism to the island, making it one of the wealthiest regions in Spain, and accounting for 80 per cent of the island's income. Unsurprisingly, such an important source of money has become closely tied to local politics. The government of the Balearic Islands has a degree of autonomy and can introduce measures—such as the now-defunct eco-tax on tourists—which affect tourism revenue. Islanders have to decide how best to manage the tourist industry and have to find a balance between encouraging ever-increasing numbers of visitors and preserving the very things, such as clean beaches and beautiful mountain landscapes, that attract people in the first place. Tourism also caused massive social upheaval in Mallorca. For centuries the island's economy was based on agriculture; it was said that in Mallorca's fields 'children worked like women, women worked like men and men worked like Titans'. In landowning families the most fertile and profitable land—always the farmland in the interior—was handed down to the eldest son, whereas coastal land was worthless. Within one generation tourism turned society upside down: building on the coast yielded huge returns, whereas in comparison cultivating almonds, olives and oranges inland seemed like hard work for little reward. Today a mere 1 per cent of the GDP comes from agriculture.

PACKAGING PARADISE
In 1960, 250,000 tourists arrived in Mallorca and the advent of affordable package holidays meant that the island was no longer the preserve of the wealthy. Today, more than 7 million people annually take their holidays on the island— and they have to have somewhere to sleep. In 1960 there were around 20,000 hotel beds, but today the figure is nearer 300,000. As befits an island that started the world's first tourist board, Mallorca has been in the vanguard of mass tourism. It's made mistakes, such as piling people into ugly, high-rise hotels, but it's also had the wisdom to rectify those mistakes. As more people book their holidays independently and the package deal loses its appeal, Mallorca is pulling down its cheap, concrete hotels and developing smaller, stylish hotels away from the main resorts.

Clockwise from above *The Jardines de Alfàbia take their name from the Arabic* 'al fabi'*, which means* '*jar of olives'; the white-arched cloisters of the Reial Cartoixa in Valldemossa; Peguera was the first resort on Mallorca to have its own artificial beach*

AGROTURISMO

The persistent image of Mallorca as a high-rise hell of concrete beachfront resorts is out of date. Look away from the coast and you'll find that the accommodation Mallorca offers is changing swiftly. The biggest development in recent years has been *agroturismo* (rural tourism): government policies have encouraged farmers and house owners inland to convert their properties into small hotels. There are now more than 120 rural properties in the scheme (▷ 212–213), from *grandes hoteles rurales* to humbler *agroturismos* (often working farms) and renovated town-house hotels. All offer something special, whether it is sumptuous bedrooms in an old manor house, fantastic Mallorcan cooking, or simply the chance to stay in glorious silence deep in the countryside.

TOAD IN A HOLE

There is no more amazing survivor than the critically endangered Mallorcan midwife toad. Long thought extinct, a pocket of surviving toads was discovered high in the Serra de Tramuntana in 1980. The mountain range is the only place in the world where this diminutive 3.5cm (1.5in) amphibian lives; a tadpole-breeding programme by Gerald Durrell's Wildlife Conservation Trust has returned many young *ferrerets* (the toad's local name) to remote mountain-top crevices. The species is unusual because once the female has laid her eggs, the male takes over, winding the strings of eggs around his legs and nurturing them until they hatch. It is hoped that more populations of this toad, a special part of Mallorca's natural heritage, will be established around the island in spite of mass tourism.

MONEY, MONEY

Money talks, and nowhere can you hear it speaking louder than in the yacht clubs and marinas of the Bay of Palma. The island has 20,000 yacht moorings and Palma is one of the largest and most prestigious marinas in Europe. Harbours such as Puerto Portals are where the rich and famous berth their magnificent yachts for the summer. Here they have all their essential support services: designer boutiques, hideously expensive restaurants and luxury apartments. But what makes Mallorca unusual is that the super-rich and the average holidaymaker co-exist in close proximity. One minute you can be in chic Portals Nous, but walk around the next point and you'll be among the theme pubs and souvenir shops of Magaluf.

MALLORCA AND THE ENVIRONMENT

To replace the unpopular eco-tax that surfaced, and sank, briefly in 2002, Mallorca has introduced a Green Card that offers various admission discounts with funds raised going towards environmental projects and sustainable development (▷ 196). There has also been a drive to preserve more green areas on the island with the result that, currently, around 40 per cent of the land mass is protected, including the Illa de Cabrera archipelago. Endangered species, including birds, tortoises and the midwife toad are increasing in number due to conservation funding and efforts, while environmental groups continue to canvas for building restrictions, particularly those involving golf courses.

There's much more to Mallorca than sunshine and sand: the arts and artists thrive on the island and contemporary culture is as strong now as it has ever been. Two auditoriums, in Alcúdia and Cala Millor, host theatre, dance and musical productions, and Palma's auditorium attracts high-profile performers to its adventurous seasonal programmes. There are 10 cultural centres in Palma alone, with modern art in the city's galleries and Modernist architecture in its streets. This wealth of art and culture is not restricted to Palma. Throughout the island there are towns and villages where visitors can enjoy the arts, ranging from the famous mountain village of Deià to the east coast town of Artà, where several (mainly German) artists have set up art galleries. Traditional performances at festivals throughout the year (▷ 207) make for interesting days out, while crafts such as glass-blowing and the making of clay whistles *(siurells)* are continued for the benefit of tourists. So, if you fancy a break from the beaches, you can always hunt down paintings by Picasso, sculptures by Rodin and buildings by Gaudí.

MIRÓ IN MALLORCA
Evidence of Joan Miró's (1893–1983) impact in Mallorca is everywhere: the mural in the Parc de la Mar (▷ 69), an urban space in front of Palma's cathedral, is based on his art. And, if you use the Spanish or Mallorcan tourist boards, you will spot his own work; he designed their logos. The Barcelona-born artist moved to Mallorca in 1956 and the island has claimed him as its own. Prior to settling in Mallorca he had explored Dadaism and Surrealism, but his work post-1960 is characterized by bold, colourful, but precise paintings; he is regarded as a father of Abstract Expressionism. You'll also find sculptures by Miró in the King's Garden in Palma and more work at his former studio, now a museum (▷ 62).

Clockwise from above Evocative statuary in the grounds of La Granja; detail of Gaudí's impressive canopy in Palma Cathedral; inside elegant Can Marquès, a rare seigneurial mansion in Palma

MALLORCA TO MALI

Miquel Barceló is the most celebrated contemporary Mallorcan artist—and the most adventurous. He was born in Felanitx in 1957 and studied at the Arts and Crafts School of Palma. Notable for being the youngest painter to have exhibited at the Louvre in Paris, Barceló's larger paintings can sell for almost £1 million—and he also creates sculptures and pottery. Clear traces of Spain's artistic traditions, such as mysticism and fatalism, can be seen in his figurative work, but look closely at the subject matter—goats, insects and skulls—and you'll find clues to his second home outside Mallorca. In 1988 Barceló crossed the Sahara and settled in Mali, where he built his own hut in a Dogon village in the desert.

THROUGH THE KEYHOLE

The old town of Palma, the streets around the cathedral, is the perfect place for nosing around other people's houses. The area is packed with the mansions of Palma's movers and shakers, and when the owners move on, many of their residences are opened for all to see. One of the most intriguing houses to be restored is Can Marquès (▷ 59), once the home of a rich coffee merchant, and you can still appreciate his taste in interior design and art. The wallpaper dates from the 19th century and the Modernist staircase is marvellous. But the centrepiece of any Mallorcan town house is its courtyard, invariably a feast of graceful sandstone arches, staircases and exotic foliage—all of which you can spy from the doorways on the street.

SHADY DEALINGS

The March family is to Mallorca what the Guggenheim family is to New York: enormously wealthy, influential philanthropists. In 2003 the family mansion, Palau March, opened to the public and immediately dazzled visitors. The linchpin of the March empire was Joan March, born in Santa Margalida in 1880. Having amassed a huge personal fortune that made him one of the world's richest men during Franco's regime, he spent much of it on art (▷ 67). But there are increasing indications that some of his early wealth was based on tobacco smuggling and arms dealing. Accounting books have been discovered that detail, under the heading 'Tobacco Expenses 1902', the bribes to be paid to policemen: sergeants pocketed 150 pesetas. There are even payments to spies listed, some of whom charged 50 pesetas for their services.

GAUDÍ'S SIGNATURE

In some respects Palma resembles a miniature Barcelona. Both are attractive cities with a strong Catalan culture, famous shopping streets and spectacular cathedrals by Antoni Gaudí. In 1904 Gaudí was commissioned to restore Palma's Gothic cathedral and during the 10 years he spent working on the interior his presence in the city undoubtedly helped fire the imagination of Mallorcan architects and designers. Soon Modernism's motifs—natural imagery, elaborate ironwork, colourful tiling—were appearing on buildings everywhere. Gaudí's assistant Joan Rubió designed some of the Modernist landmarks in Mallorca, while another Catalan architect, Lluís Domènech i Montaner, created the most famous Modernist building in Palma—the Fundació La Caixa, previously the Gran Hotel (▷ 63).

Mallorca has long been a rich hunting ground for paparazzi. The island attracts an eclectic mix of celebrities and you can see many of their famous haunts today. Australian-born American actor Errol Flynn was arguably the island's first lager lout, raising hell at the Bon Sol hotel in the 1950s. Rock stars, such as Rod Stewart, Annie Lennox and Elton John, have also let their hair down on the island, and Mallorca is even more popular with actors: Alec Guinness, Jack Nicholson, Charlie Chaplin, Peter Ustinov, Grace Kelly and Ava Gardner have all stayed. Michael Douglas liked Mallorca so much he opened a visitor centre in Valldemossa. Couples, from Frédéric Chopin and George Sand to Antonio Banderas and Melanie Griffiths, come and go. Royalty, racing-car drivers and Richard Branson have all bought property in Mallorca—although the British business tycoon has now sold La Residencia, his exclusive hotel in Deià. Writers make up a significant contingent of visitors to Mallorca. Both Kingsley Amis and Gabriel García Márquez made short pilgrimages to Robert Graves' home in Deià and Agatha Christie was a regular guest at the Hotel Formentor, setting a short story in nearby Pollença Bay. It all adds up to a lot of free publicity for the island.

SUN, SAND AND CHOPIN

George Sand (the pen name of Aurore, Baronne Dudevant) and her lover Frédéric Chopin retreated to Valldemossa (▷ 110–113) in 1838 in the hope of improving the tubercular composer's health. It wasn't successful: his favourite Pleyel piano failed to arrive and he was forced to compose *Preludes, Op. 28* on a ropey local instrument. The Mallorcans were unfriendly to the couple, the relationship foundered and a bitter Sand wrote about the experience in *A Winter in Majorca*, a book that is still proudly sold throughout the island despite being a dispiriting tale of miserable weather, truculent locals and primitive conditions: how it became such a central part of the marketing of Mallorca remains a mystery.

Clockwise from above The Spanish royal family frequently spend their summer holidays on Mallorca; Camp de Mar is a fast-growing resort; Ca N'Alluny—Robert Graves' house in Deià—is now a museum

TOP MODELS TO TENNIS CHAMPS

Of the 50,000 Germans who call Mallorca home, former supermodel Claudia Schiffer is perhaps the most eye-catching. For several years she has owned a hilltop apartment in the upmarket, celeb-friendly resort of Camp de Mar, where neighbouring residents include Formula One star Michael Schumacher. Claudia is rumoured to have spent £6 million on her apartment here, which is not so unusual on an island where you won't find many houses for sale under £100,000. Spain's star tennis player Rafael Nadal is a native of Manacor. His father Sebastian is a business partner with two brothers in running a restaurant, Sa Punta in Port Verd. Other celebrities with a home here include Anna Friel, Andrew Lloyd Webber, poet Roger McGough and the Corrs' drummer, Caroline Corr.

HOLLYWOOD GLAMOUR

You're a world-famous film star, with Catherine Zeta-Jones for a wife, and a young family. What do you do with your spare time? Well, if you're Michael Douglas you represent Mallorca's tourist board. In 2003 he agreed to become the world's glitziest ambassador, promoting Mallorca at unglamourous travel trade fairs around the world for four years. There's no doubt Douglas loves the island: in the 1980s he bought the S'Estaca estate, which was once owned by Archduke Ludwig Salvator, and in 2000 he opened Costa Nord (▷ 113), a cultural centre in Valldemossa, devoted to the Serra de Tramuntana. Here, every summer, he hosts the eclectic Mediterranean Nights arts festival, with a line-up that reflects new musical trends and a great fusion of styles and traditions.

INSPIRATION IN DEIÀ

A rather happier literary connection occurred just up the road from Valldemossa in Deià (▷ 98). Having lived briefly in Mallorca with Laura Riding, the poet Robert Graves (1895–1985) moved to the island permanently in 1946 with his second wife, Beryl Hodge (1915–2003). They settled in Deià, in a house called Ca N'Alluny. As readers of Graves' *The White Goddess* know, the prolific writer argued that female muses were essential for a poet's inspiration; while Graves laboured over some of his most distinctive love poems, his wife tolerated the steady stream of muses passing through their house.

ROYAL RETREAT

For such a small island, Mallorca has a high concentration of royal visitors. When King Juan Carlos of Spain was still a prince, a group of local businessmen presented him with the Palau Marivent, a glorious Moorish palace next to Palma's cathedral. It has been his summer retreat ever since, and venue for some of Palma's most elegant soirées. The king, a keen sailor, crosses the road to his favourite hang-out, Palma's Real Club Náutico. He's a patron of the club's Copa del Rey sailing regatta (▷ 85). He's not the only keen royal sailor: King Harald of Norway is a regular visitor too.

It's no exaggeration to say that, whatever your sporting interests, you'll find a way to pursue them in Mallorca. Whether you're into cliff diving or rock climbing, the island has an excellent infrastructure for sports. But it does specialize in a few: golf, bicycling and most watersports. Hiking in the mountains is a major activity in autumn, winter and spring. There are 20 top-class golf courses in Mallorca, and a dozen yacht clubs, 10 horse-riding schools, 6 kayaking schools and 1 wrestling pavilion. Perhaps the most visible sport in Mallorca is bicycling (▷ 202). Northern European bicyclists visit the island for winter training sessions and many hotels provide special facilities for bicyclists. Casual bicyclists can hire bicycles throughout the island, but shouldn't expect to emulate the professionals, who scarcely seem to notice that the roads of the Serra de Tramuntana mountains have gradients. Yachting is another high-profile sport, with clubs and schools around the coast offering tuition and charters. Dinghies and wind- and kite-surfers can be hired from most beaches. Less active pursuits in Mallorca include birdwatching, at places such as the marshes of S'Albufera wildlife park. Or you can stick to a gentle game of beach volleyball.

FLYING HIGH
With a wingspan of 3m (9ft), the black vulture is Europe's largest bird of prey—with a lifespan of 40 years. Impressive it may be, but only a handful remain in existence: some in mainland Spain and about 100 in Mallorca. The birds congregate around Lluc Monastery (▷ 102–105) in the Serra de Tramuntana and you'll probably spot them soaring on the thermals above the Cúber and Gorg Blau reservoirs. Mallorca is one of Europe's best birdwatching locations, so there's plenty of other birdlife worth looking out for, too. Resident and migrant species include Eleonora's falcons, marsh harriers, hoopoes, egrets, bitterns, eagles, greater flamingoes and the purple swamp hen.

Clockwise from above Fishing in Port de Pollença; jet-skiing is just one of many watersports on offer; *Mallorca has excellent bicycling opportunities across the island*

THE KING'S CUP

Palma's status as the capital of Mediterranean yachting was confirmed by the creation of the Copa del Rey competition in 1982. The regatta was founded by the Real Club Náutico and benefited from a blend of factors: offshore sailing conditions are superb; the marina is close to the centre of the city and the Spanish royal family are fanatical about the club, the city and the sport. The event's royal patronage is key to its success. In 2008, the regatta marked its 25th anniversary with the king and his son Prince Felipe competing in the race together. The competition showcases two races each day for a week with prizes awarded in each event. Palma's year-round tropical climate, miles of open Mediterranean sea and the position of the Bay of Palma all help fuel the love of sailing here.

PEDAL POWER

Visit Mallorca in winter or spring and you'll find the roads teeming with bicyclists on the mountain roads. Professional teams, such as T-Mobile, amateur clubs and keen individuals all come to the island to train. Noticing this rapidly growing group of visitors, the government of the Balearic Islands stepped in to co-sponsor a Spanish road-bicycling team in 2003, putting up most of the multi-million-euro budget. Now named Illes Balears-Caisse d'Épargne, the professional team, made up of mainly Spanish and some Mallorcan riders, competes in top races. It got off to a flying start in its inaugural season, winning the annual five-day Tour of Mallorca in February 2004. However, the team failed to win in 2005 and 2006, and the title was reversed to Caisse d'Epargne-Illes Balears.

WALK THIS WAY

La Ruta de Pedra en Sec, the Dry Stone Route for walkers, (▷ 120), is a 150km (93-mile) path from Andratx to Pollença in the east, passing through some of the prettiest towns and villages, including Sóller, Deià and Escorca. It runs mainly via historic bridleways that cling to the higher peaks of the mountain range. It's divided into eight stages and, at the end of each stage, hikers can use the refuges run by the Consell de Mallorca (book in advance). The route can be walked partially or as a whole, allowing hikers to tailor it to their own needs. A reasonable level of fitness is required, as well as good walking boots and certain essentials, including a water bottle, compass and map. Check www.conselldemallorca.net/mediambient/pedra.

ALMONDS, ALMONDS, EVERYWHERE

There's much to thank the humble almond tree for. Mallorca's traditional dessert, almond cake, is on most menus and you'll also be tempted by almond ice cream, almond milk and almond milk liqueur, crushed almonds as garnishes and almond sweets. In fact, although the Moors brought the almond tree to Spain centuries ago, it wasn't until the last 200 years that almond cultivation became widespread in Mallorca. Now, although almond farming has suffered a downturn, the orchards will be preserved. And this is what visitors to Mallorca will be most grateful for, because in January and February white blossom blows in the wind like snowflakes and carpets the countryside.

One of the most striking aspects of modern Mallorca is the way in which age-old festivals and traditions have survived and adapted in the face of threats from Fascism, global culture and the decline of the Catholic faith. During the Franco dictatorship traditional folk dances were discouraged because of their sensual nature and pagan roots, or sanitized and turned into tourist-oriented folklore performances, yet now they are once again seen at village fiestas. Many festivals are religious in origin, usually based around a local saint's day, yet as church attendance declines, the fiestas grow in popularity, with bonfires, street parties, pop concerts and sports competitions alongside traditional religious processions. Even the *romería*, an annual pilgrimage to a local shrine, is a jolly community occasion with music, dancing and a picnic. The fact that every town or village in Mallorca outside Palma has a saint's day during the summer months suggests that this is merely a return to the days when each village celebrated the harvest. Other traditions are still deeply religious. At midnight on Christmas Eve in churches across the island, a young boy dressed in a tunic and holding a sword sings the *Cant de la Sibilla*, a medieval chant foretelling the end of the world.

DEVIL OF A TIME
Horned and masked *dimonis* (devils) are an integral part of many Mallorcan festivals. At one stage, these eye-catching characters were banned by the Catholic Church but they are now tolerated as harmless fun—even if they do occasionally frighten the children. Ironically, their original purpose was probably religious, to symbolize the battle between good and evil. One of the oldest traditions in Mallorca is the *cossiers* dance, performed at Algaida and Montuïri and possibly dating back to Moorish times. Six men and one woman, dressed in white and with bells sewn onto their tights, dance while the devil tries to disrupt them with impudent remarks. The woman, symbolizing virtue, leads the fight against the devil and, of course, triumphs in the end.

Clockwise from above *Re-enactment of the Moors versus the Christians battle in Pollença; dressing up as a* dimoni *is an essential part of many traditional festivals; Mallorca's famous* siurells—*distinctive clay figurines with whistles, in white with red and green flashes*

SIURELLS

The miniature earthenware figures known as *siurells* have been made in Mallorca since Moorish times. Painted white with bright flashes of red and green, they typically take the form of a man on horseback or playing a guitar, but more unusual designs might include *dimonis* (devils) or even cars and planes. Every *siurell* incorporates a crude whistle at its base, making them great gifts for children. Although you can buy *siurells* in souvenir shops across the island, it is more rewarding to make the trip to the villages of Sa Cabaneta and Pòrtol, where you can still find artists making and painting the figures by hand. While you are there, look into the Museu del Fang (Pottery Museum), inside an old windmill in Sa Cabaneta, with its exhibition of around 900 ceramic pieces.

TIR DE FONA

The ancient art of the *foners* (Balearic slingers), banned under Franco, has been revived and the slingshot is now taught in Mallorcan schools—using tennis balls instead of stones. There are active clubs in Palma, Sóller, Lloseta, Sa Pobla and Campanet, and regular competitions are held. The leading slinger of the modern era is Joan Guerrero of Lloseta, who was Mallorcan champion 10 times between 1990 and 2002. Antonia Reynes Pons of Campanet has won the women's title eight times. To find out when the slingers are in action, ask at the Bar Espanya, Carrer dels Oms 31, Palma (tel 971 726250), or check out www.tirdefona.com.

PILGRIMAGE TO LLUC

One night in 1974, Tolo Guëll and friends set off from Bar Guëll in Palma to walk the 48km (30 miles) to Lluc Monastery. The following year they made the trip again, joined by more friends, and more the year after that, until the overnight pilgrimage had grown into a mass movement. Some people participate to give thanks for recovery from illness or for the birth of a child, others join in for the camaraderie. All night long, spectators line the route offering food and drink to tired walkers. In 1985 up to 40,000 people took part; in 1993 King Juan Carlos gave the traditional greeting. The pilgrimage takes place on the first Saturday in August, leaving Palma at 11pm.

TORO TORO

There is very little tradition of bullfighting in Mallorca— it has a much greater following in southern Spain than in the Catalan-speaking regions—but bullfights are held once a year during the patronal festivals at Muro and Felanitx. The bullring at Muro is a spectacular sight, chiselled out of the white rock in a former sandstone quarry between 1910 and 1920, with seats for 6,000 spectators. In the past, Muro had its own version of the bullfight, pitting bulls against hounds; these days a more conventional *corrida* takes place during the feast of Sant Joan Baptista on 24 June. Similarly, the bullring at Felanitx is used once a year during the festival of Sant Agustí on 28 August.

Ever since the Balearic Islands gained regional autonomy on 22 February 1983, Mallorcans' pride in their island has been resurgent. During General Franco's regime regional identities in Spain were suppressed: local dialects such as Mallorquí were banned and traditional fiestas were cancelled. However, since 1983 the Mallorquí language, a Catalan dialect, has been reinstated as the island's official language and local festivals have returned to the island's calendar. In other areas too, including cuisine, culture and sport, Mallorcans have been highly effective in promoting their island's interests.

SPORTING HEROES

Soccer club Real Club Deportivo Mallorca, also known as Real Mallorca, has twice come third in the league, reached the final of the European Cup Winners' Cup in 1999 and won the Copa del Rei (King's Cup) in 2003. Their greatest victory was a 5-1 triumph in 2003 at the Bernabeu, home of formidable Real Madrid. However, Rafael Nadal is arguably Mallorca's most famous sporting export in recent years. Crowned Wimbledon Champion 2010, he is Spain's greatest tennis player of all time and comes from Manacor. Find out more about this popular player at www.rafaelnadal.com.

LANGUAGE WARS

Hard though it may be for foreigners to understand, the difference between *plaça* and *plaza* has become an issue of cultural identity. Since the formation of the Balearic government in 1983, Catalan has replaced Spanish as the first language in Mallorca, so that you will now see signs to the *platja* rather than *playa* (beach). To add to the confusion, most locals speak Mallorquí,

which is essentially a dialect of Catalan with one or two important differences, such as the use of the definite articles *es*, *sa* and *ses* instead of *el*, *la* and *els*. Following 2007's elections, bilingualism is in fashion, and it is now common to hear politicians mixing Mallorquí and Castilian.

WINNING WINES

Years after the dark days of Franco, Mallorca's wine is finally a sought-after, prize-winning product. And because of the limited land available for growing grapes, it tends to be in short supply and consequently rather expensive. Two wine-producing regions are protected by *Denominació d'Origen* (DO) status: Binissalem and neighbouring villages, and the Pla I Llevant, covering Algaida, Felanitx, Manacor, Petra and Porreres. As you pass through these areas, look out for a sprig of vine over doorways: this means that the place is a *bodega* (wine cellar or maker) with wine to sell. A fresh green cutting indicates that the wine is fresh; a withered old cutting says that it is aged.

Above *Vineyard near Binissalem, centre of Mallorca's wine industry*

THE STORY OF MALLORCA

Prehistory, Romans and Moors   26
    Prehistory–1229
The Golden Age   28
    1229–1349
Catalonia and Spain   30
    1349–1850
The Modernist Era   32
    1850–1936
Dictatorship to Democracy   34
    1936–2000
Into the Future   36
    2000–today

The first human beings to arrive in Mallorca are thought to have been fishermen or sailors who came over from the Iberian Peninsula around 5000BC. These early inhabitants lived in caves, hunting with crude tools of flint or stone. By 2000BC the Beaker culture—named after the practice of burying ceramic cups with the dead—had taken hold on the island, but the first organized settlements, such as those at Artà and Capocorb Vell, were built during the Talaiotic era, which flourished between 1400 and 800BC. Phoenician and Greek traders were attracted to the island and in 123BC the Roman consul Quintus Caecilius Metellus led a successful invasion—despite an attack on his fleet by the famed Balearic slingers. The Romans established cities at Palmaria (now Palma) and Pollentia (now Alcúdia), named the island Balearis Major and incorporated it into their Mediterranean empire. With the decline of this empire some 500 years later, periods of Vandal and Byzantine rule followed. When the Moors conquered Mallorca in AD902 the island became part of the Emirate of Córdoba, ushering in three centuries of Moorish rule—the legacy of which can still be seen today.

MYOTRAGUS BALEARICUS

In 1909 British palaeontologist Dorothea Bates first discovered evidence that this goat-like mammal, a distant relative of the antelope, with eyes at the front of its head, had inhabited Mallorca. Having probably migrated to the island about 6 million years ago during a fall in the sea level of the Mediterranean, Myotragus continued to thrive until the appearance of the first humans. Evidence from a cave in Sóller suggests that the animal co-existed with man for a time, but domestication and the introduction of goats, sheep and pigs eventually contributed to its demise. Skeletons of Myotragus balearicus are displayed at the Museu de Mallorca in Palma (▷ 64) and the Natural History Museum in Sóller (▷ 109).

Clockwise from above *A bronze warrior in the Museu de Mallorca in Palma; ruins at Roman Pollentia, near Alcúdia; the statue of a hondero or Balearic slinger*

TALAIOTIC LIFE

Archaeologists generally divide the Talaiotic era into three periods. During the pre-Talaiotic period (2000–1400BC) the island's inhabitants lived in caves and made crude bronze and pottery utensils. The Talaiotic period (1400–800BC) saw the development of sophisticated bronze weaponry, as well as the building of walled villages and fortified stone towers known as *talaiots*. In the post-Talaiotic period (800–123BC) there was greater contact with other Mediterranean civilizations. The Mallorcans traded with the Carthaginians and their pottery began to imitate Roman styles; they also developed a cult of bull worship similar to that found in Sardinia. The bronze statues of warriors seen in the Museu de Mallorca were probably brought back as booty by mercenaries fighting in the Punic Wars.

MEDINA MAYURQA

From about AD500 to AD1000 Moorish Palma, then known as Medina Mayurqa, was a civilized, elegant city with street lights and heated baths, as well as a typical Arab souk. The city also maintained a close alliance with the rest of the Muslim world. Under Moorish rule the walled city began to take on its present shape, with a castle on the site of the Palau de l'Almudaina and a great mosque on the site of the cathedral. Orchards and market gardens were planted outside the city walls to supply the traders in the souk. The Moors introduced oranges and almonds to Mallorca, which are both important crops today, along with windmills and irrigation techniques. Mallorca's rich Moorish legacy also survives in the names of several of its towns and villages, including Alcúdia, Algaida, Binissalem and Deià.

THE OLDEST SLINGERS IN TOWN

The Talaiotic people were renowned for their skill with the slingshot, and it is said that fathers taught their sons to sling by placing their food high in a tree and forcing them to go hungry until they were able to bring it down with a catapult. The great Carthaginian general Hannibal was so impressed by this prowess that he recruited Mallorcan slingers as bodyguards for his epic journey across the Alps on elephant-back, paying them in wine and women rather than in gold. This skill with the sling was praised by the Roman historian Livy, and even gave its name to the islands—Balearic probably derives from the Greek verb *ballein* (to throw).

ROMAN REMAINS

Roman settlers introduced vines and olives to Mallorca and were responsible for building the first roads, bridges and aqueducts on the island. Their capital, Pollentia (Alcúdia), was a sophisticated example of town planning, with handsome villas, porticoed streets, a central forum and a theatre. For five centuries the people of Mallorca used Roman currency, spoke in Latin and adopted the Roman styles of dress; they also worshipped Roman gods until the arrival of Christianity in the second century. With the Vandal invasion of around AD425, however, virtually all traces of Roman Mallorca were wiped out, leaving just wine and olive oil as lasting reminders of their stay.

One of the dates etched onto every Mallorcan schoolchild's mind is 31 December 1229—the day Jaume I of Aragón entered Palma to capture the island from the Moors. To reward his nobles for their loyalty, the victorious king divided the island up between them in proportion to the number of men each had supplied, thus populating the island with members of the Catalan nobility and importing the Catalan language. On his death in 1276, Jaume I bequeathed his kingdom to his sons—the elder son, Pedro, received Aragón and Catalonia, while the younger son, Jaume II, had to make do with Mallorca, and Montpellier and Roussillon (both now part of southern France). However, this arrangement was not to last. Pedro's son Alfonso III captured Mallorca in 1285, forcing Jaume II into exile for 13 years before the restoration of the kingdom in 1298. When Jaume II died in 1311 the crown passed to his asthmatic son, Sancho. Having died childless in 1324, Sancho was succeeded by his nine-year-old nephew, Jaume III, but Jaume III's brother-in-law Pedro IV of Aragón felt he had a stronger claim to the throne and seized the island in 1343. When Jaume III, now an adult, tried to return, he was killed at the battle of Llucmajor in 1349, bringing the kingdom of Mallorca to an end.

Clockwise from above *King Jaume II's Palau de l'Almudaina; the death of Ramón Llull in Tunisia; Jaume I's conquest of Palma, by Pedro Nisart*

JAUME THE CONQUEROR

'The best thing man has done for a hundred years past' was how 21-year-old Jaume I described his conquest of Mallorca. In part he was driven by the spirit of the Crusades and the *Reconquista* (Reconquest) of land from the Moors, which was sweeping southwards through Spain; in part, no doubt, by youthful exuberance and greed. His appetite was whetted by a great banquet in Tarragona at which the seafarer Pere Martell served Mallorcan olives and spoke of the bounty of the island; shortly afterwards, the king gathered together his nobles to plan an invasion. He set sail from Salou in September 1229 with a party of 150 ships, 1,500 horses and 16,000 men. Three months later, Mallorca was his.

PEDRO THE GIGOLO

Jaume I's commitments on the mainland meant that he had little time to devote to Mallorca so he entrusted the rule of the island to others. One of those chosen was Don Pedro, Crown Prince of Portugal, who had previously helped the young king out of a difficult situation. In 1228, in an attempt to bring the Catalan county of Urgell into his kingdom, Jaume had taken its heiress, the beautiful Countess Aurembiaix, as his mistress. However, having tired of her, he needed to engineer an acceptable way of ending the affair. Don Pedro came to the rescue by marrying the countess and was rewarded after her death with the lordship of Mallorca. He served as lord of Mallorca from 1231 to 1244, playing a key role in the conquest of Ibiza.

JAUME RULES OK

His father, Jaume I, may have been the hero of the Reconquest, but it was Jaume II, the first true king of Mallorca, who steered the island into its Golden Age. Jaume ordered the building of the cathedral, the Castell de Bellver and the Palau de l'Almudaina, and the construction of Alcúdia's city walls. The finest Gothic churches of Palma, including Santa Eulàlia, Sant Miquel and Sant Francesc, were also begun during his reign. He established royal palaces at Sineu and Valldemossa, and also in the French city of Perpignan, and founded the towns of Felanitx, Llucmajor and Manacor. Jaume was an enlightened as well as a visionary ruler, introducing a weekly market at Palma and setting minimum wages for agricultural workers.

RAMÓN LLULL

Although he is now revered as a missionary and scholar, Ramón Llull (c.1235–1315) was little more than a dissolute courtier until a salutary incident changed his life at the age of 40. Chasing a married woman through the streets of Palma on horseback, he followed her into church and down the aisle, whereupon she tore open her bodice to reveal diseased breasts. Much chastened, he took a vow of poverty and retired to Puig de Randa (▷ 169) as a hermit. Recalled to the court by his patron Jaume II, he founded a school of languages at Miramar (▷ 101) and wrote widely on everything from philosophy to poetry. He is said to have been stoned to death while attempting to convert Muslims in Tunisia.

CHEEKY KID

One of the most gruesome episodes in the history of Mallorca is remembered on the island chiefly for the verbal spat it engendered. During his conquest of the island in 1285, Alfonso III met with fierce resistance at Castell d'Alaró (▷ 97), whose commanders remained loyal to Jaume II. The story goes that as the king of Aragón attempted to take the castle, the sentry, Cabrit, asked him his name. When the king replied that his name was Alfonso, Cabrit turned it into an impudent pun. 'We like our *anfós* grilled,' he called out, referring to a grouper-like fish. 'And I like my *cabrit* [goat kid] roasted,' replied the king, promising to burn Cabrit and his companion Brassa alive on a spit. And he did.

From the 14th century, when it lost its status as an independent kingdom, Mallorca began a long decline. By the 19th century it was no more than a poor provincial outpost of Catalonia and Spain. The noble Catalan families who had arrived after the conquest returned to their mainland estates as the kingdom of Aragón grew into a major Mediterranean power incorporating Corsica, Sardinia and Naples. Mallorca's fortunes worsened in 1479 when Fernando V of Aragón married Isabel I of Castile, uniting the two royal houses and paving the way for the creation of modern Spain. The defeat of the Moors at Granada in 1492 completed the process; at the same time, explorer Christopher Columbus was setting out on his journeys for the New World, reducing Mediterranean influence and turning attention towards trade across the Atlantic with America. The 16th century saw renewed attacks on Mallorca from Turkish and North African pirates, which led to watchtowers being built around the coast. Mallorca also picked the wrong side during the War of the Spanish Succession (1701–14), supporting the Habsburg emperor Charles III against the victorious candidate Felipe V and becoming the last province to surrender in 1715. The island was punished by being stripped of its historic privileges and by the imposition of the Castilian language over Catalan.

Clockwise from above A map of Palma c.1572; portrait of the explorer Christopher Columbus; a wall tile in Valldemossa depicting Santa Catalina Thomàs, Mallorca's only saint

JEWISH PALMA

During the 14th century Jews were active in Palma as merchants, bankers, tailors, dyers, goldsmiths, butchers and bakers. Jewish cartographers Abraham and Jafuda Cresques produced the *Atles Català* here in 1375, a map of the known world now held at the Bibliothèque Nationale in Paris. However, although the Jews of Palma were granted special legal and financial privileges, they were also discriminated against, were forced to live in ghettoes and had to wear distinctive dress. An anti-Semitic riot in 1391 led to an attack on the Jewish ghetto in which up to 300 people were killed. This marked the start of the forced conversions to Christianity, which continued with the setting up of an Office of the Inquisition to denounce heretics in 1484.

JUNÍPERO SERRA

Many people emigrated from Mallorca in the 18th century, but no one from the island had more influence beyond its shores than Junípero Serra (1713–84), a farmer's son from Petra, who is honoured in the Capitol in Washington as 'the founder of California'. After studying in convents in Petra and Palma, Serra was ordained as a priest and in 1749 set off for Mexico as a missionary. Two decades later, after an epic trek from Mexico, he established his first Californian mission at San Diego. Over the next 15 years he was to found eight more missions—one of which grew into the city of San Francisco—and to baptize more than 5,000 Native Americans into Catholicism. He was beatified in 1988.

RATS!

In 1809 thousands of French soldiers landed on the island of Cabrera (▷ 161), off Mallorca's southern coast, following their defeat at the Battle of Bailén. The Spanish victors needed somewhere to keep their prisoners and this uninhabited island provided the answer. A ruined castle was turned into a prison camp, and meagre rations of bread, beans and oil were delivered every few days by boat. In their desperation, the soldiers foraged for wild food: an account tells how a mouse could be bought for seven or eight beans, and a rat for four times as much. Violence and disease were common. Of the 9,000 men who arrived, barely a third survived. Visitors today can still see the prisoners' graffiti on the walls.

CARNIVAL REVOLT

In February 1521, during Palma's traditional Carnival celebrations, peasants and traders marched on the capital to protest at high taxes, grain shortages and the concentration of power in a few hands. Forming themselves into a *Germanía* (brotherhood), bound together by oath, the protesters quickly occupied the city, forcing many of the nobles to flee to Pollença. Others took refuge in the Castell de Bellver but the rebels soon took the castle by storm. It was two years before Charles V, the Holy Roman Emperor and King of Spain, managed to organize a fleet to recapture Palma from the *Germanía*. After agreeing terms for a surrender he reneged on the deal and executed 500 rebels, including their leader, Joan Colom.

A MALLORCAN SAINT

As you walk around Valldemossa (▷ 110–113) look for the painted tiles on houses with the message *Santa Catalina Thomàs pregau per nosaltres* (Santa Catalina Thomàs, pray for us). Numerous legends are told about the life of this pious girl (1531–74), who, as a child, preferred long walks with her rosary to toys and games. In the interests of fasting she refused to eat more than one meal a day, going so far as to mix sand with her soup to avoid the sin of gluttony. At the age of 22 she entered the Santa Magdalena in Palma, where she was known as a model of humility, chastity and obedience. Beatified in 1792 and canonized in 1930, she is Mallorca's only saint to date. The house where she lived in Valldemossa has been turned into a shrine.

SANTA CATALINA THOMAS PREGAU PER NOSALTRES

THE MODERNIST ERA

In the late 19th century many Mallorcans grew rich on the booming export trade in almonds and wine, which was aided by the opening in 1875 of a railway line from Palma to Inca and the establishment of a regular steamship service from Palma to Barcelona. Unfortunately this prosperity was short-lived as a phylloxera plague in the 1890s virtually wiped out Mallorca's wine industry, and the loss of Spain's last colonies, Cuba and the Philippines, in 1898 led to a reduction in export markets and widespread emigration. Despite these setbacks, the turn of the 20th century was a confident time, fuelled by the *Renaixença*; this Catalan cultural renaissance saw a flowering of the arts, music and literature, and a revival of the Catalan language. One of the products of this was the *Modernista* architectural movement (▷ 74–75). At the same time, adventurous travellers started arriving in Mallorca; the Gran Hotel opened in Palma in 1903; and in the same year Thomas Cook began offering package tours to the island. Authors such as Gordon West *(Jogging Round Majorca*, 1929) and Santiago Rusinyol *(The Island of Calm*, 1922) depicted a tranquil, rural island yet to be disturbed by mass tourism or political upheavals.

THE DUKE OF MALLORCA
Of the many foreigners who have been attracted to Mallorca, one in particular has lodged in the hearts of the Mallorcans. Ludwig Salvator (1847–1915), an Austrian archduke, first came to the island at the age of 20 to escape the stuffiness of Viennese court life, and immediately felt at home. An early ecologist (and a renowned womanizer), he bought up most of the land between Valldemossa and Deià, laid out a network of walking trails—which is still in use—and refused to allow any trees on his estates to be cut down. When he wasn't having affairs with local women, he studied Mallorcan history, culture and flora. One of his houses, S'Estaca, built for his lover Catalina Homar, now belongs to the American actor Michael Douglas.

Clockwise from above Joan Rubio's fine Banco de Sóller, in Sóller; the Duke and Duchess of Windsor were frequent visitors to Mallorca; Modernist detail on Can Forteza Rey, in Palma

WALLS COME TUMBLING DOWN

Until 1902 the outline of Palma had scarcely changed in a thousand years—then the tragic decision was taken to destroy the city walls in order to expand the city. Although the walls had stood since the time of the Moors and had been reinforced after the Catalan conquest, the city needed to expand and their destruction was seen as the logical solution. At first it was hoped that the northern gate, through which Jaume I's forces entered the city in 1229, would be saved, but in the name of progress even that had to go. All that remains of the original walls is the bastion of Sant Pere and a section beneath the cathedral which is clearly visible; the rest has been incorporated into the ring road and the city's famous tree-flanked promenade.

A GOOD TIP

In 1929 the opening of the Hotel Formentor was announced to the world with illuminated advertisements on the Eiffel Tower in Paris. The first guests were two English women, who arrived following a storm at sea. They were helped ashore by the Argentinian owner, Adan Diehl. Assuming he was the porter, they gave him a one-peseta tip; he later joked that this was the only money he ever earned from the hotel. During the 1930s this was the most fashionable address in Mallorca, the haunt of visitors such as statesman Winston Churchill, comic actor Charlie Chaplin and novelist Agatha Christie. The hotel also saw its share of scandal when Edward, Prince of Wales (the future Edward VIII of Britain) stayed there with his lover, Mrs Simpson.

GAUDÍ IN THE CATHEDRAL

The Modernist architect Antoní Gaudí (1852–1926) is best known for his unfinished Sagrada Família cathedral in Barcelona, and few people realize that he also worked on Palma's cathedral (▷ 70–73). Modernism was a democratic movement, and in 1904 Bishop Campins brought Gaudí in to open up the interior of the cathedral through the careful use of light and space. Among his reforms was the introduction of electric lighting and the moving of the choirstalls from the centre of the nave to their current position in the chancel, thus removing a barrier between congregation and priest. Gaudí worked on the cathedral for 10 years; his assistant Joan Rubió stayed behind in Mallorca and brought Modernist architecture to Sóller (▷ 108–109), such as the church of Sant Bartomeu.

EUROPE'S FIRST TOURIST BOARD

Businessman Enrique Alzamora Goma, the president of Mallorca's chamber of commerce, founded the Fomento del Turismo de Mallorca (Mallorca Tourist Board) in 1905 as a private organization representing hoteliers and transport companies. Initially, it concentrated on promoting Mallorca to Mallorcans, improving roads and communications, and publishing the first guide to the island in 1908. Among its first projects was the construction of a road between Andratx and Estellencs, and the building of *miradors* (viewpoints) overlooking the north coast. By the 1930s it was producing tourist brochures and posters, organizing excursions for visitors, and even posting a representative to Paris to market Mallorca as a summer holiday destination.

In 1936 General Francisco Franco led a military rebellion that heralded three years of civil war and almost 40 years of Fascist dictatorship across Spain. The army in Mallorca supported Franco's Nationalists from the start, though atrocities were committed on both sides. Despite its support during the Spanish Civil War, Mallorca was not immune from the reprisals unleashed by Franco when he finally took power. The Catalan language was banned, expressions of regional culture were suppressed, and Mallorca was used as a testing ground for mass tourism with little thought given to the impact on the islanders. Franco's death in 1975 was followed by the restoration of the monarchy and a rapid return to democracy. A new constitution granted limited autonomy to the regions and Spain entered the European mainstream, joining Nato in 1982 and the European Union in 1986. At the same time, the strict Francoist alliance of Church and State gave way to a relaxation of social and sexual mores as the people threw off the enforced power of the Catholic Church. After decades of suppression, Mallorca began to rediscover its own voice—the Mallorquí language was once again heard on the streets and road signs in Spanish were replaced with those in Catalan.

POOR TOURISM

At first, Franco was happy to keep foreigners out, fearing an influx of bikini-clad visitors with loose morals, but later he embarked on an aggressive policy of marketing Spain as a tourist destination. Regional identity went out of the window as the clichés of bullfighting, flamenco and *sangria*—none of which have much relevance to Mallorca—appeared on posters to promote the island. This was the era of 'poor tourism', when high-rise hotels sprung up overnight, transforming fishing villages into concrete resorts and turning property values and the social order upside down. Suddenly, a strip of rocky coastline was worth more than a fertile field and the prime farmland traditionally inherited by the eldest child became worthless in comparison.

Clockwise from above *Santa Ponça has developed into a bustling mega-resort; mass tourism brought many sunseekers to Mallorca; Sa Dragonera—centre of a conservation controversy in 1977*

THE BATTLE FOR SA DRAGONERA

In 1977, two years after Franco's death, plans were made to build a luxury tourist resort on the island of Sa Dragonera (▷ 106). In one of the first protests of its kind, environmentalists from the Grup Ornitològic Balear (GOB), an ornithological group with wider conservation interests, occupied the island. Eventually, the authorities gave in—the Mallorcan government purchased Sa Dragonera and declared it a wildlife park. The victory for the campaigners is widely seen as a turning point, the moment when Mallorca realized that mass tourism was reaching its limit and that the island's natural heritage had to be protected. The GOB has now become a powerful political voice and an influential member of the Green lobby. Despite its designation as a protected park, the island is accessible to visitors.

THE NEW POLITICS

Eight years after the death of Franco, the Statute of Autonomy passed in 1983 gave a degree of self-government to the Balearic Islands, with powers in a wide range of areas such as education, transport and the environment. At the same time, Catalan was given equal status to Spanish as an official language of the Balearic Islands, with priority given to Catalan in the areas of education and local government. The Balearic parliament has representatives from Menorca, Ibiza and Formentera, though Mallorcans are in the majority. Each island also has its own local council, the Consell Insular. For 16 years from 1983 the Balearic Islands were governed by the centre-right Partit Popular. In 2007, Socialist Francesc Antich formed a coalition government known as Mallorca's Bloc (Bloc per Mallorca).

MULTICULTURAL MALLORCA

The large number of African traders selling wood carvings and djembe drums at street markets in Mallorca might give the impression of a highly integrated society, but this is a very recent phenomenon. For about 750 years after the defeat of the Moors there were few non-white faces in Mallorca and the island is only just coming to terms with its new multi-racial existence. In the late 1990s, many immigrants from Senegal and Morocco arrived to work on the Pla Mirall, a government-funded project to restore the centre of Palma. At first, the workers faced hostility and were forced to live in hostels with alcoholics and drug addicts; only now are they starting to be accepted as equal members of society. According to a recent poll, 17 per cent of Mallorca's population is foreign-born.

ICH BIN EIN MALLORCAN

In 1998 the author Carlos Garrido published *Mallorca de los Alemanes*, a satire about an island populated by Germans in 2013. This was not entirely a joke—it caught the public mood and coincided with a wave of anti-German sentiment in Mallorca. Much of this was directed at rich German landowners, including model Claudia Schiffer, tennis player Boris Becker and racing driver Michael Schumacher, all of whom have houses in Mallorca (▷ 19). The biggest estate agent in Mallorca was a German company and it was estimated that Germans owned 20 per cent of all property, including 80 per cent of rural manor houses. There was even talk of launching a German political party. 'Germans are buying up our island,' complained Balearic president Jaume Matas.

The challenge facing Mallorca in the 21st century is how to maintain its role as Europe's leading tourist destination without destroying its fragile environment. Thanks to tourism, Mallorca has become one of the richest regions of Europe but there is general agreement that the limit has been reached. A ban on any new hotels under three stars was introduced in 2008, while boutique hotels and *agroturismos* (rural accommodation) have been concurrently encouraged. Business travellers are also finding new appeal in Mallorca, with the emergence of modern convention centres, while those seeking a more active holiday have plenty of sports and activities to choose from.

UNDERGROUND RUBBISH

As you stroll around the old quarter of Palma, bear in mind that more than the remains of the Roman city lie beneath your feet. An innovative waste disposal system has made refuse sacks and dustcarts a thing of the past. Residents place their rubbish in robotic-looking grey containers on street corners. From here, rubbish is pumped pneumatically along a network of underground pipes to a central collection point outside the city, where it is sorted and compressed for recycling and disposal. This has made Palma's centre a tidier place to live and reduced pollution and damage to historic buildings by keeping lorries out of the old town's narrow lanes.

THE PALMA BUZZ

According to a recent survey in *El Pais,* the Spanish daily newspaper, Palma provides its residents with some of the highest quality of living in the country. Of course the people who live there know this already—from its seaside setting to its vibrant cafe culture, Palma has all the ingredients of the perfect city. These days, the city has a tangible buzz about it, with new restaurants, bars and designer boutiques opening almost every week. Previously run-down districts, such as Santa Catalina and Sa Gerreria, are being repopulated by young professionals and trendy shops. Low-cost flights from Britain and Germany have made Palma a popular weekend break destination, a trend reinforced by the opening of the Museu Es Baluard (▷ 63) and Palma Aquarium (▷ 68).

THE COALITION SPIRIT

The local elections in 2007 were very close. Despite the right-wing Partido Popular (PP) winning most of the island's municipalities, the then leader, Jaume Matas, failed to win an absolute majority in the regional elections. A coalition was subsequently formed under the Socialist rule of Francesc Antich. Among their pledges was to stamp out illegal rural construction and the corrupt issuance of building licences, particularly in the Tramuntana. Despite the ETA bombings of July 2009 when two Guardia Civil officers lost their lives, Mallorca remains one of Europe's top destinations, particularly Palma. New hi-tech facilities such as Palma's Congress Palace (scheduled to open in 2011) also help guarantee that the island similarly remains a top business travel destination.

Above *Palma's innovative waste disposal bins*

ON THE MOVE

On the Move gives you detailed advice and information about the various options for travelling to Mallorca before explaining the best ways to get around the island once you are there. Handy tips help you with everything from buying tickets to renting a car.

Arriving	38
By Air	38
By Sea	39
Getting Around	40
Buses	40
Trains	42
Boat Trips	43
Driving	44
Motorcycles and Bicycling	46
Taxis	47
Visitors with a Disability	48

BY AIR

Most visitors to Mallorca arrive at Palma's Son Sant Joan airport (code PMI), some 8km (5 miles) east of the city. Once a small provincial airport, this is now one of the busiest in Europe, capable of handling more than 25 million passengers per year. There are daily flights from Palma to Madrid, Barcelona and other Spanish cities, to Menorca and Ibiza, and also to London, Paris and Berlin. During the summer season these are complemented by numerous budget airlines bringing visitors from all over northern Europe.

The main terminal at Son Sant Joan is vast, and the walk from the arrivals gates to the baggage hall can take up to 30 minutes. Once you have collected your luggage, you pass through to the arrivals hall on the ground floor, where there is an information desk, a tourist information office, a newsagent, a cafe, ATMs and car rental agencies. A post office is situated on the second floor. There is a larger range of shops, cafes and restaurants in the pre-departure area on the fourth floor, including a branch of La Caixa bank (open 9–2), a pharmacy and shops selling alcohol, food, fashion, jewellery, glassware, CDs and electronic equipment. These shops are landside and are open to arriving passengers, though to buy certain items you will need a boarding card for a departing flight.

CAR HIRE

The major international car-hire firms have offices at the airport. These are situated inside the baggage hall and the arrivals hall (beyond customs).

>> It is usually advisable to reserve a car in advance, especially in the peak summer season. You can often get a better deal this way and you can compare rates from different companies.

>> Remember to check the small print of the contract, especially with regards to insurance. Most policies include an excess payment of up to €300 for accident damage, although this can sometimes be waived on payment of an additional premium.

>> Local companies may offer more competitive rates than the big international chains. Firms such as Serra (tel 971 865492) can save money by not having an airport office, but they will meet you at the airport or deliver a car to your hotel.

>> There are also car-hire companies in all the main towns and resorts. In some cases, these offer very attractive rates, though it is important to check the details of the contract as the cheaper deals are more likely to have exclusions.

>> To hire a car, you must be over 21 and you will need a passport, driver's licence and credit card. Keep your passport and driver's licence with you whenever you use the car, as well as the car hire documents. Never leave these documents in the car while it is parked.

>> Check the car carefully before you set off, and make a note of any visible signs of damage on the hire documents.

Above *Estacio Intermodal—Palma's main train station*

>> Ask about a 24-hour emergency contact number in case of accident or breakdown.

>> The majority of rental cars take standard unleaded petrol, though some do take diesel fuel. It is usual to pay for a full tank and return the car full, though some policies vary.

>> Most cars hired in Mallorca are not allowed be taken on ferries to Menorca and Ibiza.

>> Never leave any valuable items on display inside the car, and, if possible, remove any obvious signs that indicate it is a hire car as thieves tend to target them.

>> Ask about the arrangements for returning the car. Most companies have designated car parking spaces on the ground floor of the car park opposite the terminal.

>> It is essential never to give the keys to anybody other than an authorized employee of the car-hire company.

>> Some foreigners have become targets for car theft by criminals posing as employees of car-hire firms in this way.

LEAVING THE AIRPORT
>> Most people arriving on package holidays are taken to their final destination by transfer bus, accompanied by their tour operator's representative.

>> The taxi rank is directly outside the terminal. There are fixed fares to destinations across the island and these should be checked in advance. Taxi journeys into central Palma are metered and will usually cost around €18.

>> Bus No. 1 leaves for Palma from the bus stop opposite the terminal,

between the taxi rank and the multistorey car park. Departures are every 20 minutes from 6.10am to 2.15am in summer, 6.10am to 1am in winter. The bus takes around 20–30 minutes to reach central Palma, with a flat fare of €2. In Palma, it travels around the Avingudas ring road before continuing along the seafront to the port. The most useful stop is Plaça d'Espanya, which is close to the city centre and has bus and train connections within Palma and across the island. There is a tourist information office close to the bus stop at Plaça d'Espanya, in the Parc de les Estacions (tel 971 754329).

BY SEA
Up to a million people a year arrive in Mallorca by sea, mostly from the

Spanish mainland and the other Balearic Islands.

>> Car and passenger ferries from Menorca, Ibiza, Barcelona and Valencia arrive at the commercial port at Palma.

>> Baleària and Iscomar operate ferries between Ciutadella on Menorca and Port d'Alcúdia.

>> Cruise ships frequently dock at the harbour at Palma.

>> There is a taxi rank outside Palma's maritime station. Bus No. 1 runs to the centre of Palma and the airport every 20 minutes from 6.15am to 2.30am in summer, 6.10am to 1am in winter. There is a flat fare of €1.25 to Palma and €2 to the airport.

Below *Boats depart regularly from the small jetty at Sant Elm for Sa Dragonera*

FERRY COMPANIES

NAME	TELEPHONE	WEBSITE
Acciona–Trasmediterránea	902 454645	www.trasmediterranea.es
Baleària	902 160180	www.balearia.com
Iscomar	902 119128	www.iscomar.com

AIRPORT GUIDE

Ground floor: Arrivals, tourist information, car hire.
Second floor: Check-in, post office, first aid.
Fourth floor: Departures, bank, shops, restaurants.
Website: www.aena.es
Telephone numbers:
Son Sant Joan airport tel 902 404704
Tourist information office tel 971 789556

AIRPORT CAR HIRE FIRMS

NAME	TELEPHONE	WEBSITE
Avis	971 789187	www.avis.com
Centauro	902 104103	www.centauro.net
Europa	971 745390	www.drivespain.com
Europcar	971 789135	www.europcar.com
Hasso	902 203012	www.hasso-rentacar.com
Hertz	971 789670	www.hertz.es
Record	971 743705	www.recordrentacar.com
Serra	971 865492	www.serra-rent.com

BUSES

GETTING AROUND PALMA

Palma's compact city centre is best explored on foot, but there is a good network of buses connecting the city with the outlying suburbs. Buses are operated by EMT (Empresa Municipal de Transports).

Information

Carrer Josep Anselm Clavé, 5, tel 971 214444; www.emtpalma.es

>> The city tourist offices have maps and itineraries of all bus routes operating within Palma.

>> Buses are blue and are of the low-floor type, making them accessible for passengers in wheelchairs.

>> Enter by the front door and buy your ticket from the driver. Disabled passengers may enter via the middle doors. Passengers must leave by the middle doors.

>> The standard fare is €1.25 for most journeys though there are a few variations (see box).

>> Children under the age of five travel free.

>> If you are going to be using the buses a lot, it may be worth getting a *targeta* (card, €10), which is valid for 10 journeys. The card must be validated on each trip in the machine behind the driver's cabin.

>> Most bus stops have information panels with a full list of timetables and routes, as well as electronic display boards showing waiting times for the next buses.

>> The hub of Palma's bus network is at Plaça d'Espanya, where you can transfer between routes and also to island-wide buses and trains.

>> Bus No. 1 runs at 20-minute intervals from the airport to the port, via the Avingudas ring road and Plaça d'Espanya.

>> Bus No. 2 makes a regular circuit of the old centre. You can pick it up at Plaça d'Espanya, Avinguda Jaume III, or at the foot of Passeig des Born. It does not run on Sundays.

Other Routes

3 Palma to Cas Català
6 Palma to Sant Agustí
8 Palma to Son Roca (via Moix football stadium)
15 Palma to Platja de Palma
17 Palma to Can Pastilla
20 Palma to Palma Nova
23 Palma to S'Arenal (and to Aquacity in summer)
25 Palma to Platja de Palma (via *autopista*)
46 Palma to Genova

Night Bus

Bus No. 41 (also known as the Bus de Nit) operates on Friday and Saturday nights during the summer months from 11pm to 6am. It runs along the seafront from Parc de la Mar to Porto Pí, with stops outside all the main discos and clubs. There is a flat fare of €1.25.

Metro

The metro entrance is conveniently located at Plaça d'Espanya. There is just one line that runs from the Plaça to the University taking around 13 minutes, with several stops, including Gran Via Asimi. A single journey costs €0.90.

City Sightseeing Bus

>> The open-top City Sightseeing bus makes a complete circuit of Palma and its outlying sights, including Castell de Bellver.

>> The 80-minute tour begins at the port, on the jetty facing the cathedral and Parc de la Mar. You can pick it up at any of 13 stops, including Plaça d'Espanya and Avinguda Jaume III.

>> There is a headphone commentary in Spanish, Catalan, English, French, German, Italian, Portuguese and Swedish.

➤ Tickets are valid for 24 hours and you can get on and off as many times as you like.

➤ Tickets cost €13 for adults and €6.50 for children aged 5 to 15. Children under 5 travel free.

➤ The bus runs every 20 minutes from 10am. From November to the end of April the service finishes at 6pm; from March to the end of May and from mid-September to the end of October it stops at 8pm and from June to mid-September at 10pm.

ORGANIZED EXCURSIONS

Tour operators offer a range of organized coach trips to popular attractions such as waterparks and caves, as well as shopping trips to Palma and local markets. These tend to be considerably more expensive than using public transport, but they may make a good alternative if you have limited time for exploring the island. For the longer tours, a meal is generally included in the price. Take a bottle of water with you, especially in the summer months. Entrance tickets to the attractions are usually included in the price. The majority of tours include a visit to a leather or glass factory, or a gift shop, though be aware that as the tour guide will get a commission on any sales, the prices may be higher than in local shops. It is usual to tip the driver at the end of an excursion.

GETTING ACROSS THE ISLAND

All bus services across Mallorca are operated by Transports de les Illes Balears (TIB, tel 971 777777, http:// tib.caib.es), an integrated public transport network that also includes trains. Most buses are painted in the red and yellow livery of TIB, though some older buses retain the livery of private companies.

➤ Buses from Palma to towns and villages across the island depart from the bus station on Carrer Eusebi Estada, which is situated behind the railway station on Plaça d'Espanya. Several information boards here show maps, lists of destinations and departure points.

➤ Local buses to Palma Nova, Magaluf, Illetes and Andratx depart from stops on Carrer Eusebi Estada.

➤ Facilities at Palma bus station include toilets, a cafe, a newsagent and an information counter (open daily 9–1 and 3–7), which can issue timetables for various routes.

➤ Many routes, particularly those to and from coastal resorts, operate reduced timetables between November and the end of April.

➤ In summer, extra buses link all the main resorts with each other and with nearby towns.

➤ Bus stops across Mallorca are recognizable by the red and yellow colours of TIB.

➤ Tickets can be bought from the driver on the bus.

➤ Smoking, eating and drinking are not allowed on board.

PALMA BUS FARES	
Standard tariff	€1.25
10 journeys	€10
To Palma Nova	€1.50
To or from airport	€2
Children under 5	Free

Left *Sóller's delightful vintage tram*
Opposite *There are regular boat trips to Mallorca's outlying islands*

THE SÓLLER TRAIN

The opening of the Sóller tunnel in 1997 means that this train is no longer used by commuters, but it remains viable thanks to its popularity with visitors. Everything about the 27km (17-mile) journey is delightfully old-fashioned, from the hoots and whistles as it pulls out of the station to the vintage walnut carriages and leather upholstery in first-class. The train rattles down Palma's streets before crossing the countryside of the plain and rising gently to Bunyola. After leaving the 3km-long (2-mile) Tunel Major, it twists down the mountainside to Sóller in a dizzying series of gradients, tunnels, viaducts and bends. From Sóller, an antique tram, which began service in 1913, rattles down to the port.

➤➤ Five trains a day run in winter and seven in summer, with a journey time of one hour. The first departure from Palma is at 8am and from Sóller at 7am.

➤➤ The single fare is €10, return €17.

➤➤ The 10.50am departure from Palma (and also the 12.15pm in summer) is a *tren panoramic*, with an additional stop at a viewpoint overlooking the Sóller Valley. The single fare for this journey is €10.

➤➤ Bicycles and wheelchairs cannot be taken on the train.

➤➤ Smoking is not allowed.

➤➤ There are toilets and cafes at Palma and Sóller stations.

➤➤ Trams leave Sóller for Port de Sóller every half-hour in summer and every hour in winter. The single fare is €4.

INFORMATION

For timetables, tel 902 364711 or visit www.trendesoller.com.

TRAINS

There are two separate railways in Mallorca. The first, which is publicly owned and operated by Transports de les Illes Balears (TIB), has a fleet of modern trains connecting Palma with Inca, Manacor and Sa Pobla. The second is the privately owned Ferrocarril de Sóller, which has been going over the mountains from Palma to Sóller since 1912 and continues to provide an enjoyable day out for visitors. In Palma, the two railway stations are on the north side of Plaça d'Espanya, a short walk from the bus station.

THE INCA TRAIN

➤➤ Around 32 trains a day run from Palma to Inca (journey time around 45 minutes). Between Palma and Inca, there are stops at Marratxí, Santa Maria del Camí, Alaró-Consell, Binissalem and Lloseta.

➤➤ Half of the trains continue to Manacor (64 minutes) via Sineu and Petra; the others continue via Llubí and Muro to Sa Pobla (53 minutes).

➤➤ An integrated rail-and-bus service provides connections to outlying villages, for example from Santa Maria del Camí to Santa Eugènia and Sencelles.

➤➤ Tickets can be bought at Palma railway station, at other main stations or from the conductor on the train.

➤➤ There are toilets at Palma and some other stations.

➤➤ All trains are accessible for wheelchairs.

➤➤ Bicycles may be carried on most trains.

➤➤ Smoking is not allowed.

ON TRACK FOR THE FUTURE?

The reopening of the line to Manacor in 2003 has prompted further investment in the rail network and there are plans to open several new routes in the future. These could include the extension of the Sa Pobla line to Alcúdia, the extension of the Manacor line to Artà and Cala Rajada, and a line from Palma to Llucmajor, Campos and Santanyí.

SOME TYPICAL FARES	
Palma to Inca	Single €1.80, return €3.60
Palma to Sa Pobla	Single €2.85, return €5.70
Palma to Manacor	Single €3.70, return €4.40

BOAT TRIPS

Regular ferry services link Mallorca to the Spanish mainland and the other Balearic Islands, and there is a wide choice of pleasure boat trips for summer visitors. The tourist office provides a comprehensive list; just ask.

MENORCA AND IBIZA

Fast ferries and catamarans link Mallorca to Menorca and Ibiza, making it possible to visit either of them for a day. The main services are from Port d'Alcúdia to Ciutadella in Menorca, and from Palma to the Ibizan capital Eivissa. Both these historic cities are small enough to explore in a day.

CABRERA AND SA DRAGONERA

The offshore nature reserves of Sa Dragonera (▷ 106–107) and Cabrera (▷ 161) can be visited by boat. Depending on weather conditions, it is usually possible to visit Sa Dragonera throughout the year but trips to Cabrera operate from April to the end of October only. In addition to the regular trips from Cruceros Margarita in Sant Elm, there are extra departures in summer for Sa Dragonera from Palma Nova, Peguera and Port d'Andratx.

OTHER TRIPS

▶ Several boat trips operate in summer from beaches, harbours and resorts around the coast. These range from cruises around Palma and Alcúdia bays to 'glass-bottomed' boat trips along the east coast, day trips to remote beaches and coves, and evening 'pirate' cruises with food, drink and entertainment. In most cases, you can simply turn up at the jetty and see what is on offer, but for the more popular trips it is advisable to book in advance.

▶ One trip that runs throughout the year is from Port de Sóller to Sa Calobra (▷ 101), operated by Barcos Azules (tel 971 630170; www.barcosazules.com). From April to October there are four daily ferries leaving from Port de Sóller at 10am, 11.15am, 1pm and 3pm. The return fare is €22 for adults and €12 for children aged 6 to 12; children under 6 travel free. There are extra departures in summer as well as cruises along the coast to Cala Deià (▷ 98) and Formentor (▷ 138).

TIP

▶ The sea can be unpredictable and boat trips are always dependent on the weather, which can change suddenly even in summer. It is always worth checking the forecast before setting out.

SOME POPULAR TRIPS

ROUTE	TELEPHONE
Around Palma Bay	659 636775
Cala Millor to Porto Cristo (optional visit to Coves del Drac)	971 810600
Cala Rajada to Canyamel (optional visit to Coves d'Artà)	971 563622
Palma to Sant Elm	971 717190
Palma Nova to Portals Vells (dinner included)	971 131211
Port d'Alcúdia to Formentor	971 545811
Port de Pollença to Formentor	971 864014

FERRY COMPANIES

NAME	TELEPHONE	WEBSITE	ROUTES	COST
Baleària	902 160180	www.balearia.com	Fast ferries from Palma to Ibiza (2 hours) and Port d'Alcúdia to Ciutadella (1 hour)	Day return from €61
Acciona–Trasmediterránea	902 454645	www.trasmediterranea.es	Fast ferries from Palma to Ibiza (2 hours)	Day return from €55
Iscomar	902 119128	www.iscomar.com	Ferry from Port d'Alcúdia to Ciutadella (2.5 hours)	Day return from €53
Ferry booking websites		www.directferries.es; www.ticket.es/ferries.htm; www.aferry.com		

DRIVING

Despite Mallorca's excellent and extensive public transport network, to explore the island thoroughly you will need a car. Bus services are limited in the less populated rural villages, and there is much pleasure to be gained from striking off the beaten track on remote mountain roads. Spanish drivers have a reputation for reckless overtaking and the accident rate in Mallorca is high, but in practice much of the danger comes from visitors in hired cars.

It is possible to take your own car to Mallorca by ferry from mainland Spain, but in most cases it will be easier and cheaper to fly to Palma and hire a car on arrival (▷ 38). If bringing your own car, ensure you have adequate breakdown cover and accident insurance. These can be obtained from your usual insurer or from a motoring organization such as the Automobile Association (www.theAA.com).

Above *Main road network on Mallorca*

RULES OF THE ROAD

>> Drive on the right and overtake on the left.

>> At roundabouts, give way to traffic coming from the left.

>> The minimum age for driving is 18, though you will probably have to be over 21 to hire a car.

>> Speed limits are 120kph (75mph) on motorways, 90kph (56mph) on main roads and 50kph (31mph) in built-up areas, unless otherwise indicated.

>> The drink-drive limit is 50mg alcohol per 100ml blood, which is lower than in the UK. The only sensible advice is never to drink and drive.

>> The Guardia Civil and Policía Nacional have the power to impose large on-the-spot fines on speeding motorists and to remove licences from drunk drivers.

>> Motorcycle and moped riders must wear a helmet at all times.

>> Car drivers and passengers must wear seat belts at all times.

>> Children under 12 may not travel in the front seat of a car; instead they must be strapped into a child seat attached to the rear seat of the vehicle.

>> The use of mobile phones while driving is prohibited. It is also illegal to use mobile phones, headlights or car radios while stationary at a petrol station.

>> Use dipped headlights in tunnels.

>> Drivers are required to carry two warning triangles, a spare set of light bulbs and a reflective vest—which should be worn if you have to get out of the car on the road or the hard shoulder of a motorway. Hire cars should be provided with these items.

MOTORWAYS

>> Mallorca has one main stretch of motorway, from Palma to Inca, as well as the Via Cintura (ring road) around Palma and short sections of motorway to Palma Nova and Llucmajor. There are long-term plans for a second, outer, ring road around Palma.

>> When joining the motorway from a slip road, give priority to traffic already on the motorway.

>> Always overtake on the left.

>> Do not exceed the 120kph (75mph) limit, and keep a safe distance from the vehicle in front.

>> Do not drive on the hard shoulder except in an emergency.

TOLLS

>> Mallorca's only toll road is the Sóller Tunnel, which costs €4.45 for cars and €2.50 for motorcycles, payable by cash or credit card.

FUEL

>> All petrol stations should sell high-octane unleaded petrol and diesel. Most hire cars take 95-octane unleaded fuel.

>> There are petrol stations on all main roads and in major towns. Many are open 24 hours and these are listed in the newspaper *Diario de Mallorca*.

>> There are a growing number of self-service stations, but the majority have petrol attendants. Most accept payment by cash or credit card.

PARKING

>> Parking spaces in towns and cities are marked out by blue lines. Never park where you see yellow lines or any other form of markings.

>> Most spaces are pay-and-display during working hours, approximately 9–1 and 4–8 on weekdays and Saturday mornings. At these times, buy a ticket from a nearby machine and display it in your windscreen.

>> Pay-and-display street parking is usually limited to a maximum of two hours.

>> The public car parks in Deià, Valldemossa, Fornalutx and Port de Sóller are pay-and-display at all times.

>> Parking in Palma is particularly difficult. There is a large car park on the jetty facing the cathedral and an underground car park beneath Parc de la Mar. This is central and secure, and there are no time limits, but it is costly for longer periods. If you can walk a short way into the city, there is free parking on the seafront to the west of the city centre, beyond Avinguda Argentina.

>> In central Palma, freelance car parking 'attendants' will often guard free spaces for motorists. If you see someone guiding you into a free space, he will expect a tip (€1 is sufficient). There is no danger in doing this, but be aware that many of these people are drug addicts using the money to fund their habit.

>> Hotels, especially in Palma, will not necessarily have free car parking spaces for their guests. Ask about this when you book—it may be necessary to use a public car park or to pay for space in the hotel garage.

SECURITY

>> Take common-sense security precautions as you would anywhere else. Never leave anything on display inside the car; all valuables should either be taken away or locked out of sight in the boot.

>> Hire cars can be targets for thieves, so remove obvious signs.

>> Never leave keys in the ignition while parked at a petrol station or unloading luggage at a hotel.

>> If you are involved in an accident that you suspect may be deliberate, drive on to the nearest well-lit petrol station before stopping.

WHAT TO DO IN AN ACCIDENT

Your car-hire company should give you an emergency contact telephone number for use in the event of a breakdown or accident. Make sure you inform them as soon as possible. If it's your own car, contact your insurers.

>> Write down the name, address, registration number and insurance details of any other parties involved.

>> If anybody is injured or there is any dispute about the facts, call the police or emergency services on 112.

>> If the car cannot be moved, and if you can safely do so, place a warning triangle on the road approximately 50m (164ft) to either side of your vehicle.

Chart showing distances in kilometres (green) and duration in hours and minutes (blue) of a car journey between major towns

Duration (blue), upper-right triangle, reading from Alcúdia row:

```
055 141 043 139 058 030 049 106 049 108 124 037 025 124 017 122 037 126 150
    052 100 047 037 027 047 016 033 028 046 026 051 025 040 042 023 044 042
        206 042 118 051 131 053 119 035 020 112 116 043 105 120 101 055 040
            147 041 055 132 101 024 129 146 031 108 105 044 059 044 043 147
                113 044 150 048 114 034 052 104 103 038 059 115 054 017 008
                    052 106 027 021 053 121 025 107 041 052 021 036 112 107
                        022 037 041 030 052 027 030 034 019 059 016 035 038
                            100 105 101 113 048 024 112 143 128 038 040 105
                                036 028 050 031 101 016 050 028 033 050 042
                                    056 116 016 055 049 040 039 028 108 109
                                        015 048 054 017 043 053 040 035 028
                                            107 124 034 110 120 056 050 040
                                                045 042 029 042 012 056 058
                                                    059 020 123 038 052 103
                                                        048 043 041 040 032
                                                            107 021 050 053
                                                                046 117 110
                                                                    047 049
                                                                        025
```

Distances in kilometres (green), lower-left triangle:

```
Alcúdia
Algaida       46
Andratx       84  54
Artà          36  50 105
Deià          83  46  43  89
Felanitx      48  32  82  34  73
Inca          25  23  59  46  44  43
Lluc          41  39  76  77  42  55  18
Llucmajor     55  13  58  51  50  24  30  50
Manacor       41  31  82  20  73  14  36  54  32
Palma         57  24  30  74  30  51  33  51  27  51
Palma Nova    70  38  17  88  43  68  43  61  42  63  13
Petra         31  26  73  26  58  20  24  40  30  13  43  56
Pollença      21  48  84  57  63  57  27  20  55  46  58  70  37
S'Arenal      70  23  48  54  39  38  42  60  14  46  16  28  41  68
Sa Pobla      15  36  72  37  56  43  15  36  43  32  46  58  25  16  55
Santanyí      69  36  82  49  73  21  56  74  25  30  50  67  38  80  38  58
Sineu         31  22  66  37  50  29  14  32  30  23  40  47  11  37  40  17  41
Sóller        72  38  51  36  14  64  36  33  48  63  28  42  51  52  38  50  72  42
Valldemossa   92  39  39  89   7  67  37  54  43  66  23  33  52  63  33  51  67  44  21
```

Above and left *Two wheels are an excellent way of getting around the island*
Opposite *Taxis are easy to find in Palma*

MOTORCYCLES AND BICYCLING

For some holidaymakers, hiring a car on this small island is unnecessary. Mopeds are fine for short trips from resorts, while many prefer pedal power: bicycling is a very popular activity in Mallorca.

SCOOTERS AND MOTORCYCLES

The island is popular with touring motorcyclists who come for the Tramuntana's twisty mountain roads. You can bring your motorbike to Mallorca on the ferry services from northeast Spain (▷ 39), but this can be an expensive option. The alternative is to hire a motorcycle on the island. Several firms offer powerful touring motorcycles. It's possible to hire anything from a 50cc scooter to a BMW or Harley Davidson motorcycle in Mallorca. Scooter rental firms proliferate in the seaside resorts, where they are popular with young Mallorcans and tourists alike.

However, there are risks associated with riding scooters and avoidable accidents occur each year. It is mandatory to wear a helmet when riding a scooter or motorcycle and firms will typically include a helmet in the price of the rental. You'll need to show a valid driving licence to hire a scooter, which means that you have to have passed a driving test and be at least 17 years of age. Insurance should also be included in the package and is essential. The price of hiring a small 50cc scooter starts from about €25 per day, but you can expect to spend more hiring a motorbike.

RIDING A SCOOTER SAFELY

›› Helmets are mandatory.
›› Use your lights at night.
›› Watch out for car doors opening without warning.
›› Make other road users aware of your intentions by using the indicators.
›› Avoid riding along the inside of traffic when there is a right turn ahead.
›› Don't drink alcohol before riding a scooter; you can be breathalyzed.
›› Don't carry a passenger unless the scooter is designed for two people.

BICYCLING

Bicycling is a popular activity in Mallorca and winter and spring see many bicyclists on the roads. Traffic levels at this time of year are relatively low but it is still recommended to seek out quieter roads and avoid the fast main roads.

Many of Mallorca's administrative districts have developed extensive networks of bicycle lanes and created bicycle routes along scenic rural roads (▷ 174–175). Maps of these routes are available from local tourist information offices. The routes are usually clearly signposted and road quality is generally good, but watch out for potholes on some of the minor mountain roads. Palma itself has a number of bicycle lanes but the best bicycling is to be found outside the island's capital on the flat Pla I Llevant, around the coast and in the mountainous Serra de Tramuntana. Wherever you are based, there will be a bicycle rental firm nearby. You might have to look a little harder to find specialist racing or mountain bikes (▷ 202). Each year bicyclists are killed and injured in traffic accidents; despite local drivers' good awareness of bicyclists, always ride cautiously.

BICYCLING SAFELY

›› Helmets are not mandatory but are strongly advised.
›› Wear bright clothing and use lights at night.
›› Don't cut corners on mountain descents.
›› Watch out for car doors opening without warning.
›› Make other road users aware of your movements.
›› Avoid bicycling along the inside of traffic when there is a right turn ahead.

TAXIS

Taxis are plentiful in Palma and all the main towns and resorts. Although they are a relatively expensive way of getting around, they are useful for short journeys and airport transfers. Locals rarely tip, but more is expected of tourists. A local would round up to the nearest euro at the most.

IN PALMA

➤➤ Palma's taxis are either black or cream.

➤➤ You can hail one on the street whenever the green light is illuminated, pick one up at taxi ranks, or order a taxi by telephone (supplement payable).

➤➤ There are taxi ranks at the bus and train stations, on Avinguda d'Antoni Maura and Avinguda Jaume III.

➤➤ Fares are metered. Between 6am and 9pm on weekdays, the minimum fare is €2.50, plus €1 per km, rising to €3, plus €1.20 per km for journeys outside the city limits.

➤➤ Fares are higher at night and at weekends and public holidays. There is a supplement of €3 for journeys to the airport and €2.20 to the port.

➤➤ Wheelchairs and prams are carried free of charge.

OUTSIDE PALMA

➤➤ The livery of taxi companies varies around the island. Taxis can usually be hailed on the street, or hired at taxi ranks in town centres or outside the main hotels.

➤➤ Fares for local journeys are usually metered though it's wise to check in advance.

➤➤ There are supplements for late-night and weekend travel.

➤➤ A list of fares for longer journeys is usually displayed at taxi ranks. A taxi journey across the island from Alcúdia to Palma will cost around €80, but ask for a quote.

PALMA TAXIS	
NAME	TELEPHONE
Fono Taxi	971 728081
Radio Taxi	971 764545
Taxi Palma Radio	971 401414
Taxi Teléfono	971 743737

ISLAND TAXIS	
TOWN	TELEPHONE
Alcúdia	971 549870
Pollença	971 866213
Santa Ponça	971 680970
Sóller	971 638484

Mallorca has made great efforts to cater for disabled visitors.

>> All new buildings must be accessible to wheelchair users. Most older buildings have been adapted, though attractions such as castles and caves can still prove difficult. Most hotels are happy to cater for disabled visitors, though it is important to discuss your needs in advance.

>> All new buses are of the low-floor variety. All Palma's buses are wheelchair-accessible, though some older buses are still in use outside the capital.

>> The Palma–Inca train line is fully accessible for disabled visitors.

>> Most car-hire companies can provide specially adapted cars.

>> Disabled parking bays are marked by a blue wheelchair symbol.

>> The majority of beach resorts have level, traffic-free promenades which are suitable for wheelchair users. At Palma Nova, Magaluf,

Illetes, Peguera and Santa Ponça, amphibious wheelchairs are available in summer for disabled swimmers.

>> Taxi drivers are generally helpful and they are required to carry wheelchairs free of charge.

INFORMATION
In Mallorca and Spain
>> Associació Balear de Persones amb Discapacitat Fisica (tel 971 289052; www.asprom.net) is based in Palma.

>> Mobility Abroad (tel 0871 277 0888; www.mallorca.mobilityabroad. com) rents out electric scooters and wheelchairs for €110 per week, as well as other aids for the disabled.

>> Easyride Mobility Hire (tel 606 543099; www.easyridermobilityhire. com) offers similar services, plus children's and household equipment, ranging from pushchairs (strollers) to electric fans.

>> ONCE (Organización Nacional de Ciegos de España; www.once.es) is

the Spanish association for the blind.

>> Taxi Adaptat (tel 971 703529) Taxis that cater for disabled passengers.

In the UK
>> Tourism For All (tel 0845 124 9971; www.tourismforall.org.uk) has an excellent website with information and advice on planning your trip, plus a directory of international accommodation that caters for the handicapped, including Mallorca.

>> RADAR (the Royal Association for Disability and Rehabilitation) tel 0207 259 3222; www.radar.org.uk has an excellent range of travel information.

In the US
>> Accessible Journey (tel 610/521-0339; www.disabilitytravel.com), based in the US, organizes vacations throughout Europe, including Spain, for travellers confined to a wheelchair.

REGIONS

This chapter is divided into four regions of Mallorca. Places of interest are
listed alphabetically in each region.

Mallorca's Regions 50–186

Palma		50
Serra de Tramuntana		94
The Northeast		130
The South		158

SIGHTS 57
WALKS 74
WHAT TO DO 78
EATING 86
STAYING 90

PALMA

Palma tends to take first-time visitors by surprise. Despite the steady influx of tourists, the island's capital has remained a very genuine Mallorquín city, with a surprising sophistication and elegance. There is also a refreshing lack of straw donkey-style souvenirs and indifferent restaurants serving so-called 'international' cuisine.

Palma exudes a tangible sense of history, particularly in its tangle of atmospheric back streets lined with sun-baked ochre buildings. The city's beguiling Modernist architecture can also be seen throughout the city, equalling fabulous facades and an eye-catching and eclectic skyline. The city appropriately reflects its capital status with the typical bustle and commerce of a Spanish working town, while the agreeable flip side includes plenty of green spaces, superb museums and galleries and the opportunity to indulge in a wide range of leisure pursuits. Palma has a great selection of dining and drinking venues, from Michelin-star gourmet restaurants to typical neighbourhood bars where flat-capped old men play dominoes and drink *anís*. The scope for shopping here is also superb, with an enticing combination of designer boutiques, national chains, gourmet delicatessens and those charming idiosyncratic family-owned shops that have remained in the same family for generations and tend to sell just one thing—like espadrilles or hats. The city is also becoming an increasingly popular venue for business travellers, with a brand-new Congress Palace due to open in 2011.

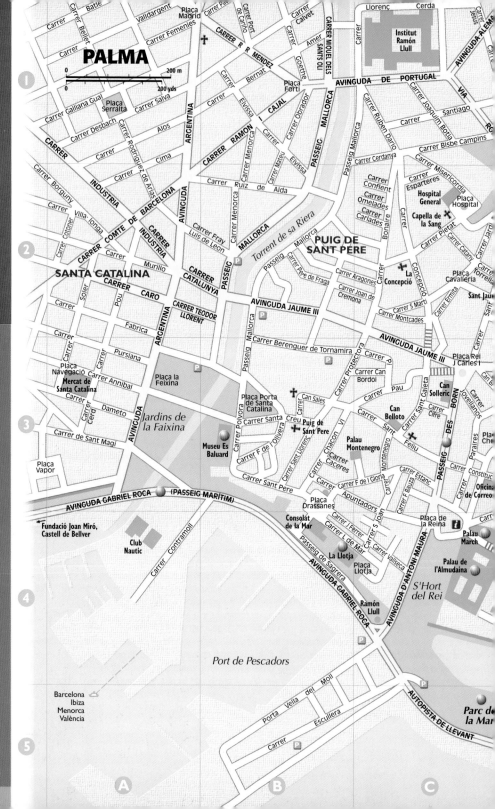

PALMA

0 ____ 200 m
0 ____ 200 yds

Plaça Madrid

Carrer Batle

Valldargent

Carrer Femenies

Plaça Serralta

Carrer Galliana Gual

Carrer Bellet

Carrer

Carrer Desbach

Carrer Salva

CARRER

Carrer Rodríguez de Arias

Alos

Cima

INDUSTRIA

Villa-longa

Carrer Cotoner

CARRER COMTE DE BARCELONA

CARRER INDUSTRIA

SANTA CATALINA

CARRER CARO

Soler

Pou

Fabrica

ARGENTINA

Carrer

Carrer

Murillo

Pursiana

Plaça Navegació

Carrer Annibal

Mercat de Santa Catalina

Carrer

Carrer Cerd

Dameto

Plaça Vapor

Carrer de Sant Magí

AVINGUDA

Jardins de la Faixina

CARRER CATALUNYA

CARRER TEODOR LLORENT

ARGENTINA

PASSEIG

MALLORCA

Plaça la Feixina

Plaça Porta de Santa Catalina

Carrer Santa Creu

Puig de Sant Pere

Museu Es Baluard

Carrer Pólvora

Carrer Sant Llorenç

Chacón VI

Carrer F de l'Olivera

Carrer Sant Pere

Carrer Cáceres

Palau Montenegro

AVINGUDA GABRIEL ROCA (PASSEIG MARÍTIM)

Fundació Joan Miró, Castell de Bellver

Club Nautic

Carrer Contramoll

Carrer

Plaça Drassanes

Consolát de la Mar

Carrer I Ferrer

Carrer L de Mar

La Llotja

Plaça Llotja

PASSEIG de Sagrera

AVINGUDA GABRIEL ROCA

Ramón Llull

AVINGUDA D'ANTONI MAURA

Apuntadors

Carrer Vallseca

Plaça de la Reina

Palau March

Palau de l'Almudaina

S'Hort del Rei

Port de Pescadors

Barcelona
Ibiza
Menorca
València

Porta Vella del Moll

Carrer

Escullera

Carrer

AUTOPISTA DE LLEVANT

Parc de la Mar

Llorenç

Cerda

Jesús

Institut Ramón Llull

AVINGUDA-ALEM

Carrer Pau de Cariño

Carrer Calvet

CARRER MIQUEL DELS SANTS OLI

Carrer

AVINGUDA DE PORTUGAL

VIA

Bernat

Plaça Forti

Amer

Coethe

Carrer R R MENDEZ

CARRER RAMON I CAJAL

Elvissa

Carrer Obrador

Carrer Mateu

Eivissa

PASSEIG MALLORCA

Carrer Rubén Darío

Carrer Joaquim Botia

Santiago

Carrer

Carrer Bisbe Campins

Carrer Misericordia

Carrer Esparteres

Plaça Hospital

Hospital General

Capella de la Sang

Plaça Pietat

Carrer Conflent

Carrer Omelades

Carrer Carlades

Bonaire

Carrer Ruiz de Alda

Carrer Menorca

Carrer Fray Luis de Leon

Carrer Menorca

MALLORCA

Torrent de sa Riera

Passeig Mallorca

Carrer Cerdanya

PUIG DE SANT PERE

La Concepció

Carrer Pere de Fraga

Carrer Aragones

Carrer Joan de Cremona

Carrer S Martí

Carrer Montcades

AVINGUDA JAUME III

AVINGUDA JAUME III

Carrer Berenguer de Tornamira

Carrer Protectora

Carrer P

Carrer Can Bordoi

Can Sales

Carrer

Pau

Can Solleric

Carrer Sant Feliu

Can Belloto

Sant

Carrer Sant Galeta

Carrer Cifre

DES BORN

PASSEIG

Carrer Montenegro

Carrer F Bauza

Carrer F de l Gloria

Carrer Estanc

Carrer Joan

Ermita

Plaça Cavallería

Plaça Torrella

Sant Jau

Sant

Carrer Catany

Plaça Jard

Plaça Rei J Carles I

Paralles

Carrer Constituc

Plaça Ch

Oficina de Correo

Carrer

Concepció

Jovellanos

Carrer Feliu

A B C

PALMA STREET INDEX

Alemanya, Avinguda	52	C1	Can Sales, Carrer	52	B3	Esparteres, Carrer	52	C2
Alexandre Jaume, Plaça	53	F2	Can Sanç, Carrer	53	E3	Estanc, Carrer	52	C3
Alexandre Rosselló, Avinguda	53	E1	Can Savellà, Carrer	53	E3	Estudi General, Carrer	53	D4
Almoina, Plaça	53	D4	Can Serinya, Carrer	52	C3	Eusebi Estada, Carrer	53	E1
Almudaina, Carrer	53	D4	Can Tagamanent, Plaça	53	D3	Fabrica, Carrer	52	A2
Alos, Carrer	52	A1	Can Troncoso, Carrer	53	E4	F Bauza, Carrer	52	C3
Angels, Carrer	53	D2	Can Vallori, Carrer	53	E3	F Chopin, Plaça	52	C3
Annibal, Carrer	52	A3	Caputxines, Carrer	53	D2	F de l Gloria, Carrer	52	B3
Antoni Maura, Avinguda d'	52	C4	Carlades, Carrer	52	C2	F de l'Olivera, Carrer	52	B3
Antoni Planas i Franch	53	F4	Carme, Carrer	53	D2	Femenies, Carrer	52	A1
Antoni Ribas, Carrer	53	F3	Caro, Carrer	52	A2	Ferreira, Carrer	53	E3
Apuntadors, Carrer	52	B3	Catalunya, Carrer	52	A2	Foners, Carrer	53	F3
Aragon, Carrer de	53	F2	Catany, Carrer	52	C2	Font Monteros, Carrer	53	D1
Aragones, Carrer	52	B2	Cavalleria, Plaça	52	C2	Forti, Plaça	52	B1
Argenteria, Carrer	53	D3	C Danus, Carrer	53	D3	Francesc de Borja Moll, Carrer	53	D1
Argentina, Avinguda	52	A3	C Dusai, Carrer	53	E4	Frares, Carrer	53	E2
Autopista de Llevant	52	C5	Cecili Metel, Carrer	53	D1	Fray Luis de Leon, Carrer	52	A2
			Cerd, Carrer	52	A3			
Baro de Pinopar, Carrer	52	C1	Cerdanya, Carrer	52	C1	Gabriel Alomar I Villalonga,		
Bastio de Princep, Carrer	53	E5	Chacon VI, Carrer	52	B3	Avinguda	53	F3
Bastio d'en Berard, Carrer	53	E5	Cifre, Carrer	52	C3	Gabriel Roca (Passeig Marítim),		
Batle Llorenç Bisbal, Plaça	53	F4	Cima, Carrer	52	A2	Avinguda	52	A3
Batle, Carrer	52	A1	C Jaquotot, Carrer	53	D2	Galliana Gual, Carrer	52	A1
Bellet, Carrer	52	A1	C Malla, Carrer	53	E3	Gerreria, Carrer	53	E3
Berenguer de Tornamira, Carrer	52	B3	Coll, Plaça	53	E3	Gilabert de Centelles, Carrer	53	F1
Bernat Amer, Carrer	52	B1	Comtat del Rossello, Plaça	53	E2	Goethe, Carrer	52	B1
B Ferra, Carrer	53	F2	Comte de Barcelona, Carrer	52	A2	Graduada, Carrer	53	F3
Bisbe Berenguer de Palou, Plaça	53	D1	Concepció, Carrer	52	C2	Guixers, Carrer	53	D3
Bisbe Campins, Carrer	52	C1	Conflent, Carrer	52	C2			
Bisbe, Carrer	53	D2	Conquistador, Carrer	52	C4	H d Baulo, Carrer	53	E3
Bisbe, Carrer	53	F1	Constitucio, Carrer	52	C3	H de l'Estel, Carrer	53	E3
Blanquers, Carrer	53	E4	Contramoll, Carrer	52	A4	Horts, Carrer dels	53	D2
Bonaire, Carrer	52	C2	Convent des Caputxins, Carrer	53	E2	Hospital, Plaça	52	C2
Born, Passeig des	52	C3	Corderia, Carrer	53	E3	Hostals, Carrer	53	E3
Bosc, Carrer	53	E4	Cort, Plaça de	53	D3			
Bosseria, Carrer	53	E3	Costa i Llobera, Carrer	53	F2	Industria, Carrer	52	A1
Botons, Carrer dels	53	E4	Cotoner, Carrer	52	A2	Inf Pau, Carrer	53	F3
B Perelló, Carrer	53	E2	C Salat, Carrer	53	F3			
Brossa, Carrer	53	D3	C Sant, Carrer	53	D3	J Anselmo Clavé, Carrer	53	F2
			C Serra, Carrer de	53	D4	Jardi Botanic, Carrer	52	C2
Caceres, Carrer	52	B3	C Veri, Carrer	53	D3	Jaume II, Carrer	53	D3
Calatrava, Carrer de la	53	E5				Jaume III, Avinguda	52	B2
Calvet, Carrer	52	B1	Dameto, Carrer	52	A3	Jaume Lluis Garau, Carrer	53	F4
Campana, Carrer	53	E3	Desbach, Carrer	52	A1	Jeroni Antic, Carrer	53	D1
Can Bordoi, Carrer	52	C3	Drassanes, Plaça	52	B3	Jeroni, Carrer	53	F4
Can Brondo, Carrer	52	C3	Ducs de Palma de Mallorca,			Jesus, Carrer	52	C1
Can Campaner, Carrer	53	D2	Rambla dels	53	D2	J Ferrer, Carrer	52	B4
Can Carrio, Carrer	53	E2				J M Bover, Carrer	53	F1
Can de Sant Francesc,			Eglesia de Santa, Carrer	53	F4	Joan de Cremona, Carrer	52	B2
Carrer	53	D3	Eivissa, Carrer	52	B1	Joan Lluis Estelrich, Carrer	53	D1
Can Gater, Carrer	53	E2	Enric, Carrer	53	F2	Joan Maragall, Carrer de	53	F5
Canisseria, Carrer	53	E3	Ermita, Carrer	52	C2	Joan March, Carrer	53	E1
Can Maçanet, Carrer	53	D1	Escoles, Carrer de les	53	E4	Joan Maura, Carrer	53	F1
Can Oliva, Carrer	53	D2	Escullera, Carrer	52	B5	Joan XXIII, Carrer	53	E2
Can Pueyo, Carrer	53	D2	Espanya, Plaça d'	53	E1	Joaquim Botia, Carrer	52	C1

Street	Page	Grid	Street	Page	Grid	Street	Page	Grid
José Tous y Ferrer, Carrer	53	E2	Palau Reial, Carrer	53	D4	Sant Antoni, Plaça	53	F3
Josep Maria Quadrado, Plaça	53	E3	Palau, Carrer	53	D4	Sant Bona Ventura, Carrer	53	E4
Josep Rover Mota, Carrer	53	F4	Paraires, Carrer	52	C3	Sant Elies, Carrer	53	D1
Jovellanos, Carrer	52	C3	Parellades, Carrer	53	D1	Sant Espirit, Carrer	53	E2
Justicia, Carrer	53	F3	Pau, Carrer	52	B1	Sant Feliu, Carrer	52	C3
la Feixina, Plaça	52	A3	Pau, Carrer	52	C3	Sant Francesc, Plaça de	53	E4
la Unió, Avinguda de	53	D3	P de Jesus, Carrer	53	D1	Sant Gaieta, Carrer	52	C3
l'Artesania, Plaça de	53	E4	P de Montserrat, Carrer	53	E4	Sant Jaume, Carrer	52	C3
L de Mar, Carrer	52	B4	Pere de Fraga, Carrer	52	B2	Sant Jeroni, Plaça de	53	E4
Llorenç Cerda, Carrer	52	C1	Pere Dezcallar i Net, Carrer	53	D1	Sant Llorenç, Carrer	52	B3
Llorenç Villalonga, Plaça	53	E5	Pere Nadal, Carrer	53	E4	Sant Magí, Carrer de	52	A3
Llotgeta, Carrer	53	E3	Perez Galdos, Carrer	53	F4	Sant Miguel, Carrer	53	E2
Llotja, Plaça	52	C4	Pes de la Palla, Plaça del	53	E4	Sant Nicolau, Carrer	53	D3
Lluis Marti, Carrer	53	F2	Pi, Carrer	52	C3	Sant Pere, Carrer	52	B3
Llums, Carrer	53	D3	Pietat, Carrer	52	C2	Santa Creu, Carrer	52	B3
			Pols, Carrer	53	D2	Santa Eulàlia, Plaça	53	D4
Madrid, Plaça	52	A1	Polvora, Carrer	52	B3	Santa Magdalena, Plaça	53	D2
Major, Plaça	53	E3	Pont I Vich, Carrer	53	D4	Santiago Rusiñol, Carrer	52	C1
Mallorca, Passeig	52	B2	Port de Cariño, Carrer	52	B1	Sastre Roig, Carrer	53	D2
Man Guasp, Carrer	53	F4	Porta de Santa Catalina, Plaça	52	B3	S Bart, Carrer	53	D3
Manacor, Carrer	53	F3	Porta d'es Camp, Plaça	53	F4	S de S Jaume, Carrer	53	D2
Maneu, Passeig	53	F2	Porta Pintada, Plaça	53	E1	Seminari, Carrer del	53	E4
Margarita Caimari, Carrer	53	F1	Porta Vella del Moll	52	B5	Serralta, Plaça	52	A1
Marie Curie, Carrer	53	E1	Portella, Carrer de la	53	D4	S F Neri, Carrer	53	D4
Marques de la Fontsanta, Carrer	53	F1	Portugal, Avinguda de	52	B1	S Joan, Carrer	52	C4
Marquès del Palmer, Plaça del	53	D3	Posada de la Real, Carrer	53	D2	Sindicat, Carrer des	53	E3
Marti Feliu, Carrer	53	E3	Possada de Terra Sant, Carrer	53	E3	S Marti, Carrer	52	C2
Mateu Enric Llado, Carrer	53	F4	Pou, Carrer	52	A3	Socors, Carrer del	53	F4
Mateu, Carrer	52	B2	Previssi, Carrer	53	D3	Sol, Carrer del	53	E4
Menorca, Carrer	52	B2	Protectora, Carrer	52	B3	Soler, Carrer	52	A3
Mercadal, Plaça del	53	E3	Puresa, Carrer	53	D4	Son Campos, Carrer	53	F1
Mercat, Plaça	53	D3	Pursiana, Carrer	52	A2	S Pere Nolasc, Carrer	53	D4
Merce, Carrer de la	53	E2				S Sebastia, Carrer	53	D4
Merce, Plaça	53	E2	Quartera, Plaça	53	E3			
Miquel dels Sants Oli, Carrer	52	B1				T d'en Ballester Escola	53	E3
Miquel Marqués, Carrer	53	F1	R Ankerman, Carrer	53	F4	Temple, Carrer	53	E4
Miramar, Carrer	53	D4	Ramon I Cajal, Carrer	52	B2	Teodor Llorent, Carrer	52	A2
Misericordia, Carrer	52	C1	Ramon Llull, Carrer	53	E4	Tereses, Carrer	53	D2
Missio, Carrer de la	53	D2	Rei J Carles I, Plaça	52	C3	Tomas Forteza, Carrer	53	F5
Mistral, Carrer	53	F3	Reina Esclarmunda, Carrer	53	D1	Torrella, Carrer	52	C2
Moliners, Carrer	53	D2	Reina Maria Christina, Carrer	53	E1	Tous I Maroto, Carrer	53	D3
Monges, Carrer	53	D3	Reina, Plaça de la	52	C4			
Montcades, Carrer	52	C2	Rodriguez de Arias, Carrer	52	A1	Uruguay, Carrer	53	D4
Montenegro, Carrer	52	C3	Roma, Via	52	C1			
Monti-Sion, Carrer	53	E4	Rosa, Carrer	53	D3	Valldargent, Carrer	52	A1
Morer, Carrer	53	E3	Rosari, Plaça	53	D3	Vallseca, Carrer	52	C4
Morey, Carrer d'en	53	D4	R R Mendez, Carrer	52	B1	Vedra, Carrer	53	F4
Murillo, Carrer	52	A2	Ruben Dario, Carrer	52	C1	Velazquez, Carrer	53	E2
			Rubi, Carrer	53	E3	Victoria, Carrer	53	D3
Navegació, Plaça	52	A3	Ruiz de Alda, Carrer	52	B2	Vilanova, Carrer	53	E2
Nuredduna, Carrer	53	F2				Villalonga, Carrer	52	A2
			Sagrera, Passeig de	52	B4	Vinyassa, Carrer de	53	F1
Obrador, Carrer	52	B1	S Agusti, Carrer	53	F3			
Oli, Carrer	53	E3	Salva, Carrer	52	A1	Weyler, Plaça	53	D3
Olivar, Plaça	53	E2	Samaritana, Carrer	53	E3			
Omelades, Carrer	52	C2	S Andreu, Carrer	53	E3	Zanglada, Carrer	53	D4
Oms, Carrer dels	53	D1	Sant Alonso, Carrer de	53	E4			

INTRODUCTION

During the summer months, the stretch of coastline that runs for around 25km (16 miles) around Palma Bay seems to be little more than an endless expanse of sand populated by sunburnt northern Europeans who rarely venture beyond their high-rise hotels or the resort bars serving bratwurst, burgers and chips. Generally, the east side of the bay around S'Arenal and Platja de Palma has been colonized by German visitors, while the west side around Palma Nova and Magaluf has long been the preserve of the British. But there is something for everyone here: quiet coves with a handful of sunbeds; beaches where locals outnumber visitors; glitzy marinas and gritty fishing districts, and in the middle of it all there is Palma itself. During the summer season the best way to get a feel for Palma Bay is to take a boat cruise (▷ 43).

WHAT TO SEE

PORTITXOL AND CIUTAT JARDÍ

Portitxol, a traditional fishermen's quarter to the east of Palma, has become trendy, with the result that harbourside shops selling fishing tackle now rub shoulders with designer bars and hotels. You can get there by following the waterfront walk from Palma. The promenade curls around the small crescent beach of Es Portitxolet, passing the fishing district of Es Molinar on its way to Ciutat Jardí, whose lively beach is popular with local families in summer.
➕ Off map 53 F5, 223 E6

CASTELL DE SANT CARLES

Avinguda Gabriel Roca follows the broad sweep of Palma's seafront. Named after the engineer who supervised its building in the 1950s, it is more popularly known as Passeig Marítim (▷ 69). Both the path and the road come to an end at Porto Pí, the historic entrance to the port. The castle above Porto Pí was built by Felipe III in 1612; it is now a military museum. You can wander around the star-shaped fortress with its bastions, moats and sea views, and admire the collections of military uniforms, flags, lead soldiers and portraits of generals.
➕ 223 D6 ✉ Carretera Dic de l'Oest ☎ 971 402145 🕐 Mon–Fri 9–1, Sat 10–1 💷 Adult €3, child (under 18) free 🚌 1 🛒

INFORMATION

➕ 223 D7 ℹ Tourist information offices at S'Arenal, Platja de Palma, Palma, Illetes, Palma Nova and Magaluf

TIP

➤➤ Parking in any of the resorts around the bay can be very difficult in summer so it is better to use the excellent network of local buses. The Palma city bus lines (Nos. 15, 17, 23) extend east to Platja de Palma and S'Arenal, while the Calvià area has its own network connecting Palma to Portals Nous, Palma Nova, Magaluf, Illetes and Andratx.

Above *A quiet moment on the usually bustling beach at Illetes*
Opposite *The beautiful cove at Portals Vells, with golden sands and rocky cliffs*

PUERTO PORTALS

www.puerto-portals.com

This marina has been a magnet for celebrities since opening in 1986. Members of the Spanish royal family have been spotted at the waterfront restaurants and bistros, while millionaires shop at the boutiques on the promenade. It's fun just to wander around here, admiring the sleek yachts. The harbour was built beside the scruffy resort of Portals Nous, and the beach to the east of the marina is popular with locals.

✚ 222 D6

PALMA NOVA

One of Mallorca's earliest holiday resorts, 'New Palma' is often unfairly linked with its neighbour Magaluf. While Magaluf remains a raucous nightlife capital, Palma Nova is quieter and better suited to families with young children. Two beaches, divided by a headland, shelve gently into the sea around a broad sandy bay backed by a promenade with restaurants and bars. Touristy it certainly is, but tacky it isn't.

✚ 222 D6 🛈 Passeig de la Mar 13 ☎ 971 682365 🕓 Mon–Fri 9–6, Sat–Sun 9–2

MAGALUF

There's no escaping the fact that Magaluf is Mallorca's equivalent of Benidorm or Torremolinos. All-day English breakfasts, karaoke and English football on the big screen are what you can expect here, as well as a vigorous nightlife that especially appeals to a steady stream of hen and stag night revellers from the UK. Europe's largest disco, BCM, is also located here, which typically crams in up to 4,000 revellers a night during the summer months. On the plus side, Magaluf's sweep of European-Blue-Flag-awarded white sandy beach is well maintained, the sea is shallow and safe for children and several of the island's best family-geared theme parks can be found here. Adults may prefer a flutter at the more grown-up themed entertainment available at the island's only casino: the Casino Mallorca.

✚ 222 D7 🛈 Carrer de Pere Vacquer Ramis 1 ☎ 971 131126 🕓 Mon–Sat 9–6, Sun 9–2

PORTALS VELLS

Beyond Magaluf you get a glimpse of how Palma Bay used to look. South of the town, a lane winds through pine woods to the west of the bay. Narrow roads lead down to Platja El Mago, a sheltered cove that contains Mallorca's first official nudist beach, and Portals Vells, a lovely beach hiding beneath the cliffs. From Portals Vells a path leads around the cliffs to Cove de la Mare de Déu. The road from Magaluf fizzles out before you reach the lighthouse at Cap de Cala Figuera.

✚ 222 C7

MORE TO SEE

PLATJA DE PALMA

This 5km (3-mile) long, nondescript beach with a palm-lined promenade and views across Palma Bay is just a few minutes from the airport. The resort has swallowed up the nearby villages of Can Pastilla and S'Arenal. Mallorca's best waterpark, Aqualand El Arenal (May–end Oct daily 10–6, ▷ 84), is here, and is very popular with families.

✚ 223 E6 🛈 Plaça Meravelles ☎ 971 264532 🕓 Mon–Sat 9.30–1.30, 4–6.30

ILLETES

On weekend afternoons the people of Palma flock to this lovely, low-rise resort. Two beaches look out over two rocky islets, one of them crowned by a watchtower.

✚ 223 D6 🛈 Carretera Andratx 33 (summer only) ☎ 971 405444 🕓 Mon–Fri 9–3

BANYS ÀRABS (ARAB BATHS)

Palma's 10th-century Arab bathhouse is one of the few surviving examples of Moorish architecture in the city and probably formed part of a nobleman's palace in the city of Medina Mayurqa. The design, copied from the Romans, is identical to those found across the Arab world, with a series of chambers acting as changing rooms, and hot and cold baths. Best preserved is the *caldarium* (hot room), with a hemispherical dome pierced by 25 skylights and supported by 12 columns and horseshoe arches. Hot air was circulated beneath the floor from an underground furnace and water channelled from a spring was splashed onto the stone to produce steam. The small garden, with its palms and orange trees and Arab-style pots, is a good place to relax. ✚ 53 D4 ✉ Carrer de Can Serra 7 ☎ 971 721549 🕙 Apr–end Nov daily 9–7.30; Dec–end Mar daily 9–6 ✋ Adult €2, child (under 10) free

BASÍLICA DE SANT FRANCESC

This Franciscan church and convent dates from 1281, though the baroque facade was rebuilt in the 17th century after the original Gothic facade was struck by lightning. Outside the church is a statue of the Mallorcan missionary Junípero Serra (▷ 31) with a young Native American boy. You enter the complex through the convent on the right to reach a peaceful Gothic cloister of orange and lemon trees, with an old well at the centre and tall cypresses standing guard. Take your time here—this is by far the most impressive cloister in the city. The interior of the church is spoilt by the overblown baroque altarpiece topped by a statue of St. George on horseback. The tomb of the Mallorcan mystic Ramón Llull (▷ 29), completed in 1448, is in a chapel behind the main altar. ✚ 53 E4 ✉ Plaça de Sant Francesc ☎ 971 712965 🕙 Mon–Sat 9.30–12.30, 3.30–6, Sun 9–12.30 ✋ Adult €1, child free

CAN MARQUÈS

www.canmarques.net

A visit to Can Marquès, a rare seigneurial mansion in Palma that is open to the public, offers a glimpse into the lives of the Mallorcan aristocracy. It was built in the 14th century, though most of what you see today is the creation of Don Martín Marquès, who, having made his fortune from coffee in Puerto Rico, returned to his native Palma in 1906. The Marquès family continued to live here until the death of Don Martín's daughter in 1969. The guided tour includes the two public rooms (used for entertaining guests), the private family rooms, the chapel, the kitchen and the servants' quarters. The *Modernista* staircase, one of the highlights of the tour, and the wrought-iron candelabra are splendid. ✚ 53 D4 ✉ Carrer Zanglada 2A ☎ 971 716247 🕙 Apr–end Oct Mon–Fri 10–6, Sat 10–2; Nov–end Mar Mon–Fri 10–3 ✋ Adult €6, child (under 12) free 🏠

CASA MUSEU J TORRENTS LLADÓ

www.jtorrentsllado.com

The Catalan artist Joaquín Torrents Lladó (1946–93) settled in Mallorca in 1968, living at first in Valldemossa and later in Palma. Among his admirers was the English poet Robert Graves (▷ 19 and 98), who wrote: 'Most painters think they are painters but Joaquín Torrents really is a painter.' After his death, Torrents' house and studio in Palma were turned into a museum. The permanent collection contains a wide spectrum of his work, from his early flirtation with abstract art to more conventional portraits, landscapes, still lifes, stage sets and graphic design. His studio on the first floor has been preserved much as he left it, with sketches of female nudes and an intimate portrait of his young son, born just two years before the artist's premature death. ✚ 53 D4 ✉ Carrer de la Portella 9 ☎ 971 729835 🕙 Jun–end Sep Tue–Fri 11–7; Oct–end May Tue–Fri 10–6, Sat and holidays 10–2 ✋ Adult €3, child (under 10) free. 📖 €36 🏠

CASA OLESA

The 16th-century Casa Olesa has the finest of all Palma's patios. Although this former merchant's mansion cannot be visited, the doors are usually left open and you can peer through the heavy iron gates. The house takes its name from the Olesa family, one of the noble Catalan dynasties that arrived in Mallorca at the time of the Christian conquest (▷ 28). They acquired it in the late 17th century and restored the patio in baroque style. Ionic columns on the ground floor support flattened arches, and a staircase leads to a gallery with a balustrade featuring the Olesa coat of arms. Note the paving stones set into the floor in a geometric pattern and the octagonal cistern. All the elements come together here in perfect architectural harmony. Keep an eye out as you stroll in the old town—many of the houses in nearby streets have similar patios. ✚ 53 D4 ✉ Carrer d'en Morey 9

Below *The interior of Casa Olesa*

CASTELL DE BELLVER

INFORMATION

➕ Off map 52 A4, 223 D6 ✉ Carrer Camilo José Cela s/n ☎ 971 730657 🕒 Apr–end Sep Mon–Sat 8.30–8.15; Oct–end Mar 8.30–7.15. The castle is open on Sun and public holidays (Apr–end Sep 10–7, Oct–end Mar 10–5) though the museums are closed ✋ Adult €2, child (under 12) €1; free on Sun 🚌 City Sightseeing bus or Nos. 3 and 6 to Plaça Gomila

TIPS

➤➤ The easiest way of getting to the castle is on the City Sightseeing bus, so try to combine the two in one day.
➤➤ Entry is free on Sundays, though the museum and classical sculpture collection are both closed.
➤➤ Classical music concerts are held in the courtyard on summer evenings—check the local press or ask at tourist offices for details.

Above *Palma's squat, circular castle was built to defend the island's royal family*

INTRODUCTION

Bellver Castle stands among pine woods overlooking Palma Bay, dominating the skyline as you look across the water from the cathedral. Because it is some distance from the centre of town, it can be quite difficult to get to unless you have your own car. A road leads up to the castle from Avinguda Joan Miró, but the only public transport is the City Sightseeing bus (▷ 40). Alternatively, you can take a bus to Plaça Gomila and walk up to the castle, a steep 20-minute climb through woods. The name of the castle means 'lovely view', and many visitors come up here just for the vistas from the terrace. For the best views of all walk around the moat then climb onto the rooftop: all of Palma is visible.

WHAT TO SEE

THE CASTLE

Bellver Castle was begun in 1300 on the orders of Jaume II and completed some 10 years later. The original architect, Pere Salvà, also built the Palau de l'Almudaina (▷ 65–66). Although the castle was designed as a royal residence, it has hardly ever been used as such and served as a prison for almost 600 years. The first prisoner was the uncrowned Jaume IV, after his father, Jaume III, was defeated at the battle of Llucmajor in 1349, bringing to an end the short-lived kingdom of Mallorca. Many years later the castle became a military prison housing Napoleonic officers and the liberal general Luis de Lacy, who was executed here by firing squad in 1817. Another famous prisoner was Gaspar Melchor de Jovellanos, Treasury Minister to Carlos IV, a captive for six years in a single room. In more recent times the castle was used to house Republican prisoners during the Spanish Civil War.

Have a good look at the castle building before you go in by walking around the perimeter of the moat. Uniquely among Spanish castles, Bellver Castle is circular, with three semicircular buttresses and the round Torre de Homenaje, the keep connected to the main castle by a drawbridge. Once inside, all the rooms lead off Patio de Armas, a central courtyard and parade ground with a well for collecting rainwater. Note the differing architectural styles of the two storeys: the ground floor, designed for the soldiers, has semicircular arches with a flat roof, while the royal family's upper gallery has Gothic arches and rib vaulting. The upper floor also contains the chapel, dedicated to St. Mark, as well as the throne room and the kitchens, still blackened by woodsmoke. From here steps lead up to the roof terrace and its views of the courtyard. Step inside the towers and you may be able to make out the inscription 'Vive Napoleon', carved by French prisoners of war.

THE DESPUIG COLLECTION

Cardinal Antoni Despuig (1745–1813), one of eight children of Ramón Despuig, count of Montenegro, was born in Mallorca. He went on to become Archbishop of Valencia and Seville and a Minister of State at the Vatican. During his time in Italy he amassed a large collection of antiquities—mostly classical Roman sculpture—that he displayed in the garden of his estate at Raixa near Palma. In 1922 Palma City Council acquired part of the collection and it is now displayed in three rooms on the upper floor. The first room looks at the Cardinal's life; the other two rooms contain marble busts, statues and fragments of sculpture. In 2005, a statue of the cardinal by Damià Ramis Caubet was erected in the Santa Magdalena square, in front of the church of the same name, where his remains are buried.

CITY HISTORY MUSEUM

A set of rooms on the ground floor houses Palma's municipal history museum. The displays start with archaeological finds from prehistoric caves around Palma, including Son Oms, destroyed during the expansion of Son Sant Joan airport. There are displays relating to Roman and Moorish Palma and the Catalan conquest, as well as Palma's courtyards and Modernist architecture. Although not as comprehensive as the Museu de Mallorca (▷ 64), it does provide a quick overview. Take a look upstairs at the former historic kitchen.

CASTLE GUIDE
Ground Floor
City History Museum
Room 1: Introduction
Room 2: Prehistory
Room 3: Roman Palma
Room 4: Medina Mayurqa
Room 5: The Catalan Conquest (13th–15th centuries)
Room 6: Expansion (16th–19th centuries)
Room 7: Modernist architecture and the 20th century
Room 8: Tourism

First Floor
Capilla de San Marcos (St. Mark's Chapel)
Sala de Jovellanos (Jovellanos Room)
Salón del Trono (Throne Room)
Sala de las Reinas de Mallorca (Queens' Room)
Cocina (Kitchen)
Colección Despuig (Despuig Collection)

Below *The two-tiered courtyard of the castle, viewed from above*

INFORMATION

www.miro.palmademallorca.es
✚ Off map 52 A4, 223 D6 ✉ Carrer
Joan de Saridakis 29, Cala Major ☎ 971
701420 🕓 Mid-May to mid-Sep Tue–Sat
10–7, Sun 10–3; mid-Sep to mid-may
Tue–Sat 10–6, Sun 10–3 ✋ Adult €5,
child (16–18) €2.80, child (under 16) free
🚌 6 🚊 €12 ⬛ 🏧 ❓ Camera/video
fee €5 (no flash)

TIPS

▶▶ Entry is free on 18 May (international
museum day), 24 June (Joan Miró's
saint's day) and 19 December (the
museum's anniversary).
▶▶ A 50-minute video on Joan Miró is
shown hourly in the auditorium. It is
usually shown in English at 12 and 3pm.

Above *Miró's collection includes more
than 100 paintings, 25 sculptures and
3,000 studio pieces*

FUNDACIÓ JOAN MIRÓ

The Catalan artist Joan Miró (1893–1983), one of the greatest artists of the
20th century, was heavily influenced by Mallorca and he moved permanently
to the island in 1956 (▷ 16). As a child, he spent his summer holidays here
with his Mallorcan mother, who came from Sóller, and he often spoke of
the inspiration that he drew from the Mediterranean light and the changing
colours of the sea and sky. In 1981 Miró donated his studio to Palma City
Council; following his death, his widow donated the remainder of the land
and commissioned the architect Rafael Moneo to design a museum to house
Miró's work.

THE PAINTINGS

The permanent collection contains more than 130 paintings and numerous
sketches, but only a small number are on display at any one time. They are
shown in the Sala Estrella, the central exhibition space. Inevitably, there is
a strong focus on the later period of Miró's life and the work produced in
Mallorca during the 1960s and 1970s. These paintings demonstrate Miró's love
of simple forms; there are similarities with the naïve peasant tradition seen in
siurells (▷ 23).

THE SCULPTURES

During his time in Mallorca Miró became interested in sculpture and several of
his works are displayed in the grounds. *Personnage Gothique* (1974), outside
the main entrance to the museum, is characteristic of his style. The large
bronze figure has a head shaped like a bird, a torso like a television and legs
cast from a donkey's yoke. Look out too for *Femme et Oiseau* (*Woman and
Bird*, 1962), in the Sala Estrella, and *Femme* (1981), in the gardens behind
the museum.

THE STUDIO

Miró's studio was designed by a friend of his, Catalan architect Josep Lluís
Sert. It has been left virtually untouched since Miró's death and you can almost
feel his presence; the unfinished canvases seem to be awaiting his return.
Behind the studio is Son Boter, Miró's 17th-century farmhouse.

FUNDACIÓ LA CAIXA (GRAN HOTEL)

www.fundacio.lacaixa.es

The grand building that houses the headquarters of La Caixa cultural foundation is interesting for two reasons. One, it was designed in 1903 as Palma's first luxury hotel, the Gran Hotel, at a time when the city was just waking up to the possibility of a future in tourism, and two, it was the first significant example of *Modernista* architecture in Palma (▷ 74–75 for further buildings). Leading Catalan Modernist architect Lluís Domènech i Montaner (1850–1923), who is best known for his Palau de la Música Catalana in Barcelona, designed the Gran Hotel. The facade of the five-storey building displays typical Modernist features such as multicoloured ceramics and extravagant floral motifs on the balconies, arches and bay windows.

The ground floor, previously occupied by the hotel's reception rooms, now houses a bookshop and light and airy cafe, while the upper floors are used as exhibition space. It is always worth checking to see what is on as the exhibitions are rarely disappointing and frequently fascinating.

A large gallery on the first floor showcases the paintings of Hermen Anglada Camarasa (1871–1959), founder of the so-called Pollença school of artists. Only two of the works are permanently on display, and both reveal his fascination with gypsy themes. *Valencia* (1910) is a monumental canvas depicting Valencian gypsy dancers wreathed in flowers, while *El Tango de la Corona* (1910) is of Argentinian tango dancers.

✚ 53 D3 ✉ Plaça Weyler 3 ☎ 971 178500 🕐 Tue–Sat 10–9, Sun 10–2 ✋ Free 🍴 🖥 🏛

LA LLOTJA

This 15th-century mercantile trading exchange marks the high point of Gothic civil architecture in Palma. Designed by Guillem Sagrera, who also worked on the cathedral (▷ 70–73), it combines elements of both military and ecclesiastical styles. The turrets and battlements resemble a castle, while the gargoyles, the windows with their pointed arches, and the angel over the door could all have come from a church. Today, the spiralling columns and rib vaulting of the interior make a striking setting for the art exhibitions held here. The area around La Llotja, where the city's tapas bars and clubs are concentrated (▷ 79–81), is particularly lively at night.

✚ 52 B4 ✉ Plaça Llotja 🕐 Tue–Sat 11–2, 5–9, Sun 11–2 ✋ Free

MUSEU D'ART ESPANYOL CONTEMPORANI

www.march.es/arte/palma

An 18th-century mansion close to Plaça Major houses a comprehensive collection of 20th-century Spanish art. The house was rebuilt in the early 20th century for the Mallorcan banker Joan March (▷ 67). From the covered patio, with its elaborate skylight and mosaic floor, a grand marble staircase leads to the galleries. Room 1 contains the biggest names, including an early portrait by Picasso (*Tête de Femme*, 1907) and works by Joan Miró (*Le Perroquet*, 1937), Salvador Dalí (*Composition*, 1946) and Juan Gris (*Carafe et Bol*, 1916). Room 2 is devoted to the Dau Al Set group of abstract artists from Barcelona, such as Antoni Tàpies, whose large-scale canvases can also be seen in Room 4. Among the other artists whose work appears in the museum are the sculptor Eduardo Chillida (1924–2002) and the painter Eduardo Arroyo (born 1937).

Don't miss Miquel Barceló's canvases, in Room 13, which explore the themes of water and space. Look too for his *Large Pot with Skulls* (2000). This is a recurring image in Barceló's work, which has been influenced by his trips to Mali, West Africa (▷ 17).

✚ 53 E2 ✉ Carrer Sant Miguel 11 ☎ 971 713515 🕐 Mon–Fri 10–6.30, Sat 10.30–2 ✋ Free 📖 €18 🏛

MUSEU ES BALUARD

www.esbaluard.org

This stunning museum inside the 16th-century bastion of Sant Pere imaginatively combines historic military architecture with modern art. If you do not want to go into the museum, you can still visit the terrace, which is open to the city as a semi-public space. Sculptures are scattered around the ramparts, and you can take in the view of the castle and the cathedral. The museum is based on the modern art collection of newspaper magnate Pere Serra. Displays vary, but they are likely to include works by Joan Miró and Miquel Barceló.

A highlight is the walk around the Passeig de Ronda (wall walk). The *Aljub* (cistern) in the basement supplied water to ships arriving in Palma. It is now a space for art installations.

✚ 52 B3 ✉ Plaça Porta de Santa Catalina 10 ☎ 971 908200 🕐 Jun–end Sep daily 10am–midnight; Oct–end May Tue–Sun 10–8 ✋ Adult €6, child (under 12) free; reduced price of €4.50 on Tue; free entry on 20 Jan, 1 Mar, 18 May, 12 Sep 🎧 Audiotour included 🍴 🖥 🏛

Below The grand staircase in the Museum of Contemporary Spanish Art

INFORMATION

✚ 53 D4 ✉ Carrer de la Portella 5
☎ 971 717540 🕐 Tue–Sat 10–7, Sun
10–2 🖐 Free 🏛

TIP

❯❯ If time is short, skip the upper floors
and concentrate on the prehistory and
Moorish galleries.

MUSEU DE MALLORCA

The Museum of Mallorca is housed in the 17th-century palace of the count of Aiamans. Although the collections serve as a useful introduction to the various stages of Mallorcan history, the museum's main draw is its stunning displays of objects in authentic contexts—especially those in the prehistory section. The museum is currently undergoing restoration, so some galleries—all on the upper floor—are closed.

TALAIOTIC TREASURES

The tour of the museum is arranged chronologically, beginning in the basement. Here there are archaeological finds from the pre-Talaiotic and Talaiotic periods, when the people of Mallorca lived in caves and built stone towers *(talaiots)* like those at Capocorb Vell (▷ 163). There are actual models of the caves and burial chambers, with bones, ceramics and utensils. Also on display is a complete skeleton of *Myotragus balearicus* (▷ 26), which was wiped out soon after the arrival of the first human beings on the island. A dimly lit room contains the highlight of the museum, a collection of small bronze statues of warriors, probably used in religious rituals. The figures, dating from the fourth century BC, are naked apart from their helmets. Each has one arm raised as if holding a sword and his left arm around a shield.

ROMANS AND MOORS

The Roman and Moorish sections are on the ground floor. Besides a Roman mosaic pavement from a Christian basilica near Campos, highlights include the Almohad Treasure, a remarkable cache of coins and jewellery. It was hidden in a clay pot and buried in a cave by a Muslim family during the Catalan invasion of Mallorca in 1229. The gold coins, minted in Morocco at the end of the 12th century, have Arabic inscriptions. Among items of jewellery are a beautiful pair of gold earrings with delicate filigree work.

GOTHIC TO MODERNIST

The two upper floors cover Gothic, Renaissance and baroque religious art, together with Modernist furniture and 20th-century paintings. The Gothic painting gallery is currently the only one open to the public.

Above *Detail of a glazed plate showing the profile of a Moorish figure*

PALAU DE L'ALMUDAINA

INTRODUCTION

Like the cathedral, the palace is best seen from the seafront, from where it takes on a distinctly Moorish feel, a reminder of its earlier days as an Arab fortress. The entrance is on Carrer Palau Reial, opposite the cathedral's west front. The complex is divided into two distinct parts, the Palau del Senyor Rei (King's Palace) and Palau de la Senyora Regina (Queen's Palace), together with common areas such as the chapel, Great Hall and royal baths. Only the King's Palace and some of the common areas are open to the public. The state rooms contain treasures such as Flemish tapestries, and it is worth taking the audiotour for a detailed description. The Palau de l'Almudaina is the official residence of King Juan Carlos whenever he is in Palma, which means that it is sometimes closed for royal functions. Although the palace is used for ceremonial occasions, the king prefers to stay at Marivent, his summer palace in Cala Major.

WHAT TO SEE

PASEO DE RONDA

This narrow corridor (first discovered during restoration work in 1967) is where the tour of the palace begins. Note the black-and-white coffered ceiling, typifying Mudéjar architecture. The style, which combines both Moorish and Gothic elements, was developed in Spain by Moorish craftsmen living under Christian occupation.

HALL OF KINGS

The Great Hall of the palace originally occupied two floors, but following the collapse of the roof in 1578 it was rebuilt on separate levels and the ground floor was divided into smaller chambers. One of these is now known as the Hall of Kings, after the modern portraits of the kings of Mallorca on the walls.

INFORMATION

www.patrimonionacional.es

✚ 52 C4 ✉ Carrer Palau Reial
☎ 971 214134 ◷ May–end Sep
Mon–Fri 10–6.30, Sat 10–2; Oct–end
Apr Mon–Fri 10–2, 4–6, Sat 10–2
💶 Adult €3.20, child (5–16) €2.30; free
for European Union citizens on Wed
🎧 Guided tours €4 including admission;
audiotours €2 in English, French, German,
Italian and Spanish 📖 €7.20 🏛

TIP

➤➤ The main entrance can only be reached
by a flight of steps, so disabled visitors
need to alert the staff or one of the
soldiers on guard in order to gain access
to a separate entrance to the right.

Above *This palace, originally home to
the Moorish rulers and expanded for the
medieval Catalan kings, is now King Juan
Carlos's official residence in Mallorca*

MIRADOR DEL MAR

This sea-facing terrace offers fine views over the port. From here you can see the Arc de la Drassana, a 10th-century Moorish archway that served as the entrance for vessels to the royal dockyards.

ARAB BATHS

Discovered during restoration, these baths date back to Roman times. With a cold room, a warm room and a hot room heated by an underground furnace, they are similar in style but much better preserved than the Banys Àrabs (▷ 59). The small size of the chambers suggests that they were designed as private baths for the king.

PATIO DE ARMAS

The palace's central courtyard is also known as the Patio de Honor (Main Courtyard). At the centre, hidden beneath four palm trees, a fountain gushes from a stone lion dating from Moorish times. St. Anne's Chapel, built in 1310, dominates the west side of the courtyard. The doorway is a rare example of Romanesque art in Mallorca; mythological figures decorate the marble columns. From the courtyard there is a good view of the Torre del Angel, the central keep of the Moorish fort.

THE KING'S STUDY

The Royal Staircase leads up the state rooms on the first floor. After passing through anterooms you reach the King's Study, still used by King Juan Carlos. This was where Jaume I met secretly in 1229 to receive the surrender of the last Moorish *wali* of Palma. Next to the study is the Sala de Tinell (Throne Room), or Great Hall. The king holds receptions here during his annual visit.

MORE TO SEE

S'HORT DEL REI

Although no longer a part of the palace complex, the King's Garden is closely linked to the history of the Almudaina. At one time it was used as a kitchen garden, supplying oranges, lemons and grapes for the royal table. Wild beasts such as lions and bears, gifts to the king from visiting dignitaries, were also kept here. In the late 19th century the garden was sold for development and a hotel and theatre were built on this site, but in 1967 the land was returned to public use. Now, beneath the walls of the palace, alongside Avinguda d'Antoni Maura, is a peaceful area of fruit trees and tinkling fountains. Sculptures include a statue of a Balearic slinger and the egg-shaped *Monument* by Joan Miró. At the southern end of the gardens black swans can be seen swimming beneath the Arc de la Drassana.

Above *The palace contains fine Flemish tapestries among its many treasures*

PALAU MARCH

The opening of the Palau March museum in 2003 caused a sensation in Palma, revealing previously unseen vistas of the cathedral. The house was built in the 1940s for the Mallorcan financier Joan March (1880–1962), who was popularly known as 'Franco's banker' and rose to become one of the world's richest men. The legitimacy of his fortune has often been questioned but he knew how to spend it. This museum reflects his eclectic tastes and those of his son Bartolomé March (1917–1988), another passionate art collector.

THE SCULPTURE TERRACE

It is difficult to imagine a more spectacular setting for this collection—an open courtyard in the shadow of the cathedral. In front of the main door, on a mosaic pavement, is a bronze torso by Auguste Rodin (1840–1917). Among the other artists whose work is on display are Henry Moore (1898–1986) and Barbara Hepworth (1903–75). But two large abstract works by contemporary Spanish sculptors steal the show. *Orgue del Mar* (*Sea Organ*) by Xavier Corberó (born 1935) combines marble columns with a series of golden balls. *Línies al Vent* (*Lines to the Wind*) by Andreu Alfaro (born 1929) is a wavy steel sculpture set on a balcony directly beneath the cathedral.

EL BELÉN NAPOLITANO

The museum contains a collection of nativity scenes, with 2,000 figures made of wire, wood and clay. Beside the traditional figures of Jesus, the Holy Family, angels, shepherds and kings are innkeepers, gypsies, slaves, fishermen and musicians, all sculpted in great detail.

MUSIC ROOM

On the top floor you can see the original murals by Josep Maria Sert, completed in 1944. The highlight is the Music Room, decorated with exotic images of musicians and Carnival dancers, with billowing curtains and acrobats flying through the sky with balloons.

MAPS AND CHARTS

The museum's magnificent 16th-century maps and navigational charts are exhibited on the first floor. Compiled by Mallorcan cartographers, they are richly illustrated and considered to be some of the finest ever produced during medieval times.

INFORMATION

www.fundbmarch.es

➕ 52 C4 ✉ Carrer Palau Reial 18
☎ 971 711122 🕐 Apr–end Oct Mon–Fri 10–6.30, Sat 10–2; Nov–end Mar Mon–Fri 10–5, Sat 10–2 ✋ Adult €3.60, child (under 12) free ☕ Cappuccino Palau March 🗓

TIP

>> Cappuccino Palau March, in the same building but reached by the steps to the corner of Carrer del Conquistador, is a terrace cafe serving excellent sandwiches, salads and snacks.

Below *Xavier Corberó's contemporary* Orgue del Mar *sculpture*

INFORMATION

www.palmaaquarium.com

➕ 223 E6 ✉ Carrer de Manuela de los Herreros i Sorà ☎ 971 264275 🕐 Daily 10–6 🖐 Adult €19.50, child (3–18) €13.50, child (under 3) free 🚌 15, 17, 23 🖥 📅

PALMA AQUARIUM

Palma's magnificent aquarium opened in 2007 and is one of the largest in Europe, with 55 tanks filled with five million litres of sea water. From the dramatic modern building to the state-of-the-art exhibits, it is hailed as one of the finest aquariums in Europe. Don't miss it!

A WATERY WONDERLAND

A visit to the aquarium follows a straightforward route, which leads you through several themed exhibits. The highlight is a transparent tunnel where you are surrounded by sharks. Refreshments and more substantial meals are available and younger children will enjoy visiting the playground, complete with replica pirate ship.

The aquarium has a total of 8,000 sea creatures from 700 different species, which are divided into several sections. These include creatures from the Mediterranean, such as sea horses, anemones and rays, together with superb examples of flora. The tanks are well labelled and factual and include intriguing titles, like Sea Secrets, where the so-called holy fish takes a starring role with its unusual lifestyle. Apparently when the male dies, a female simply changes sex and replaces him.

In the Indian Ocean section there are beautiful corals, as well as dramatic tropical fish, such as zebra and butterfly fish. While the Discovery Zone is more educational, the stunning rooftop Jungle section replicates a rain forest, complete with waterfalls, tropical vegetation and even the occasional piranha. The final exhibit is the Big Blue aquarium, the deepest in Europe, featuring the walk-through tunnel surrounded by sharks. Cushions are provided if you want to relax and get up close and personal. The aquarium curator, Aharon Miroz, worked for many years with Phillippe Cousteau, son of the late Jacques Cousteau, possibly the most famous oceanographer ever. Little wonder that the Palma Aquarium is such a class act.

Above *Pull up a cushion and enjoy the aquarium's state-of-the-art tanks*

PARC DE LA MAR

This public space was created in the 1960s on land reclaimed from the sea during the construction of the dual carriageway linking Palma to its port. Before the building of the road the cathedral had been reflected in the sea so an artificial lagoon was built to restore this image. At the time, the park was criticized as a misguided attempt to cover up a disastrous mistake, but over the years it has become accepted—even loved—by the people of Palma. The mural on the south side of the park was created by local artist Lluís Castaldo from a Joan Miró painting. From this side of the lake the views of the Palau de l'Almudaina and the cathedral rising out of the Renaissance walls are stunning. On the north side, beneath the walkway along the ramparts, is Ses Voltes, an imaginative open-air theatre staging free concerts on summer evenings. Nearby, in the vaults of the old walls, is the Ses Voltes art gallery (Tue–Sat and Sun am). Both the theatre and gallery were built during the 1980s; since then Parc de la Mar has become a popular meeting place. There are plans to extend the park to the seafront by burying the road in an underground tunnel.

🔳 52 C5 ❓ Summer Nights programme of free concerts and films at Ses Voltes (☎ 971 724090) 🔲

PASSEIG DES BORN

Es Born has always played a significant role in Palma's life and today the short street, which connects the main shopping districts to the cathedral and the sea, acts as a focal point for visitors. The name harks back to the Middle Ages, when the street was an arena for jousting contests. Originally, this was a narrow creek and the promenade you see today was created in 1613 after the river was diverted in an attempt to prevent floods. The stone sphinxes at either end, and the fountains at the north end, were added in 1833. Es Born has become not only a place for strolling but also for concerts,

demonstrations and fairs. Can Solleric (Tue–Sat 10–2, 5–9, Sun 10–1.30), at the north end, is a modern art gallery, bookshop and cafe housed in an 18th-century baroque mansion. It was built for a family of oil merchants from Alaró and now houses a tourist office.

🔳 52 C3 🔲

PASSEIG MARÍTIM

Aside from Parc de la Mar, the building of the dual carriageway along Palma's seafront has had one positive effect—the creation of a waterside walk between the cathedral and the port. The footpath and bicycle track extends 5km (3 miles) east to the harbour at Portitxol and west to Porto Pí, though the most popular stretch is just west of Avinguda d'Antoni Maura. It is easiest to begin this walk on the north side of the road, following the palm-lined Passeig de Sagrera past La Llotja (▷ 63) and the 17th-century Consolat de la Mar. This former maritime tribunal, with a pair of cannons outside the door, is now the headquarters of the Balearic government. From here you can cross to the fishing port, where an auction takes place each morning and fishermen can be seen mending their nets.

Between the fishing harbour and the yacht club the path follows the coast as it curves around the bay,

offering superb views of both the cathedral and Castell de Bellver (▷ 60–61) across the water. A good place to take in the views is El Pesquero, a boardwalk cafe beside the fishing port.

🔳 52 A3 🔲

PLAÇA MAJOR

This large, open plaza, at the centre of a shopping district, is one of the liveliest places in town. It is home to a changing cast of portrait painters, musicians, street vendors, mime artists and 'living statues', who spring to life when you drop a coin into their hat. The cafes around the square are mostly overpriced and of poor quality, but they nevertheless make good vantage points. The square, with a portico at ground level and four storeys of mustard-coloured, green-shuttered housing, was laid out in the 19th century on the site of the previous headquarters of the Spanish Inquisition. The Inquisition's infamous Casa Negra (Black House) was demolished, along with a neighbouring convent. This was the site of Palma's main fish and vegetable markets until 1951. Today, craft markets are held daily in summer and at weekends throughout the year. Carrer Sant Miguel is excellent for shopping.

🔳 53 E3 🔲

Below *Fountain in the Parc de la Mar*

LA SEU (CATEDRAL)

INTRODUCTION

It is hard to imagine a church with a more spectacular setting than that of Palma Cathedral, commonly known as La Seu (the bishop's seat). Originally built on a cliff overlooking the harbour, the cathedral still stands out from its surroundings—despite the construction of a highway that separates it from the sea. For the best views of the cathedral, walk around to the seaward side or drop down to Parc de la Mar (▷ 69), where the pinnacles, gargoyles and flying buttresses are reflected in an artificial lake. Although nothing inside the cathedral matches this first impression from outside, it is worth paying the fee to look around. The entrance is on the north side, in Plaça Almoina, facing the Palau de l'Almudaina (▷ 65–66). Unless you are attending a service, you must enter through the ticket office inside the old almshouse, Casa de l'Almoina. From here you pass through the museum to emerge in a side aisle beneath the main organ. After seeing the cathedral you can return to the museum before leaving.

WHAT TO SEE

PORTAL DEL MIRADOR

Built between 1385 and 1430, this delicately carved doorway facing the sea was originally known as the Door of the Apostles, but its present name reflects its position as a vantage point. Five statues—of St. James, St. John the Baptist, St. Peter, St. Paul and St. Andrew—stand to either side of a double doorway, separated by a sculpted Virgin and Child. There should be statues of all the Apostles, as the empty niches indicate. The tympanum, above the portal, features a scene of the Last Supper presided over by God; around this, archivolts (ornamental mouldings around the arches) depict Old Testament prophets and angels blowing trumpets. A gable with the head of Christ at its centre surmounts the entire doorway.

INFORMATION

www.catedraldemallorca.org
✚ 53 D4 ✉ Plaça Almoina ☎ 971 723130 ◷ Jun–end Sep Mon–Fri 10–6; Apr–end May and Oct 10–5.15; Nov–end Mar 10–3.15; all year Sat 10–2.15
🖐 Adult €4, child (under 11) free 🏧

TIPS

›› To fully experience the cathedral's atmosphere, go to High Mass at 10.30am on Sunday.
›› Look up from the otherwise disappointing cloister for the best view of the three-storey belltower, which is generally hidden from view.
›› As you walk out of the cloister towards the gift shop, be sure to look down through a glass panel in the floor that reveals excavated remains of the Roman city.

Above *Detail of Gaudí's canopy*
Opposite *Night-time view of the cathedral from Passeig de Sagrera*

CATHEDRAL GUIDE
Key to floor plan
A Almshouse
B Belltower
C New Chapter House
D Old Chapter House
E Cloister
F Pulpit
G High Altar
H Bishop's Throne

Key to chapels
1 Trinitat
2 Sant Pere
3 Sant Antoni de Padua
4 Mare de Déu de la Corona
5 Sant Martí
6 Sant Bernat
7 Mare de Déu de la Grada
8 Sagrat Cor de Jesus
9 Sant Benet
10 Baptisteri
11 Animes
12 Immaculada Concepció
13 Sant Sebastià
14 Sant Josep
15 Todos los Santos
16 Pietat (with organ above)
17 Sant Crist
18 Sant Jeroni
19 Corpus Christi

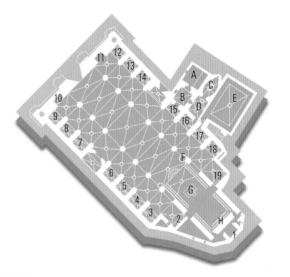

THE NAVE

Although the side chapels lining the aisles are filled with intricate details and religious art, it is the nave's overall impression of light and space that commands attention. Light streams in through stained-glass windows, and the rose window above the chancel is more than 12m (39ft) in diameter, making it one of the largest in the world. In it you can make out the shape of the Star of David. The window consists of more than 1,200 individual stained-glass panels—the glass has had to be replaced a number of times, most recently following damage caused during the Spanish Civil War. At the request of the bishop, Catalan architect Antoni Gaudí made a number of modifications to the cathedral between 1904 and 1914. Among his revolutionary changes were the opening up of windows that had previously been blocked off from view, and ringing the columns of the nave with wrought-iron electric candelabra in the shape of crowns. He was also responsible for moving the choirstalls from their position in the centre of the nave in order to open up the view of the altar, and for the restoration of the original 14th-century Gothic altarpiece, which now hangs in the southern aisle over the interior of the Portal del Mirador.

THE BALDACCHINO

Gaudí's most controversial addition was this altar canopy, designed in the shape of an octagonal crown and thought to represent the crown of thorns placed on Jesus's head. It is decorated with vine leaves and ears of corn, clear symbols of the bread and wine used at the Eucharist. A candelabrum, suspended from the ceiling by a series of ropes and pulleys, holds 35 brass lamps to illuminate the altar. The materials used, which include cardboard, cork, wood and silk brocade, were not intended to be permanent—this was in fact a provisional model for a project that was never finished, but has become an irremovable fixture. Behind the altar, look out for the 14th-century marble bishop's throne. When Gaudí began work on the cathedral this had been hidden from view, but he returned it to its rightful place in the centre of the chancel and surrounded it with his own ceramic designs featuring plant motifs and diocesan coats of arms.

CAPELLA DE SANT PERE

Miquel Barceló's (▷ 17) first major public work in Mallorca was the remodelling of the 14th-century chapel to the right of the main altar. To begin with, the entire chapel was covered with a second skin of terracotta, which was produced in a ceramic workshop in Italy and decorated with images of the parable of the loaves and fishes. Stained-glass windows 12m (39ft) high filter the changing light onto the terracotta walls. Barceló was also responsible for the altar, the candelabrum and the sculpture of the crucified Christ. The project, begun in 2002, was scheduled for completion by 2003, but was subject to delays, partly caused by the contentious nature of Barceló's work. The cathedral authorities objected to the original sculpture because it was thought to be too sexual. The chapel finally opened to the public in early 2007.

MUSEUM

Three rooms close to the cathedral entrance house its museum. The first room that you come to is the Vermells sacristy, at the foot of the belltower. Here the centrepiece is a great 16th-century processional monstrance (receptacle used for displaying the consecrated body of Christ) encrusted with silver and precious stones. Here too is the Book of Silver, a reliquary once believed to have been a portable altar carried by Jaume I during his conquest of the island. The most interesting exhibit, however, is the pair of 14th-century rimmonim, used in synagogues to keep the pages of the Jewish scriptures in place. They came from a synagogue in Sicily and are thought to be the oldest of their kind in the world. Leaving this room to the left, you come to the Gothic chapter house. Here are Gothic altarpieces and the lavish tomb of Bishop Gil Sánchez Muñoz (1360–1447), a former bishop of Mallorca who assumed the title of Clement VIII, an antipope set up in opposition to the pope during the schism in the Roman Catholic Church. The final room in the museum is the baroque chapter house, an oval chapel with an extravagant domed ceiling. The collections here are equally ornate, and include ivory crucifixes, silver candelabra and a 16th-century relic of the True Cross.

MORE TO SEE

CAPELLA DE LA TRINITAT

The Chapel of the Trinity, dating from 1327, is one of the oldest parts of the cathedral. Situated behind the high altar, it is notable for its fine alabaster tombs of the Mallorcan kings Jaume II and Jaume III, which were placed here when the chapel was restored in 1946. The tombs, by the Catalan sculptor Frederic Marès, are rich in detail; note the weeping lions supporting the royal sarcophagi. The chapel opens approximately once a month for guided tours—ask at the tourist office for details.

MUSEU DIOCESÀ

The Diocesan Museum is located in a wing of the bishop's palace. The most emblematic item is a 15th-century painting of St. George slaying a dragon. St. George is said to have appeared on his white charger when the Catalan army entered Palma in 1229. Don't miss the fabulous altarpiece depicting the Passion of Christ, with its fine craftsmanship and detail.

✚ 53 D4 ✉ Carrer del Mirador 5 ☎ 971 213100 🕐 Tue–Fri 10–2 ✋ Adult €3, child (under 10) free

Below left *The cathedral museum displays a variety of treasures and religious artefacts*
Below *Gaudí's unfinished Crown of Thorns canopy above the altar*

MODERNIST PALMA

Modernist architecture and modern art—plus foodie and shopping treats—between the old town and Palma's most up-and-coming district, are highlighted on this walk.

THE WALK

Distance: 4km (2.5 miles)
Time: 2 hours
Start/end at: Plaça de la Reina
Parking: Underground car park beneath Parc de la Mar

HOW TO GET THERE

Several bus services stop at Plaça de la Reina, including 6, 15, 17 and the City Sightseeing bus

★The best-known Modernist, Spanish architect, Antoni Gaudí (1852–1926), worked on Palma's cathedral (▷ 70–73) and his influence can be seen across the city. This walk takes in some of the leading examples of Modernist architecture in Palma before ending in Santa Catalina, a buzzing district of restaurants and bars.

Start at the northern end of the S'Hort del Rei gardens and climb the steps towards the cathedral, emerging alongside Palau March (▷ 67). Turn left at the top of the steps, passing the Balearic Parliament building on your left to

Above *The façade of Can Corbella, designed by Nicolás Lliteras*

arrive at Plaça de Cort in front of the Ajuntament (city hall). Turn left beside a huge old olive tree to enter the pedestrianized shopping district.

❶ On reaching the first street corner of the pedestrianized district, look up to your left at the façade of Can Corbella, one of the forerunners of Modernism in Palma. Note the Moorish-style horseshoe arches and stained-glass windows on the ground floor, the undulating wooden façade and octagonal tower.

Turn right along Carrer Jaume II. The street ends at Plaça del Marquès del Palmer.

❷ On Plaça del Marquès del Palmer, step back to admire Palma's most distinctive Modernist building, Can Forteza Rey. Lluís Forteza Rey designed it in 1909. The upper half of the façade is covered with *trencadís* (fragments of broken ceramic). Note the grotesque face set between a pair of winged

dragons. The neighbouring building, Can Aguila, was built at the same time, as a department store, but is now a shoe shop. It is notable for the extensive use of iron and glass in its façade. The archway in front of you leads into Plaça Major (▷ 69). Instead, take the steps down to your left to arrive on Plaça Weyler, where there are two more Modernist classics.

On your left is the Forn des Teatre, a bakery with a charming art nouveau shopfront. Across the street is the Gran Hotel, the first Modernist building in Palma, now home to Fundació La Caixa (▷ 63).

Continue a short way ahead to Plaça Mercat, on your left.

❸ Plaça Mercat occupies the site of the city's oldest market place, used as a souk in Moorish times. On the square is Can Casasayas, a pair of matching Modernist mansions— separated by a narrow lane—with balconies in the shape of carnival masks.

Keep ahead along Avinguda de la Unió, passing the top of Passeig des Born (▷ 69) to reach the boutiques and arcades of Avinguda Jaume III.

❹ This is Palma's principal shopping street. After passing the department store El Corte Inglés on your left, look for Carrer Baró Santa Maria de Sepulcre on the opposite side of the road. If you feel like a break, stop at Ca'n Joan de S'Aigo, a smart coffee house at Baró Santa Maria de Sepulcre 5. (You'll pass the sister establishment of the same name on the Jewish Quarter walk, ▷ 76–77.)

Continue to the top of Avinguda Jaume III, then turn left and walk along Passeig Mallorca, a promenade following the line of the medieval walls. Ahead is the Museu Es Baluard (▷ 63). Cross the bridge to reach Jardins de la Faixina.

❺ The Jardins de la Faixina, popular with children, has a seating area for seniors, as well as some low-impact exercise installations.

Cross at the traffic lights and walk a short way up Avinguda Argentina. Turn left onto Carrer de Sant Magí.

❻ On the corner of Carrer de Sant Magí is Hostal Cuba, a Modernist hotel of Moorish inspiration with a minaret-shaped tower. You are now in the Santa Catalina district, built as a fishing village in the early 20th century. The mix of old-style neighbourhood shops with trendy modern restaurants and bars gives it a cosmopolitan, villagey feel.

Continue along Carrer de Sant Magí, passing the last working coalyard in Palma at No. 35 and Ferreteria La Central at No. 37, an ironmonger's shop with a Modernist facade decorated with ornamental flower and vegetable motifs. Turn

left into Plaça Vapor and walk to the viewpoint overlooking the harbour.

❼ Several old windmills have been restored and now house nightclubs, a cultural centre and the Museu dels Molins/Molí d'en Garleta (call to arrange visits, tel 971 429555).

Turn right to follow the sea walls before returning to Carrer de Sant Magí along a narrow alley, and cross the road. Follow Carrer Mir to the right of the church to Plaça del Progrès.

❽ On the left of Plaça del Progrès is Bar Progreso, dating from 1920, and almost opposite is Ca'n Palmer at Carrer Quetglas 5, with ceramic mosaics on the facade.

Turn right along Carrer Dameto to reach Mercat de Santa Catalina **❾**, a thriving local market. Continue to the end of the street, then turn right on Avinguda Argentina and return to the centre of Palma's old town along the seafront.

WHERE TO EAT
There are many restaurants and bars around Santa Catalina market. For a snack, try the seafood *tapas* at El Pilón (▷ 88).

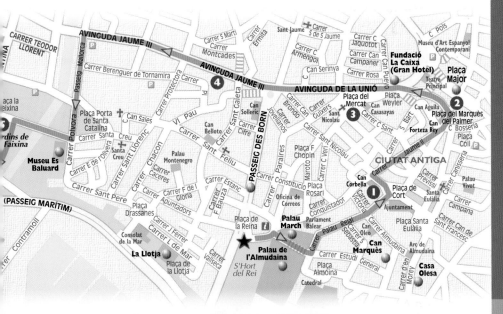

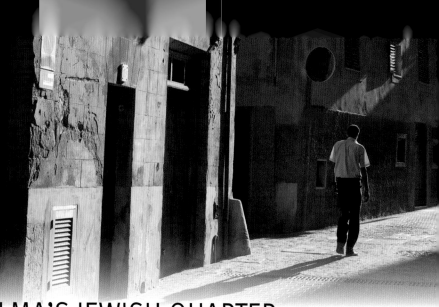

PALMA'S JEWISH QUARTER

An easy walk through one of the lesser-known parts of the old town explores the dark, narrow back streets of what was once a thriving Jewish neighbourhood.

THE WALK

Distance: 3.2km (2 miles)
Time: 2 hours
Start/end at: Parc de la Mar
Parking: Underground car park beneath Parc de la Mar

HOW TO GET THERE

Buses stopping on Passeig des Born and Avinguda d'Antoni Maura (6, 15, 17) are just a short walk from Parc de la Mar

★During the 14th century the district known as El Call was one of the most important Jewish quarters in Europe, an enclave of silk merchants, silversmiths, synagogues and scholars. The Jews of Palma were distinguished in many fields, including medicine, astronomy, navigation and cartography—in the 14th century a map of the known world was produced by father and son Abraham and Jafuda Cresques (▷ 30). An anti-Semitic riot in 1391 led to the decline of the Jewish quarter and the start of the forced conversion of Jews to Christianity. It is only since the 1970s that an active Jewish community has returned to Palma, though the former Jewish neighbourhood now has its own mosque—a sign of changing times.

Begin the walk on the south side of Parc de la Mar, facing the cathedral. Head east, walking beside the lake with good views of the cathedral to your left. Beyond the lake, climb to the road and continue across another small section of park with a playground beside the Renaissance walls. At the end of the park, look for a gap in the wall to enter the city through the 16th-century Porta de la Murada.

❶ Porta de la Murada is the gate to Sa Calatrava, one of Palma's most traditional areas and home to its tanning industry in the 15th century.

Keep straight ahead, going gently uphill, and take the first turning left, Carrer de la Calatrava, to enter a maze of narrow alleyways and streets. Turn right along Carrer de Can Salom and continue uphill onto Carrer d'en Calders. The street ends in Plaça de Sant Jeroni.

❷ To the right of Plaça de Sant Jeroni are the church and convent of Sant Jeroni, with the restored battlements and tower of the only surviving section of Arab walls beyond.

Fork left across the square and continue ahead along Carrer dels Botons. It was along here that the cartographer Jafuda Cresques was born, around 1350. At the end of the street, cross the road and continue slightly to the right along Carrer del Socors, across Plaça del Pes de la Palla, formerly the city's straw market. Keep right along Carrer dels Socors to reach a small square, Plaça Batle Llorenç Bisbal.

Above *Palma's Jewish quarter is full of atmospheric little back streets*

❸ On entering Plaça Batle Llorenç Bisbal, note the pair of churches on your right. The first, the 15th-century Nostra Senyora de Gracìa (Our Lady of Grace), was founded by a group of converted Jews. It takes its name from its abandonment in the 17th century, when the Augustinian order built the neighbouring church of Nostra Senyora dels Socors (Our Lady of Mercy).

Turn left across the square and walk through an archway to enter Passeig per l'Artesania.

❹ Passeig per l'Artesania is a modern complex of craft workshops and shops where artists sell Mallorcan glassware, pottery, woodwork, leatherwork and recycled goods.

Cross Plaça de l'Artesania and turn right to reach Plaça Josep Maria Quadrado.

❺ As you enter Plaça Josep Maria Quadrado look up at the facade of Can Barceló, the four-storey apartment block on your left. The most notable feature of this *Modernista* (Catalan art nouveau) building is the set of ceramic panels, produced in a local factory, depicting female artists, architects, writers and musicians.

Keep right across the square and continue along a narrow alley to reach Carrer Samaritana, where there is a small mosque. Turn left here and then immediately right to reach Palma's most elegant coffee house, Ca'n Joan de S'Aigo. Founded in 1700, it is now famed for its almond ice cream. Retrace your steps to Carrer Samaritana and turn right, then fork left to return to Plaça Josep Maria Quadrado. Turn right to reach Plaça de Sant Francesc ❻, dominated by the Basílica de Sant Francesc (▷ 59). Cross the square, keeping to the right, then turn right and immediately left along Carrer Pere Nadal. Continue to the crossroads at the junctions of Carrer

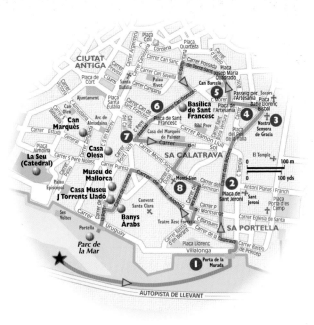

del Call, Carrer del Sol and Carrer Monti-Sion.

❼ This crossroads was the main gate to the Jewish quarter. It was through here that a mob burst on 2 August 1391, killing 300 Jews and consigning this district to history.

The main streets of El Call lead off left from here. Take a sharp left along Carrer del Sol, passing the 14th-century palace of the count of La Cova. Farther along on the left is Casa del Marquès de Palmer, a 16th-century mansion with delicate, carved Renaissance windows. Turn right along a narrow alley, Carrer de la Criança, to emerge opposite the Jesuit church of Monti-Sion.

❽ The church of Monti-Sion was built on the site of an old synagogue. Note the elaborate portal of 1683, its columns decorated with motifs and statues of the Jesuit saints St. Ignatius and St. Francis Xavier.

Turn left along Carrer del Seminari and right along Carrer de les Escoles

beside the walls of the old seminary. Continue down to a small square where you will see the Teatre Xesc Forteza, opened in 2003. Turn right and follow the lane around to reach Carrer de Sant Alonso, with two stone benches beneath a tree. Keep straight on along this street to a crossroads, and turn left along Carrer de Can Serra. Follow this street past the Banys Àrabs and around to the right, then turn left under an archway. Keep straight ahead through the Portella gate to return to Parc de la Mar, or turn right to walk along the top of the Renaissance walls.

WHERE TO EAT
LA TABERNA DEL CARACOL
For great tapas, try this cosy backstreet bar near the end of the walk. It has daily specials on the chalkboard and a convivial traditional ambience with its strings of garlic and racks of local wine. The fried aubergine slices drizzled with honey come particularly recommended.
✉ Carrer de Sant Alonso 2 ☎ 971 714908
🕐 Mon–Sat 7.30–11.30

SHOPPING

BOSSA

One of the upmarket designerwear shops on Plaça de Cort, Bossa eschews the mainstream and specializes in innovative jewellery by designers from Spain and the rest of Europe. Designers include Raquel Moreno, who is very successful in Spain (earrings cost from €100). The shop also sells perfumes and accessories. There are several branches around the city.

✉ Plaça de Cort 3, 07001 Palma ☎ 971 213565 ⏰ Mon–Fri 10–8, Sat 10–3

LA CASA DEL MAPA

All kinds of maps, from reproductions of historic maps of Mallorca to up-to-the-minute walkers' maps, are sold at this useful shop, under an archway between Plaça Rosari and Carrer Jaume II. The shop also sells a selection of walking guides, postcards and stationery.

✉ Carrer de Sant Domingo 11, 07001 Palma ☎ 971 225945 ⏰ Mon–Fri 10–1.30, 5–7.30, Sat 10–1

CHOCOLAT FACTORY

www.chocolatfactory.com
Enjoying a fine position on this scenic square, this tiny shop is a chocoholic's fantasy, selling superb Belgian chocolates ranging from the more conventional truffles to mint-infused and chocolaty lemon drops. Samples happily available!

✉ Plaça Mercat 9, 07001 Palma ☎ 971 229493 ⏰ Mon–Sat 10.30–9

COLMADO SANTO DOMINGO

This shop sells Mallorcan speciality foods, mainly *sobrassadas* (▷ 210), to tourists. Prices and quality are typical for Palma, but it is an entertaining place to visit, as you fight your way through a forest of sausages hanging from the ceiling. It also sells fig loaves, wines, fruit and vegetables.

✉ Carrer de Sant Domingo 1, 07001 Palma ☎ 971 714887 ⏰ Mon–Sat 10–8

DIALOG

www.dialog-palma.com
Dialog is the city's largest international bookshop, with a superb range of books, including fiction, children's books, travel and health in English and German. There's a laid-back cafe here, as well as a year-round programme of Spanish language courses.

✉ Carrer Carme 14, 07001 Palma ☎ 971 719994 ⏰ Mon–Fri 9.30–2, 4.30–8.30, Sat 10–1.30

EL CORTE INGLÉS

www.elcorteingles.es
A Spanish institution, the El Corte Inglés department stores (there are two in Palma) offer a high-quality selection of all the goods you'll find up and down Avinguda Jaume III: designer clothes ranges, handmade shoes, electronics, sports equipment, household items and a section selling gourmet food, including excellent examples of Mallorcan specialities.

✉ Avinguda Jaume III 15, 07012 Palma ☎ 971 770177 ⏰ Mon–Sat 9.30–9.30

FORN DES TEATRE

Forn des Teatre is as notable for its mouthwatering pastries and pies as it is for its fabulous art deco facade. It's a famously good place to buy traditional *ensaïmadas* (▷ 210). They have a cafe next door.

✉ Plaça Weyler 9, 07001 Palma ☎ 971 715254 ⏰ Mon–Sat 8–8, Sun 9–2

FRASQUET

Those with a sweet tooth will find themselves ignoring the elaborate gold-lacquered decoration of this chocolate shop on the corner of Carrer Orfila and Can Danus, and homing in on Frasquet's amazing array of sweets and chocolates.

As well as traditional sweets such as *panellets*, balls of almond paste coated in toasted pinenuts, the chocolatier is famous for producing Mallorca's finest chocolate.
✉ Carrer Orfila 4, 07001 Palma ☎ 971 721824 🕐 Mon–Fri 9.30–2, 4.45–8, Sat 9.30–2

LIBRERIA RIPOLL
This is an excellent place to buy arty, out-of-the-ordinary postcards, antique maps and aged prints of Mallorcan scenes, fauna, flora and landscapes. You can also find rare books here, although they are mostly in Spanish. It's a quirky shop on an otherwise mainstream shopping street.
✉ Carrer Sant Miguel 12, 07002 Palma ☎ 971 711191 🕐 Mon–Fri 10–1.30, 4.30–8, Sat 10–2

LOEWE
www.loewe.com
Loewe is a mainstay of Spain's fashion scene; the luxury Spanish fashion house was founded in 1846 and is now part of the Louis Vuitton group, with stores throughout the world. The Palma store sells beautiful leather goods and accessories for men and women, such as handbags, luggage, belts and purses. Styling is classic but contemporary and the workmanship is typically excellent.
✉ Avinguda Jaume III 1, 07012 Palma ☎ 971 715275 🕐 Mon–Fri 9.30–8, Sat 9.30–2

MAJORICA
Majorica is one of the two main producers of Mallorca's famous man-made pearls. Branches throughout the island sell pearl jewellery, from earrings to strings of coloured pearls. Prices start from about €20 for earrings. There is another branch of Majorica at Avinguda Jaume III 11.
✉ Plaça Mercat 9, 07001 Palma ☎ 971 722919 🕐 Mon–Sat 10–8

PICAROL
Sandals are one of the few traditional products still made in Mallorca and this small shop has a bright selection, plus other shoes. It is particularly strong on children's sizes. Carrer Forn del Racó is a narrow side street close to Carrer Jaume II.
✉ Carrer Forn del Racó 1, 07001 Palma ☎ 971 711196 🕐 Mon–Sat 10.30–8.30

VIDRIERÍAS DE GORDIOLA
The best place in Palma to buy Algaida's famous glassware, Vidrierías de Gordiola stocks glasses, candlesticks, vases and ornaments in coloured, hand-blown glass. Prices are slightly more expensive than buying direct from the factory in Algaida (▷ 161).
✉ Carrer Victoria 2, 07001 Palma ☎ 971 711541 🕐 Mon–Fri 10–1.30, 5–8, Sat 10–1.30

VINOTECA BONS VINS
For an outstanding selection of wines, especially Mallorcan and Spanish vintages, head for this shop on the northern side of La Llotja. The staff are very knowledgeable and helpful and there are regular tastings, including evening get-togethers to help make up your mind. Bottles start from €7 to €8, but expect to spend upwards of €12 for the really good wines.
✉ Carrer Sant Feliu 7, 07012 Palma ☎ 971 727185 🕐 Mon–Sat 10.30–2, 6–late

ZARA
You'll find good-quality, well-cut clothing for men, women and children at affordable prices in this branch of the well-known Galician fashion chain on the Born. Styles are very fashionable, so purchases may look dated next year, but Zara is an excellent destination for bargain hunters.
✉ Plaça Rei Carles I, Passeig des Born, 07012 Palma ☎ 971 719828 🕐 Mon–Sat 10–8.30 winter; Mon–Sat 10–9 summer

ENTERTAINMENT AND NIGHTLIFE
ABACO
If Abaco has a theme, it is probably all about fall-of-the-Roman-Empire decadence. Behind a heavy wooden door in La Llotja, the whole of this palatial town house has been converted into a surreal nightspot. Classical music plays quietly in the background, flower garlands cascade from marble stairways and the main courtyard is decorated with mountains of fresh fruit, art, candles, busts and mirrors. All the rooms are similarly fantastical; the kitchen has colossal copper pans and vegetable displays covering every surface; the garden has fountains and caged birds. You'll be snapped back to reality by the drink prices—cocktails cost from €15, champagne up to €150 per bottle—but it is definitely worth one drink to see everything.
✉ Carrer Sant Joan 1, 07012 Palma ☎ 971 714939 🕐 Nightly 8pm–1am (2.30am summer)

Below *Forn des Teatre's art deco facade*

ABRAXAS
www.abraxasmallorca.com
Formerly Pacha, this huge club may have changed its name, but its remains as popular as ever. The music policy is adventurous, the clientele trendy (if youthful) and the setting fabulous: it overlooks the Bay of Palma from a low cliff on the Passeig Marítim. With an outdoor terrace, two dance floors and several bars, there's somewhere to go whether you want to chill out or dance.
✉ Passeig Marítim 42, 07015 Palma ☎ 971 455908 🕐 Summer, nightly 10pm–late

ART DÉCO
www.artdecodisco.com
This bar-club in Santa Catalina overlooks the Passeig Marítim. The playlist is mostly pop music from the '70s, '80s and '90s and attracts smartly dressed professionals who are noticeably older than the clubbers on the promenade below. It also holds regular salsa classics.
✉ Plaça Vapor 20, 07011 Palma ☎ 650 391915 🕐 Thu–Sat midnight–late

AUDITORIUM DE PALMA
www.auditoriumdepalma.es
The largest auditorium in Mallorca, with 1,700 seats, opened in 1969 and occupies a central position on Palma's seafront. The Mozart room hosts the principal shows, with ballet, theatre and classical concerts featuring in most programmes.
✉ Passeig Marítim 18, 07014 Palma ☎ 902 332211 🖐 €15–€80 🍴 🍷

BCM
BCM, one of Europe's largest nightclubs, promises sensory overload. With capacity for 5,500 people, a 10,000-watt sound system and a 400,000-watt light show, you know if you'll love it or hate it. The mainly young, British crowd dances to house, garage and techno played by star DJs on the high-ceilinged upper floor; over-30s prefer the lower floor.
✉ Avinguda S'Olivera s/n, 07182 Magaluf ☎ 971 711856 🕐 Nightly 10pm–late

BLACK CAT
This popular, well-established gay club is at the heart of Palma's gay scene, surrounded by other gay-friendly venues, and has a dark room and drag acts.
✉ Avinguda Joan Miró 75, 07015 Palma 🕐 Nightly midnight–5am (show 3.30am)

BLUESVILLE
Musically literate youngsters and older hipsters arrive for live sounds at Bluesville after 12am. Blues, bluesy rock and world music are the soundtrack and the standard of the live acts is generally high. Beers cost €3. It's down an easily missed side street in La Llotja.
✉ Ma del Moro 3, 07012 Palma 🕐 Daily 10.30pm–4am, live performances from midnight

LA BODEGUITA DEL MEDIO
www.labodeguitadelmedio.es
This is one of a chain of Havana-themed bars (another is in Puerto Portals). Many of the 20- to 40-something customers come for the Cuban cocktails, and there's Cuban music on the stereo.
✉ Carrer Vallseca 16, 07012 Palma ☎ 971 717832 🕐 Daily from 8pm. Closes Mon–Thu 12am, Fri–Sat 3am, Sun 1am

CAFÉ ANTIQUARI
www.cafe-antiquari.com
A quintessential European cafe where you can check your emails and grab a quick espresso daytime, and spend the evenings enjoying a selection of beers and wines, along with tasty light snacks. There's live music as well as regular art exhibitions and thematic evenings.
✉ Carrer Arabi 5, 07013 Palma ☎ 971 719687 🕐 Mon–Sat 10am–3am

CASINO MALLORCA
www.casinodemallorca.com
High-rollers will head to the casino for poker, roulette, blackjack and slot machines. For entry to the casino you will need to dress smartly; don't forget ID, such as a passport.
✉ Urbanización Sol de Mallorca, Carretera Andratx, 07181 Palma ☎ 971 130000 🕐 Casino: nightly 5pm–5am 🍴 🍷

ES FOGUERÓ
www.esfoguero.com
This is a very popular dinner show featuring African dancers and flamenco ballet. Tickets can be organized through most holiday tour-operators but it is also possible to attend independently. It's located 10km (6 miles) from Palma and 2km (1.2 miles) from the airport.
✉ Carretera S'Aranjassa, km 10, Can Pastilla, 07610 Palma ☎ 971 265260 🕐 Shows on Wed, Thu and Sat eves 🖐 From €32 (show only), or from €49 (for dinner) 🚗 Take the airport motorway, turn off at exit 10, and follow signs

FUNDACIÓ LA CAIXA
A wide range of activities and events, including art exhibitions,

are held at the centrally located Fundació La Caixa.

✉ Plaça Weyler 3, 07001 Palma
☎ 971 178500 🕐 Tue–Sat 10–9, Sun 10–2 💻

GARITO CAFÉ
www.garitocafe.com
Garito is one of the most fashionable bars in Palma. DJ Nacho Velasco plays jazzy deep house to pre-club drinkers at the end of the week, but you'll hear an eclectic selection of music, from drum 'n' bass to soul and funk, on other nights.

✉ Dársena de Can Barbarà, 07015 Palma
☎ 971 736912 🕐 Daily 7pm–4.30am

HAVANA
Laid-back bar with a rustic stone floor, comfortable seats and daily international papers. Equally inviting for morning coffee or cocktails, accompanied by chill-out jazz.

✉ Carrer de Sant Magi, Santa Catalina, 07013 Palma ☎ 971 425658 🕐 Mon–Sat 8am–3am, Sun 10am–2am

IB'S
Ib's is another of the city's big nightclubs, but it doesn't have the views of its rivals, Abraxas and Tito's, primarily because it is under the seafront promenade.

✉ Passeig Marítim 32, 07014 Palma
☎ 971 733671 🕐 Thu–Sat 10pm–late

JAZZ VOYEUR CLUB
www.jazzvoyeur.com
The live music at this excellent small venue ranges from Cuban to trad jazz. It's a cosy place with couches and low stools, black walls and a good sound system, but there is little room to stand or dance. You'll find the club up a flight of stairs on La Llotja's main street. The bar staff are friendly but will expect you to listen to the music rather than shout over the top of it. The club hosts an excellent annual jazz festival—see the website for details.

✉ Carrer Apuntadors 5, 07012 Palma
☎ 971 720480 🕐 Nightly from 10pm
🖐 €8–15 (including one drink)

Left Abaco, Palma's most famous bar

PIRATES ADVENTURE
www.piratesadventure.com
This swashbuckling show is one of the Magaluf originals, dating back to the mid-1980s. An exuberant combination of acrobatics, dance, comedy and suspense, the show takes place in a purpose-built theatre and is slick and professional. A more recent adults-only Pirate Uncut show promises to 'unlock the pirate within!' Tickets are expensive, but the price includes dinner, *sangría* and soft drinks during the show. Check the website for more details and a trailer.

✉ Avinguda Sa Porrassa 12, 07182 Magaluf ☎ 971 130411 🕐 Shows from 6–11, times vary. Matinee performance 3pm 🖐 May, Jun, Sep, Oct, adult from €30, child (2–12) from €20; Jul–Aug, adult from €35, child €30. Pirates Uncut: adults €46 🍴 🥂

RIU PALACE
www.riupalace.com
In the heart of the predominantly German resort of S'Arenal, RIU Palace is as raucous as its British counterpart in Magaluf, with live acts, dancers and top DJs. Music is mainstream house and techno, but the Soul Suite plays R & B, funk and soul in July and August. The club has a capacity of 2,000.

✉ Carrer Llaud, Las Maravillas, 07610 Playa de Palma ☎ 971 743474 🕐 Jul, Aug nightly 10pm–late

TEATRE MUNICIPAL
There's something for everyone, from contemporary dance, drama and film to children's activities, at this theatre to the west of Palma's centre.

✉ Passeig Mallorca 9, 07011 Palma
☎ 971 739148 🖐 €8–€40, some events are free 🥂

TEATRE PRINCIPAL
www.teatreprincipal.com
This grand 19th-century theatre in the centre of Palma (on Plaça Weyler) stages theatrical productions all year round, as well as annual opera and ballet seasons. It has recently benefited from extensive renovation.

✉ Carrer de la Riera 2, 07003 Palma
☎ 971 713346 🖐 €10–€40

TITO'S
www.titosmallorca.com
Tito's heyday was in the days when Ray Charles and Marlene Dietrich were on the guest list: today it's a popular option for a less sophisticated night out. There are six bars in which to escape the hen and stag parties, and exciting views across the Bay of Palma. The clientele is marginally less youthful than that of Abraxas, but not as mature as Art Déco's (▷ 80).

✉ Passeig Marítim 33, 07014 Palma
☎ 971 730017 🕐 Summer, nightly 11pm–6am; winter, Thu–Sat 11pm–6am

SPORTS AND ACTIVITIES
BICYCLING
Palma is not the best place for bicycling; although there are bicycle lanes along the seafront, the roads are busy with both pedestrians and

Below *Dining out in Palma's traffic-free, arcaded Plaça Mayor*

Above *The dolphin show at Marineland*

vehicles. But if you do want to hire a bicycle, try the following Palma-based firms:
Belori Bike ☎ 971 490358;
www.belori-bike.com
Palma on Bike ☎ 971 918986;
www.palmaonbike.com

CITY SIGHTSEEING BUS TOUR
www.city-sightseeing.com
See Palma from the top of a double-decker bus (▷ 40). The tour lasts 80 minutes and takes in all Palma's major sights, including Castell de Bellver. There are 13 stops and you can jump on or off at any of them. You can book online.
🕐 May–end Sep daily 9.30–8, Oct–end Apr 9.30–7 ✋ Adult €13, child (5–15) €6.50

CLUB DE VUELO LIBRE MALLORCA
club2006@cvlmallorca.com
www.cvlmallorca.com
Mallorca's main hang-gliding club is a good source of information on flying locations and equipment hire.

CLUB NÁUTICO CALA GAMBA
www.cncalagamba.com
Cala Gamba's sailing school has Optimist dinghies for children. Kayaking is also possible.
✉ Paseo Cala Gamba, 07007 Palma
☎ 971 261849 🕐 All year

CLUB NÁUTICO EL ARENAL
www.cnarenal.com
Whether you want to master navigation or learn to use a trapeze, there's something for everyone at this large, German-biased club. Also swimming and kayaking in summer.
✉ Carrer Roses, 07600 S'Arenal
☎ 971 440142 🕐 Courses Jul–end Sep
✋ Non-members: adult €160, child (0–15) €140–€150 per 10-day course

CLUB NÁUTICO EL PORTITXOL
El Portitxol's sailing school has Optimist dinghies for children.
✉ Paseo Barceló I Mir 2, 07006 Portitxol
☎ 971 242424 🕐 All year

CRUESA MALLORCA YACHT CHARTER
www.cruesa.com
The fleet of this upmarket yacht charter firm is next to the city's Reial Club Náutico de Palma. Take your pick from yachts, motor boats or catamarans.
✉ Office at Passeig Marítim 16, 07014 Palma ☎ 971 282821 ✋ €1,100–€4,700 per week

ESCUELA NACIONAL DE VELA DE CALANOVA
http://calanova.caib.es
The national sailing school offers courses in a variety of disciplines.
✉ Avinguda Joan Miró 327, Cala Major, 07015 Palma ☎ 971 402512

ESTADIO SON MOIX
www.rcdmallorca.es
Home to Real Mallorca (▷ 24), the Son Moix stadium seats 23,000 spectators and is a good place to see some of the top teams in Spain's *Primera Liga*. Tickets may be in short supply for big matches, but should be generally available. Matches are played on alternate Sunday afternoons.
✉ Camí dels Reis, 07011 Palma ☎ 971 221221 🕐 Jun–end Sep ✋ €20–€45
🚌 No. 8

GOLF DE PONIENTE
www.ponientegolf.com
This 18-hole, par-72 course is just 1km (0.5 miles) from Magaluf. The wide fairways and large greens can be deceptive, and the 10th hole is regarded as one of the best golf holes on Mallorca. There's no shortage of bunkers and lakes.
✉ Carretera Cala Figuera, 07182 Magaluf
☎ 971 130148 ✋ Green fee €75 🍴 ▢

HIPÓDROMO SON PARDO
www.hipodromosonpardo.com
Trotting races *(carreras)* with horse and trap are the most popular form of horse-racing in the Balearic Islands and have been practised in Mallorca for 200 years. Betting on the races is considered an essential part of the experience.
✉ Carretera Palma–Sóller, km 3, 07009 Palma ☎ 971 763853 🕐 Summer Fri 9pm; winter Sun 4.30

PLAÇA DE TOROS
Palma's bullring dates from 1929 and is the island's main venue for bullfights. You can choose to sit in the sun *(sol)* or the shade *(sombra)*—the recommended (but more expensive) option.
✉ Avinguda Gaspar Bennazar Arquitecte 32, 07011 Palma ☎ 971 755245
🕐 Mar–end Oct

PUERTO PORTALS MARINA
www.puertoportals.com
There are 670 moorings at one of Mallorca's flashiest marinas.
✉ Puerto Portals, 07181 Portals Nous
☎ 971 171100

REAL CLUB NÁUTICO DE PALMA
www.realclubnauticopalma.com
Learn to sail at the sailing club patronized by Spanish royalty and which hosts the famous Copa del Rey event each summer (▷ 85). Courses range from beginner initiation to tuition for racing yachtsmen. Kayaking is also available.

✉ Muelle de Sant Pere, 07012 Palma ☎ 971 726848 🕐 Courses Jul–end Sep ✋ Non-members from €250 per 5-day course

REAL GOLF DE BENDINAT
www.realgolfbendinat.com
A tricky 18-hole, par-71 course, thanks to tree-lined fairways, steep slopes and testing greens. It is located between Palma and Ses Illetes and close to Puerto Portals.

✉ Urbanización Bendinat, Carrer Campoamor, 07015 Calvià ☎ 971 405200 ✋ Green fee €75 🍴 🛒

SEGWAY TOURS
These two-wheel motorized scooters are a great way to zip around town.

✉ Carrer Marbella 22, local 42, 07610 Playa de Palma ☎ 605 666365 ✋ One-hour guided excursion €35

SKI CLUB CALANOVA
This club offers water-skiing tuition at Santa Ponça and Magaluf and water-skiing by the hour.

✉ Carrer Condor 22, Son Ferrer, 07180 Santa Ponça ☎ 971 130965 ✋ 1 hour approx €80

SON VIDA GOLF
www.sonvidagolf.com
Son Vida was opened in 1964, making it the oldest golf course in Mallorca. The 18-hole, par-71 course is frequented by guests at the two on-site luxury hotels and the owners of some of Palma's most exclusive nearby properties. Make reservations one month in advance for spring and autumn. Son Vida's sister course, Son Muntaner, is reserved for guests of the Arabella Sheraton Golf Hotel Son Vida (▷ 90), the Castillo Hotel Son Vida and the Mardavall Hotel and Spa (▷ 91).

✉ Urbanización Son Vida, 07013 Palma ☎ 971 791210 ✋ Green fee €70–€95 🍴 🛒

HEALTH AND BEAUTY
AYURVEDA
This is one of a chain of stylish hairdressers and beauty salons, with other branches in Portals Nous (tel

971 676026) and Archduque Luis Salvador 2 (tel 971 757554). Men's haircuts start at €13.50, women's at €29, manicures at €10.50 and pedicures at €18.50.

✉ Carrer Conquistador 8, 07001 Palma ☎ 971 713631 🕐 Mon–Sat 10–8

ILLES FITNESS CENTRE
www.illescf.com
One of a small chain, this modern sports centre is opposite El Corte Inglés. There's gym equipment, a pool and squash courts. You can also join classes, including yoga, pilates, taekwondo and body pump.

✉ Carrer Nuredduna 9, 07012 Palma ☎ 902 076655 🕐 Mon–Fri 6.30am–10.30pm, Sat 9–8.30; closed Sat–Sun Jul, Aug

SALONES LLONGUERAS
www.llongueras.com
This chain of upmarket hair salons founded by Luis Llongueras, Spain's most famous hair stylist, has two branches in Palma:

✉ Passeig Mallorca 14, 07001 Palma ☎ 971 715137 🕐 Mon–Fri 9.30–7, Sat 9.30–12.30
✉ Carrer Tous i Maroto 15, 07001 Palma ☎ 971 721862 🕐 Mon–Fri 9.30–7, Sat 9.30–12.30

FOR CHILDREN

AQUALAND EL ARENAL
www.aqualand.es

This waterpark has an exciting assortment of attractions, including the twisty waterslide Anaconda, Surf Beach, with 1m-high (3ft) waves, the Congo River cruise, the Mini Park for children and the Black Hole. Newer attractions are the Tsunami, a 50kph (30mph) waterslide and a Polynesian-themed children's area. There's also a small zoo and a petting farm.

✉ Carretera Palma–Arenal exit 13, km 15, 07600 S'Arenal ☎ 971 440000 🕓 May, Jun, Sep 10–5; Jul, Aug 10–6 ✋ Adult €22, child (3–12) €15, under-3s free 🚌 No. 23 and shuttle bus from Plaça d'Espanya, Ca'n Pastilla, Playa de Palma and El Arenal 🍴 📷

AQUALAND MAGALUF
www.aqualand.es

This large waterpark in Magaluf has waterslides, rides and pools, including the Tornado, a tubular slide that funnels you into a whirlpool. The children's area includes an Enchanted Castle.

✉ Carretera Cala Figuera, 07182 Magaluf ☎ 971 130811 🕓 May, Jun, Sep, Oct 10–5; Jul, Aug 10–6 ✋ Adult €19.50, child (3–12) €12.50, under-3s free 🚌 Catalina Marqués 2 and 10 🍴 📷

GOLF FANTASIA
www.golf-fantasia.com

Perhaps the best mini-golf complex on the island, Golf Fantasia is a cleverly landscaped complex of three 18-hole courses set around waterfalls, caves and tropical gardens.

✉ Carrer Tenis 3, 07181 Palma Nova ☎ 971 135040 🕓 All year, daily 10am–midnight ✋ Adult from €8.90, child (under 11) €5.40 🍴 📷

HOUSE OF KATMANDU
www.houseofkatmandu.com

Visitors walk through a series of chambers in this bizarre upside-down house and enjoy an interactive experience in the quest for a legendary red jewel.

✉ Avenida de Pedro Vaquer Ramis 9, 07181 Magaluf ☎ 971 134660 🕓 Daily 10.30–6 ✋ Adult €15.90, child (3–12) €9.90

KARTING MAGALUF
www.kartingmagaluf.com

Children can let off steam at this go-karting course to the west of Palma.

✉ Carretera Sa Porrassa, 07182 Magaluf ☎ 971 131734 🕓 May–Oct Tue–Sun 10–sunset ✋ Adult €30 for 15 mins, child (9–15) €25, child (2–7) €9

MARINELAND
www.aspro-ocio.es

There's a reptile house, penguin pool, aviary and monkeys at this marine park, as well as rides on pirate ships and miniature trains. The main attractions are the performing dolphins and sealions. Many people don't approve of such shows, but this park puts money into conservation and educational programmes. There are up to four exhibitions daily.

✉ Carrer Garcilaso de la Vega 9, 07184 Costa d'en Blanes ☎ 971 675125 🕓 End Mar–end Nov daily 9.30–6 (last admission 4.45) ✋ Adult €22, child (4–12) €16, under-3s free 🍴 📷

NEMO SUBMARINE
www.nemosub.org

Prospective submariners meet in Magaluf for the boat trip to Isla del Sech, where they board the Nemo mini-submarine for a 50-minute dive to a depth of 30m (100ft). Undersea action visible from its 1m (3ft)-wide portholes includes fish, wrecks and a fish-feeding show by scuba divers. Free pick-ups are available from most resorts. It is advisable to book ahead by telephone in the summer months.

✉ Carrer Galeon 2, 07181 Magaluf ☎ 971 130244 🕓 Mar–end Oct 9–8 ✋ Adult €62, child (3–12) €52

WESTERN PARK
www.western-park.com

Opposite the larger Aquapark, Western Park has Wild West-themed attractions including waterslides, plus a cowboy family show and a bird of prey exhibition. Western Park's version of a Wild West town has a jail, a saloon, a theatre and fast-food restaurants.

✉ Carretera Cala Figuera, 07182 Magaluf ☎ 971 131203 🕓 Jun–end Sep daily 10–6, Oct–end Jun 10–5 ✋ Adult €24, child (3–15) €16, under-3s free 🚌 Palma 10 🍴 📷

Below *Waterslides at Western Park*

PALMA

CAVALCADA DE REIS (PROCESSION OF THE THREE KINGS)

5 January
A family-friendly event in which the Three Kings arrive by boat and lead a procession through Palma to hand out presents to good children.
✉ Palma

SANT ANTONI ABAT

16–17 January
Known as the Blessing of the Animals, this is a procession of pets and farm animals that takes place in three locations: Palma, Artà and Sa Pobla.
✉ Palma, Artà and Sa Pobla

SANT SEBASTIÀ

19 January
On the night before the Saint's Day, bonfires with fireworks and barbecues are held in Palma's squares and in Costitx. The festivities, which celebrate Palma's patron saint, continue for two weeks in the Mallorcan capital.
✉ Palma and Costitx

SA RÚA

Weekend before Lent
Bonfires, processions and fancy dress constitute this carnival held on the last weekend before Lent.
✉ Palma and rest of island

SETMANA SANTA (HOLY WEEK)

Easter
Easter is taken very seriously in Mallorca. The week begins with the blessing of palm and olive branches at churches across the island, followed by daily processions in Palma (the biggest is on Maundy Thursday) and other towns and villages. A figure of Christ is lowered from his cross in Pollença on Good Friday evening and carried down the town's Calvary steps; a similar ritual takes place in Felanitx.
✉ Palma and rest of island

Above *The Copa del Rey sailing regatta*

PRINCESS SOFIA TROPHY

April
www.trofeoprincesasofia.org
This dinghy sailing regatta attracts around 600 boats from 50 nations.
✉ Palma

TEMPORADA DE BALLET DE MALLORCA

June–end February
www.temporadadeballet.es
Mallorca's annual ballet season is held in the Auditorium de Palma (▷ 80).
✉ Palma ☎ 971 402612 ✋ €39–€60

FESTIVAL DE MÚSICA CASTELL DE BELLVER

June
www.simfonica-de-balears.com
This annual music festival in Castell de Bellver is staged by the Balearic Symphony Orchestra, which also plays regularly during seasons at the Auditorium de Palma (▷ 80).
✉ Palma

DIUMENGE DEL ANGEL (ANGEL SUNDAY)

Sunday after Easter
Angel Sunday is celebrated in Palma with processions and feasts.
✉ Palma

INTERNATIONAL BOAT SHOW

April, May
www.firesicongressos.com
The Mediterranean's yachting capital is the perfect venue for this annual boat show. Visitors can

ogle the beautiful and seriously expensive boats lining Palma's port area.
✉ Palma 🕐 Daily 10–8 ✋ €5

COPA DEL REY (KING'S CUP)

End July–August
www.realclubnauticopalma.com
The largest and most prestigious cruising regatta in the Mediterranean is the year's yachting highlight. Based at the Real Club Náutico in Palma, the event, founded in 1982, attracts royal patronage and hundreds of amazing yachts.
✉ Palma

BALEART CRAFT FAIR

Mid-December
www.firesicongressos.com
This long-standing annual fair exhibits handicrafts from all the Balearic Islands, and sells everything from pottery to handmade shoes.
✉ Palma

FESTA DE L'ESTENDARD

31 December
The anniversary of the Christian conquest of the city by King Jaume I in 1229 is commemorated every New Year's Eve. There's a tremendous procession from the town hall to the cathedral for a special Mass.
✉ Palma

PRICES AND SYMBOLS

The prices given are the average for a two-course lunch (L) and a three-course dinner (D) for one person, without drinks. The wine price is for the least expensive bottle.

For a key to the symbols, ▷ 2.

AFRIKANA

Chef Zamam from Ethiopia turns out wonderful dishes from all corners of Africa and the Caribbean at this cosy restaurant near Santa Catalina market. Start with aniseed-flavoured flatbread with a selection of dips, followed by aromatic beef from Madagascar, Kenyan peanut and vegetable curry, chicken Senegalese-style or king prawns with vanilla and rum. There are always plenty of vegetarian choices. Dessert might be banana and ginger tart and you can finish your meal with coffee brewed in a clay pot. The owners also make their own ginger beer, hibiscus wine and Ethiopian honey wine. For a real treat, splash out on the five-course Ethiopian banquet at around €18 per person. A small selection of African crafts is on sale.
✉ Carrer Dameto 17, 07013 Palma ☎ 971 287007 ⊙ Mon–Sat 12.30–4, 8–12 ✋ L €15, D €20, Honey wine €3.50

APTC

www.restauranteaptc.com
A sophisticated restaurant with punchy modern decor in this culinary street near the Santa Catalina market. Dishes here are Asian inspired, with starters like satsuma salad with tuna, bean sprouts and tangerine-spiked vinegar (€8.95), while mains run the gamut from lamb stroganoff (€12.95) to Japanese-style pork (€11.95) and lamb chops with red peppers, potatoes and a spicy chilli sauce (€17.50 for two people). If you are part of a group of eight or more there are three well-priced *menus de degustacion*, from €22 to €26. There is also regular soothing live music and an attractive terrace at the back.
✉ Carrer Annibal 11, 07013 Palma ☎ 971 289165 ⊙ Mon–Sat 1–4, 8–11.30 ✋ L €15, D €20, Wine €9

ARAMÍS

The entrance to this chic restaurant, in a small group of shops at the top end of the La Llotja area, is easy to miss. Once you're inside, you'll find a smart, minimalist interior with a high, arched ceiling, candlelit tables, soft music, a bar and faux-arty black-and-white photographs on the wall. The cuisine is international Mediterranean, with an Italian slant. Since revising its prices downwards, Aramís is better value, with starters such as crayfish in tempura with caramelized onion for €12, and main courses costing from €12.50 for pasta dishes, including spaghetti carbonara and pasta with salmon and lemon sauce. Fish dishes include roasted fillet of sea bass. Panna cotta with mango sauce makes a tempting dessert. As you'd expect from a restaurant that offers wine-tasting evenings, the wine list has been thoughtfully compiled, with Riojas from €20.80. Although there's a €14.50 three-course *menú del día*, Aramís is better suited to romantic evening meals than lunching.
✉ Carrer Montenegro 1, 07012 Palma ☎ 971 725232 ⊙ Mon–Fri 1–3.30, 8–11, Sat 8–11 ✋ L €20, D €40, Wine €16.20

BISTRO FÁBRICA 23

Young British chef Alexei Tarsey is making waves at this fashionable restaurant in the buzzing Santa Catalina district. At lunchtime, it is full of trendy office workers enjoying one of the best deals in town, while at night it attracts a cosmopolitan yachting crowd from the nearby port. The food is Mediterranean with diverse influences from Asia, but always features fresh market ingredients. Starters might be salmon tempura with mango, ginger and coriander (cilantro), watercress and potato cream soup, or grilled asparagus with rocket, watercress, Parmesan cheese and mustard. Mains might include duck confit with apple and rosemary, monkfish red curry with coconut milk, or a roast red-pepper tart. The *menú del día* is €15. Desserts are all home-made, such as hot chocolate fondant with vanilla ice cream. The wine list includes several good Mallorcan labels.

✉ Carrer Cotoner 42–44, 07013 Palma
☎ 971 453125 🕐 Tue–Sat 1–3.30,
9–11.30, Sun 1–3.30. Closed 1 Aug–7 Sep
✋ L €18, D €30, Wine €10

LA BODEGUILLA

www.la-bodeguilla.com
'Traditional Spanish cuisine with a creative touch' is how this restaurant near the top of Passeig des Born describes itself. There are actually two parts to La Bodeguilla. One side is a wine bar, perfect for a pre-dinner aperitif, with plates of ham and cheese to nibble and a selection of over 200 wines. The main restaurant, which stays open throughout the day, features classics such as garlic soup, venison with mushrooms and goose liver in puff pastry, and roast suckling pig. A popular starter is the *pica-pica* of gourmet tapas to share at €22 per person. Portions are generous, and the service is friendly but discreet. La Bodeguilla makes a good venue for a romantic meal.

✉ Carrer Sant Jaume 1–3, 07012 Palma
☎ 971 718274 🕐 Mon–Sat 1–11
✋ L and D €25, Wine €17.90

BON LLOC

Vegetarian cookery has been slow to take off in Spain but Palma's original vegetarian restaurant proves that meat-free eating does not have to be dull. Low lights and soft music create a soothing atmosphere. Popular with local office workers, the four-course lunchtime menu offers exceptional value and might feature salad, cream of fennel or beetroot soup, followed by jacket potatoes in a rich herb sauce and strawberry sorbet for dessert. The menu changes daily and there are always two choices for each course. This is part of a small foodie enclave near Passeig des Born; the same building houses a smart restaurant, a wine and tapas bar and a funky breakfast cafe.

✉ Carrer Sant Feliu 7, 07012 Palma
☎ 971 718617 🕐 Mon–Sat 1–4
✋ L €13.50, Wine €9

LA BÓVEDA

This popular Palma institution near La Llotja has a deserved reputation for serving the best tapas in town, and at busy times you will often find queues outside the door. This is just what a tapas bar should look like, with a lovely old tiled counter and customers standing at wine barrels demolishing platefuls of ham, chorizo and *tortilla* (potato omelette). Standard tapas dishes range from €5 to €12 and include dates wrapped in bacon, garlicky grilled prawns and red peppers stuffed with cod. There are also more complete meals such as steak in pepper sauce. For a one-plate snack, it's hard to beat the *pa amb olí* topped with thin slices of Iberian ham. If you want to eat out of doors, there is a second branch around the corner with tables on a sea-facing terrace (Taberna de la Bóveda, Passeig Sagrera 3, tel 971 714963).

✉ Carrer Boteria 3, 07012 Palma ☎ 971 714863 🕐 Mon–Sat 1.30–4, 8.30–12.30
✋ L and D €25, Wine €8

CA'N CARLOS

The traditional Mallorcan cooking served up at Ca'n Carlos is of above-average quality and includes some out-of-the-ordinary dishes. But if you don't like the sound of *sipia amb sobrassada*—cuttle fish chunks in tomato sauce with raisins, pine nuts, brandy and *sobrassada*—there are mainstream favourites such as stuffed aubergine, baked cod and *frit mallorquí* on the menu. The restaurant has a fine reputation but some diners report that service can be slow. You'll find it in a side street off the north side of Avinguda Jaume III.

✉ Carrer de S'Aigua 5, 07012 Palma
☎ 971 713869 🕐 Mon–Sat 1–4, 8–11
✋ L and D €30, Wine €12

CANDELA RESTAURANTE

This restaurant, on the main street through La Llotja, is perfectly placed to pick up a lot of custom from people leaving the many neighbouring tapas bars. It's a handsome place, with a large, subtly lit interior and a stylish design. Candela's cuisine is modern Mediterranean: simple starters, such as chicken consommé, are a surprisingly costly €9–€10, while main courses, such as fillet of perch with mushroom risotto and chicory, cost from €18.50. Desserts, such as semolina pudding with vanilla and strawberries, are more inventive than usual. The location and trendy ambience perhaps justify the slightly inflated prices. Service, from the youthful staff, is efficient.

✉ Carrer Apuntadors 14, 07012 Palma
☎ 971 724428 🕐 Daily 1–4, 7.30–12
✋ L €29, D €30, Wine €12

CELLAR SA PREMSA

Dating from 1958 and a culinary institution in Palma, this cavernous restaurant is high on atmosphere, its walls lined with enormous barrels and faded bullfighting posters, together with a mishmash of quirky ornaments, from a mounted goat's head to a grandfather clock. The menu is solidly traditional, with dishes like *frito Mallorquín* (fried lamb and pork; €6.25) and *pollo asado* (roasted chicken; €11.70). At lunchtime there are two inexpensive daily set menus.

✉ Plaça Obispo Berenguer de Palou 8, 07003 Palma ☎ 971 723529 🕐 Mon–Sat 12–4, 7–11 🍴 *Menus del día* €11.70 and €12.65, D €20, Wine €7.95

LA CUCHARA

This restaurant, on the east side of Passeig Mallorca close to Avinguda Jaume III, serves rustic Mallorcan dishes with a Basque twist. Expect starters such as black pudding with red peppers and spicy Basque sausage. Mains cost €12–€14.50 for a hearty lamb dish flavoured with onion and bacon. Dessert includes praline mousse. Portions are not large—you'll wish there was more of the wild mushrooms with Roquefort sauce—but the cooking is fine. Look out for a few tongue-twisting Basque dishes such as *esqueixada* (marinated cod with tomato and black olives). La Cuchara's interior draws on classic rustic elements: red-and-white tablecloths, wine racks lining the walls and a tiled floor. Extras—bread, olives and oil—cost €1.85. The wine list has some reasonable Riojas and Navarras.

✉ Passeig Mallorca 18, 07012 Palma
☎ 971 722223 🕐 Daily 1–4, 8–12
✋ L €25, D €35, Wine €9.70

LA CUEVA TAPAS BAR

Choosing between tapas bars in La Llotja is a Sisyphean task. But you should certainly try La Cueva if you like fish and seafood: the bar's specialities are *gambas al ajillo* and *gambas a la plancha*. You'll also find one of the tastiest treats in Palma here: a plate of fried whitebait for €8. It's a mountain of hot, crispy and very fresh fish; just douse them in lemon juice and devour. La Cueva's *pa amb olí*, with crunchy, crusted bread, is just as good. The *raciones* selection also includes Moorish kebabs for €8, pigs' trotters for €8 and battered squid rings for €8. The house red is a good buy at €9, with Mallorcan wines going for a pricey €24.

✉ Carrer Apuntadors 5, 07012 Palma
☎ 971 724422 🕐 Mon–Sat 12–12
✋ *Raciones* from €7 per person, Wine €9

MANGIAFUOCO

Flamboyant owner Daniele hails from Lucca in Tuscany, so you can guarantee that the food here is authentic Italian, as well as

the decor, with jolly red gingham tablecloths and walls hung with Italian football and Ferrari memorabilia. Truffles are a speciality here, as well as non-pasta Italian dishes like *carpaccio de ternera* (€13) and *scaloppini al vino blanco* (€14.50).

✉ Plaça Vapor 4, 07013 Palma
☎ 971 451072 🕐 Wed–Mon 12–4, 7–12
✋ L €18, D €20, Wine €9

+NATURAL (MAS NATURAL)

www.masntrl.com

This bright, modern cafe with colourful murals depicting waterfalls and natural scenes is a good choice if you're looking for a healthy snack. They do tasty salads (including classics like the Waldorf or Caesar salads), or you can make your own starting with a base such as mixed leaves or pasta, with prices from €7.70 for five additional ingredients. For something a bit more substantial, try a stir fry (€9) prepared with a choice of salmon, beef or chicken. Curiously, although there is plenty of choice for vegetarians at the salad bar, there are no strictly veggie stir fries. There are home-made cakes and artisan ice cream to finish up. There's also a terrace outside—a good people-watching spot on one of Palma's busiest squares.

✉ Plaça d'Espanya 8, 07012 Palma
☎ 971 722232 🕐 Mon–Sat 12–11
✋ L and D €15, Wine €8

EL PILÓN

This terrific tapas bar specializes in seafood and has an open kitchen so you can see the chefs at work. Its seafood selection, displayed on a counter, includes king prawns, battered squid and octopus. Individual tapas cost from €5 while themed selections cost from €13.10 for the vegetarian option (*tumbet*, *pimientos de padrón*, cauliflower, aubergine and battered artichoke) to €19.20 for wild Mallorcan mushrooms, prawns, mussels and small squid. Watching the waiters is like watching a veteran chat-show host work a guest; they're friendly,

amusing and very professional. The decor piques interest if not appetite—turtles, sharks and gourds hang from the ceiling, and there are two house piranhas in an aquarium.

✉ Carrer Cifre 4, 07012 Palma ☎ 971 717590 🕐 Mon–Sat 9–4, 6–12
✋ Tapas from €5 per person, Wine €10

RESTAURANTE LIVING

In the ever-fashionable *barri* of Santa Catalina, this street is fast becoming one of the best for contemporary cuisine in Palma. The acclaimed Bistro Fábrica 23 (▷ 86–87) is close by, but this stylish restaurant is also a good choice. The plain walls are dotted with contemporary art, shells and natural objects, and the chunky wooden chairs and tables are laid with pale linen. The menu features delectable fusion cuisine, which includes dishes such as guinea fowl ravioli with ceps, artichokes and rosemary sauce (€12.50), or dorado with saffron risotto (€14.50). A *menú de degustació* (tasting menu) is available for €22.

✉ Carrer Cotoner 47, 07013 Palma ☎ 971 455628 🕐 Mon 8.30pm–midnight, Tue–Sat 1.30–4, 8.30–12 ✋ *Menú del día* €11.50. L €20, D €22, Wine €12.50

SA LLIMONA

This pair of restaurants in Santa Catalina raises *pa amb olí* to an art form. You choose from a wide range of toppings—ham, salami, cured duck breast, smoked salmon, anchovies, cheese—and then it is make-your-own-meal. The waiter will bring you a side dish of salad, consisting of grated carrot and cabbage, olives, capers, pickled samphire, plus garlic and a tomato to rub on your bread. A basket on the table contains salt and a jug of olive oil. Finally the bread arrives, and the rest is up to you. If you don't fancy do-it-yourself, there is a small menu of ready-made salads and desserts, but really the whole point here is the *pa amb olí*.

✉ Carrer Fabrica 27A; also at Carrer de Sant Magí, 80, 07013 Palma ☎ 971 280023 🕐 Daily 8pm–midnight ✋ D €10, Wine €7

S'EIXERIT

This popular restaurant in Cuitat Jardí has a terrace overlooking the sea and a walled garden at the back. Inside the converted town house, a series of cosy dining rooms, decorated with paintings and antiques, make an indoor alternative if the weather prevents alfresco dining. Locals come to S'Eixerit for the fresh seafood and the house speciality, paella. The *menú del día* at €12 is good value and includes a glass of wine, but it means that lunchtimes can be busy. The tasty desserts are homemade or order a platter of the Menorcan cheese, specially imported by head chef Ruben Perez.

📧 Carrer Vicari Joaquin Fuster 73, 07012 Palma ☎ 971 273781 🕐 Daily 1–4, 8–11 ✋ L €18, D €26, Wine €8 (jug of house wine)

SIMPLY FOSH

www.simplyfosh.com
The former El Refectori has benefited from the new owner, celebrated UK Michelin chef Marc Fosh (ex Read's Hotel). He has introduced an exciting new affordable menu with innovative, Mediterranean-inspired dishes, including starters like chilled yellow gazpacho with marinated salmon and avocado sorbet (€13.25), followed by a choice of mains, including slow-cooked guinea fowl with smoked rice, apricot purée and

red wine shallots (€21). The desserts are sumptuous; the raspberry and hibiscus crème brûlée is highly recommended. Regarding the decor, think lashings of white accentuated by black Starke-style seating and dramatic artwork and photography. The gallery near the entrance sets the creative tone perfectly.

📧 Carrer de la Missio 7A, 07003 Palma ☎ 971 720114 🕐 Sun–Fri 12–4, 7–11, Sat 7–11 ✋ L €35, D €55, Wine €12

LA TABERNA DEL CARACOL

The 'tavern of the snail', hidden away in the back streets behind the cathedral and the Arab Baths, is worth seeking out for its first-class tapas. The atmosphere is one of rustic chic, with Gothic stone arches, wooden beams, whitewashed walls and strings of garlic and dried chillies hanging from the ceiling. The simple things are the best here, and with most dishes costing around €6 you can order several to share, from *frito marinero* (fried seafood) to *pimientos de padrón* (deep-fried spicy green peppers), scrambled eggs with Jabugo ham and the eponymous snails, which come dressed in garlic and olive oil. If you still have room afterwards, they also serve excellent home-made cakes and desserts.

📧 Carrer de Sant Alonso 2, 07001 Palma ☎ 971 714908 🕐 Mon–Sat 7.30–11.30pm ✋ D €25, Wine €8

TAJ MAHAL

There are several Indian restaurants in Palma, but this one near the main train station is arguably the best. The Balti dishes are delicately spiced and include biryanis, vegetarian dishes, tandooris and specialities like *pollo tikka dansak* (€9.95), chicken with a sauce of lentils, pineapple, herbs and spices. If you like your curry hot, ask, as these cater for locals who generally do not like their food too spicy. The decor is pleasant, with ochre-washed walls and ethnic wall hangings.

📧 11 Carrer Blanquerna 4, 07003 Palma ☎ 971 751408 🕐 Daily 12–4, 7–12 ✋ L €15, D €18, Wine €8

VECCHIO GIOVANNI

This welcoming Italian restaurant, in a busy street near the seafront, is a popular place, catering mainly for tourists, so don't expect to be amazed by the food: red peppers stuffed with shrimp, stone bass and angler are smothered in tomato sauce. Mains are inexpensive, with pasta or pizza costing €8–€11. Desserts include the Mallorcan staple, almond cake. There are lots of tables for two, but it's more family-orientated than romantic. Diners might find the Daliesque paintings on the walls interesting.

📧 Carrer Sant Joan 3, 07012 Palma ☎ 971 722879 🕐 Daily 12–12 ✋ *Menú del día* €11, D €18, Wine €12

PRICES AND SYMBOLS

Prices are the lowest and highest for a double room for one night. Breakfast is included unless noted otherwise. All the hotels listed accept credit cards unless otherwise stated. Note that rates vary widely throughout the year.

For a key to the symbols, ▷ 2.

ARABELLA SHERATON GOLF HOTEL SON VIDA

www.luxurycollection.com
The Arabella Sheraton Golf Hotel is located to the west of Palma, beyond the Son Rapinya district and north of the restaurant-packed Genova district. The key attraction is the 18-hole, 72-par Son Vida golf course, which has almost as many water hazards as palm trees. Buggies and equipment are available for hire, but most golfers will bring their own kit. Bedrooms at the Spanish-styled building all have television, telephone, stereo and WiFi. Decor is better than the usual

bland designs of the luxury hotel chains; rooms are colourful and cosy. The hotel now has a fitness centre and spa.
✉ Carrer de la Vinagrella–Urbanización Son Vida, 07013 Palma ☎ 971 787100 🕔 All year ♨ €361–€380 🛏 93 ✦ 🏊 Indoor ▼

BENDINAT

www.hotelbendinat.es
In the wealthy enclave of Bendinat, 9km (6 miles) west of Palma, near Portals Nous, Hotel Bendinat offers guests traditional—if rather expensive—accommodation. The restaurant serves Mediterranean-Mallorcan cuisine and even the breakfast has a Mallorcan slant. Clifftop views from the terrace are superb. Bedrooms are all well equipped, and there are extensive gardens, a swimming pool outside and direct access to the beach.
✉ Andrés Ferret Sobral 1, 07181 Portals Nous ☎ 971 675725 🕔 End Feb–1 Nov ♨ €196–€256 🛏 52 ✦ 🏊

BON SOL

www.hotelbonsol.es
Once a haunt of film idol Errol Flynn, this family-owned hotel 8km (5 miles) west of Palma offers a variety of large, individually decorated bedrooms. They're all luxuriously furnished and fitted with television, telephone, central heating and tea- and coffee-making facilities. Beyond the sleeping quarters the hotel offers tennis courts, a swimming pool, a squash court and a gym, and other outdoor activities. Inside, guests can use a Moorish-styled spa with massage rooms, a sauna and Turkish bath. But the highlight of the hotel is outside: the subtropical gardens are spectacular. Lush and mature trees and plants line narrow winding paths which are intercepted by lily ponds, waterfalls and even fresh water pools where you can take a cool dip.
✉ Paseo de Illetes 30, 07181 Illetes ☎ 971 402111 🕔 Mid-Dec to mid-Nov ♨ €103–€118 🛏 92 ✦ 🏊 ▼

BORN

www.hotelborn.com

Palma has a shortage of mid-range hotels and this is by far the best place to stay if you want character and a central location at a reasonable price. It is housed in a converted 16th-century palace at the top of Passeig des Born, but unlike other similar establishments it has not gone for the luxury end of the market. Rooms are simply furnished but comfortable, and are set around a courtyard where breakfast is taken beneath the palm trees in summer. The Born is extremely popular, so it's worth booking well ahead.

✉ Carrer Sant Jaume 3, 07012 Palma
☎ 971 712942 🕐 All year 💶 €60–€120
🛏 29 🔳

CIUTAT JARDÍ

www.hciutatj.com

The hotel Ciutat Jardí is 4km (2.5 miles) east of Palma, five minutes from the airport and just a few steps from the beach. It has been managed by the same Mallorcan family since 1934. The building is a fine example of 1920s architecture and the best rooms are in the two domed wings—the largest, the 'Gran Cúpula' (Great Dome), has 12 windows for a panoramic view—while other rooms have generously sized terraces. All the bedrooms have telephone, television, central heating, a hydro-massage bath and WiFi. Access for disabled guests is much better than average.

✉ Illa de Malta 14, 07007 Ciutat Jardí
☎ 971 260007 🕐 21 Jan–21 Dec
💶 €110–€130 🛏 20 🔳 🏊 Outdoor

CONVENT DE LA MISSIÓ

www.conventdelamissio.com

Don't be surprised if you feel less stylish than the black-clad staff at this slick boutique hotel in central Palma. The spartan hotel, once part of a church, is one of Palma's trendiest places to lay your head. There's fashionable Simply Fosh (▷ 89), a bar, wine cellar, chapel and an art gallery in the old refectory. Bedrooms have gorgeous marble bathrooms and WiFi.

✉ Carrer de la Missío 7A, 07003 Palma
☎ 971 227347 🕐 All year 💶 €225–€390 🛏 14 🔳 Plus jacuzzi and sauna

DALT MURADA

www.hoteldaltmurada.com

For a top hotel in Palma, Dalt Murada is unquestionably outstanding value. Entrance to the hotel, in a mansion in the old town, close behind the cathedral, is through a gate on a side street off Carrer Conquistador. Dalt Murada's rooms are grand, if appealingly frayed around the edges, with antiques, tapestries, high ceilings and fairytale beds, but the hotel retains a warm homeliness. Bedrooms have telephone, television, central heating and WiFi. Large en-suite bathrooms are a highlight, with enormous oval baths or jacuzzis and stone floors.

✉ Carrer Almudaina 6, 07001 Palma
☎ 971 425300 🕐 All year 💶 €95–€159
🛏 3 doubles and 5 suites 🔳

FERMINUS

Dating from 1924, this no-frills place has real character, with original tiled floors, high ceilings, the occasional chandelier and a soothing neutral colour scheme. The rooms are large, with dark wood wardrobes, fans and good mattresses; the bathrooms could do with updating, however. The hotel also owns the adjacent cafeteria, where breakfast is served either inside or out on the terrace. Ferminus is very handy for the airport bus, which stops right across the road. Rooms sharing a bathroom are also available for €10 less. Free WiFi available.

✉ Plaça d'Espanya 5, 07002 Palma
☎ 971 750014 🕐 All year 💶 €60 all year 🛏 24 🔳

HOSTAL BRONDO

www.hostalbrondo.net

Few guesthouses are as centrally located as this one: it's in a narrow lane between the Passeig des Born and Carrer de la Unió. Prices are about right for such a location. Rooms are available with or without en-suite bathrooms. Those without bathrooms have use of a clean shared bathroom and all rooms have a basin. There's also a communal lounge with television and drinking water. Note that reception is open only 9–2 and 6–8, so make sure you arrive between these times or you may find yourself locked out with your suitcases.

✉ Carrer Can Brondo 1, 07001 Palma
☎ 971 719043 🕐 All year 💶 €50 all year (without bathroom) 🛏 10

HOTEL CA SA PADRINA

www.hotelcasapadrina.com

A stone's throw from the Plaça Major, this simple but delightful hotel is located in a newly renovated 16th-century town house. It offers characterful rooms furnished with antique furniture and oil paintings for a very reasonable price—so book early, as bargains are hard to find in this popular city. It's worth splashing out on Room 5, which has a jacuzzi and a private terrace (€130). Breakfast is not served, but there are numerous cafes and bars close by.

✉ Carrer Tereses 2, 07003 Palma
☎ 971 425 300 🕐 All year 💶 €67–€130
🛏 6 🔳

MARDAVALL

www.mardavall-hotel.com

It's no use coming to the Mardavall to escape the workplace; bedrooms at the high-tech hotel are equipped with ISDN, fax and internet connections, and there's even an IT 'butler' to help with technical problems. Other features in the bedrooms are similarly extravagant: bathrooms are lined with marble, sheets are Egyptian cotton and duvets are down-filled. Hotel services include babysitting, limousine travel and a butler. There are several restaurants and bars: Es Fum serves gourmet meals in the evening, S'Aigua is a brasserie for lighter meals during the day and tapas are served in Es Vent. The AltiraSPA, with hammams set around a blue-tiled saltwater pool, provides Ayurvedic and thalassotherapy treatments. Of course, the problem with such places is that you can easily forget which country you are staying in—combat this by at least getting out of the hotel for a round of golf at one of the courses nearby.

✉ Passeig Calvia, 07181 Costa d'en Blanes ☎ 971 629400 🕐 All year 🖐 €250–€400 ⓘ 133 🔣 🏊 🍴

MARICEL
www.hospes.es
Swathed in leather and cased in acres of marble, the Maricel's modern minimalist interior attracts a wealthy but youthful crowd of jet-setters. The grand old building itself has been through a number of incarnations and was once a decadent nightclub. It has a wonderful views of the sea; views that the infinity-edge swimming pool and the steps leading through the rocks and into the sea capitalize upon. Sandstone from Santanyí has been used to create arches and alcoves to hide away in. Catalan architect Xavier Claramunt designed the bedrooms to emphasize light

and space, but he's found a place for a television, DVD player, hi-fi and WiFi in each room.

✉ Carretera d'Andratx 11, Cas Catalá, 07184 Calvia ☎ 971 707744 🕐 All year 🖐 €192–€374, excluding breakfast (€30) ⓘ 29 🔣 🏊

MISIÓN DE SAN MIGUEL
www.hotelmisiondesanmiguel.com
Yet another chic new boutique hotel in Palma's elegant old city, this one adheres to the winning formula of fusing historic architecture with contemporary decor. The rooms are all bright, modern and comfortable with extras including free WiFi. The hotel restaurant Trébol serves light and delicious Mediterranean cuisine.

✉ Carrer Can Maçanet 1a, 07003 Palma, ☎ 971 214848 🕐 All year 🖐 €67–€160 ⓘ 32

PALACIO CA SA GALESA
www.palaciocasagalesa.com
This was the place that started the trend towards boutique hotels in Palma when it opened in 1996, and it continues to set the standards for others to follow. The hotel occupies

a 16th-century palace behind the cathedral, whose restoration has won an award from Palma city council. Each of the 12 rooms and suites, all named after composers, is individually decorated with antiques and modern art; in addition to all the facilities you would expect from a 5-star hotel, the rooms have WiFi. Most impressive of all are the public areas. The great hall is decorated in a mixture of Mallorcan, French and British styles, with polished floors, elegant furniture and dark Puerto Rican wood. There is a library where a fire is lit every evening in winter, and guests are encouraged to help themselves to free sherry. Afternoon tea is served in a replica of Monet's kitchen at Giverny; on warm days you can take it outside to a patio with a tinkling fountain. There is a small indoor pool and a spa which opened in March 2010. The owners have filled the hotel with their own private art collection, including works by Joan Miró and contemporary Spanish artists Eduardo Arroyo and Lorenzo Quinn. Parking is available for €16.85 per day.

✉ Carrer Miramar 8, 07001 Palma
☎ 971 715400 🕒 All year ✋ €348 all year (breakfast €24.75) 🛏 5 doubles and 7 suites ≋ ⊙

PALAU SA FONT
www.palausafont.com

A 16th-century palace on the outside, Palau Sa Font is a hip confection of funky colours, modern furniture and distressed ironwork on the inside. Best of all, the youthful guests find it perfectly placed for bar crawls in La Llotja. All the rooms have WiFi or high-speed adsl connection and central heating. Breakfast, like the decor, is slightly more imaginative than the standard hotel buffet, with *tortilla*, Serrano ham and smoked salmon. Don't miss the exciting views across Palma from the tower.

✉ Carrer Apuntadors 38, 07012 Palma
☎ 971 712277 🕒 1 Feb–2 Jan ✋ €155 all year 🛏 19 ⊙

PORTITXOL
www.portitxol.com

Scandinavian cool meets retro-50s architecture at this Swedish-owned design hotel, situated right by the harbourside in the up-and-coming district of Portitxol. Following a major refit in the 1990s, the shell of the building has been retained, but the interior has been completely redesigned, with clean white lines and a strong minimalist feel. There is a large outdoor pool, and a restaurant that has developed a reputation for its first-class seafood and fish dishes—some of which, such as the sashimi, betray a clear Japanese influence. Many of the rooms look out over the harbour, and a pleasant half-hour walk along the promenade leads to the city centre, with views of the cathedral throughout. Public parking is available nearby.

✉ Carrer Sirena 27, 07006 Portitxol
☎ 971 271800 🕒 All year ✋ €170–€230 🛏 26 ⊙ ≋ 📺

Above *The Portitxol hotel's pool area*
Opposite *The dining room at the Bon Sol hotel (see page 90)*

SAN LORENZO
www.hotelsanlorenzo.com

This town house hotel in a quiet street north of La Llotja in the centre of Palma has a friendly, lived-in ambience. The rooms are cosy rather than fashionable and each has television, telephone, minibar, safe and WiFi. the three suites are located away from the main building and are more romantic: they're large, private and have their own terraces. A small, well-tended swimming pool has a few sun loungers around the edge and there's an outdoor bar. Excellent breakfasts are a hallmark of the San Lorenzo. Their menu offers bacon and eggs in various combinations, all cooked to order; fruit juice is freshly squeezed. Note that parking in this central area can be a problem—there's a car park nearby on the Passeig Mallorca.

✉ Carrer Sant Llorenç 14, 07012 Palma,
☎ 971 728200 🕒 All year ✋ €150 all year (breakfast from €12) 🛏 6 doubles and 3 suites ⊙ ≋

SANTA CLARA
www.santaclarahotel.es

This sumptuous boutique hotel is housed in an exquisitely restored 18th-century manor house. Perks include a sun terrace with sea and cathedral views, a small spa, bicycle hire, free newspapers and WiFi. Rooms are minimalist yet intimate, with original beams, a warm colour scheme and exposed stone walls. Superior rooms have hydrojet jacuzzi baths and 42-inch plasma TV screens. However, who needs the latter with views like this!

✉ Carrer de Sant Alonso 16, 07001 Palma
☎ 971 729231 🕒 All year ✋ €180–€200 🛏 20 rooms ⊙

SARATOGA
www.hotelsaratoga.es

This central downtown hotel has been slickly updated, starting from the lobby where the walls are painted a warm yellow, contrasting with glossy cream marble floors and regency-style furniture. This is one of the rare city hotels with two pools. The guest rooms vary and are stylishly decorated with warm neutral tones with balconies – ask for a sea view. There's a rooftop solarium and pool, a small spa and the added perk of a jazz club with live music Thursdays to Saturdays. The breakfast buffet is more generous than most.

✉ Passeig Mallorca 6, 07001 Palma
☎ 971 727240 🕒 All year ✋ €120–€140 🛏 187 ⊙ ≋

TRES
www.hoteltres.com

The remnants of a 16th-century mansion have been spectacularly converted into this sleek, Swedish-owned design hotel. Scandinavian design is evident in the chic, minimalist rooms, which are fitted with every 21st-century amenity. You can breakfast under the palm trees in the delightful courtyard, relax by the rooftop plunge pool, which has great views or drowse peacefully in a hammock.

✉ Carrer Apuntadors 3, 07012 Palma
☎ 971 717333 🕒 All year ✋ €170–€208 🛏 41 rooms and suites ⊙ ≋ 📺

SIGHTS 97

WALK AND DRIVES 114

WHAT TO DO 120

EATING 124

STAYING 127

SERRA DE TRAMUNTANA

This is Mallorca's most picturesque region, where the unspoiled landscape seems to stretch to the horizon, making it easy to forget that you are on a comparatively small island. This big landscape includes dramatic mountain ranges that have an almost alpine feel: their peaks cloaked in pines and coniferous trees and punctuated by stone farmhouses and unspoiled hilltop villages. Drivers take note, the mountain roads here are not for the faint-hearted. They twist and turn spectacularly with, fortunately, plenty of strategically placed *miradors* (look-out points) affording a welcome rest, as well as stunning valley views with the Mediterranean backdrop beyond. The highest peak is lofty Puig Major at 1,445m (4,741ft), followed by the Puig de Massanella (1,365m/4,478ft), which is the highest climbable peak on the island; snow typically covers these mountaintops in winter.

As well as being a scenic driving area, the Serra de Tramuntana is superb for walking and cycling, with many truly lovely hiking trails winding through woodland. Those who prefer pedal power are similarly well catered for, with an abundance of well marked cycle paths. Fortunately, strict legislation and the sheer unsuitability of the landscape mean that the Serra de Tramuntana region has not succumbed to over-zealous bulldozing and overbuilding, even around the most popular tourist spots like Deià and Fornalutx. Several stylish town houses have been tastefully restored into chic boutique hotels here without impacting the vernacular architectural look of these historic villages. The pristine beauty of the Serra landscape is particularly vivid during the springtime, when the countryside is carpeted with a colourful dazzle of wild flowers.

ANDRATX

Like other towns on the Mallorcan coast, Andratx was built inland from its port to protect it from pirate raids. These days visitors converge on the port, but Andratx retains a sleepy provincial feel, really only coming alive on market day. Two buildings dominate the town—the 13th-century church of Santa Maria and the 15th-century Castell Son Mas, now the town hall. Beyond the castle, in the village of Sa Coma, is the Centro Cultural Andratx (Mar–end Oct Tue–Sat 10.30–7, Sun 10–4.30), which hosts exhibitions of contemporary art. There is a sculpture court and artists' studios, a café and art bookshop, together with extensive gardens of orange, lemon and fig trees.

The biggest draw is Port d'Andratx, once a quiet fishing village but now a stylish harbour-side town. There is not much to do but stroll along the promenade admiring the yachts and sit at the waterfront cafes watching the sunset. The nearest beach is across the hills at Camp de Mar.

✚ 222 C6 🚍 Buses from Palma to Port d'Andratx, Andratx and Camp de Mar

BANYALBUFAR

This village, whose Arabic name means 'vineyard by the sea', has been known for its fertile soil since Moorish times. Moorish settlers built the terraced hillsides sloping down towards the coast and the irrigation channels and cisterns. The village was once famous for wine, supplied to the royal house of Aragón, but these days the main crop is tomatoes. West of the village, the Torre de Ses Animes is a 16th-century watchtower offering marvellous views along the coast.
✚ 222 C5 🚍 Occasional buses from Palma to Estellencs

CASTELL D'ALARÓ

Imaginations can run wild at this ruined castle and atmospheric chapel perching on a rocky peak.

The ruined castle of Alaró seems to grow out of the landscape, so that from below it is hard to distinguish its walls from the rocky peak on which it stands. The Moorish fort that stood on this site was so well protected that its commander was able to defend it for two years after the Christian conquest. In 1285 this was the setting for the resistance of the soldiers Cabrit and Brassa (▷ 29).

The road to the castle begins just outside Alaró, winding up through terraces of olive trees to Es Verger. This farmhouse restaurant is popular with local families, who eat roast lamb here at weekends. The road continues beyond Es Verger but its condition worsens, although it is drivable unless wet. Eventually you arrive at a clearing, Es Pouet, which is the farthest you can travel by car.

Above *The terraced hillsides of Banyalbufar, irrigated by a network of gushing water channels, slope down to the sea*
Opposite *Yachts and boat in Port d'Andratx*

From here it is a short, steep walk to the castle. There is not much left to look at, though there are fine views across the plain framed by the ruined windows and arches. However, this is not the end of your walk. Keep going for a few more minutes and you will reach a small chapel and sanctuary, Nostra Senyora del Refugio, founded as a hermitage in 1622. This is one of the most atmospheric spots in Mallorca. Candles are lit in the chapel, alongside *ex votos* and notes of thanks to the Virgin for everything from recovery from illness to the birth of a child. There are majolica tiles on the walls, a pink-and-white stuccoed ceiling and an altar carved from a single slab of marble. You can clamber up onto the rocks behind the belltower for views across the sierra. From the terrace you can see as far as Palma, with Cabrera shimmering across the sea. If the walk hasn't taken your breath away, then the views certainly will. Spend the night in the simple hostel at Nostra Senyora del Refugio, above the castle, to experience the true tranquillity of this place.
✚ 220 F4 ✉ Puig d'Alaró ☎ 971 182112 🍽 Es Verger (▷ 124) and at Nostra Senyora del Refugió (▷ 213)

INFORMATION

http://deia.info

⊞ 220 D4 🚌 Buses from Palma, Valldemossa and Sóller

TIP

➤➤ A 30-minute walk from the village leads down to Cala Deià, a shingle cove with a small beach and a couple of fish restaurants that open in summer. You can also bring a car down here—take the main road out of Deià towards Sóller and turn left at the sign saying 'Depuradora'.

DEIÀ

There are many pretty villages in Mallorca, but, thanks to the English poet and novelist Robert Graves (1895–1985), Deià, a beautiful village huddling beneath the Teix Mountains, attracts most attention. Graves lived in Deià for some years in the 1930s, returning in 1946 to spend the rest of his life in the village.

BOHEMIAN VILLAGE

The presence of Graves attracted a stream of writers, artists and muses to Deià—among the visitors to his home were Ava Gardner, Anthony Burgess, Kingsley Amis and Anaïs Nin. Although the golden-stoned village has become a retreat for wealthy visitors, the bohemian spirit lives on. About half of the residents are foreigners, many of them artists and ageing hippies. Graves himself would probably have deplored this trend, but there is no doubt that he started it. Among the residents today is his son Tomás, a printer, author and musician.

TOMB WITH A VIEW

Climb Carrer d'es Puig to the parish church of Sant Joan Baptista. Beside the church is the small cemetery where Robert Graves is buried. His tomb is inscribed 'Robert Graves, Poeta, 1895–1985, EPD' (*En Paz Descanse*, Rest In Peace). Graves' second wife, Beryl Pritchard, died in 2003 and is buried at the other end of the graveyard. The names on the tombstones here reveal the cosmopolitan nature of Deià.

CA N'ALLUNY

Following the death of Graves' widow, Beryl, the poet's house and garden in Deià were converted into a museum (tel 971 636185; www.lacasade robertgraves.com; open Tue–Sat 10–5, Sun 10–3, public holidays 10–5; admission €5, children under 13 €3.50). Beryl Graves barely changed the house for the two decades in which she lived in it alone, and it still has furniture and artefacts from the 1950s. Graves' small office has been left intact. It was here that he wrote his best-selling novel *I, Claudius*—the proceeds of which paid for the road which links the village to the small cove. Highlights of the visit include the original printing press with which Graves published his own poems, and a short video directed by Graves' son, William.

Above *The small shingle beach at Cala Deià, set in a pretty cove*

LA GRANJA

The rows of tour buses in the car park attest to the popularity of this place, one of Mallorca's oldest agricultural estates and now a living museum of rural crafts and traditions, which is heavily promoted as an example of 'the other Mallorca'. Not everything that you see is authentic and it certainly feels more like a tourist attraction than a working farm, but nevertheless a visit to La Granja gives a genuine insight into traditional rural life.

THE FARM

The natural spring that spouts 10m (33ft) into the air here has been used for irrigation since Roman times. A Moorish farmhouse stood on the site and after the Catalan conquest the land was given to Count Nuno Sanç, a lieutenant of Jaume I. In 1239 he passed the farm to the Cistercian order, which founded its first convent here, but in 1447 it reverted to its role as a manorial estate. Today La Granja is a working farm with pigs, turkeys, chickens and goats, and displays of farm implements in the old farm buildings. The gardens contain a thousand-year-old yew tree and an 18th-century bathhouse, and there is also the option of a short walk (1.2km/0.7 miles) in the woods.

THE HOUSE

The tour of the house begins on the first floor, among drawing rooms and halls filled with family portraits. There is a theatre and a children's room filled with period toys. The ground floor rooms, where the servants worked, contain a wine press, an oil mill and workshops where you might see displays of embroidery, carpentry and basket-making. You may also be offered a tasting of *empanadas* (pasties) and *coca* (Mallorcan pizza) in the medieval kitchen. Finally, go down to the cellar, with its prison cells and gruesome torture chamber. The latter is interesting in a harrowing sort of way, but it does seem to be a little out of place here.

FOLK FIESTA

On Wednesday and Friday afternoons musicians in folk costume play bagpipes, flutes and drums, and women dance the *ball de pages*, a traditional matriarchal dance performed at village festivals. Blacksmiths and candlemakers work in the courtyard, and there are tastings of sausages, cheese, wine, liqueurs, fig cake and *bunyols* (▷ 210).

INFORMATION

www.lagranja.net

✚ 222 D5 ✉ 2km (1 mile) west of Esporles ☎ 971 610032 🌐 Apr–end Oct daily 10–7; Nov–end Mar 10–6

✋ Adult €11, child (4–14) €6

📖 €1.50 ❓ Folk fiesta Wed and Fri 3.30–5 🍴 🅿 🏛

TIPS

>> Come on a Wednesday or Friday and you can save the cost of lunch by helping yourself to all the free samples of food. Otherwise, the restaurant serves traditional Mallorcan cuisine, with a good three-course lunch menu for €12.

>> The shops in the courtyard sell pottery, perfume and other gifts, but they are rather pricey.

Below *La Granja's open-sided gallery looks out over delightful gardens*

INFORMATION

www.jardinesdealfabia.com

✚ 223 E4 ✉ Carretera de Sóller, 17km (11 miles) ☎ 971 613123 🕐 Apr–end Oct Mon–Sat 9.30–6.30; Nov–end Mar Mon–Fri 9.30–5.30, Sat 9.30–1 💶 Adult €4.50, child (under 10) free 📖 €2.50 📷

TIPS

>> The gardens make a good place to relax before or after the drive over the Coll de Sóller.

>> Ses Porxeres, an elegant restaurant beside the car park, serves excellent Mallorcan cuisine.

JARDINES DE ALFÀBIA

The peaceful, landscaped gardens at Alfàbia, at the southern entrance to the Sóller tunnel, almost certainly date back to Moorish times. There is evidence of an Arab house since the 12th century; following the Catalan conquest, the estate belonged to Ben-Abet, a Moorish official who had converted to Christianity. The water is supplied by a mountain spring originating 60m (197ft) above the house in the foothills of the Serra d'Alfàbia.

FOUNTAINS AND CASCADES

An avenue of plane trees leads from the car park to the ticket office. The tour of the gardens begins to the left of the house, climbing a stairway lined with irrigation ditches to reach a fountain and a pair of stone lions. At the top of the stairway the facade gives on to the spray pergola, rebuilt in the 18th century and the most notable feature of the gardens. These days the water jets are controlled by an electric switch and you can turn them on and off as you please.

TO THE LAKE

From the spray pergola a covered walkway leads through an ornamental garden created for Isabel II when she visited the gardens in the 19th century; it is known as the Jardinet de la Reina (the Queen's Little Garden). A double stone stairway takes you down to the lake and the biggest area of the gardens, with palm trees, acacia, eucalyptus, bamboo, cedar, citrus trees, lily ponds and shady walks. You'll find plenty of hidden corners, and seats beside the lake, where you can relax. There is a delightful shady bar where you can enjoy a little refreshment.

INSIDE THE HOUSE

The way out of the gardens takes you through the house, a combination of Moorish, Gothic and Renaissance styles. The highlights are the library with its manuscripts and the 15th-century Flemish oak chair in the salon, carved with scenes of the lovers Tristan and Isolde. There is also a typical *tafona* (oil press) in the inner courtyard, once considered an essential household item for houses of this grandeur.

The coffered Mudéjar ceiling (the only one of its kind on the island), inside the porch, with the coats of arms of Moorish families and Arabic inscriptions in praise of Allah, dates from the 13th century.

Above *The tranquil gardens make a perfect retreat from the hustle and bustle of the island*

LLUC MONASTERY

▷ 102–105.

MIRAMAR

Archduke Ludwig Salvator (▷ 32) bought Miramar in 1872. The site was originally occupied by a monastery and the school of languages founded by Jaume II in 1276—at the request of Ramón Llull (▷ 29)—to teach Arabic to missionaries. The present house incorporates a small section of cloister and the original Gothic columns from the Santa Margalida convent in Palma. It is now a museum dedicated to Llull and the Archduke. The gardens contain the pool where the Archduke swam, benches arranged in the shape of a Byzantine cross, and a promenade with sea views. A carved wooden sculpture of Ramón Llull is set inside a geometric cube, said to represent the cosmos, a gift from the hermits of Ermita de la Trinitat (▷ 113).

✚ 223 D4 ✉ Carretera Valldemossa–Deià ☎ 971 616073 🕐 May–end Oct Tue–Sun 10–7; Nov–end Apr 10–5 👊 Adult €3, child (under 12) free

ORIENT

This village, one of the smallest in Mallorca, is the only settlement in the Vall d'Orient, a 'golden valley' of almond and olive groves. The most dramatic approach is from Alaró, where the mountains of Puig de S'Alcadena and Puig d'Alaró loom on either side of the road. The village has a population of just 30, yet supports two hotels and several restaurants thanks to weekend trippers from Palma. Some good walks start from here. The ascent to Castell d'Alaró (▷ 97) begins on a marked path 200m (656ft) beyond the hotel L'Hermitage.

✚ 220 E4

LA RESERVA

www.lareservaaventur.com

This private nature reserve and outdoor activity centre is on the slopes of Puig de Galatzó, believed to be the most magnetic mountain in Europe. Revered across Mallorca,

it is home to many legends, including that of El Comte Mal (The Wicked Count), a 17th-century nobleman whose ghost is said to haunt the valley. Bring strong shoes and warm outdoor clothing for the 3.7km (2-mile) walking trail. It follows marked paths through typical mountain scenery, with waterfalls, caves and streams. La Reserva calls itself a 'paradise of plants' and it is worth buying a booklet to identify the flora along the way. Mammals to look out for include Pyrenean brown bears, *mouflon* (wild sheep) and emus. The centre arranges activities from horse-riding to rock climbing; there is also an adventure trail with rope bridges and zip slides. Bird of prey flying displays take place daily at 2pm.

✚ 222 C5 ✉ On slopes of Puig de Galatzó, 3.5km (2 miles) from Puigpunyent ☎ 971 616622 🕐 Jun–end Aug daily 10–7; Sep–end May 10–6; last entrance two hours before closing 👊 Adult €11, child (3–10) €5.95 📖 Plant guide €1 ❓ Adventure trail €26.50 (minimum age 8) 🖐

SA CALOBRA

The small cove at Sa Calobra has been spoiled by thoughtless tourism development and these days the best part of a visit is the journey there. You have two choices—the boat trip from Port de Sóller (▷ 43) along the deserted north coast, or the heart-stopping drive down from the M710—look for the snack bar on your right. The road drops 800m (2,624ft) in just 12km (7 miles), with endless hairpin bends and one particularly dramatic switchback where it turns 270 degrees to pass under itself. Once at the coast, ignore the souvenir stands and overpriced restaurants and take the path through the rock tunnels to Torrent de Pareis. A small pebble beach lies at the entrance to a tall, narrow canyon that channels a fast-flowing torrent of water after rain.

✚ 220 F3 🚤 Boat from Port de Sóller ☎ 971 633109 👊 Return €20

SA DRAGONERA

▷ 106–107.

SÓLLER

▷ 108–109.

SON MARROIG

www.sonmarroig.com

Archduke Ludwig Salvator (▷ 32) owned most of the land between Valldemossa and Deià, but his favourite home was Son Marroig. He bought it in 1877 and lived there between 1908 and 1913. On his death the house passed to his secretary Antoni Vives, to whose family it still belongs. The house is rather gloomy but it does contain a good collection of memorabilia and books from the Archduke's library. There are also paintings by Antoni Ribes Prats, the son-in-law of Antoni Vives. Most people make for the garden and its white marble rotunda, imported from Italy. Admire the views over Na Foradada, a jagged peninsula with a hole in the rock offering a window onto the sea. To walk to the peninsula you need to buy a ticket and ask for permission at the house. The 3km (2-mile) path begins at a green gate to the left of Son Marroig; when the path divides, keep right and follow the trail down to the sea.

✚ 223 D4 ✉ Carretera Valldemossa–Deià ☎ 649 913832 🕐 Apr–end Sep Mon–Sat 9.30–7.30; Oct–end Mar 9.30–5.30 👊 Adult €3, child (under 10) free 🍴 Mirador de Na Foradada, closed Thu 🖐

Below La Reserva is a natural paradise of streams, waterfalls and caves

INFORMATION

www.lluc.net
✚ 220 F3 ☎ 971 871525 🕔 Daily
10–1.15, 2.30–5.15 ♿ Monastery and
botanical gardens free, entrance charge
for museum (€4) 🚌 Buses from Palma via
Inca; also from Port de Pollença and Port
de Sóller (May–Oct) 🍴 ⬛ 🏛

Above *Looking out over the rooftops
of Lluc and the basilica*

INTRODUCTION

Lluc Monastery, Mallorca's holiest and loftiest shrine, stands in the heart of the Serra de Tramuntana mountain range, surrounded by wooded hills, valleys and, further to the northeast, steep sea cliffs. Although you could visit the monastery in under an hour, it is best to allow half a day here. Most people time their visit to take in a service and hear the choirboys sing during morning Mass. If you want to soak up the atmosphere of the place, it is better to come late in the day after most of the day-trippers have left, or do as many Mallorcan pilgrims do and stay the night. The monastery is the focal point of what has become a small village, with restaurants, shops and banks. Other attractions include an interesting museum, a botanical garden, an environmental exhibition centre and walks in the nearby hills.

The first evidence of a shrine at Lluc dates from 1268; by the end of the 13th century it was attracting pilgrims from across the island and miracles were being attributed to the Virgin of Lluc. Eight centuries later Lluc continues to hold a special place in the Mallorcan psyche, both religious and secular (it is a popular honeymoon destination). A mass overnight pilgrimage to Lluc takes place in August (▷ 23).

WHAT TO SEE
THE BASILICA

The large Plaça dels Pelegrins (Pilgrim Square) leads to the monastery complex, where an avenue of yew trees links a stone cross at one end with a fountain at the other. To the right is Els Porxets, a beautiful arcade built in the 16th century to provide pilgrim accommodation. Rooms are on the first floor along a wooden balcony with stabling for animals underneath. To reach the basilica, you have to enter the monastery through the main door and continue past the reception office and along the corridor to a courtyard. Just beyond the courtyard, in a small room on the right, an exhibition describes the history and iconography of Lluc. At a second courtyard look right to see the facade of the church, inscribed with the words *Ave Maria*. Dating from 1622, the basilica was built on the plan of a Latin cross with a single nave and a central dome. A path to the right of the altar leads around the back to a small chapel where La Moreneta (The Little Dark One) is kept. This statue of blackened sandstone depicts Mary, the Virgin of Lluc, cradling the Infant Jesus in her arms as he holds open the Book of Life with the Greek letters alpha and omega on its pages. Her crown, encrusted with precious stones including diamonds, rubies, emeralds, sapphires and pearls, was a gift from the people of Mallorca in 1884—which is why the coats of arms of every Mallorcan town are displayed on the walls. You can climb the staircase for a close-up look at the Virgin, though be aware that for many visitors this is a sacred ritual. During services the statue is swivelled round so that it can be seen in a niche above the high altar.

THE CHOIR

For many people the highlight of a visit to Lluc is the chance to hear the choirboys of the Escolania, who sing most days during Mass at 11.15am and again during vespers at 7.30pm. The prior of Lluc founded the choir, popularly known as Els Blauets after the choristers' blue cassocks, in 1531. He stipulated that it should be 'composed of natives of Mallorca, of pure blood, sound in grammar and song'. Although the morning service has become something of a performance, it should be remembered that this is primarily an act of worship. To listen to the music without distraction, and to experience a greater sense of spirituality, attend an evening service.

MUSEU DE LLUC

The museum occupies the upper floors of one wing of the main building. It begins with a gallery devoted to archaeology, which includes a sarcophagus from the nearby burial cave Sa Cometa des Morts, discovered by one of the monks (you pass this cave on the Camel Rock walk, ▷ 118–119). Also on

TIPS

▶▶ The Eastern Tramuntana drive (▷ 116–117) and the Camel Rock walk (▷ 118–119) both start from here.
▶▶ It is usually possible to get a room in the guest quarters, which are basic but comfortable (▷ 213). Telephone in advance or ask at reception.
▶▶ The best place to eat here is Sa Fonda, which serves local cuisine beneath the stone arches and wooden beams of the former monastic refectory.

Below left *La Moreneta (The Little Dark One)*, set in her chapel
Below *Bust of Father Antoni Maria Alcover outside the monastery cloister*

display is fifth-century BC Greek pottery found on a shipwreck near Puerto Portals. The next room, featuring liturgical treasures and vestments, is largely missable, but it is worth going upstairs to see the varied art collection with paintings by Joan Miró and the Catalan artist Santiago Rusinyol. A long gallery of Mallorcan pottery leads to the highlight of the museum, the rooms dedicated to Josep Coll Bardolet (born 1912). This Catalan painter settled in Mallorca in 1940 and the museum contains a wide range of his work: bright, colourful, impressionist paintings of Mallorcan landscapes and seascapes, olive trees, festivals, folk dancers and his travels in Venice, Rome and England.
🕐 Mon–Sat 10–2 ♿ Adult €4, child (under 10) free

THE WAY OF THE ROSARY

A pilgrim path, the Pujada dels Misteris (Way of the Rosary), begins beside a huge elm tree to the left of the monastery complex. Constructed in the early 20th century, the path is lined with granite monuments depicting the Stations of the Cross. It takes about 10 minutes to climb to the summit, with pauses along the way to enjoy panoramic views over the Albarca Valley, where lush farmland nestles in a fold beneath the sheer bulk of Puig Roig. The path leads up to a huge replica of a wooden cross brought from Jerusalem by Spanish pilgrims in 1910. Near here is a sculptural relief with a twisted, wrought-iron frame that bears the unmistakable stamp of the architect Antoni Gaudí. It was while Gaudí was working on his changes to Palma's La Seu (▷ 70–73), that his patron, Bishop Campins, commissioned him to work at Lluc.

MORE TO SEE

JARDÍ BOTÀNIC

This botanical garden was laid out in 1956 and restored between 1993 and 2001 under the direction of Brother Macià Ripoll, with the support of former choirboys and friends of Lluc. On the short trail around the garden you can see around 200 native species of plants, together with fig, quince and walnut trees. One section is devoted to medicinal plants and herbs, and there are several small pools attracting aquatic plants and birds. The garden is reached through an archway in Plaça dels Pelegrins, between Els Porxets and the gift shop.
🕐 Daily 10–1, 3–6 ♿ Free

CA S'AMITGER

Ca S'Amitger, a small building near the entrance to the car park, houses the Serra de Tramuntana information centre. Pick up leaflets here on local walks; a small museum describes the ecology and wildlife of the sierra. One room is devoted to the *ferreret*, the Mallorcan midwife toad (▷ 15), discovered as a fossil in a cave near Sóller in 1978 and subsequently found to be still living in Mallorca. The rehabilitation of the black vulture is illustrated in another room.
☎ 971 517070 🕐 Daily 9–4 ♿ Free

FONT CUBERTA

The 'covered fountain' is situated at the top of the car park, at the farthest distance from the monastery. You will often see a queue of people here waiting to collect water from a natural spring.

ONE PEOPLE?

The Catholic Church may have been closely associated with the Spanish government during the Franco dictatorship, but these days it has become a powerful force for Catalan nationalism. At the end of the Way of the Rosary, on the site of the original chapel, look for a ceramic plaque depicting a map of the historic Catalan-speaking regions, including the Balearic Islands, Andorra and Catalunya Nord (Roussillon in France). The caption reads *Un Poble, Una Llengua, Una Cultura* (One people, one language, one culture).

Opposite *La Moreneta—the Virgin cradles the Infant Jesus in her arms as he holds open the Book of Life*
Below *A statue of Bishop Campins stands in the monastery courtyard*

INFORMATION

✚ 222 B6 ℹ Parc Natural de Sa
Dragonera ☎ 639 617545 ⛴ Boat
trips from Sant Elm: May–end Sep 10.15,
11.15, 12.15, 1.15 daily, last return 4pm;
Nov, Feb–end Apr 10.15, 11.15, 12.15,
1.15 daily, last return 3pm ✋ Return
boat trip: adult €10, child (under 10) €7

TIPS

➤➤ There are no facilities on Sa
Dragonera, so take plenty of food and
water, and check the time of your
return trip.
➤➤ Boats operate from Sant Elm, Peguera,
Port d'Andratx and Palma Nova during
the summer.

Above *View of Sa Dragonera, whose
shape is said to resemble a dragon*
Opposite *Beach on Sa Dragonera*

SA DRAGONERA

The islet of Dragonera, almost 4km (2.5 miles) long and 700m (2,296ft) wide,
is a continuation of the Tramuntana range, separated from the rest of Mallorca
by a narrow channel at Sant Elm. It takes its name from its shape, said to
resemble a sleeping dragon. During the 16th century the island played host to
the notorious Turkish corsair Barbarossa (Redbeard), who used it as a base for
his attacks on Mallorca and Menorca. Today it is a protected nature reserve—
Parc Natural de Sa Dragonera.

GETTING THERE

Boats depart from the small jetty at Sant Elm (for details, contact Cruceros
Margarita, mobile tel 639 617545) and take 20 minutes to reach the island. You
land at the harbour at Cala Lladó, where there is a visitor centre that issues
maps and information on walking routes.

WHAT TO DO

There is a stark contrast between the two sides of Dragonera; vertical cliffs
drop straight into the sea along the west coast, while narrow inlets and coves
form a gentler coastline on the east side. Two paved routes are open to
visitors: the road that runs the length of the island along the east coast, and
the road that climbs west from Cala Lladó to the lighthouse at the summit
of Puig de Na Pòpia (353m/1,158ft). Cap de Tramuntana, at the northern tip,
offers dramatic views along the north coast of Mallorca—allow about an hour
for the return hike from Cala Lladó. The walks from Cala Lladó to Cap des
Llebeig on the southern cape and across the island take a little longer. There
are two additional tiny islands considered part of the Sa Dragonera nature
reserve: Illa Mitjana and Es Pantaleu. Visitors are allowed on the latter; contact
the reception centre in Cala Lladó for more information.

WHAT TO LOOK FOR

Sa Dragonera was designated a nature reserve in 1995 to protect Balearic
wildlife. Among the native plants here are the dwarf fan palm and the cliff
violet. Seabirds such as shearwaters and cormorants are frequently seen
during the spring and autumn migrations, and the island is home to Europe's
largest colony of Eleanora's falcons. Look out too for Balearic lizards, which
have died out on the mainland but continue to flourish both here and on the
island of Cabrera (▷ 161).

INFORMATION

www.sollernet.com

➕ 220 E4 ❗ Plaça d'Espanya (in an old railway wagon outside the station)

☎ 971 638008 🕐 Mar–end Oct Mon–Fri 10–2, 3–5, Sat 9–1; Nov–end Feb Mon–Fri 9–3, Sat 9–1 🚌 Buses from Palma, Valldemossa and Deià 🚆 From Palma

INTRODUCTION

Sóller, set in an aromatic valley of orange groves and surrounded by the highest peaks of the Serra de Tramuntana, is the only sizeable town along the north coast. It is also one of Mallorca's most appealing towns, and getting there is part of the fun. These days it is a lot easier, thanks to the opening of a road tunnel in 1997, which made Sóller much more accessible, but there is nothing to beat arriving by train. The 27km (17-mile) journey from Palma, in a vintage wooden carriage that rattles down the mountainside, is a throwback to an earlier age of travel (▷ 42).

Once in Sóller, most people stroll around the close-knit maze of narrow streets, visit the market and sit in the main square admiring the Modernist architecture. If you want more stimulation, though, there are good walks into the countryside through a valley of orange trees and an enjoyable tram ride to the port.

WHAT TO SEE

THE RAILWAY STATION

The first place that many people see on arrival in Sóller has a claim to fame as the oldest railway station building in the world. The house, Can Mayol, was built in 1606. Steps lead down to the inner courtyard with a stone well once used for watering horses.

PLAÇA CONSTITUCIÓ

The central plaza is a delightful place to sit with a glass of freshly squeezed orange juice from one of the cafes. On the south side is the neo-Gothic church of Sant Bartomeu, with a Modernist facade by Gaudí's pupil Joan Rubió. Rubió also designed the Banco de Sóller next door, with its twisted iron window grilles, circular corner balcony, and a gargoyle of a lion. His house, Can Prunera, with more decorative ironwork, can be seen at Carrer de Sa Lluna 90, in an attractive shopping street off the northeast corner of the square.

Above *Fishing nets drying on the quayside in Port de Sóller*

JARDÍ BOTÀNIC

www.jardibotanicdesoller.org

This botanical garden is divided into several zones planted with Mediterranean flora. Zones 1 to 6 contain plants of the Balearics, while other sections are devoted to the Canary Islands, Corsica, ornamental and medicinal plants, and fruit trees. Attached to the garden, and included on the same ticket, is the Museu Balear de Ciències Naturals, a small museum of geology and botany. Among the exhibits is a skeleton of the extinct *Myotragus balearicus*, discovered by English palaeontologist Dorothea Bates in 1909 (▷ 26).

✉ Carretera Palma–Sóller, 30km (19 miles) ☎ 971 634014 ⏰ Tue–Sat 10–6, Sun 10–2
💶 Adult €5, child (under 12) free

PORT DE SÓLLER

The tramline from Sóller to Port de Sóller opened in 1913 and trams still trundle down to the port, passing so close to the orange groves that you can almost reach out and pluck fruit from the trees. The port has benefited from being tastefully restored in 2007. It is a popular haunt of watersports' enthusiasts with windsurfing, waterskiing and diving available. A low-key resort, overall, it is busy with coach trips during the day, but reverts to calm at night. You can walk up to the lighthouse on the west side for superb sunset views, then order locally caught prawns from a quayside restaurant

✚ 220 E3 🛈 Carrer Canonge Oliver 10 ☎ 971 633042 ⏰ Mar–end Oct

BINIARAIX AND FORNALUTX

From Plaça Constitució, walk along Carrer de Sa Lluna and you will reach the orchards and olive groves of the foothills of Puig Major. Keep straight ahead at a crossroads, follow signs across a bridge, and after 2km (1 mile) you will find the quiet hamlet of Biniaraix; 2km (1 mile) further is Fornalutx, often voted Spain's prettiest village. It is not a secret—there are several restaurants with terrace views where you can eat lunch before walking back—but the setting is undeniably beautiful.

MORE TO SEE

MUSEU DE SÓLLER

Also known as the Casa de Cultura, this old town house contains displays of pottery, costume, umbrellas, fans, musical instruments and works by local artists. There are occasional temporary art exhibitions here. Also of interest is the actual building, a former private nobleman's house dating from the 18th century.

✉ Carrer de Sa Mar 9 ☎ 971 634663 ⏰ Mon–Fri 11–4, Sat 11–1 💶 €2

CEMENTERI

The cemetery behind the station is one of the most impressive in Mallorca, with fine sculptural monuments from the 19th century reflecting the wealth of the merchants who made their fortunes by exporting oranges. The cemetery is also a popular and attractive green space, with well-maintained lawns, plants and trees.

✉ Carrer Can Fabiol ⏰ Summer daily 8–8; winter 8–5

MERCAT MUNICIPAL

The covered market, just north of the main square, was inaugurated in 1952. Check out the typical local bar here—'Bar Mercat'—where you can sit with the vendors and try a tumbler of the local Mallorquín herb liquor. The market is also one of the cheapest places to stock up for a picnic with superb cheeses, cold meats, fresh fruit and bread. It is busiest on Saturdays, when a street market is also set up outside.

✉ Plaça del Mercat ⏰ Mon–Sat 8–1

TIPS

❱❱ Negotiating your way around the Sóller traffic can be difficult—instead, follow signs to the car park on the edge of town or leave your car outside the botanical garden and walk in.

❱❱ Pick up a delicious local ice cream from Sa Fàbrica de Gelats, opposite the covered market in Plaça del Mercat.

Below *Port de Sóller has a natural harbour set inside a fish-shaped bay*

INFORMATION

www.valldemossa.com

✚ 223 D4 ℹ Avinguda de Palma 7
☎ 971 612019 ◷ Mon–Fri 10–2, 3–6,
Sat 10–1 🚌 Buses from Palma, Deià
and Sóller

Above *Valldemossa is Mallorca's highest town at 437m (1,434ft)*

INTRODUCTION

Valldemossa, the birthplace of Mallorca's only saint, Santa Catalina Thomàs, and the highest town in Mallorca, is set in a green vale beneath the Puig d'es Teix. The best approach is from Palma—as you drive through the mountain pass Valldemossa appears ahead of you, its stone cottages and terraced fields nestling in the valley with the tiled green belfry of the monastery rising above the rooftops. Tourism has almost overwhelmed this small town of around 2,000 people and the Reial Cartoixa is second only to Palma Cathedral in the number of visitors it receives. This has come about because of a brief stay by the Polish composer and pianist Frédéric Chopin and his mistress, the French novelist George Sand, who rented rooms in the monastery during the winter of 1838. They had come to Mallorca in the hope that the climate would alleviate Chopin's tuberculosis and to continue their affair away from the gossip of Paris. Chopin wrote that it was 'the loveliest spot on earth' and Sand wrote that 'whatever poet and painter might dream, Nature has created'. But the visit was a disaster. The people of Valldemossa were very conservative and objected to Sand, a liberated woman who wore trousers, smoked cigars, refused to attend church and lived with a man who was not her husband. Sand took her revenge in her book *A Winter in Majorca*, describing the islanders as monkeys, savages and thieves.

In recent years another celebrity couple, actors Michael Douglas and Catherine Zeta-Jones, have put the town back on the map. Any visit has to centre on the Reial Cartoixa, which contains Chopin's cells as well as the municipal museum. If possible, visit out of season, and to really appreciate the beauty of the place, stay until after the coaches have left in the evening.

WHAT TO SEE
REIAL CARTOIXA

Having been given Valldemossa's royal palace in 1399, the Carthusian order founded the Royal Carthusian Monastery on the site. The community prospered and monks lived here until their expulsion in 1835. After this, the monastery was transformed into a hotel of sorts (the rooms were the original monks' cells) and became a popular place for visitors to stay. Aside from the infamous Chopin and Sand, the guests were mainly Mallorquín, from Palma. On its dissolution the monastery passed into private hands and was divided among a number of families. This joint ownership system survives today, with different owners responsible for separate areas, which is why you will find competing gift stalls in many rooms.

The tour of the monastery begins in the neoclassical church, built in the 18th century in the shape of a Latin cross. Note the frescoes by Manuel Bayeu, a brother-in-law of Spanish painter Francisco Goya, and the image of Santa Catalina Thomàs, Valldemossa's saint, over the altarpiece. From the church, you enter the whitewashed cloisters. On your left is the old Carthusian pharmacy with its frescoed ceiling and shelves of ceramic and glass jars and painted wooden pill boxes. The pharmacy continued to operate as the local chemist until 1896. A painting of the patron saints of medicine, Cosmas and Damien, hangs on one wall. The next rooms that you come to are labelled the Prior's Cell, though 'cell' is an inappropriate word to describe a suite of rooms which included a private chapel, library, bedroom, dining room and garden. Of particular interest here is the 15th-century ivory triptych in the library, where the prior would meet with the monks for half an hour each week; it was the only time they were allowed to speak. Look out too for the bedroom cabinet with its macabre display of hair shirts and whips used for penitential flagellation, and a skull that provided a constant reminder of mortality. The monastery gardens are mature and lovely for a wander around. There are also fine views from here.

✉ Plaça Cartoixa ☎ 971 612106 🕐 Mar–end Sep Mon–Sat 9.30–6.30, Sun 10–1; Oct Mon–Sat 9.30–5.30; Nov–end Feb Mon–Sat 9.30–4.30 💶 Adult €8.50, child (under 10) free
📖 €9 🏛

TIPS

➤➤ Try to get here as early as possible to visit the Reial Cartoixa before the tour groups start to arrive.

➤➤ On the road from Palma to Valldemossa, stop off at the Lafiore glass factory at S'Esgleieta (▷ 123), where you can watch glass being blown.

➤➤ Follow the twisting road for 6km (4 miles) down to the coast at Port de Valldemossa, a seaside hamlet with a small gravel beach and a fish restaurant on the quay.

REGIONS **SERRA DE TRAMUNTANA • SIGHTS**

Below *The library in the Prior's Cell in the Reial Cartoixa*

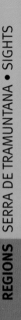

Above *Inside the Palau del Rei Sanç, built for Jaume II's son Sancho*

Above right *The belfry at Reial Cartoixa is tiled in turquoise*

CHOPIN'S CELLS

The cells were inhabited by just 13 monks and the tour illustrates how they lived their frugal live, bound by an oath of silence. The most interesting cells in the complex are those displaying mementoes of Chopin and Sand. Cell 2 contains the Mallorcan piano on which Chopin composed *Raindrop Prelude* while waiting for his own piano to arrive from Paris. Also in this room is a lock of Chopin's hair and various original scores and manuscripts autographed by Chopin and Sand. The most interesting of the latter is a signed copy of Sand's famous book, *A Winter in Majorca*, which is a none too complimentary account of her stay on the island. At the time this did little to raise the couple's standing in the local popularity stakes. Notwithstanding, you can still find copies of the book for sale both at the gift shops here, as well as throughout the island. Cell 4 was actually occupied by the couple. On the left is their bedroom, with Chopin's original Pleyel piano standing in front of a Polish flag. Glass cabinets contain correspondence and documents belonging to them. There is a reproduction of Chopin's death mask and, outside in the garden, a replica of his tombstone in Paris. On a clear day the views from the terrace stretch all the way to the south coast.

MUSEU MUNICIPAL

The Municipal Museum is housed inside the Reial Cartoixa and entered on the same ticket. The first room contains the Guasp printing press (one of the oldest in Europe), built in 1622 and in use for more than 300 years. Also on this floor is an exhibition on the life of Archduke Ludwig Salvator (▷ 32), and the Serra de Tramuntana art gallery, featuring paintings inspired by the landscapes of northern Mallorca. You may recognize scenes such as *Vista de Valldemossa* (1974) by the Catalan artist Josep Coll Bardolet (born 1912), who has lived in Mallorca since 1940 and is now an 'adopted son' of Valldemossa. Among other familiar views are *Cartoixa de Valldemossa* (2001) by Bernat Reüll. The upper floor of the museum is devoted to 20th-century art, with several works by the Mallorcan artist Juli Ramis (1909–90). They trace his career from youthful portraits and self-portraits to an impressionist view of Port de Sóller (1929), a 'blue period' represented by *Dama Blava* (*Blue Woman*, 1940) and his '*abstract drippings*' (1961). Also on display is a large collection of paintings and prints by Joan Miró, and a series of drawings by Pablo Picasso from his book *The Burial of the Count of Orgaz*.

PALAU DEL REI SANÇ

The royal palace adjoining the monastery was built in the early 14th century by Jaume II for his asthmatic son Sancho (Sanç in Catalan), believing that the pure mountain air would be beneficial for his health. Of the original palace, only the defence tower and a stairway survive. The tour of the state rooms is largely uninspiring, and the main reason for visiting is to hear the concerts of Chopin piano music, which take place hourly on the half-hour. The palace is in the same square as the Reial Cartoixa; to get there from inside the monastery, take the doorway that leads out from the cloisters beside the Prior's Cell. Afterwards you can walk around the back of the palace to the original entrance on Carrer de Jovellanos, where a stairway leads to a wooden drawbridge. There are wonderful views from the adjoining terrace, Miranda des Lledoners.

✉ Plaça Cartoixa ✋ Included on Reial Cartoixa ticket 🕐 As for Reial Cartoixa ❓ Piano concerts

COSTA NORD

www.targetaverde.com

American actor Michael Douglas, who has a home near Valldemossa, founded this multimedia cultural centre in 2000. Although it has since been taken over by the Balearic government, it retains close links with Douglas. Visitors are first shown a film in which Douglas describes his passion for the landscapes and culture of the Tramuntana, and are then taken to a replica of the *Nixe*, a yacht belonging to Archduke Ludwig Salvator, another wealthy foreigner who loved Valldemossa.

✉ Avinguda de Palma 6 ☎ 971 612425 🕐 Daily 9–5 ✋ Adult €7.50, child (5–12) €4.50
🏛 🍴 🛍

MORE TO SEE

CASA NATAL DE SANTA CATALINA THOMÀS

Mallorca's only saint, Santa Catalina Thomàs (1531–74), was born in Valldemossa but spent most of her life in a convent in Palma, where she was renowned for her piety (▷ 31). Almost every house in Valldemossa has a ceramic plaque by the front door asking her for help. An easy walk through the cobbled streets of the town leads to her birthplace, now a shrine. From the Reial Cartoixa, head east along Carrer Uetam and fork right downhill to the parish church of Sant Bartomeu. The house is in the lane to the left of the church.

✉ Carrer Rectoría 5 🕐 Daily 9–8.30

ERMITA DE LA TRINITAT

A steep, narrow lane (signposted 'Ermita') leads off the Valldemossa–Deià road to this peaceful and beautiful hermitage, founded by Joan Mir in 1648. This is one of only two places in Mallorca where hermits live in silent contemplation. The other is the Ermita de Betlem (▷ 136). A cool, whitewashed porch lined with ceramic tiles of saints leads to the patio, where an old well and a palm tree stand in front of the chapel. From the terrace there are views over the vegetable garden, tended by the hermits, and out to sea. Notices remind you to respect the silence. Outside, beneath the trees, barbecues and tables are set up for local families to enjoy weekend picnics.

✉ Carretera Valldemossa–Deià 🕐 Summer daily 9.30–7; winter 9.30–6

Below *The baroque interior of the Reial Cartoixa's church*

WESTERN TRAMUNTANA

A circuit of western Mallorca, beginning with a coastal corniche before turning inland through vineyards and olive groves, passing mountain villages and watchtowers with dramatic sea views.

THE DRIVE

Distance: 62km (38 miles)
Time: At least 2 hours
Start/end at: Andratx

HOW TO GET THERE

From Palma, take the PM-1 motorway west and continue to Andratx on C-719

★Start in Andratx (▷ 97), taking the Ma-10, which begins about halfway up the main street on the right as you approach Palma, and follow signs to Estellencs and Sóller. In about 400m (1,300ft) the road passes Castell Son Mas, a 15th-century fortress overlooking the town. Now restored, it houses the police station and town hall. At the next roundabout turn left, keeping on the Ma-10. The road begins to climb, twisting and turning through pine woods. After 5km (3 miles) you will catch your first glimpse of the sea at the foot of the cliffs to your left. The road clings to the cliff top between the forested hills and the

coast, passing through two tunnels on its way to Estellencs. Shortly before the second tunnel, pull in at the Mirador de Ricardo Roca to climb the steps to the lookout point for views over the north coast. There is a cafe here. The Mallorca Tourist Board (1905), whose first project was the construction of the road between Andratx and Estellencs, built the mirador early in the 20th century.

❶ Estellencs is a pretty village of around 400 people, with stone houses, cobbled streets and a few restaurants, bars and hotels. A path leads down through orchards to a small cove with a shingle beach.

Continue on the Ma-10 for another 7km (4 miles) until you see a circular watchtower, Torre de Ses Animes, on your left.

❷ You can stop and climb up to the 16th-century Torre de Ses Animes, one of the oldest survivors of a

line of coastal defences built along the north coast to deter pirates. Fires would be lit inside the tower to warn the villagers of danger. A ladder leads up to the roof, offering wonderful windswept views as far as Sa Dragonera to the west. A short way along the road is a small parking area (signposted with a camera symbol) from which you can admire the terraces and stone walls of the fields outside Banyalbufar.

Continue to Banyalbufar ❸ (▷ 97) and drive along the main street. Beyond the village the road leaves the coast behind and starts to climb inland once again. When the Ma-10 turns left to Sóller, keep straight ahead towards Palma and shortly afterwards turn right to La Granja ❹ (▷ 99). Leaving La Granja, turn right out of the car park on the narrow road to Puigpunyent. Stay on this road for 10km (6 miles) as it snakes through olive groves in the shadow of the Galatzó Mountain. Just after passing the Puigpunyent village sign, turn right (signposted Galilea and Palma) to bypass the narrowest streets and arrive at the centre of the village. Turn right again and continue past the church, with the option of a diversion to your right to visit La Reserva (▷ 101).

❺ Puigpunyent is a peaceful, rural village, but its proximity to Palma means it is attracting many foreigners buying second homes. The village's manor house, Son Net, is one of Mallorca's top hotels (▷ 129).

Stay on the Ma-10 for another 4km (2.5 miles) to reach Galilea.

❻ It is worth parking your car outside the village of Galilea and walking up to the church square to admire the views, which stretch from the Galatzó Mountain on one side to Palma Bay on the other.

From Galilea, the road winds slowly downhill towards the small village of Es Capdellà.

❼ A short diversion to the left of Es Capdellà leads to Calvià, the municipality that includes the beach resorts of Palma Nova, Magaluf and Santa Ponça. Once a poor rural village, Calvià mushroomed in the late 1990s and is now one of the richest towns in Spain. Despite this, it remains an unassuming place, with few signs of tourism. Glazed ceramic tiles in the church square tell the history of the town through a series of tableaux. Near here is the 13th-century church of Sant Joan Baptista, which was rebuilt in the 19th century.

Turn right in Es Capdellà and keep straight ahead at the crossroads to return to Andratx, passing carob and almond groves, with occasional glimpses of the sea. As the road levels out you pass the vineyards and bodega of Santa Catarina—one of the new generation of Mallorcan winemakers—which offers free tours and tastings. After passing the

huge new cultural centre and art gallery on the outskirts of Andratx, you will see Castell Son Mas up ahead.

PLACES TO VISIT
BODEGA SANTA CATARINA
www.santa-catarina.com
✉ Carretera Andratx–Es Capdellà ☎ 971 235413 🕐 Mon–Fri 10–6, Sun 12–2 🖐 Free

CENTRO CULTURAL ANDRATX
www.ccandratx.com
✉ Carretera Àndratx–Es Capdellà ☎ 971

137770 🕐 Easter–end Oct Tue–Sat 10–6, Sun 10–4 🖐 Adult €5, child (under 12) free (for exhibitions only)

WHERE TO EAT
There are great views at Café Bellavista (Carrer Comte Sallent 15, tel 971 618004) in Banyalbufar. The bars in Galilea are good for a snack, and lunch is served daily at La Granja (▷ 99). There is also a large terrace cafe in the Centro Cultural Andratx.

Opposite *Harvest time in Puigpunyent*
Below *Mural depicting Calvià's history*

EASTERN TRAMUNTANA

A drive into the mountains through spectacular gorges surrounded by craggy peaks. Confident drivers can take a helter-skelter journey over the Sóller Pass.

THE DRIVE

Distance: 98km (61 miles)
Time: 3 hours
Start/end at: Lluc Monastery

HOW TO GET THERE

Lluc is on the Ma-10 between Pollença and Sóller. It can also be reached via PM-213

★Start at Lluc Monastery (▷ 102–105), taking the main road out of the car park. At the first junction, turn right (signposted Inca and Palma). After 1km (0.6 miles), turn left towards Inca, passing a petrol station on the left. The road drops steeply through a succession of bends with views across the plain to the Serra de Llevant. After 10km (6 miles) you enter Caimari.

❶ The village of Caimari is home to the island's oldest olive oil co-operative, Oli Caimari (▷ 121). You can visit the oil mill. The open-air museum, at the east side of the village, focuses on Mallorcan rural

traditions, with a limekiln, a charcoal stove, a net for catching thrushes and a *casa de neu* (snow house), used for storing winter snow in the days before refrigeration. Access to the park is free at any time.

Turn right beside the olive groves on a minor road signposted to Mancor and continue between plantations of carob and olive trees. On reaching Mancor, turn left at the crossroads then left again on the main road towards Inca. After 1km (0.6 miles) turn right (signposted Biniamar and Lloseta). Pass through the hamlet of Biniamar and continue to Lloseta. Turn sharp right at a four-way junction to pass through the centre of the village.

❷ Lloseta is best known for its leather industry, in particular Bestard mountain boots (▷ 121). In the 1960s there were 32 workshops in the village. Also of interest is the 18th-century palace of the Count of Aiamans, now a smart rural hotel,

Petit Hotel Cas Comte. You can reach it by climbing the steps beside the parish church.

Leave Lloseta, and after 1km (0.6 miles) turn right, following signs for Alaró. Stay on this road, Ma-2130, for the next 7km (4 miles) through the rural foothills of the sierra. Before you reach Alaró, turn right at a crossroads (signposted Castell d'Alaró and Orient). Look up as you drive along this short road and you will see a white farmhouse on the horizon, halfway up a mountain. This is Es Verger, the restaurant on the way to Castell d'Alaró (▷ 97). To visit the castle, turn left at the T-junction at the end of this road and follow the signs. You can take your car as far as Es Verger—after that it is easier to walk. If you do not want to visit the castle, turn right at the T-junction and continue for 8km (5 miles) as the road climbs to Orient. The twin plateaux of Puig d'Alaró and Puig de S'Alcadena face each other across the road, guarding the entrance to the valley. Shortly after passing L'Hermitage, a hotel (▷ 129), you will see the tiny village of Orient (▷ 101) nestling in the valley to your right.

❸ Orient has a population of around 45 people, but its bars and restaurants attract many visitors at weekends. Park your car and wander up to the 17th-century church of Sant Jordi. If it is open, go inside to see the marble and gold altar and a wood crucifix.

Continue on the narrow, bendy road for another 10km (6 miles) into Bunyola.

❹ Bunyola is a pleasing little town, once the centre of production for Tunel, a herbal liqueur named after the nearby railway tunnel. In 1998, the company moved to Marratxí.

At the main square in Bunyola turn right and cross the railway line from Palma to Sóller. At the next roundabout turn right onto the Ma-11 to Sóller. On reaching the Jardines de Alfàbia (▷ 100) you have a choice. The easier option is

to continue straight ahead through the Sóller Tunnel (toll payable). Alternatively, turn left to head up the Coll de Sóller.

❺ The 14km (9-mile) route over the Sóller Pass is one of the scenic highlights of Mallorca—although with 57 hairpin bends to negotiate, it is not for nervous drivers. The road climbs steeply towards the pass (501m/155ft), where there is a car park and a bar. On a clear day the views from the terrace stretch down to Palma and far out to sea. Once you are over the pass the landscape changes, with huge terraces of drystone walls and views across the Sóller Valley.

The two routes are reunited at the exit from the tunnel. Drive straight ahead, bypassing Sóller ❻ (▷ 108–109). After passing the botanical gardens, turn right at the third roundabout onto the Ma-10 (signposted Pollença and Lluc). Stay on this road as it climbs to the high sierra. After passing the road to Fornalutx (▷ 109) on the right, you arrive at Mirador de Ses Barques on the left. Lunch at the terrace

SERRA DE TRAMUNTANA • DRIVE

REGIONS

restaurant or enjoy the views of Port de Sóller from the belvedere. Soon after this, the road reaches a height of 1,000m (3,280ft), then tunnels into the mountains to emerge in a military zone before carving its way through a deep gorge between Mallorca's two highest summits, Puig Major (1,447m/4,688ft) and Puig de Massanella (1,367m/4,429ft). The Cúber and Gorg Blau reservoirs are popular birdwatching spots. After a second tunnel you pass the switchback road to Sa Calobra (▷ 101) on your left. The final stretch has spectacular views, looking out to sea over the sheer limestone walls and jagged rocks of the Torrent de Pareis. Stay on the Ma-10 and follow the signs to return to Lluc.

WHERE TO EAT
RESTAURANT ORIENT
Tuck into generous portions of rustic Mallorcan cuisine here.
✉ On the main road through Orient ☎ 971 615153 ⏰ Mon, Wed–Sat 1–5, 8–11, Sun, Tue 1–5

Above *Mallorca's walkways are well signed*
Opposite *The Cúber Reservoir is a popular place for birdwatching*

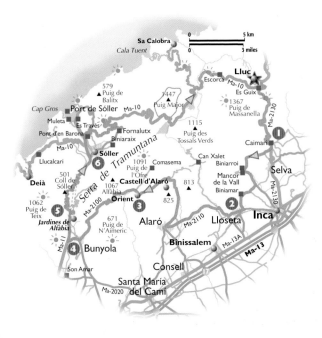

TO CAMEL ROCK

A chance to explore the magnificent scenery of the Serra de Tramuntana, with minimum effort. The route starts at Lluc Monastery and takes in odd-shaped rocks, ancient burial caves and natural water springs.

THE WALK

Distance: 3.2km (2 miles)
Time: 2 hours
Start/end at: Lluc Monastery (⊞ 220 F3)
Information: Serra de Tramuntana information centre, Ca S'Amitger, Lluc, ☎ 971 517070

HOW TO GET THERE

Lluc is on the Ma-10 between Pollença and Sóller and it can also be reached on the Ma-2130 from Inca. Allow extra time for the journey here, especially in the summer, when the difficult roads are very busy

★Lluc Monastery (▷ 102–105) is a popular base for walkers and the starting point for a number of serious hikes, including the ascents of Puig de Massanella and Puig Tomir. This easy walk, however, can be done by anybody equipped with a sturdy pair of shoes. You can pick up a map and descriptive leaflet at Ca S'Amitger, the environmental information centre in the car park.

Leave Lluc by taking the main road out of the car park, keeping to the pavement on the left-hand side. When you reach a concrete road on the left, turn off and pass through the gateposts. The way ahead, marked 'Camí Reservat', is a private access road to the monastery. Ignore this one and instead turn right and climb through a gap in the wall (signposted Santuari de Lluc–Acampades), which brings you out by a dusty football pitch.

You may spot the choirboys of the Escolania here, having exchanged their blue cassocks for football kit.

Follow the path around the outside of the fence, then enter the football pitch through a gate. Leave through another gate in the far left-hand corner to arrive at a wooden footbridge.

This bridge crosses the Torrent de Lluc, a watercourse which is bone-dry for much of the year but fills

rapidly with fast-flowing water after rain. After merging with the Torrent de Pareis the stream eventually flows into the sea at Sa Calobra (▷ 101).

Cross the bridge and clamber over boulders to begin the climb up to a rocky ridge. This is a short but steep ascent through a shady grove of oak trees, following a path marked with red dots on the signposts. Wild goats can sometimes be seen here. After 150m (165 yards) you come to an open area on your left where the ground has been artificially flattened. This was the site of a *rotllo de sitja*, a circular construction consisting of an earthen mound enclosed by stones. At one stage these were common features of the Mallorcan landscape, used by *carboners* (charcoal burners). Branches from oak trees were built up around the

Above *Lluc Monastery, with its orange-flecked roof tiles, viewed from the hills above its wooded setting*

sitja into a conical shape, then burnt slowly to obtain the fuel.

Take the narrow path to your right opposite the *sitja* (signposted Es Camell).

This short diversion leads in about 50m (55 yards) to the famous Camel Rock, which is an outcrop that has been sculpted by wind and rain over thousands of years into the shape of a camel. Follow the path and descend the steps to arrive at a flat area, where there is a stone bench from which to contemplate this natural work of art.

Retrace your steps to return to the main path. Turn right and continue to climb until you arrive at a junction with a wooden waste bin in front of you.

It is worth taking another short detour here to enjoy the best views of the walk. Turn left and follow the wide path for around 100m (110 yards) to reach the Mirador des Pixarells, where you will find more stone benches and a small sign forbidding camping and lighting fires. There are fine views across the sierra from here. Notice how the karstic limestone rock has been eroded into yet more fantastical shapes in various shades of russet and grey.

Return to the junction and keep straight ahead, passing a curious-looking pine tree whose distinctive shape has given rise to the nickname 'the witches' nest'.

Just before the path descends, look for an opening in the ground to your left. This is Sa Cometa des Morts (Cave of the Dead), a prehistoric burial cave first discovered and explored by a monk from Lluc Monastery. A sarcophagus discovered in the cave is on display in the monastery's museum.

Stay on the path as it climbs gradually through steep banks

divided by stone walls, then follows a zigzag course to reach a main road. Turn right here and walk beside the road for 200m (220 yards). Take care—the traffic can be fast here.

On your left you pass an access road to Binifaldó. This old stone farmhouse at the foot of Puig Tomir is now a forestry education centre. If the name is familiar, it is because Binifaldó is also Mallorca's leading brand of mineral water. The water comes from a nearby spring.

Turn right at a wooden gate, where the gatepost is marked with a red dot.

You are now on the old road from Pollença to Lluc, which has been in existence since at least the 13th century. At one time it was designated a *camí reial* (royal path), and a toll was levied for maintenance of the route.

Stay on the path as it twists gradually down towards Lluc. After passing a campsite, you arrive back at the football pitch from where you can retrace your steps to the monastery.

WHERE TO EAT

There are no facilities on this walk, so take plenty of water and a snack. You can stock up on provisions at a small shop near the entrance to the monastery. There are, however, several options at Lluc itself. Sa Fonda (tel 971 517022), in the old monks' refectory, offers traditional Mallorcan cuisine. Ca S'Amitger (tel 971 517046) and Sa Font Coberta (tel 971 517029) are restaurants situated at either end of the car park. For a lighter meal, you can pick up a pastry or a plate of *pa amb olí* at Café Sa Plaça in the main square.

Below *View across the Lluc Valley*

ANDRATX AND ENVIRONS

CLUB DE VELA PORT D'ANDRATX

www.cvpa.es

Sailing and kayaking are offered at this medium-sized marina.

✉ Avinguda Gabriel Roca 27, 07157 Port d'Andratx ☎ 971 671721 🕐 All year

THE FASHION HOUSE

Port d'Andratx is the realm of the astronomically expensive boutique, selling designer clothes, shoes and sunglasses. A good example is The Fashion House, home to Valentino, Moschino and Versace. If cashmere pullovers are not to your taste, you can always watch others flexing their credit cards.

✉ Avinguda Mateo Bosch 4, 07157 Port d'Andratx ☎ 971 673642 🕐 Mon–Sat 10–1, 3–8

GOLF DE ANDRATX

www.golfdeandratx.com

This 18-hole, par-72 course is made difficult by the inclusion of more than 60 bunkers, seven lakes and long, narrow fairways. One half of the course is in a residential area but the other half is set in natural surroundings.

✉ Carrer Cromlec 1, 07160 Camp de Mar ☎ 971 236280 ✋ Green fee (up to 3pm), €100 (buggies compulsory) 🍴 🖥 🏊

GOLF SANTA PONÇA I

www.habitatgolf.es

Perhaps this is the best-known golf course in Mallorca; royalty, celebrities and golfing legends have trodden its swards. The testing 18-hole, par-72 course has wide fairways and water hazards.

✉ Avinguda del Golf, 07180 Santa Ponça ☎ 971 699064 ✋ Green fee €80

🍴 🖥 🏊

RAD-INTERNATIONAL

www.rad-international.de

Racing bikes for serious bicyclists are available from Santa Ponça, Camp de Mar and Peguera, in the southwest of the island (mornings only). Most riders bring their own shoes and pedals but the Shimano system is available.

✉ Gran Vía de la Cruz 49–51, 07180 Santa Ponça ☎ 971 697692 🕐 Daily 9.30–11 ✋ From €166 per week (includes bike rental and five guided tours); €69 with own bike

RUTA DE PEDRA EN SEC

The Dry Stone Route is an on-going project to create a durable footpath along the length of the Serra de Tramuntana from Andratx to Pollença. The plan is to build eight or nine refuges on the route

where walkers can spend the night: six have been completed to date. Each refuge has about 30 bunk beds; reservations are strongly recommended. For more information contact the Department for Nature and the Environment (Carrer General riera, 111, Palma, tel 971 173700, www.conselldemallorca.net/ mediambient/pedra).

REFUGI MULETA (NEAR PORT DE SÓLLER)

www.conselldemallorca.net/mediambient/ pedra

☎ 971 173700

REFUGI TOSSALS VERDS (NEAR CUBER RESERVOIR)

www.conselldemallorca.net/mediambient/ pedra

☎ 971 173700

SA TARONJA

www.sataronja.com

This former farm, surrounded by lovely gardens, has been transformed into a dynamic cultural centre, with a busy programme of concerts, exhibitions and workshops, the latter encompassing everything from tai chi to painting, wine-tasting and cooking. All ages are catered for.

✉ Carrer Andalucia 23, 07150 Andratx
☎ 971 235268 🕐 Wed–Sun 11–9 🍴

SCUBA ACTIVA
www.scuba-activa.com
This scuba-diving school offers courses for children and adults off the coast of Sant Elm and organizes dives around Sa Dragonera. Equipment is available for hire.
✉ Plaça Monsenyor, Carrer Sebastian Grau 7, 07159 Sant Elm ☎ 971 239102 🕐 Apr–end Nov, times vary 🖐 Single dive plus equipment from €32

BANYALBUFAR
CAFÉ ES TRAST
This lively restaurant-bar on the main road through Banyalbufar serves reasonably priced innovative tapas—€2.50 for one dish, €7 for three—and cold beer.
✉ Comte de Sallent 10, 07191 Banyalbufar ☎ 971 148714 🕐 Daily 10.30am–midnight

BUNYOLA
CLUB HIPIC DE SON MOLINA
www.sonmolina.com
This horse-riding centre in the foothills of the Tramuntana has two large arenas and offers tuition in a range of disciplines, including jumping and dressage. It has expertise with handicapped riders.
✉ Carretera Palma–Sóller, km 12, 07193 Bunyola ☎ 971 613739 🕐 Mon–Fri 9–8, closed Aug 🖐 Group class €16 per person

GOLF SON TERMENS
www.golfsontermens.com
The most naturalistic course on Mallorca, Son Termens, uses the hilly landscape to craft a tough 18-hole, par-70 course. The 18th hole finishes at the clubhouse.
✉ Carretera de S'Esglieta, km 10, 07110 Bunyola ☎ 971 617862 🖐 Green fee €80 🍴 🖵

CAIMARI
OLI CAIMARI
www.aceites-olicaimari.com
Caimari is the hub of olive oil production in Mallorca. Although Mallorca's best oils are not produced here, good-quality oils are sold at

this olive mill and you can see the olives being crushed at harvest time. Other Mallorcan products are also available in the shop.
✉ Carretera Inca–Lluc, km 6, 07314 Caimari ☎ 971 873577 🕐 Mon–Fri 9.30–2, 3.30–7, Sat 10–2, 4–7, Sun 10–2 🖐 €6.50 for 500ml bottle

DEIÀ
CAFÉ SA FONDA
With jazz on the stereo, a lovely vine-covered terrace and views up to the church, Sa Fonda is a pleasant place for a drink. The old village inn appears to be the last bastion of Deià's laidback residents. You might hear live music on summer evenings.
✉ Carrer Arxiduc Lluis Salvador 5, 07179 Deià ☎ 971 639306 🕐 Daily 12–12, closed Feb

HERBORISTERÍA L'ARXIDUC
As befits a village with such a bohemian background, the most interesting shop in Deià is a health food shop, selling organic foods, homeopathic and herbal remedies, natural cosmetics, eco-friendly books and clothes.
✉ Carrer Arxiduc Lluis Salvador 2, 07179 Deià ☎ 971 639434 🕐 Mon–Sat 10–1, 5–7

SON MARROIG
www.sonmarroig.com
On summer nights at Archduke Ludwig Salvator's old mansion you can watch concerts in the gardens. Son Marroig is also the venue for Deià's classical music festival (▷ 123).
✉ Carretera Valldemossa–Deià, 07179 Deià ☎ 971 639158 🕐 Jun–end Sep, times vary 🖵

ESPORLES
LA GRANJA
www.lagranja.net
Folk music and dance shows take place at this rural museum (▷ 99) on Wednesday and Friday afternoons.
✉ 2km (1 mile) west of Esporles ☎ 971 610032 🕐 Folk fiesta Wed and Fri 3.30–5 🖐 Adult €12, child €6 on Wed and Fri 3.30–5pm 🍴 🖵 🏛

LLOSETA
BESTARD
www.bestard.com
Few products are more authentically Mallorcan than a pair of Bestard walking boots. The family firm was established in Lloseta in 1940 and today produces a high-quality range of technical footwear from multi-activity trainers to four-season mountain boots.
✉ Carrer Estació 40–42, 07360 Lloseta ☎ 971 514044 🕐 Mon–Fri 9.30–7

TEATRO DE LLOSETA
www.teatrelloseta.com
In a startling contrast to its rustic surroundings, Lloseta's arts centre is an angular marble and glass building. The venue hosts theatre, dance, concerts, book readings and festivals. There's seating for up to 350 people.
✉ Carrer Pou Nou, 07360 Lloseta ☎ 971 514452 (Town Hall) 🕐 All year (information Tue–Sun 10–2) 🖐 From €6 🖵 🔊

PALMANYOLA
SON AMAR
www.sonamar.com
Although after-dinner shows are new to Mallorca, this glitzy cabaret, an acquired taste, has been entertaining diners since 1963 with singers, dancers and magicians in a large 17th-century manor house near Bunyola. Most people arrive on an organized excursion, but seats are available independently.
✉ Carretera de Sóller, km 10.8, 07193 Palmanyola ☎ 971 617533 🕐 Daily dinner 8pm, show 9pm 🖐 Menus €60–€90, show only €40 🍴 🔊

PORT DE SÓLLER
NAUTIC SÓLLER
www.nauticsoller.com
Since 1984, this company has been providing motorboat rental, as well as canoeing and sea kayaking. Boat trips and sailing classes for beginners are also available, plus water skiing.
✉ Platja d'en Generos s/n, 07108 Port de Sóller ☎ 609 354132 🕐 May–end Oct 🖐 Canoe and kayak rental, 1 day €40; water skiing, 1 hour €110

PUIGPUNYENT

RESERVA PUIG DE GALATZÓ

www.lareservaaventur.com

This small nature reserve around Galatzó mountain (▷ 101) offers activities for groups, including archery, rock climbing, horse-riding, zip-wire rides, orienteering and bathing under the waterfalls. Individuals come here for hiking.

✉ Puigpunyent ☎ 971 616622
🕙 Jun–end Aug 10–7; Sep–end May 10–6
✋ Adult €11.90, child (3–10) €5.95

SÓLLER

ADREÇ

Browse the racks of fashionable clothes and accessories at this boutique on Sóller's main shopping street. It's particularly strong on delicate, colourful scarves and neat handbags.

✉ Carrer Sa Lluna 6, 07100 Sóller ☎ 971 630201 🕙 Mon–Fri 9.30–1.30, 4.30–8.30, Sat 9.30–2

BARCOS AZULES

www.barcosazules.com

Barcos Azules run boat trips on a large catamaran from Port de Sóller to a number of destinations including Sa Calobra, Cala Tuent, Cap de Formentor and Menorca, and circumnavigations of Mallorca. Paella is served on Sunday outings in July and August. Private boat charters are also available.

✉ Passeig Es Través 3, 07108 Port de Sóller ☎ 971 630170 ⬛ Return trips from €24, child (6–12) €12, under-6s free

BEN CALÇAT

This narrow shop is one of the few places where you can buy handmade traditional Mallorcan shoes, and the only place to watch the skilled cobbler, Ben Calçat, at work. Boots in sizes 34–47 cost €80; dapper canvas and leather shoes, with tyre treads for soles, cost €34. The traditional but stylish sandals are a good purchase.

✉ Carrer Sa Lluna 74, 07100 Sóller ☎ 971 632874 🕙 Mon–Fri 9–8, Sat 9–1

CAFÉ CENTRAL

For mid-shopping refreshments, pull up a wicker chair outside this friendly cafe on Sóller's main square. A slice of almond cake, the house speciality, costs €2.70, with coffees for €1.80. Inside there's a long bar with bench seating.

✉ Plaça Constitució 32, 07100 Sóller ☎ 971 630008 🕙 Daily 8am–9.30pm (11pm in summer). Closed Wed in winter

CAFÉ SÓLLER

Tasty tapas are dispensed from a counter at the rear of this well-regarded tapas bar in Sóller's main square. Mixed tapas start at €6. Try the good spinach and lamb tapas. Beers are served from the long bar and there's often low-key dance music playing.

✉ Plaça Constitució 13, 07100 Sóller ☎ 971 630010 🕙 Mon–Fri 8pm–1am (11pm in winter), Sat 8pm–5am

EUGENIO

Try this small shop for olive wood handicrafts, including kitchen kit such as salad bowls and salt cellars, from €8.

✉ Carrer Jeroni Estades 11, 07100 Sóller ☎ 971 630984 🕙 Mon–Fri 10.30–8, Sat 10.30–6

FINCA GOURMET

Seasonal Mallorcan specialities are sold at this delicatessen. Expect to find jars of preserved fruits and conserves in winter and fresh produce in summer. A fine selection of *sobrassadas* (▷ 210), Menorcan cheeses and sought-after Mallorcan wines is stocked all year. Gift ideas? Try orange blossom honey, jars of Sóller olives or sundried tomatoes.

Packets of almondy *carquinyol* biscuits cost around €3. Prices reflect the high quality.

✉ Carrer Sa Lluna 16, 07100 Sóller ☎ 971 630253 🕐 Mon–Sat 10–8, Sun 11–3

MALLORCA MUNTANYA
www.mallorcamuntanya.com
Two professional mountain guides, Salvador Suau and David Casajuana, offer six-day walking holidays which can be tailored to suit the fitness levels of each group. Prices do not include accommodation, although this can be arranged. Both guides speak English, German, French and Spanish.

✉ 07100 Sóller ☎ 639 713212 (Salvador), 669 334910 (David) 🕐 Mon–Sat ✋ From €210 for 6 days

OCTOPUS DIVING CENTRE
www.octopus-mallorca.com
This PADI-approved diving centre has two boats taking divers to 30 dive sites along the rocky west coast. Staff are multi-lingual. The centre offers nitrox tanks, and specialist equipment—including underwater cameras—can be hired.

✉ Carrer Cononge Oliver 13, 07108 Port de Sóller ☎ 971 633133 🕐 May–end Oct ✋ Single dive €34

TRAMONTANA CRUCEROS
www.tramontanacruceros.com
Two cruise boats and a 350-seat catamaran operate trips along the north coast, with various stopping-off points.

✉ Carrer Marina 16, 07108 Port de Sóller ☎ 971 633109 🕐 Daily 10, 11, 12.45, 3 to Sa Calobra ✋ Adult €22, child (6–12) €12

TRAMUNTANA TOURS
Organizes a wide range of adrenalin-fuelled activities in the surrounding Serra de Tramuntana countryside for people with a reasonable level of fitness. Choose from guided hikes, gentle strolls, mountain bicycling, canyoning, deep sea fishing and sea kayaking in Port Sóller.

✉ Carrer Marina 16, 07108 Port de Sóller ☎ 971 633109 🕐 Daily 10, 11, 12.45, 3 to Sa Calobra ✋ Adult €22, child (6–12) €12

FESTIVALS AND EVENTS

TOUR OF MALLORCA
February
www.vueltamallorca.com
Professional bicycling teams come to Mallorca for this pre-season competition. The tour lasts five days and takes different routes around the island each year.

✉ Serra de Tramuntana and rest of island

VINTAGE CAR RALLY
March
www.rallyislamallorca.com
This annual vintage car rally in late March attracts Porsches, Ferraris and other classic cars to the twisting roads of the Serra de Tramuntana.

✉ Serra de Tramuntana and rest of island

MOROS I CRISTIANOS
Monday after the second Sunday of August
Local Sóller women helped vanquish a band of Turkish pirates in 1561 and the battle for Sóller is commemorated with this lively re-enactment.

✉ Sóller

DEIÀ INTERNATIONAL FESTIVAL
April, May, August, September
www.soundpost.org
This chamber music festival, with spring and summer programmes,

is held at Son Marroig and boasts a lengthy roster of top-class performers.

✉ Deià ☎ 971 639178

SÁ MOSTRA INTERNATIONAL FOLKLORE FESTIVAL
Late July
www.sollernet.com/samostra/mostraen.html
Now in its third decade, this festival brings music and dance from all over the world to Sóller.

✉ Sóller

FESTIVAL CHOPIN
August
www.festivalchopin.com
Chopin's compositions dominate this festival—typically there are only a few works by other composers scheduled. It takes place every year in Valldemossa's monastery (▷ 110–113) and also includes exhibitions and talks.

✉ Valldemossa

FESTIVAL BUNYOLA
October, November
www.festivalbunyola.org
Two months of concerts bring classical music to this small mountain town.

✉ Bunyola

VALLDEMOSSA

COSTA NORD
www.costanord.com
The long-running Mediterranean Nights festival draws top flamenco, salsa and jazz acts to Costa Nord (▷ 113). The centre also occasionally hosts jazz, soul and classical concerts throughout the year.

✉ Avinguda de Palma 6, 07170 Valldemossa ☎ 971 612425 ✋ Adult €7.50, child (5–12) €4.50 🍴 🖥 🏧

LAFIORE
www.lafiore.com
Watch glass-blowers create all sorts of glassware, from colourful

contemporary designs to classic pieces at this factory shop 7km (4 miles) from Valldemossa. Prices are a little lower here than for similar items elsewhere.

✉ Carretera de Valldemossa, km 11, 07193 S'Esgleieta ☎ 971 611800 🕐 Mon–Fri 9–8, Sat 9–2

L'OR DE MALLORCA
This souvenir shop is a cut above the rest, selling distinctive gold jewellery and handicrafts such as good-quality Mallorcan glassware.

✉ Carrer Blanquerna 10–12, 07170 Valldemossa ☎ 971 616114 🕐 Summer daily 10–8.30; winter 10–5

PRICES AND SYMBOLS

The prices given are the average for a two-course lunch (L) and a three-course dinner (D) for one person, without drinks. The wine price is for the least expensive bottle.

For a key to the symbols, ▷ 2.

ALARÓ
ES VERGER

A twisting road from Alaró leads up to this famous restaurant 4km (2.5 miles) from the village, housed in a whitewashed farmhouse halfway up the mountainside on the way to Castell d'Alaró. It is possible to take a car up here, but the road deteriorates as you climb, with numerous potholes over the final stretch. On the whole it is far better to walk, taking in the fabulous views. There is really only one thing to order here—roast shoulder of lamb, slow-cooked in a wood-burning oven and served deliciously tender with roast potatoes and salad (€12). Other hearty Mallorcan specialities include *arròs brut* and roast suckling pig. You can eat outside on the terrace in summer. No credit cards.

✉ Camí del Castell, 07340 Alaró ☎ 971 182126 🕐 Daily 9–9 ✋ L €14, D €20, Wine €7

BANYALBUFAR
SON TOMÁS

A popular roadside restaurant on the outskirts of Banyalbufar, Son Tomás has wonderful views over fields, mountains and out to sea from its terrace. The rice dishes are excellent—try *arròs negre* (rice cooked with squid ink) or the shellfish paella—and they also prepare delicious fresh fish. Vegetables come from the restaurant garden and are fresh and tasty. The owners are proud of the wine list, which features wines produced using the unusual Malvasia grape which comes from the Banyalbufar region.

✉ Carrer Baronía 17, 07191 Banyalbufar ☎ 971 618149 🕐 Summer 12.30–4, 7.30–10.30; winter 12.30–4. Closed 11 Dec–25 Jan ✋ L and D €25, Wine €11

DEIÀ
ES RACÓ D'ES TEIX

Josef Sauerschell, former chef at the prestigious El Olivo restaurant in La Residencia (possibly Mallorca's smartest hotel, ▷ 128), runs this charming restaurant which specializes in Mediterranean cuisine. If you want to push the boat out while on holiday on Mallorca, this may well be the place to do it—the situation is beautiful, the staff delightful and the food is simply divine (it has been rewarded with a Michelin star). Neither fussy nor over-complicated, Sauerschell relies on using beautifully fresh local ingredients to create his flavoursome recipes. Try dishes such as sea bass with artichoke and nut risotto, or the rack of lamb with an olive crust and potato au gratin. There are set menus to choose from ranging from four dishes for €68 to six dishes for €92. Book in advance and get a table out on the stone terrace in summer.

✉ Carrer Sa Vinya Vella 6, 07179 Deià ☎ 971 639501 🕐 Mon, Wed–Sun 1–3, 8–11. Closed Dec and Jan ✋ L €50, D €70, Wine €20

JAUME RESTAURANT

This longstanding restaurant, in a smart, quiet town house on the road through Deià, has updated its appearance but the cuisine is still solidly Mallorcan. Book a terrace table (Jaume fills up from 1.30pm) for lunchtime sunshine and views over an orchard of lemon trees and the gorge leading to Cala Deià. Look out for *tumbet* and Mallorcan sausages among the starters. Main courses include grilled squid and John Dory; and their signature dish of roast suckling pig with a double carb helping of roast and puréed potatoes (€24). The ubiquitous almond cake is on the dessert menu, but three scoops of the punchy lemon sorbet with a raspberry coulis is a refreshing alternative. The nine-page wine list includes Mallorcan red wines from €15.30 for Macia Batle Crianza 2000 from Binissalem.

✉ Carrer Arxiduc Lluis Salvador 22, 07179 Deià ☎ 971 639029 ⏱ Tue–Sun 1–3, 7.30–12 🍴 L €20, D €24, Wine €8.20

FORNALUTX
CA N'ANTUNA
The views of mountains and the orange groves from the terrace of this simple restaurant make it a popular place to eat in this small Tramuntanan village. Sensibly, the cooking sticks to familiar, seasonal Mallorcan dishes such as *frit mallorquí* (potatoes and vegetables fried with chopped meat), rabbit, and pork ingredients such as *sobrassada*. Sunday brings walkers and local families to the restaurant, when it is advisable to make a reservation.

✉ Carrer Arbona Colom 8, 07109 Fornalutx ☎ 971 633068 ⏱ Tue–Sun 12.30–4, 7.30–11 🍴 L €20, D €25, Wine €9

ORIENT
MANDALA
The Genevan couple who run this restaurant at the top of the hill offer an interesting brand of fusion cooking: French-Indian-Spanish cuisine. So you'll encounter main courses such as salmon with saffron sauce, chicken with green pepper sauce or duck breast with Marsala sauce. You'll also find dishes (for example, Moroccan spiced prawns) that don't fall into either camp. Round off the meal with spiced ice cream for €6.

✉ Carrer Nou 1, 07349 Orient ☎ 971 615285 ⏱ Summer Mon–Sat 8–10.30; winter Tue–Sun 1–3, Fri–Sat 8–10.30 🍴 L €20, D €45, Wine €12

ORIENT
Despite the explosion of new-wave restaurants across Mallorca, it is good to know that there are still village bars serving traditional peasant food. Restaurant Orient is situated beside the road which passes through the village on its way from Bunyola to Alaró. Local families come up here at weekends for long, leisurely lunches, while walkers and cyclists top up their calorie counts with much-needed refreshment. The main dining room has a picture window looking out over the citrus groves, or you can eat on the roadside terrace in summer. The food is classic Mallorcan, such as *sopas mallorquínas* (meat and vegetable broth), *arròs brut* (rice soup), snails with garlic mayonnaise and roast lamb, all served in very generous portions.

✉ Carretera Bunyola–Alaró, 07349 Orient ☎ 971 615153 ⏱ Mon, Wed–Sat 1–5, 8–11, Sun 1–5 🍴 L €35, D €40, Wine €15

PORT DE SÓLLER
DOMENICO
Everything is home-made at this cosy and family-friendly trattoria. In summer, you can sit out on the sunny terrace and tuck into tasty pizza and pasta, supplemented by grilled meat and fish dishes. Most children will find something they like on the menu, and there is also plenty of choice for vegetarians. The desserts are standards like tiramisu and chocolate mousse but they are also home-made, as are the ice creams.

✉ Marina 44, 07108 Port de Sóller ☎ 971 633155 ⏱ Daily 12.15–4, 7–11.30. Open all day in summer 🍴 L €10, D €20, Wine €8

ES FARO
If there was a competition for the best view from a restaurant in Mallorca, Es Faro's widescreen panorama would be in the running for the top prize. The restaurant is adjacent to the Faro lighthouse at the top of the hill on the southern side of Port de Sóller. From up here you can gaze out to sea, across the

Serra de Tramuntana or into the harbour town. Standards (and prices) are equally lofty. Given Es Faro's location, it's no surprise that seafood is a speciality so expect to spend €18–€25 on main courses such as gilt head bream stuffed with asparagus or prawns sautéed in balsamic vinegar with an underwhelming black risotto. There's a tendency to complicate dishes but the portions won't leave you hungry and, like the quiet classical music playing in the background, the service is unobtrusive. Although there is a small car park at the top of the hill, it's a good idea to walk up because the road's narrow switchbacks can get congested.

✉ Cap Gros de Moleta 61, 07108 Port de Sóller ☎ 971 633752 ⏱ Mar–end Sep daily 10am–midnight; Oct–end Feb Mon, Wed–Sun 10–5, 7–10 🍴 *Menú del día* €25, L €30, D €40, Wine €12

LA LUA RESTAURANTE
There is a cluster of restaurants at the far (north) end of Port de Sóller's delightful harbour and La Lua is the one for fans of fish. Seating is on two floors, with the top floor offering the best views of the port. Decor is smart, with paintings for sale hanging on the walls. The restaurant seems to attract the more mature, predominantly British customer. The seafood available depends on the market prices—sea bream, prawns and sea bass are regular fixtures on the menu. No seafood is served on Sundays. Starters cost from €5.60, mains from €9.70 (for steak) and ice creams for dessert from €5.50.

✉ Santa Catalina 1, 07108 Port de Sóller ☎ 971 634745 ⏱ Tue–Sun 12.15–4, 7–11.30 🍴 L €13, D €18, Wine €8.75

SO CAPRICHOS
www.socaprichos.com
Located on the upper level boardwalk overlooking the harbour, this laid back bistro has a no-surprises menu of well-prepared dishes, including grilled fish of the day with salad and chips (€16.90), chicken salad (€14.90)

and barbecued sardines (€8.90). The salads are fresh and enticing and include the speciality of *rucola*, parmesan and sundried tomatoes.

✉ Sant Ramon de Penyafort 15, 07108 Port de Sóller ☎ 971 630095 🕐 Wed–Mon 1.30–3.30, 8–10. Closed 20 Dec–end Mar ✋ L €20, D €25, Wine €7

SANTA MARIA DEL CAMÍ
READ'S HOTEL AND BACCHUS RESTAURANT
www.readshotel.com

Bacchus restaurant at Read's is the number one destination on the island for anyone with an appetite for imaginative, skilled cooking. Launched by Michelin-star chef Marc Fosh (who left in February 2009), the style remains a blend of traditional French cuisine, modern Mediterranean techniques and Asian minimalism. Heavy sauces are absent; instead, dishes are light, fresh and forcefully flavoured. Themes are explored in each dish: fillet of salt cod with caviar, gelatine of vodka and cold celeriac and lime soup look to northern Europe, while cardamom-glazed pigeon breast on couscous with fresh herbs looks south. Expect to spend from €20 (or €8 in the bistro) for a starter, from €28 for a main course in the restaurant, or from €17 in the bistro, and about €9.30 for a dessert such as vanilla panna cotta with rhubarb sorbet (or €7 in the bistro). At these prices the seven-course tasting menu is good value at €89. The sommelier is ready to recommend bottles from the wine list for each course. Vivid wall murals brighten the cavernous dining room. For less formal dining, Marc Fosh has opened a bistro, Simply Fosh, next to the main dining room. With a similarly bold interior, it is a lot of fun and very popular (reservations essential). He offers three courses from €30, with crowd-pleasing classics such as chilli spare ribs, Thai curry and spicy chicken tagine with couscous. In the summer diners can eat on the terrace.

✉ Carretera Santa Maria–Alaró, 07320 Santa Maria del Camí ☎ 971 140261

🕐 Restaurant: Mon–Fri 8–10.30, Sat–Sun 1–3, 8–10.30. Bistro: daily 1–3, 8–10.30 ✋ Restaurant: L €53 and D €70, Wine €18. Bistro: L €30, D €30

SÓLLER
BENS D'AVALL
www.bensdavall.com

One of the best restaurants on the island, Bens d'Avall is as celebrated for its location as its food. As you drive from Sóller to Deià, look out for a right turn on a sharp corner, which will take you down a steep hill to the restaurant. When you're almost at sea level, the restaurant will be on your left, with fantastic views along the rugged Tramuntana coast. The seasonal menu is dominated by seafood, with starters such as carpaccio of Sóller prawns with herbs, lemon, olive oil and a salad of fresh pesto. The kitchen's enthusiastic attitude to desserts is more French than Mallorcan, with creations such as Cuban chocolate *millefeuille* with citrus fruit and spices. A tasting menu is available for entire tables, for €68 per person, and there are options for vegetarians. During the winter months chef Benet Vicens Mayol holds workshops and cookery courses at the restaurant (see the website for details).

✉ Carretera Sóller–Deià, 07100 Sóller ☎ 971 632381 🕐 Mon, Wed–Sat 1.30–3.30, 8–10.30, Sun 1.30–3.30 ✋ L €36, D €50, Wine €20

CA'N GATA
The main attraction here is a delightful back garden-cum-terrace with just a few tables, which, combined with the friendly service, makes it seem as if you are dining in a friend's garden. The food is nothing extraordinary, but prices are low, with a daily menu, plus a great choice of tapas, including mainstays like moist potato tortilla and fresh anchovies in vinaigrette. The dining room inside is cosy and informal with plenty of cat pictures.

✉ Carrer Sa Lluna 51, 07100 Sóller ☎ 971 638634 🕐 Mon–Sat 1–5 ✋ *Menú del día* €9.75, Wine €7.50

CA'N QUIROS
This smart restaurant in a prime position on the corner of Sóller's main square has six solid wood tables, a tiled floor and warm, low lighting. Mains include lamb shoulder (€19.95), grilled squid (€17.95) and aubergine stuffed with lamb (€15.95). There's also paella for two at €12.95 per person. Service can be less than attentive. Desserts cost from €3.50 for fruit or apple tart.

✉ Plaça Constitució 16, 07100 Sóller ☎ 971 633608 🕐 Thu–Tue 12–3.30, 7.30–12 (earlier in winter) ✋ L €25, D €30, Wine €8

SA COVA RESTAURANT
Tucked away on a corner of the main square, Sa Cova delivers fine, traditional Mallorcan meals in a cosy, pleasantly cluttered dining room. A *menú del día* is available for €12.50 or expect to spend €6.50 on salads and €9–€15 on main courses such as lamb chops and rice with codfish and vegetables. The restaurant is renowned for its paellas and rice dishes. If it's warm, sit on the terrace and watch the world go by.

✉ Plaça Constitució 7, 07100 Sóller ☎ 971 633222 🕐 Daily 1–4.30, 7–12 ✋ *Menú del día* €12.50 (Mon–Fri), L €20, D €25, Wine €8

VALLDEMOSSA
CA'N MARIÓ
Truly a well-kept secret, Ca'n Marió serves traditional Mallorcan food at keen prices to locals: paellas, *arròs brut* and *llom amb col* cost about €9. However, because the restaurant is off Valldemossa's tourist trail, you will need to speak competent Spanish when booking (recommended at weekends). The restaurant is not signposted from street level; you will have to go into the building and up one floor. The airy interior is simply furnished, with red chequered tablecloths and wooden furniture. It's part of a simple *hostal*.

✉ Carrer Uetam 8, 07170 Valldemossa ☎ 971 612122 🕐 Mon–Thu, Sun 1.30–3.30, 8–10, Fri, Sat 1–10. Closed Dec and part of Jan ✋ L €20, D €25, Wine €9

PRICES AND SYMBOLS

Prices are the lowest and highest for a double room for one night. Breakfast is included unless noted otherwise. All the hotels listed accept credit cards unless otherwise stated. Note that rates vary widely throughout the year.

For a key to the symbols, ▷ 2.

BANYALBUFAR
MAR I VENT

www.hotelmarivent.com

Now in the third generation of the Vives family, this old-style seaside hotel continues to attract a loyal following of mostly British families, many of whom return year after year and know each of the staff by name. The biggest attraction here is the setting, high above the sea, with panoramic vistas from the terraces, balconies and picture windows. All the rooms have sea views. There is an outdoor pool with a separate children's area, and a tennis court for the use of guests. The disadvantage of staying in Banyalbufar, especially for families, is that there is only a small rocky beach. The food in the restaurant here can be disappointing, catering to the tastes of visitors of a generation ago.

✉ Carrer Major 49, 07191 Banyalbufar ☎ 971 618000 ⊘ Feb–end Nov 🖐 €100–€140 ❶ 29 🏊

BUNYOLA
SA MÀNIGA

www.fincasamaniga.com

Sa Màniga is a large *agroturismo* in the foothills of the Tramuntana just outside Bunyola, with four sunlit rooms, each with telephone, television, a minibar and central heating. A pool outside is ringed with sun loungers, but the hotel is a good choice for active guests with golf, horse-riding, bicycling and hiking all available nearby. Bike rental is free. Bunyola, an otherwise unassuming town a half-hour drive from Palma, is an excellent base for exploring the central portion of the Serra de Tramuntana, and, thanks to its prosaic appearance, it has escaped the worst of the daytrippers and retains a local pace of life. The Palma–Sóller train stops there, and there are good local restaurants. The town is also famed for its olive oil and herbal liquor distillery; don't leave without having a taste.

✉ Carrer Afores, 07110 Bunyola ☎ 971 613428 ⊘ All year 🖐 €110–€130 ❶ 4 🔄 🏊

CAIMARI
BINIBONA PARC NATURAL

www.binibona.com

This is one of the best examples of eco-tourism on the island; the owners of Binibona Parc Natural, the Vicens family, are striving to make this hotel as ecologically friendly as possible. Energy comes from solar panels, water is recycled to irrigate the garden and natural fertilizers are used to grow the vegetables and fruit. All but one room enjoy jacuzzis and terraces, and all have telephone, television, central heating and WiFi.

✉ Finca Binibona, Binibona, 07314 Caimari ☎ 971 873565 ⊘ All year 🖐 €170 all year ❶ 9 suites, 2 doubles 🔄 🏊 🍽

ES CASTELL

www.fincaescastell.com

Paola Cassini and James Hiscock welcome guests to their rustic stone *finca*, set amid 300ha (750 acres) of ancient pine and olive groves on a working sheep farm. The bedrooms are cosy and decorated in traditional Mallorcan style, while original features of the house include an 11th-century olive press and a chimney. There is a small pool in the

Above *Hotel Valldemossa (see page 129)*

gardens, and dreamy views from the terrace that stretch across the plain to the mountains and the sea. Guests can reserve a four-course dinner, which will be freshly bought from the market and prepared by the Austrian chef, with an emphasis on Italian and Spanish cuisine.

This is a delightful rural retreat in an unspoiled corner of Mallorca that is fast becoming a centre for agrotourism. Caters for children.
✉ Binibona, 07314 Caimari ☎ 971 875154 ⏰ All year 🖐 €150–€190 ⓘ 12 (11 rooms and 1 suite) 🏊 ♿ 🄿 Follow signs from Selva or Caimari

DEIÀ
LA RESIDENCIA
www.hotellaresidencia.com
The country hotel was bought by the Orient Express chain from British entrepreneur Sir Richard Branson in 2002, but it has retained its atmosphere of informal luxury and remains the hideaway of choice for fashion models and A-list celebrities. It is set in two restored 16th- and 17th-century manor houses with terraced gardens overlooking the village. The two largest suites, each with their own terrace and pool, cost upwards of €2,000 per night in high season. All rooms have teddy bears, WiFi, rubber ducks in the bathroom and Molton Brown toiletries. Facilities include indoor and outdoor pools, sauna and gym, beauty treatments, Turkish baths, tennis courts, an art gallery and shuttle buses in summer to Llucalcari beach, where the hotel has its own bar. There is gourmet dining in El Olivo restaurant, upmarket bistro food at Son Fony, poolside lunches in summer and afternoon tea on the terrace. Mobile phones are strongly discouraged and children under 10 are only allowed between 1 July and 15 August, 20–31 October, and the Christmas period. A minimum stay of five nights is required from 12 May to the end of October.
✉ Finca Son Canals, 07179 Deià ☎ 971 639011 ⏰ All year 🖐 €305–€580 ⓘ 4 singles, 32 doubles and 23 suites ♿ 🏊 🄿

SA PEDRISSA
www.sapedrissa.com
With just eight rooms in a 17th-century farmhouse and olive mill once belonging to Archduke Ludwig Salvator, Sa Pedrissa is a good example of the trend towards *agroturismo* in Mallorca. Breakfast here is a treat, with eggs, home-made yogurt and jams, and olive oil straight from the farm. On summer evenings dinner is served out of doors on a terrace with views out to sea, while on chilly nights you can eat inside by the old olive press. The rooms may have rustic decor but the fittings are modern. Some are set in their own garden of olive trees; room 8, known as the Tower Suite, is a penthouse on two floors of the old tower, with sea views from the terrace and an espresso machine.
✉ Carretera Valldemossa–Deià, km 64.5, 07179 Deià ☎ 971 639111 ⏰ All year 🖐 €120–€327 ⓘ 9 ♿ 🏊 🄿 On the road to Valldemossa, just outside Deià

S'HOTEL D'ES PUIG
www.hoteldespuig.com
Mentioned, if not immortalized, in a short story by Robert Graves, 'the hotel on the hill' is a small, friendly place opposite La Residencia (▷ left) with eight simple bedrooms washed in ochre, four of them with terraces. Each has a bathroom, telephone, television, WiFi and central heating. Prices reflect its location in Deià, but standards are high. Enjoy breakfast in the attractive, simply furnished dining room or outside on the terrace. There's a small outdoor pool with mountain views.
✉ Es Puig, 4, 07179 Deià ☎ 971 639409 ⏰ All year 🖐 €122–€145 ⓘ 8 ♿ 🏊

FORNALUTX
CA'N REUS
www.canreushotel.com
A few steps away from the Petit Hotel (▷ right), Ca'n Reus is another stylishly renovated town-house hotel in this small village. Decor is more traditional and less minimalist than at the Petit Hotel, but just as pleasing. Both make good bases for hikers exploring the southern and middle sections of the Tramuntana. Bedrooms at Ca'n Reus have hair dryers, WiFi and central heating. There's an 'honesty' bar for guests. In an attempt to retain the tranquillity, children under 5 are not encouraged.
✉ Carrer de l'Alba 26, 07109 Fornalutx ☎ 971 631174 ⏰ All year 🖐 €105–€120 ⓘ 7 ♿ 🏊

CA'N VERDERA
www.canverdera.com
Quiet and effortlessly chic, this designer hotel is everything you'd expect for the price. Each of the centrally heated rooms is individually decorated in pastel colours; some even have whirlpool baths, but you have to pay €20 more for a garden view. They're all equipped with a CD player as well as telephone, satellite television and WiFi. The hotel can organize activities such as golf, bicycling and tennis, but many guests will prefer just to explore the village and its gorgeous surroundings. There's a fine restaurant, open to guests only.
✉ Carrer de Toros 1, 07109 Fornalutx ☎ 971 638203 ⏰ Mar–end Oct 🖐 €160–€200 ⓘ 11 ♿ 🏊

FORNALUTX PETIT HOTEL
www.fornalutxpetithotel.com
This small, attractive hotel looks out across Fornalutx's valley. Once a convent (and then a school), the hotel has been decorated in a modern, airy style, with lots of pale linens, tiled floors and tasteful furnishings. The Sa Capelleta suite lifts the spirits, with a high ceiling, arched alcoves and a large bed in the middle of the room. It gets better outside: there's decking among the citrus groves, tables in the shade and deckchairs around a pool and a jacuzzi (free of charge for guests). There's also a sauna. Bedrooms have central heating for the colder months.
✉ Carrer de l'Alba, 22, 07109 Fornalutx ☎ 971 631997 ⏰ Mar–end Oct 🖐 €145 all year ⓘ 8 🏊 🄿 The hotel is on a quiet, traffic-free street on the left as you enter Fornalutx from the C-710

ORIENT

L'HERMITAGE

www.hermitage-hotel.com

Parts of this former convent date back 400 years, but it is now one of the best-known hotels on Mallorca. The restaurant in the old olive mill draws many daytrippers to this serene, low-lying part of the Serra de Tramuntana, but hotel guests have the advantage of exploring the rest of the hotel, including the herb garden which supplies chef Bartolomé Bisbal. The hotel excels at organizing activities, from tai chi to painting classes, for its guests and there are also tennis courts and a spa available. Despite the sophistication of the hotel and the restaurant, the bedrooms are not as swanky as you might expect. Those in the main building offer an authentically ancient experience, with creaky doors and draughty windows. The remaining rooms are in a pair of modern buildings at the back of the hotel. All have telephone, television and central heating, but no air-conditioning.

✉ Carretera Alaró–Bunyola, 07349 Orient ☎ 971 180303 🕑 Apr–end Oct 🖐 €185–€220 🛈 24 🏊

PUIGPUNYENT

SON NET

www.sonnet.es

Opened in 1998 in a 17th-century manor house looking over a peaceful village, Son Net has become one of Mallorca's top luxury hotels. The suites here are ridiculously spacious, with huge living rooms, marble bathrooms, jacuzzis and walk-in showers; one of them even has its own garden and swimming pool. The main pool is lined with private *cabañas* (cabins), which allow guests to relax discreetly. The hotel offers honeymoon packages and also organizes various programmes based around golf, beauty treatments and learning Spanish. Artworks by Marc Chagall, David Hockney and Andy Warhol are on display in the corridors and bars. The restaurant, L'Orangerie, serves modern Mediterranean cuisine.

The Zen Zone Beauty Centre offers a comprehensive range of beauty treatments.

✉ Castillo de Son Net, 07194 Puigpunyent ☎ 971 147000 🕑 All year 🖐 €250–€350 🛈 31 doubles and 6 suites 🏊

SANTA MARIA DEL CAMÍ

READ'S HOTEL AND RESTAURANT

www.readshotel.com

There are 23 themed bedrooms at this exclusive Relais & Châteaux hotel, 20 minutes from Palma. Each is individually and vividly decorated: the furniture is antique, the beds are enormous and the toiletries are from Molton Brown. Read's is justifiably proud of its restaurant (▷ 125–126) and it has now been joined by an affordable bistro. In early 2007, a fabulous new spa was opened, with a spectacular gym and a wide range of health and beauty treatments. No children under 14 years old.

✉ Carretera Santa Maria del Camí–Alaró, 07320 Santa Maria del Camí ☎ 971 140261 🕑 All year 🖐 €220–€395 🛈 23 🏊

SÓLLER

CA'N AI

www.canai.com

Perhaps one of the most captivating hotels in the Serra de Tramuntana, Ca'n Ai is a converted manor house set in orange and lemon groves in the Sóller Valley. It's the outdoor areas that impress immediately— there are plenty of places in the spectacular gardens and terraces to find seclusion. You can also enjoy the views and the heady scent of the citrus groves from the suites, each of which has a private terrace. The bedrooms are also fitted with telephone, minibar and central heating, but don't have television—a refreshingly bold decision. Breakfast, lunch and dinner are served in the informal dining room, in which there are several levels of seating, so once again it is easy to find privacy. WiFi in public areas.

✉ Camí de Son Sales, 50, 07100 Sóller ☎ 971 632494 🕑 Mar–end Oct 🖐 €180–€237 🛈 11 🏊

CA'S XORC

www.casxorc.com

'Fantastic', 'fashionable', 'a real pain to get to'—all descriptions that apply equally to Ca's Xorc, a hip mountain-top retreat overlooking Sóller where Claudia Schiffer (▷ 19) celebrated her 30th birthday. But it's worth struggling up the twisty, narrow drive to the converted olive mill. The breathtaking views are matched by the shabby chic interior with its candles, stone-flagged floors and psychedelic art. Rooms are kitted out with a music system, WiFi and gold bath fittings; the hotel's decor has Moroccan touches throughout. Sa Tafona, the restaurant, features classy and classic Mallorcan dishes such as ravioli of oxtail, lobster with saffron risotto and a sweet pastry stuffed with pumpkin mousse and cinnamon ice cream. The five-course tasting menu costs €59. Outside there is a swimming pool, jacuzzi and several interesting, sculpture-filled gardens around the hillside. And if it matters at all, Miss Schiffer stayed in room number 8.

✉ Carretera Deià–Sóller, km 56, 07100 Sóller ☎ 971 638280 🕑 Mid-Feb to mid-Nov 🖐 €195 all year 🛈 12 🏊

VALLDEMOSSA

HOTEL VALLDEMOSSA

www.valldemossahotel.com

This tasteful hotel is situated in a restored *finca*, with its own orchards and gardens overlooking the village of Valldemossa. The hotel offers traditional luxury with modern touches, such as the large selection of DVDs available for free loan and WiFi access in the rooms. The three double rooms have their own balconies, while the suites each have a private terrace. The restaurant emphasizes the use of local produce, but some dishes are overcomplicated. In summer you can dine on the terrace. Some rooms have been adapted for visitors with limited mobility.

✉ Carretera Vieja de Valldemossa, 07170 Valldemossa ☎ 971 612626 🕑 All year 🖐 €290–€460 🛈 3 doubles and 9 suites 🏊

SIGHTS 133
WALK AND DRIVE 144
WHAT TO DO 148
EATING 152
STAYING 155

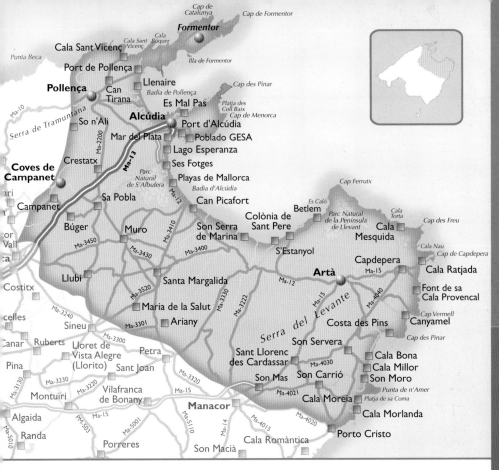

THE NORTHEAST

The northeast corner of the island is also the most diverse, with a landscape that includes dramatic sea cliffs, isolated coves, hidden valleys with ancient olive terraces, and picturesque villages and towns. The latter are home to some of the longest-established and best restaurants and hotels on the island. Add to this a tangible sense of history, with well-preserved Roman ruins and superb beaches and watersports, and it's easy to see why the northeast rates high on so many visitors' itineraries. This region is also a great family destination, with plenty of light-hearted entertainment and activities, coupled with the sandscastle-and-sunbed appeal in destinations like the Bay of Alcúdia. The agreeable flipside is the genteel resort town of Pollença, located in the beautiful foothills of the northern Tramuntana, which has a delightful traditional feel laced with a more contemporary sense of style. Easygoing Port de Pollença also has a timeless feel, despite being a popular British holiday resort for several decades.

The northeast has also long been popular with walkers, with well-marked trails and pathways crisscrossing this beautiful dramatic landscape. Don't miss the memorable farthest northeast corner of the island: the wild and mountainous Formentor peninsula, affording spectacular panoramic views. Although most places of interest are accessible via public transport or organized coach trips, your own wheels are recommended in order to explore the lesser-known villages and sights of this delightful part of the island.

INTRODUCTION

Set on a peninsula between two sandy bays, Alcúdia, one of Mallorca's
most interesting and historic towns, is divided into two distinct parts. To the
south, by the harbour, is the resort town of Port d'Alcúdia, often confusingly
referred to as Alcúdia in tour brochures. Of greater interest is the old town of
Alcúdia, just inland. Alcúdia takes its name from the Arabic *al-kudia* (the town
on the hill). The Romans recognized the strategic importance of this site and
established it as their capital after their conquest of Mallorca in 123BC. It was
sacked by Vandals, rebuilt by Moors and fortified by Christian conquerors. Much
of the town is still enclosed by its medieval walls, begun in 1298. The old town
within the walls is charming to wander around, with its handsome mansions
and atmospheric streets. The town is popular with tourists, so there are plenty
of restaurants and bars, as well as a handful of exquisite boutique hotels.
After years of neglect, recent decades have seen the rebuilding of these walls,
the pedestrianization of the old town's streets and the restoration of several
facades. Outside the walls is the Roman capital of Pollentia; excavations are
still taking place but the main areas can be visited. If you arrive by car there
is a large parking area just outside the walls, in front of the parish church, and
Roman Pollentia's remains can be seen across the road.

WHAT TO SEE

ROMAN POLLENTIA

The ruins of Pollentia are the only significant remains from the Roman
occupation of Mallorca. The visit begins in the La Portella district, where you
can see the remains of three houses. The best preserved is La Casa dels
Dos Tresors (House of Two Treasures), with rooms arranged around a central
atrium. Nearby is La Casa del Cap de Bronze, where a bronze head of a girl,
now in the museum, was discovered. A porticoed street, with some columns
still standing, separated the two houses. From here a path leads to the forum,
Pollentia's main square. Here are the remains of a temple to Jupiter, Juno and
Minerva, together with shops, workshops and inns—Pollentia's commercial
zone between the first century BC and third century AD.

✉ Avinguda dels Prínceps d'Espanya ☎ 971 897102 🕐 Tue–Fri 10–3.30, Sat–Sun
10.30–12.30 🎫 Adult €2, child (under 16) free; includes entry to Museu Monogràfic 🏛

INFORMATION

www.alcudia.net
✚ 221 H3 🛈 Edifici Ca Ses
Monges, Carrer Major ☎ 971 897100
🕐 Mon–Fri 7.45–2.25 🚌 Buses from
Palma, Pollença and Port d'Alcúdia
❓ Market Tue and Sun

Above *Alcúdia reached its heyday in the
2nd century BC when Roman invaders
made it their capital, Pollentia*
Opposite *Alcúdia's lively Old Town*

133

TIPS

>> Visit Alcúdia on a Tuesday or Sunday morning, when a large street market takes place on Passeig de la Mare de Déu de la Victòria, beside Porta del Moll.
>> Walkers should pick up the booklet *Alcudia 10 Excursions* (in English and Catalan) from the tourist office, which maps out 10 walks, including a gentle amble within the town.

TEATRE ROMÀ

The 1st-century Roman theatre is reached by taking a signed path from the south side of Avinguda dels Prínceps d'Espanya. Another path runs behind the Roman forum, linking the theatre to the Oratori de Sant Anna. Unlike the rest of the Roman city, the theatre can be freely visited at any time. Once thought to have been an amphitheatre for gladiatorial combats, it is now believed to have been used exclusively for plays. The council puts on musical and dramatic events in the theatre each summer.

MUSEU MONOGRÀFIC DE POLLENTIA

Some of the finds recovered during excavation of Roman Pollentia are displayed here, including coins, jewellery, musical instruments and toys. Of particular note are the marble statue of an army officer, a bust of the emperor Augustus, and the Cap de Nina, a fine bronze head of a girl dating from the second century. The museum is housed in a 14th-century Gothic hospital beside the parish church of Sant Jaume.

✉ Carrer Sant Jaume 30 ☎ 971 547004 ⊙ Tue–Fri 10–3.30, Sat–Sun 10.30–12.30 ✋ Adult €3, child (under 16) free; includes entry to Roman Pollentia

MUSEU DE SANT JAUME

Located within the 13th-century church of the same name (later re-modelled in neo-Gothic style), this museum has all sorts of religious items on display, including some beautifully ornate vestments.

✉ Plaça de Jaume Ques ☎ 971 548665 ⊙ Mon–Sat 10–1 ✋ Adult €1, child (under 16) free

THE OLD TOWN AND THE WALLS

Inside the medieval walls, Alcúdia is a delightful maze of narrow, traffic-free lanes and carefully restored Gothic and Renaissance mansions. A good example is Can Torró at Carrer d'en Serra 15 (Tue–Fri 10–1, 5–8, Sat, Sun 10–1), a 14th-century mansion that is now a public library and sculpture garden. The walls around Alcúdia were begun by Jaume II in 1298; to make a complete circuit, follow Camí de Ronda, a path that goes right around the town inside the walls. You will pass three gateways, including Porta de Mallorca, the original entrance to the town from Palma, and Porta del Moll, the historic entrance from the port. Carrer Major, with its trendy bars and restaurants, runs between the two, passing the 1929 town hall, with its Modernist clock tower, before reaching the main square.

MORE TO SEE

ORATORI DE SANT ANNA

A footpath from the Roman theatre leads to this 13th-century chapel, seen opposite the cemetery beside the main road to Artà. Built by Diego Espanyol, it was one of the first churches on Mallorca after the Christian conquest. Above the doorway is a statue of the Virgin and Child known as the Mare de Déu de Bona Nova (Our Lady of Good News).

PORT D'ALCÚDIA

The original port town and fishing village is now a mega-resort stretching south from the port beside Mallorca's longest beach. The area down by the harbour still has an enjoyable nautical feel, with a wide, palm-lined promenade. East of here are the docks, where ferries depart for Menorca and Barcelona.

✚ 221 H3 🚌 2 ℹ Passeig Marítim ☎ 971 547257 ⊙ Mon–Sat 9.30–8

PENINSULA DE LA VICTÒRIA

This wild headland between Alcúdia and Pollença bays is the setting for some wonderful walks (▷ 146–147).

ARTÀ

Two enormous monuments—the parish church and the castle-sanctuary at the summit—dominate this ancient town. It is possible to drive all the way to the castle, but a better alternative is to leave your car near the tourist office in the old railway station on the edge of town. From here you can walk along Artà's main street, Carrer del Ciutat, lined with cafes, restaurants and arty shops. Keep going uphill, passing the town hall on Plaça d'Espanya, until you reach the parish church of the Transfiguració del Senyor (Lord's Transfiguration) with its small museum (Mon–Sat 10–2, 3–5). From the church, a cypress tree-lined flight of steps leads to the castle walls.

CROWNING GLORY

The Santuari de Sant Salvador (daily 8.30–8 in summer, 8.30–6 in winter) is inside a walled enclosure, parts of which date from Moorish times. You can walk around the battlements and climb onto the tower for views over Artà's rooftops. The chapel dates from 1825, but the statue of the Virgin behind the altar is much older. Probably brought over by Catalan soldiers during the conquest of Mallorca, it was worshipped in a shrine on this spot. In 1820, the old chapel was used as a hospital during a plague epidemic and then burned down, with only the Virgin being saved. The paintings on the wall, by Salvador Torres, depict Jaume I receiving the surrender of the Moorish *wali* and Ramón Llull (▷ 29) being stoned to death in Tunisia.

TALAIOTIC VILLAGE

Just outside Artà, signposted from the road to Capdepera, are the remains of Ses Països (Apr–end Oct Mon–Sat 10–1, 2.30–6.30; Nov–end Mar Mon–Sat 9–1, 2–5; closed 20 Dec–2 Jan; admission €2), a walled Talaiotic village occupied between the 12th and first centuries BC. The entire site, set in a holm oak wood, is still surrounded by a perimeter wall 374m (1,227ft) long, 3.5m (11.5ft) high and 3.6m (12ft) thick. The main entrance gate is particularly impressive, built from three massive stone blocks. A well-marked path leads around the ruins, and you can climb onto the central circular *talaiot* to peer inside. The village was abandoned after the Roman occupation of Mallorca and its inhabitants moved to the foot of the hill, the site of modern Artà.

INFORMATION

➕ 225 K5 ℹ Estació del Tren, Avinguda Costa i Llobera ☎ 971 836981 🕐 Mon–Fri 10–2 🚌 Buses from Palma and Cala Ratjada ❓ Market Tue

TIP

▶▶ The coastline north of Artà contains some of Mallorca's wildest and least-known beaches. From the petrol station on the eastern outskirts of Artà, on the road to Capdepera, follow signs for Cala Torta. A rough country lane leads down to the coast where you will find the horseshoe-shaped coves of Cala Torta and Cala Mitjana, and the narrow creek of Cala Estreta.

Above *The Santuari de Sant Salvador has panoramic views extending beyond Artà*

CALA MILLOR

In contrast to much of the east coast, which is made up of a succession of narrow creeks and coves, Cala Millor has a long sandy beach that stretches for some 2km (1 mile). A promenade runs the length of the beach, continuing north to Cala Bona, a smaller-scale resort based around a fishing and yacht harbour. At the south end of the beach a footpath leads up to Punta de n'Amer, a wild headland and protected nature reserve with dunes, pine woods and rocky scrub. There is a 17th-century watchtower at the summit, and a cafe with views along the coast. Cala Millor has grown to become a busy resort in summer but out of season it has a much quieter feel. In summer you can take boat trips along the coast—north to Cala Ratjada or south to Porto Cristo.

➕ 225 K6 ℹ️ Parc de la Mar ☎ 971 585409 🕐 Mon–Fri 9–5 🚌 Buses from Palma; also from Cala Ratjada and local resorts in summer

CALA RATJADA

A quiet fishing port on Mallorca's eastern tip has developed into a major resort popular with German visitors, who crowd out its beaches in summer. A short walk south from the harbour leads to the town beach, Platja de Son Moll, though there are better choices to the north and east, including the small cove of Cala Gat and the broad curve of Cala Agulla. A walk of about 2km (1 mile) through pine woods leads across a headland to the lighthouse at Punta de Capdepera, the most easterly point on the island. If you feel like a complete change of scenery, fast ferries depart from the harbour for Ciutadella in Menorca (▷ 43).

➕ 225 L4 ℹ️ Plaça dels Pins ☎ 971 563033 🕐 Mon–Fri 9.30–2, 3.30–6.30, Sat 9.30–2 🚌 Buses from Palma via Artà; also from Cala Millor in summer

CASTELL DE CAPDEPERA

www.castellcapdepera.com
This 14th-century fortress, the largest in Mallorca, completely dominates the village over which it stands. At one stage the castle was the village, as everyone lived within its walls. It is possible to bring a car up here, but parking is limited and it's best to climb the long flight of steps, which begins near the village square, Plaça de l'Orient. You can walk right around the battlements and the crenellated walls, though take great care if you have children with you as there are holes large enough to fall through, and no rails. Within the walls is the Gothic chapel of Nostra Senyora de la Esperança, with an image of Our Lady of Hope over the altar. According to legend, during a siege of Capdepera, the villagers placed the statue on the castle walls and the invaders were driven away by fog.

➕ 225 L4 ✉ Plaça del Sitjar 5, Capdepera ☎ 971 556479 🕐 Apr–end Oct daily 10–8; Nov–end Mar 10–5 ✋ Adult €2, child (under 13) free 🅿️ €2 🚌 In Plaça de l'Orient

COVES D'ARTÀ

www.cuevasdearta.com
French geologist Édouard Martel first explored the underground grottoes at Cap Vermell in 1876, though they had been known for centuries as a haunt of pirates and smugglers, and a hiding place for Moors after the Christian conquest. Like the other cave systems at Campanet (▷ 137) and Coves del Drac (▷ 164–165), this is a fantasy land of stalactites and stalagmites forming outlandish shapes, complete with music, coloured lighting and special effects. The guides point out chambers with names like Paradise, Purgatory and Hell, and conjure up images of elephants and organ pipes in the stone. One of the stalagmites, known as the Queen of Columns, is 22m (72ft) tall and reaches just 50cm (20in) from the ceiling.

➕ 225 L5 ✉ Carretera de les Coves, Canyamel ☎ 971 841293 🕐 May–end Oct daily 10–6; Nov–end Apr 10–5 ✋ Adult €10, child (7–12) €5 🅿️ €1.50 🚌 Tours every 30 minutes 🚤 Boat trips from Cala Ratjada and Font de Sa Cala in summer 🚗

COVES DE CAMPANET

▷ 137.

ERMITA DE BETLEM

A winding road from Artà, beginning behind the Santuari de Sant Salvador, leads through a wooded valley to this small hermitage founded in 1805. It is one of only two in Mallorca where monks still live according to the rules laid down by the Venerable Joan Mir in 1648 (the other is the Ermita de la Trinitat at Valldemossa, ▷ 113). From the car parking area a path lined with cypress trees leads to the chapel. Inside, an altarpiece by Manuel Bayeu depicts the nativity of Christ. You can climb to the belvedere behind the church for views over Alcúdia Bay, or take the path from the car park (signposted 'font') to a spring, where there's a shrine to the Virgin inside a cave and a fountain for collecting spring water. The path continues down to the coast at Colònia de Sant Pere, a pleasant fishing village and beach resort.

➕ 221 K4 ✉ 10km (6 miles) north of Artà 🕐 Daily 8.30–6 ✋ Free ❓ Mass on Sun at 10am

Below *Just over 50 years ago this was a lonely dune-covered shore, now Cala Millor is one of Mallorca's major east-coast resorts*

COVES DE CAMPANET

These intriguing limestone caverns in the foothills of the Serra de Tramuntana might be smaller in scale than Mallorca's other cave systems, but they are still fascinating. Most visitors to Mallorca take in one set of caves and it is a matter of personal preference which you choose. Although the cave system at Campanet is the smallest of those open to the public, it is every bit as impressive as the better-known Coves d'Artà (▷ 136) and Coves del Drac (▷ 164–165). The caves cover a staggering 3,200sq m (34,450sq ft), with several chambers reaching up to 300m (984ft) in depth.

SUBTERRANEAN TREASURES

A local shepherd discovered the caves by chance in 1945 and three years later they were opened to visitors. The passage of underground water over thousands of years has eroded the limestone into curious shapes, and created extraordinary stalactites and stalagmites. In some places the two meet to make columns up to 5m (16ft) tall.

PALM TREES AND PASTA

The 40-minute guided tour takes you through three separate chambers. It begins in the Sala de la Palmera (Palm Tree Chamber), so called because of a large stalagmite said to resemble a palm trunk. With imagination, you will probably be able to discern many different shapes in the rocks, but the guides have their own ideas. They will show you Spaghetti Cave, with stalactites like thin strips of pasta, and the Chapel of the Virgin, where you can make out an image of the Madonna and Child set in stone.

STAR-CROSSED LOVERS

The next room is the Sala del Llac (Lake Chamber), where a pair of seated Buddhas overlooks an underground pool. The tour ends in the Sala Romàntica (Romantic Chamber), the largest chamber of all. Some 50m (164ft) underground, it takes its name from the figures of Romeo and Juliet said to be seen here. There are stalactites in the shape of a church organ and a cascade where the guides play tunes on the hollow columns. Afterwards, back in the real world, you can relax on the terrace with views over the countryside and the nearby oratory of Sant Miquel.

INFORMATION

www.covesdecampanet.com
✚ 221 G4 ✉ In the village of Campanet, signposted at Carretera Palma-Alcúdia, 39km (24 miles) ☎ 971 516130 🕐 Apr–end Sep daily 10–6.30; Oct–end Mar 10–5.30 💳 Adult €10.50, child (5–10) €5 📷 €1 🚌 Every 40 minutes 📷

TIPS

▶▶ Photography is not allowed inside the caves.
▶▶ The last tour of the day starts 45 minutes before closing—6.15pm in summer and 5.15pm in winter.

Above *Campanet's caves are just as impressive as the more well-known Coves d'Artà and Coves del Drac*

INFORMATION

✚ 221 J2 ℹ Carrer de les Monges 9, Port de Pollença ☎ 971 865467
🕒 Mon–Fri 8–3, 5–7, Sat 9–1 🚌 From Palma and Pollença to Formentor beach in summer 🚢 From Port de Pollença in summer 🅿 At lighthouse; also on Formentor beach in summer

TIPS

➤➤ As the car park at the lighthouse gets very full, it is better to come early or late in the day.
➤➤ About 12km (7 miles) from Port de Pollença you will see a lone pine tree on the right. This is El Pi de Formentor, immortalized in poetry, painting and song. The path opposite leads to Cala Figuera.

FORMENTOR

Nervous drivers should not even think about tackling the 20km (12-mile) journey from Port de Pollença to Cap de Formentor, where the Serra de Tramuntana finally drops into the sea. Those that do, however, will be rewarded with some of Mallorca's most dramatic scenery, including heavenly beaches, as well as a peek at Mallorca's original luxury hotel. There are also walking options on the peninsula, with several trails leading to beautiful secluded beaches. The Port de Pollença tourist office can provide maps.

POINTS OF VIEW

After ascending via a series of bends you arrive at a car park at Mirador des Colomer. Climb the steps for views over Es Colomer (The Dovecote), a rocky islet so named because of the seabirds it attracts. Below you the cliffs drop 200m (656ft) down to the sea, while to the left there are views of Cala Bóquer, a small cove beneath the jagged limestone ridge of Cavall Bernat. On the far side of the road a rough track leads up to Talaia d'Albercutx, a restored watchtower 375m (1,230ft) high. You can climb to the top for fabulous 360-degree views. The ruined buildings beneath the tower are former barracks, used to house the prisoners who built the Formentor road.

ON THE BEACH

The road levels out and travels through pine woods on its way to the cape. On the right is Formentor beach. Nowadays the beach is popular with daytrippers who arrive by boat from Port de Pollença, but it was previously the private beach of the Hotel Formentor, opened in 1929 by Argentinian entrepreneur Adan Diehl (▷ 33). This was once the place to stay in Mallorca; visiting celebrities have included Elizabeth Taylor, as well as royalty and politicians such as Winston Churchill. The hotel, part of the Spanish Barceló chain, has lost its exclusivity, and the beach is now public; in the summer the hotel employs a beach manager to prevent the masses from spoiling the guests' view.

TO THE LIGHTHOUSE

The road continues to twist and turn all the way to the lighthouse at the end of the cape. Just before the tunnel, look left for a glimpse of Cala Figuera, an isolated cove reachable only by boat or on foot. The lighthouse's cafe has views from the terrace to the island of Menorca.

Above *View of Cap de Formentor from the Mirador des Colomer*

MUSEU ETNOLÒGIC DE MURO

A 17th-century palace in Muro houses the ethnological section of the Museu de Mallorca (▷ 64). Most of the building has been preserved, with rooms leading off the entrance hall and a courtyard with a waterwheel. Rural history and crafts are the mainstay of the collection. Musicians, devils, animals and men on horseback feature in the collection of *siurells* (▷ 23), made in Marratxí between 1955 and 1970. The reconstructed rooms include a kitchen, bedrooms and a pharmacy. In the child's bedroom, look out for the model of a church with the priest in the pulpit, altar boys and a congregation of men and women seated separately.

➕ 221 H4 ✉ Carrer Major 15, Muro ☎ 971 860647 🕐 Tue–Sat 10–2.30 (also Thu 5–7), Sun 10–2 💶 Adult €2.40, child (under 12) free

PARC NATURAL DE S'ALBUFERA

www.mallorcaweb.net/salbufera
The most important wetland reserve in the Balearic Islands attracts 200 species of migrant and resident birds, and an audience of birdwatchers.

Until the 18th century this area was a swamp, but much of it was drained for agriculture to create the fertile farmland that still exists around Sa Pobla today. The British-owned New Majorca Land Company built the network of canals in the 19th century, and the land was subsequently used for growing rice and harvesting reeds for the manufacture of paper. It was only in 1988, as the sprawling tourist development of Port d'Alcúdia began to spread south, that the Balearic government declared S'Albufera a nature reserve.

Cars are not allowed in the reserve, so park at the designated car park beside the Pont dels Anglesos bridge and walk 1km (0.6 miles) to Sa Roca information centre, where you must register. Here you can pick up a map and a list of recent bird sightings, and look into the small museum, Can

Above *Potato fields around Sa Pobla, known as Mallorca's vegetable basket*

Bateman, with its audiovisual displays of birds. There are footpaths and bicycle paths around the reserve, but most visitors stick to a short circuit around Sa Roca, with birdwatching hides overlooking a lagoon. Among the species that breed here are osprey, kestrel, night heron, red-crested pochard and purple gallinule; summer visitors include purple heron and Eleanora's falcon; in winter flocks of wigeon, teal and grey heron can be seen.

➕ 221 H4 ✉ Carretera Alcúdia– Artà, 5km (3 miles) ☎ 971 892250 🕐 Apr–end Sep daily 9–6; Oct–end Mar 9–5; visitor centre 9–4 daily ✋ A free visitors' pass is required for entry. These are available from the visitor centre

POLLENÇA

▷ 140–143.

SA POBLA

Sa Pobla stands at the heart of Mallorca's richest agricultural area, on the drained land around the Parc Natural de S'Albufera. The potato harvest attracts migrant workers and Sa Pobla has the only mosque on Mallorca outside Palma. The one real attraction is Can Planes (Tue–Sat 10–2, 4–8, Sun 10–2), at Carrer Antoni Maura 6, north of the town. The ground floor features work by Mallorcan artists of the late 20th century. Upstairs (admission €4) is a delightful toy museum, with dolls' houses, toy cars and even a model bullring. Buses from Palma stop outside the museum.

➕ 221 H4 🚌 Buses from Palma, Inca, Muro and Alcúdia 🚂 From Palma and Inca; 15-minute walk from the railway station ❓ Market Sun

INTRODUCTION

Pollença, at the eastern end of the Serra de Tramuntana, is an attractive town of 17th- and 18th-century houses built in a maze of narrow, medieval streets, with historic churches, interesting musuems and a pretty, cafe-lined square. Most of the action takes place around Plaça Major, the central square that springs to life each Sunday as the setting for one of Mallorca's busiest markets. The lanes around the square are perfect for strolling, with numerous art galleries, restaurants and speciality shops. Pollença was built between two hills, each of which is topped with a sacred site. A stairway from the town centre climbs to the Calvari chapel, and a longer walk leads to the sanctuary on the summit of Puig de Maria. Port de Pollença, 6km (4 miles) away, is an enjoyable, old-style holiday resort with a fine beach set in a horseshoe bay.

During the 20th century Pollença established a reputation as an artists' colony, based around Hermen Anglada Camarasa (1871–1959), the founder of the Pollença school, who lived on the seafront at Port de Pollença. Another artist drawn to Pollença was the British violinist Philip Newman (1904–66), who founded the Pollença Festival in 1962. This international music festival (▷ 151), supported by the Spanish royal family, continues to attract performers of the calibre of Montserrat Caballé and the London Symphony Orchestra; concerts are held each July and August.

WHAT TO SEE

PLAÇA MAJOR

Plane trees surround Pollença's main square, which is built on two levels. Dominating the northern side is the church of Nostra Senyora dels Àngels, an 18th-century replacement of a church established in 1236 soon after the Catalan conquest of Mallorca. Alongside the church, the Café Espanyol is a popular meeting place. Among the bars lining the east side of the square is

INFORMATION

www.pollensa.com
✚ 221 G3 ℹ Carrer Guillem Cifre de Colonya (next to Museu de Pollença)
☎ 971 535077 🕐 Mon–Fri 8–3, 5–7, Sat 9–1 🚌 Buses from Palma and Alcúdia ❓ Market Sun

Above *The Way to Calvary; there are 365 steps up to the chapel*
Opposite *Pollença lies at the northern tip of the Serra de Tramuntana*

141

Above *Fishing boats vie with cruisers for space at Port de Pollença*

Club Pollença, housed in a 19th-century manor house on the corner of Carrer del Mercat. This old-timers' cafe, known to everyone as El Club, hosts concerts and art exhibitions, and is home to a number of active sports clubs. On Sunday mornings the upper level of Plaça Major is taken over by a colourful market that attracts visitors, locals and a large number of British residents. Fresh produce and flowers are sold on the square, while artists set up their stalls in the lanes behind the church.

EL CALVARI
To the right of the church, Carrer del Temple leads to Plaça de l'Almoina, a small square where you will find La Font del Gall, a stone fountain dating from 1827. It is topped with a cockerel, the heraldic symbol of Pollença. From here, Carrer de Monti-Sion climbs to a former Jesuit convent, now used as the town hall. To the left of the building a flight of 365 steps, lined with cypress trees, leads to the Calvary chapel, built in 1799 and containing a 14th-century carving of the Mare de Déu del Peu de la Creu (Mother of God at the foot of the cross). After the Catalan conquest a gallows was built on this site and convicted criminals would climb the steps to their deaths. From the top of the steps there are fine views across the rooftops towards Puig de Maria, and a nearby belvedere offers views over Pollença Bay. The stairway has been extended into the town centre where it ends in an open square, Plaça Seglars.

MUSEU MARTÍ VICENÇ
www.martivicens.org
The artist Martí Vicenç (1926–95) specialized in the Mallorcan fabric known as *roba de llengües* (cloth of tongues), and his brightly coloured woven patterns continue to be produced at his workshop, Galeries Vicenç, on the roundabout at the junction of the Port de Pollença road. After his death his widow, Antònia Capllonch, opened a museum in his memory in their town house near the foot of the Calvari steps. As well as examples of his textiles, the museum includes his paintings and wooden sculptures, together with a display of old looms, spindles and kitchen equipment. The gift shop sells an interesting range of contemporary Mallorcan crafts.
✉ Carrer Calvari 10 ☎ 971 532867 🕐 Tue–Sat 10–1.15, 3.15–7, Sun 10–1.30 ✋ Free 🏛

MUSEU DE POLLENÇA
www.ajpollenca.net
Pollença's municipal museum is housed in the former Dominican convent, built between 1588 and 1616. Most of the displays are situated on the first floor. The eclectic collection includes modern art (the winners of the Salón Estival de Pintura, an annual competition held in Pollença since 1962), archaeology and a Buddhist mandala, a meditative pattern created out of coloured sand by Tibetan monks and presented by the Dalai Lama. Two rooms are devoted to Atilio Boveri (1885–1949), an Argentinian painter who spent four years in Pollença and produced a number of local landscapes. Afterwards you can look into the baroque cloisters of the convent, the venue for Pollença's international summer music festival (▷ 151).
✉ Carrer Guillem Cifre de Colonya ☎ 971 531166 🕐 Jul–end Sep Tue–Sat 10–1, 5–9, Sun 10.30–1; Oct–end Jun Tue–Sun 10.30–1 ✋ Adult €1.50, child (under 12) free

PUIG DE MARIA
From the outskirts of Pollença, a twisting road leads in about 2km (1 mile) to the summit of 'Mary's mountain' (333m/1,092ft). Although you can take a car most of the way, it is not advisable as the road is in poor condition and there are several sharp bends, plus very limited parking space at the top. In any case, you will have to walk the final section on a medieval, stone-flagged mule path. The first sanctuary here was founded in 1348; it was abandoned

three centuries later but hermits returned in 1917 and stayed until 1988. The present church dates from the 14th century, as does the nearby defence tower. Although monks no longer live here the place retains its spiritual atmosphere and you can look around the old monastery buildings, including the refectory with its arched Gothic ceiling. If you are inspired, you can stay the night in the simple hostel and wake to a view of Pollença Bay.

➕ 221 H3 ☎ 971 184132 🍽 🏛

PORT DE POLLENÇA

Like other towns around the Mallorcan coast, Pollença was built back from its harbour to protect it from piracy and invasion. Until the 20th century Port de Pollença was no more than a fishing village with a handful of summer cottages and a daily stagecoach to Pollença, but all that changed in the 1920s, when it became one of Mallorca's earliest beach resorts. Today, the charm of that period remains, with old-style villas along the seafront and few high-rise hotels. South of the harbour a wide beach runs around the bay, dramatically situated between the Cap de Formentor and Peninsula de la Victòria. To the north, the Passeig Anglada Camarasa, a wide promenade named after the local painter whose work can be seen in the Fundació La Caixa (▷ 63) in Palma, leads to the Pine Walk, a romantic seafront path where pine trees lean across tiny beaches and small jetties. Port de Pollença is popular and at times it is a little too crowded, but it is hard to beat for an old-fashioned, bucket-and-spade holiday.

➕ 221 H2 🛈 Carrer de les Monges 9 ☎ 971 865467 🕐 Mon–Fri 8–3, 5–7, Sat 9–1 🚍 Buses from Palma and Pollença ❓ Market Wed

MORE TO SEE

CALA SANT VICENÇ

When the people of Pollença head to the beach, they choose Cala Sant Vicenç, where four small coves huddle together beneath the limestone ridge of Cavall Bernat. Although the setting has been somewhat spoilt by the appearance of a few ugly hotels close to the beach, this is still a beautiful spot. For pounding surf and great views head for Cala Molins.

➕ 221 H2 🚍 1 🛈 Plaça Sant Vicenç (Jun–end Sep only) ☎ 971 533264 🕐 Mon–Fri 10.15–2, 3–6 🚍 Buses from Pollença

CALA BÓQUER

An easy walk of 3km (2 miles) from Port de Pollença leads through a wild valley to this peaceful cove beneath the ridge of Cavall Bernat. The path begins on Avinguda Bocchoris, just behind the promenade, and climbs past the fortified Bóquer farmhouse before continuing down to the sea. In spring, several species of wild flowers and migrating birds can be seen along the way.

➕ 221 H2

PONT ROMÀ (ROMAN BRIDGE)

Situated near the northern entrance to Pollença from the C-710 to Lluc, the so-called Roman bridge spans the Torrent de Sant Jordi, a seasonal river. The bridge has been heavily restored and little of the original remains, but there is evidence that this may have been part of a system of bridges and aqueducts built to carry water from the mountains to the Roman capital at Pollentia.

CASA MUSEU DIONÍS BENNÀSSAR

www.museudionisbennassar.com

This 17th-century house, once the home of the painter Dionís Bennàssar (1904–67), has been restored and furnished in period style. It now houses an exhibition of the artist's work; his early works are on show downstairs and include some intricate etchings.

✉ Carrer Roca 14 ☎ 971 530997 🕐 Mon–Fri 10–2, 5–8, with prior notification ✋ Free

>> If you can, make it to Pollença on the evening of Good Friday when the statue of Jesus is taken down from the cross and carried down the Calvary steps by hooded penitents in a torchlit procession. El Davallament, as it is known, is one of the oldest religious festivities in Mallorca.

>> Early August sees another memorable event: the Moors and Christians festival when locals dress up in suitable garb and engage in mock battles against a background of drums. There is also live music in Plaça Major and plenty of partying in the streets.

POLLENÇA AND ALCÚDIA BAYS

Enjoy farmland, moorland, marshes, dunes and coast on this tour of northeast Mallorca, perhaps combined with a walk in the S'Albufera nature reserve, a visit to a historic town, or an afternoon on the beach.

THE DRIVE

Distance: 90km (56 miles)
Time: 2 hours
Start/end at: Port de Pollença
Tourist information: Carrer de les Monges 9, Port de Pollença ☎ 971 865467

HOW TO GET THERE

Take the Ma-2200 from Port de Pollença

★Start on the seafront at Port de Pollença (▷ 143) and head south around the bay in the direction of Alcúdia.

❶ As you leave the harbour behind, the villas on the promenade gradually give way to the modern apartments and hotels of Llenaire. Beyond here, the beach gets narrower and less crowded. There are fine views across the Bay of Pollença, sheltered by Cap de Formentor and the Peninsula de la Victòria on either side. To your right is the S'Albufereta wetland reserve; to your left the fishing village of

Barcarès, where many Mallorcans have weekend homes.

Turn left at the roundabout to enter Alcúdia ❷ (▷ 133–134). When you see the medieval walls and gateway ahead, keep to the right-hand lane. After rounding a bend, turn right at the traffic lights in front of the church (signposted Can Picafort and Artà). You can see the remains of the Roman city of Pollentia next to the car park on your left.

After passing the cemetery you reach a roundabout dominated by a large statue of a prancing horse. Take the second exit to the right, following signs for Artà. On your right you will see a football ground and the waterslides at Hidropark, clearly visible from the road. Keep straight ahead at the next roundabout to enter the sprawling resort area of Port d'Alcúdia. You are now on the Ma-12 coast road, which leads around the Bay of Alcúdia, cutting the main hotel and shopping districts off from the beach. Despite

driving parallel to the longest beach in Mallorca, you will get only occasional glimpses of the sea. The road crosses a bridge beside the entrance to the Parc Natural de S'Albufera (▷ 139), and the car park is about 50m/55 yards further on).

❸ Parc Natural de S'Albufera is a rare and precious area of coastline with a variety of habitats, including marshland, pine woods and dunes. Sadly, from an ecological point of view, the boundary of the natural park does not extend as far as the shore and a number of large hotels have been built on the seaward side of the road in a district known as Platja de Muro.

Keep straight ahead at the next roundabout to pass through the resort of Can Picafort.

❹ The main reason for stopping at Can Picafort, apart from the beach, is to visit the Son Real necropolis, which dates back to the 7th century.

You can reach it by walking south along the beach and crossing the Son Bauló torrent. A short distance farther south a modern defence tower gives views over S'Illot des Porros (Leek Island), an offshore island with another prehistoric cemetery.

Leaving Can Picafort, the Ma-12 continues uphill to a roundabout where you should keep straight ahead. You now leave the coast behind and the massif of Artà dominates the views. After swinging around two wide bends and passing a side road leading to Son Serra de Marina, a sign welcomes you to the Península de Llevant nature reserve. Shortly afterwards, on seeing a Campsa petrol station ahead, turn right towards Petra. Stay on this road for the next 14km (9 miles) as it crosses moorland and woods. As you approach Petra (▷ 168), you will see the Ermita de Bonany ahead of you, perched on a hill. Turn right at the roundabout and stay on this road as it bypasses the Roman village of Santa Margalida.

❺ From Santa Margalida you can make a worthwhile diversion to Maria de la Salut, a small village chiefly notable for its unusual Byzantine-style domed church. Signs in the village point the way to Embotits Matas, the shop of an artisan sausage-maker. Here you can taste and buy products such as *sobrassada de porc negre*, a spicy sausage made with the meat of Mallorca's indigenous black pig. Beyond Santa Margalida the Ma-12 continues across open farmland to Muro ❻, where you can visit the Museu Etnològic de Muro (▷ 139). Follow signs through Muro towards Sa Pobla (▷ 139).

❼ The land between Muro and Sa Pobla, behind the Parc Natural de S'Albufera, has been reclaimed from the marshes to become farmland, with vegetables thriving in the red earth. All around are abandoned windmills (although

some have been restored) that were used to extract water for irrigation. Modern evidence of Sa Pobla's agricultural importance is provided by the potato warehouse at the entrance to the town.

Skirt Sa Pobla on the new ring road, following signs for Pollença. Eventually you reach a roundabout beside a chapel with a multicoloured tiled dome and a cemetery. Leave the roundabout by heading north in the direction of Pollença. Keep straight ahead at the next roundabout. After passing a golf club on your right, the holy mountain of Puig de Maria (▷ 142–143) will be visible ahead. Follow this road around the foot of the mountain and turn right at the roundabout to return to Port de Pollença.

WHERE TO EAT

There are several restaurants along the seafront at Port de Pollença. One of the best is Stay (▷ 154), with a superb location on the harbourside.

Above *Windmills once provided power for the area's water supply*
Opposite *Alcúdia's Porta del Moll*

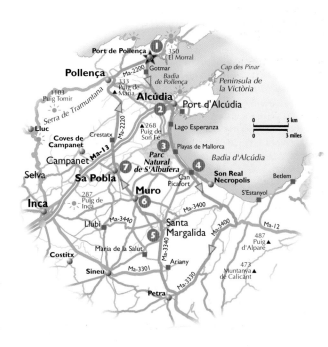

PENINSULA DE LA VICTÒRIA

Peaceful walking and magnificent coastal views can be enjoyed on a wild and lonely cape just a short distance from some of Mallorca's busiest beaches.

THE WALK

Distance: 13km (8 miles)
Total ascent: 480m (1,574ft)
Time: 3–4 hours
Start/end at: Ermita de La Victòria
(➕ 221 J3)
Tourist information centre: Carrer Major, Alcúdia ☎ 971 897100

HOW TO GET THERE

Take the road out of Alcúdia towards Mal Pas. Continue to the yacht club at Bonaire. Turn right here and follow the coast road past a pair of small beaches. When the road divides, keep right to climb to the hermitage.

★The long finger of the Peninsula de la Victòria pokes into the sea between the bays of Pollença and Alcúdia. Apart from the headland around Cap des Pinar, which is an official military zone, much of the rest of the peninsula has been designated a nature reserve and offers superb walks. Most of these walks (described in a series of leaflets available from the tourist

office in Alcúdia) start from the Ermita de la Victòria, a 17th-century hermitage overlooking the sea; there is also a car park, a restaurant and public toilets.

Start the walk by taking the forest track that leads out of the car park, behind the hermitage. This is a steep climb but you are soon rewarded with fine views over Pollença Bay.

After about 750m (800 yards), following a sharp right-hand turn, the path divides. The track on the left leads to Penya des Migdia, a rocky outcrop with the remains of an old watchtower and an abandoned cannon at the summit. You can climb to the top for views of the Cap de Formentor and the pine forest from which Cap des Pinar takes its name. On a clear day you can see as far as the neighbouring island of Menorca.

The main path continues ahead, soon reaching a plateau with views out to sea on both sides.

Pollença (▷ 140–143) is visible to your right, tucked between two hills. Beyond are the mountains of the Serra de Tramuntana.

At a junction with a wooden signpost, keep straight ahead, following the twisting path to the summit of Talaia d'Alcúdia (445m/1,460ft).

You are now at the highest point of the Peninsula de la Victòria. The ruined defence tower, of which only the base remains, dates from 1567. At one stage there were more than 30 of these watchtowers in Mallorca, strategically sited around the coast to guard the main entry points by sea. Across the bay to the north you can make out the Talaia d'Albercutx (▷ 138), watching over the Cap de Formentor and the north coast.

Retrace your steps down the mountainside and turn right at the junction (signposted Platja des Coll

Baix). The narrow path runs along a ridge on the slopes of Puig des Boc. After a while the path starts to descend, gently at first and then in a succession of sharp zigzags.

Keep an eye out over the cliff as you drop down towards the pass. At one point you have a dizzying vertical view over the idyllic cove of Coll Baix, whose sandy beach is framed by an unfeasibly turquoise sea.

Continue down this path to reach Collet des Coll Baix.

Here you will find a picnic area and a fountain supplying drinking water. A path to the left leads to the beach that you saw earlier from above. The descent is fairly straightforward, although it does involve some scrambling. This is a lovely spot, but swimming is not recommended because of the powerful currents.

To stay on the main route, turn right at the picnic area onto a forest track. Pass through a gate and into a car parking area. Follow this track through the woods for about 1km (0.6 miles), then take the path to the right (signposted Coll de Ses Fontanelles). The path is wide at first but soon narrows, crossing a dry riverbed several times before ascending steeply to a pass. Look carefully for the cairns that define the path. After reaching a ridge the path starts to descend, with good views across Pollença Bay to Port de Pollença in the distance. Eventually you arrive at a small dam and the path widens into a track. Pass behind the houses of Bonaire and continue for 1km (0.6 miles) to a junction.

The path to your left leads to La Victòria campsite. Turn right here. Almost immediately, you come to a path to your left, signposted to Ermita de la Victòria. This is not the quickest way back—if you take this path you will drop down to a beach and have a long uphill walk to the hermitage. Instead, keep straight

ahead and take the second path to your left. The path narrows, rising and falling before climbing steeply to the car park.

PLACES TO VISIT

The carved wooden statue of the Virgin above the altar in the Ermita de la Victòria (Wed–Sun 11–5, Tue 5–8) is venerated as Our Lady of the Victory. A chapel has stood on this site since the 13th century. According to legend, during a siege of Alcúdia one of the brothers held up the statue, causing the rebel army to retreat. In 1644 Our Lady of the Victory became the patron saint of Alcúdia and 50 years later the hermitage was rebuilt in her honour. Pilgrims still visit annually during the feast of La Mare de Déu de La Victòria on 2 July.

WHERE TO EAT

The Mirador de la Victòria restaurant (Camí Vell de la Victòria, tel 971 547173, closed Mon) has one of the best settings in Mallorca, with sweeping sea views from the terrace. It serves classic Mallorcan cuisine (about €30–€40 per person). There is also a small cafe beside the church selling sandwiches, snacks and drinks.

WHERE TO STAY

If you want to stay the night, the first two floors of the historic Ermita de la Victòria have been converted to a a small hotel (tel 971 549912; www.lavictoriahotel.com).

Above *The exterior of Ermita de la Victòria*
Opposite *The walk along the Peninsula de la Victòria offers superb views*

ALCÚDIA AND PORT D'ALCÚDIA

ALCUDIAMAR
www.alcudiamar.es

Much more than just a marina, Alcudiamar runs the town's busy quay area in the port. Tourists throng the bars and restaurants in the summer: Chili is good for pizzas and international-style cuisine, while San Marcos is more typically Spanish and has an excellent range of inexpensive tapas. There are 730 moorings at the marina with nautical shops for sailors.

✉ Paseo Marítimo 1, 07410 Port d'Alcùdia
☎ 971 546000 🕐 Daily 10am–late

AUDITORI D'ALCÚDIA
www.alcudia.net

This contemporary, 496-seat auditorium hosts music, theatre and other events. You can listen to a simultaneous translation of what is being said onstage.

✉ Plaça de la Porta de Mallorca 3, 07400 Alcúdia ☎ 971 897185 🕐 Box office: Mon–Sat 10–1, 6–9 💶 €5–€36 🎫 🎭

DIDI'S COAST ADVENTURE
www.coastadventure.net

This adventure sports' company offers several interesting packages, including one-day mountain bike tours, with bike rental and hotel pickup from €39.90 and one-day Nordic walking tours, including the supply of Nordic walking sticks, from €39.99 to €155.

✉ Carrer Salicornia 4, 07410 Port d'Alcúdia
☎ 971 184380

ESCOLA DE PARAPENTE ALFÀBIA (IN ALCÚDIA)
www.parapentealfabia.com

Adrenaline junkies could try their hand at hang-gliding lessons while in Mallorca—and get a stunning bird's-eye-view of the island. Lessons are geared to all levels, from beginners to experienced hang-glider pilots. If you don't want a lesson, go for a two-person descent; passengers are free to enjoy the scenery while the flight is left in the capable hands of one of the school's qualified instructors.

☎ 687 626536 🕐 All year round
💶 Prices available upon request

GOLF ALCANADA
www.golf-alcanada.com

This 18-hole course, designed by Robert Trent Jones, borders Alcúdia's bay and has views of the tiny island of Alcanada and its lighthouse. Groves of olive, oak and pine trees add interest to the par-72 course, which is more suited to experienced players than beginners.

✉ Carretera del Faro, 07410 Port d'Alcùdia
☎ 971 549560 💶 Green fee €95–€105
🍴 🚻

HIDROPARK
www.hidropark.com

This theme park on the north coast is smaller than those in S'Arenal and Magaluf but still has plenty of waterslides in the waterpark and three 18-hole mini-golf courses, adding up to a massive 54-hole complex that will keep most children amused for several hours.

✉ Avinguda Tucán, 07410 Port d'Alcúdia
☎ 971 891672 🕐 Apr–end Oct 10–6
💶 Adult €17, child (3–11) €8, under-3s free
🍴 🚻

HÍPICA FORMENTOR
www.hipicaformentor.com

On the edge of the Albufereta wildlife reserve, this riding school offers treks and excursions for riders of all ages and abilities. There are one- or two-hour excursions for less advanced riders, while those with experience can trek around some of the most beautiful stretches of Mallorcan countryside for between three and eight days. Children are welcome and are accommodated with smaller ponies. The most popular trips are those with a ride along the beach.

✉ Apt 182, 07400 Alcúdia ☎ 609 826703 (mobile) 🕐 All year ✋ From €18 per person for the 1-hour excursion

MALLORCA YACHT CHARTER & TRAINING

www.myct.co.uk
Mallorca Yacht charter offer Royal Yachting Association-approved courses, yacht charter and organize sailing holidays. Courses range from those catering for beginners all the way up to RYA Yachtmaster. The RYA Competent Crew course costs €850 for five days and courses have a maximum of five pupils. The cheapest six-berth yacht costs from €700 per week in low season and from €1,800 in high season. The most expensive yacht is available for €3,500 in high season. Skippers can also be hired from €250 per day plus expenses. Courses run from March to the end of November, with a charter available year round.

✉ Puerto Alcudiamar 5-A, 07410 Port d'Alcúdia ☎ 971 549394

SA CISTERNA

A delicatessen and wine shop, this is a good place to pick up picnic supplies or choose some local produce as gifts. These include *sobrassada* (▷ 210), *embutits* (cured meats), oils and conserves as well as a good range of regional and Spanish wines.

✉ Carrer Cisterna 1, 07400 Alcúdia ☎ 971 548606 🕐 Mon–Fri 10–2, 5–8, Sat 10–2

WATERSPORTS MALLORCA

www.watersportsmallorca.com
This is currently the sole operator on the island for kite-surfing tuition and equipment rental. Prices start at €50 for a 1-hour private course and range to €280 for a 9-hour course or €360 for a 12-hour course. Kitesurfing gear can be rented for €8 per hour or €20 for 3 hours. The company runs similar courses for windsurfing

(1 hour €15, 10 hours €180) and rents out equipment, as well as surfboards (1 hour €20).

✉ Hoteles Esperanza, Platja de Muro, 07458 Port d'Alcúdia ☎ 606 353807 🕐 Mon–Fri 10–2, 5–8, Sat 10–2

ARTÀ
ARTÀ TEATRE

www.teatrearta.com
This modern theatre in a quiet courtyard on Artà's main street puts on a wide range of productions from contemporary to classic drama. It's the best place in the northeast of the island to see theatre. Dance and theatre workshops are available.

✉ Carrer de Ciutat, 07570 Artà ☎ 971 829700 🕐 Daily 9–8. Closed Aug ✋ €20–€60 ☕ 🍷

CAPDEPERA GOLF

www.golfcapdepera.com
One of the cluster of courses around Artà, this scenic par-72 course has 18 holes, six artificial holes and a varied selection of fairways.

✉ Carretera Artà–Capdepera, km 3.5, 07570 Artà ☎ 971 818500 ✋ Green fee €49.50–€79 🍴 ☕

ES PASSEIG

While this busy tapas bar on Artà's main street has some outside tables, most of the action is around the small bar. You can start the day here (breakfast costs from €2.50) or arrive in the evening for tapas and a drink. There's also a menu for children.

✉ Carrer Ciutat 22, 07570 Artà ☎ 971 829275 🕐 Daily 9am–midnight

CALA MILLOR
AUDITÒRIUM SA MÀNIGA

www.samaniga.es
One of the three principal auditoriums in Mallorca, Sa Màniga has a 466-seat theatre for drama, music and comedy performances. There are also four booths in which you can hear simultaneous translation.

✉ Carrer de Son Galta 4, 07560 Cala Millor ☎ 971 587373 🕐 Box office: Tue–Sat 11–1, 6–9 ✋ Adult €12–€20, child (under 16) €5–€6 ☕ 🏆

AUTO–SAFARI

Mallorca's only zoo is a 44ha (108-acre) safari park with giraffes, zebras, tigers and monkeys, among other animals. Children won't want to miss the 'baby zoo' of young animals. It's a 4km (2.5-mile) drive through the park, or take an expensive mini-train.

✉ Carretera Porto Cristo–Son Servera, km 5, 07680 Cala Millor ☎ 971 810909 🕐 Apr–end Sep 9–7; Oct–end Mar 9–5 ✋ Adult €13, child €9 🚌 Shuttle bus from Cala Millor in summer 🍴 ☕

CHEERS

This popular bar offers food until 10.30pm, entertainment for children and adults, television screens for sports events, Playstations for children and free internet access.

✉ Carrer Son Corp 20, 07560 Cala Millor ☎ 971 586079 🕐 9.30am–late

CRUCEROS CREUERS

www.cruceroscreuers.com
Boat trips on the glass-bottomed *Sea Odyssey* catamaran depart from Cala Rajada, Cala Millor, Cala Bona, Sa Coma and Porto Cristo during the summer months.

✉ Carrer Baladres, Edificio Rossello, 07560 Sa Coma ☎ 971 810600 ✋ Return trips from €10

CALA RATJADA
MALLORCA BALLOONS

www.mallorcaballoons.com
One-hour or 30-minute hot-air balloon trips are offered by Mallorca Balloons. Departures, from the east coast, are weather dependent.

✉ Ca'n Melis 22, 07590 Cala Ratjada ☎ 971 818182 ✋ 1 hour: adult €150, child (6–11) €90

CAPDEPERA
CANYAMEL GOLF

www.canyamelgolf.com
Reckoned by some to be the most difficult course on the island, 18-hole, par-73 Canyamel has one of the best settings of all the courses in Mallorca, close to the northeast coast. There are sea views on the way out (on a clear day you can see Menorca from the fifth tee) and

views of the hills around Artà on the way back. Watch out for the house in the middle of the ninth fairway.

✉ Urbanización Canyamel, Avinguda d'Es Cap Vermell, 07580 Capdepera ☎ 971 841313 ✋ Green fee €72–€88 🍴 ☕

MURO

SALA FÒNICA
www.salafonica.com
Sleepy Muro is the surprising location of one of Mallorca's best-loved clubs, with excellent resident and guest DJs playing minimal, electro, house and techno for a young, hip crowd.

✉ Carrer Germanies s/n, 07440 Muro ☎ 678 723746 (mobile) 🕐 Sat 11am–4am

POLLENÇA AND PORT DE POLLENÇA

AGATA
A wonderland of minerals, stones and gems with more than 250 types, either rough, polished, cut or faceted. A great place for gifts, from jewellery to glittering mobiles.

✉ Passeig Anglada Camarassa 73, 07470 Port de Pollença ☎ 971 867606 🕐 Mon–Fri 9.30–1.30, 3.30–7.30, Sat 10.30–1

AINA
Buy smart clothes and shoes for children at this delightful shop, plus high-chairs, cots and teddy bears. Cardigans cost from €10, shoes are €20–€70 and duffel coats €90.

✉ Plaça Vella 1, 07460 Pollença ☎ 971 530686 🕐 Summer Mon–Sat 9.30–1.30,

4.30–9, Sun 9.30–2; winter Mon–Sat 9.30–1.30, 4–8, Sun 9.30–2

L'ARGENTERIA
L'Argenteria glitters with beautiful designer jewellery in silver, gold and steel by artists from all over the world. Most pieces are one-offs and you can also commission your own designs. Prices range from €20 to €700 for chunky amber necklaces. The jeweller also sells silver picture frames and jewellery boxes.

✉ Antoni Maura 22, 07460 Pollença ☎ 971 533716 🕐 Summer Mon–Sat 10–1.30, 5–10; winter 4.30–8.30

ARTESANIA
www.artesania-mallorca.com
The name says it all—this is the place to come to if you are looking for typical Mallorquín souvenirs, ranging from locally produced jams and preserves to brightly coloured ceramics, woven baskets, candles, jewellery and accessories.

✉ Carrer Temple 6, 07460 Pollença ☎ 971 531381 🕐 Mon–Fri 10–2, 5–8, Sat–Sun 10–2

BENNASSAR GALERIES
www.galeriesbennassar.com
This brand-new contemporary art gallery is squeezed between the sprawling pavement cafes on the square, with white well-lit galleries and regular exhibitions showcasing primarily local contemporary artists.

✉ Plaça Major 6, 07460 Pollença ☎ 971 533514 🕐 Tue–Sat 10–1.30, 5.30–9, Sun 11–1.30

LA BIRRERIA
www.labirreria.com
This bar is popular with a young, trendy local crowd, who come for the enormous range of beers (both Spanish and international) and the *pinxos* (delicious Basque-style snacks made of slices of crusty bread with a variety of toppings). It's not a big space, but there's always room for the regular live gigs played here most weekend nights from 10.30pm.

✉ Carrer Colón 3, 07460 Pollença ☎ 659 932887 (mobile) 🕐 Tue–Sun 7pm–late

CHARTER TUDOR DAWN
Tudor Dawn, a 15m (50ft) schooner, can be chartered, with skipper Simon, for day trips around Port de Pollença. The boat sets out from the quay and you sail it, under Simon's guidance, around the coastline for a picnic lunch. Buoyancy aids and snorkelling and fishing gear are provided. Additional activities, including water-skiing and jet-skiing, can be arranged.

✉ Moll Vell, 07470 Port de Pollença ☎ 649 875151/616 775958 🕐 Jul, Aug ✋ Adult €80, child (under 16) €70 per day

CLUB NÁUTICO PORT DE POLLENÇA
www.rcnpp.net
Few places are better for learning to sail than the Bay of Pollença and children will soon be taking out Optimists and Laser Picos. Windsurfing, canoeing and fishing trips are also available during the summer.

✉ Moll Vell, 07470 Port de Pollença ☎ 971 864635 🕐 Courses Jul–end Sep ✋ Non-members: adult €115, child (6–16) €80 per 5-day course

GALERÍA MAIOR
www.galeriamaior.com
Galería Maior is reckoned, by locals, to be the best art gallery in north Mallorca. Displays are varied, the emphasis on modern painting and sculpture.

✉ Plaça Major 4, 07460 Pollença ☎ 971 530095 🕐 Jun–end Sep Tue–Sat 10.30–1.30, 5.30–9, Sun 11–1.30; Oct–end May Tue–Sat 10.30–1.30, 5–8, Sun 11–1.30

GOLF POLLENSA
www.golfpollensa.com
There are only nine holes at this sandy par-35 course, but they form perhaps the most beautiful course on the island, overlooking the Bay of Pollença and with the Serra de Tramuntana for a backdrop. The twisting fairways, stone walls and groves of olive and oak trees present a challenge to golfers of all abilities.

✉ Carretera Palma–Pollença, km 49.3, 07460 Pollença ☎ 971 533216/533265

Green fee €70 summer, €45 winter

JK'S BAR
This family-run bar, with its two huge screens, is the place to come if you are suffering from football match deprivation. Named best bar in a local annual poll, there is a broad range of local and imported beers, as well as wines and spirits. Free WiFi available.
✉ Carretera Formentor 18, 07470 Port de Pollença ☎ 971 865458 ⏰ Mon–Sat 10am–late, Sun 12pm–late

MALLORCAN WALKING TOURS
www.mallorcanwalkingtours. puertopollensa.com
Pollença is a superb base for many of the island's most established walks. Maps can be picked up from the tourist office or the specialist walking shop in Carrer Roger de Flor, Port de Pollença. Alternatively, you can call one of the specialist walking companies, such as Mallorcan Walking Tours, which is run by Rich Stutt, who organizes a variety of walks geared to varying levels of fitness.
✉ 07470 Port de Pollença ☎ 609 700826 ✋ Day walks from €28

MUSIC BAR DUNA
With live music and no-frills decor, this cavernous first-floor bar is popular with Pollença's youth and close enough to the central squares to be convenient for a late-evening visit. There's often live music from local rock bands.
✉ Carrer Alcúdia 1, 07460 Pollença ☎ 971 532800 ⏰ Tue–Sun 9pm–late

NORD ESPORT
www.nordesport.com
Nord Esport is a smart health and fitness centre in Pollença offering spa treatments, massage and physiotherapy. Aerobics, pilates and capoeira classes are held in the well-equipped gym.
✉ Cecili Metel 6, 07460 Pollença ☎ 971 531145 ⏰ Mon–Fri 8.30–10.15, Sat 9.30–1.30, closed Sat in summer ✋ Sessions start from €8 per hour

FESTIVALS AND EVENTS

SETMANA SANTA (HOLY WEEK)
Easter
▷ 85, Palma

FESTIVAL DE POLLENÇA
July, August
www.festivalpollenca.org
This major classical music festival was founded in 1962 by British violinist Philip Newman, who moved to Pollença when he retired. It is held in Pollença annually during July and August in the cloisters of Sant Domingo. Many famous artists have appeared at the festival; the programme includes everything from solo musicians to orchestras (▷ 141).
✉ Pollença ☎ 971 281559 ✋ Seats €20–€50

PRO CYCLE HIRE
www.procyclehire.com
Mountain bikes, racing bikes and touring bikes for adults and children are available for rent and can be delivered directly to your hotel or villa. The owners can also organize group rides and excursions.
✉ Carrer Temple Fielding 3, 07470 Port de Pollença ☎ 971 866857

PRO DIVE
www.prodive-mallorca.de
Scuba diving geared for all levels, including PADI-approved courses for beginners. There are also more challenging dive trips and night dives for experienced divers. Equipment available for rent.
✉ Carrer Elcano 9, 07470 Port de Pollença ☎ 971 867978 ⏰ Apr–end Nov daily 10–7 ✋ Prices range from €40 for 1 dive to €250 for 10 dives (5 boat trips)

RANCHO GRANDE
www.ranchograndemallorca.com
Lessons, guided rides and long-distance hacks can be organized at this equestrian centre near Port de Pollença.
✉ Son Serra de Marina, 07459 Port de Pollença ☎ 971 854121 ⏰ Daily 9–1, 3–7 ✋ 2-hour ride with guide €40, full day €100, group lesson €13 per person, 2-day winter hack €200

SCUBA MALLORCA
www.scubamallorca.com
This PADI-approved, British-owned dive centre takes divers out to spots around Pollença Bay and Cap de Formentor. Scuba diving courses are offered; hotel pick-up arranged.
✉ Carrer d'El Cano 23, 07470 Port de Pollença ☎ 971 868087 ⏰ Mar to mid-Nov ✋ 1 day, 2 tanks from €70

PORTO CRISTO
AQUARI DE MALLORCA
Piranhas, moray and electric eels, and fish from coral reefs can be found at this small aquarium opposite the Coves del Drac (▷ 164–165). There are 115 tanks over two floors.
✉ Carrer Gambi 7, 07680 Porto Cristo ☎ 971 820971 ⏰ Apr–end Oct daily 10.30–6; Nov–end Mar daily 11–3 ✋ Adult €6, child (4–8) €3, under-4s free

CLUB NÁUTICO PORTO CRISTO
www.cnportocristo.com
The sailing school has Optimist dinghies for children.
✉ Carrer Vèlla 29, 07680 Porto Cristo ☎ 971 821253 ⏰ All year

SON SERVERA
ALBATROS DIVING
www.albatros-diving.com
Albatros is a well-respected dive centre in Cala Bona, boating divers to about 20 dive spots on the east coast. Staff are multilingual and equipment is well maintained. Nitrox tanks and PADI courses are available.
✉ Puerto de Cala Bona 18, 07559 Son Servera ☎ 971 586807 ⏰ Apr–end Oct ✋ From €30

PRICES AND SYMBOLS

The prices given are the average for a two-course lunch (L) and a three-course dinner (D) for one person, without drinks. The wine price is for the least expensive bottle.

For a key to the symbols, ▷ 2.

ALCÚDIA

L'ARCA D'EN PETER

Located in a renovated 19th-century town house (and small hotel), this restaurant occupies the ground floor with an inner courtyard. The cuisine is modern Mediterranean with a definite Mallorcan influence. Choose from dishes like brochette of monkfish with prawns served with black rice and a swirl of colourful sauces or lamb and creamy polenta with fresh mint. Vegetarians are also catered for with choices that include hot and crispy vegetable tempura and millefeuille *escalibada* (grilled vegetables, Catalan style). There is an excellent wine list of both local and imported wines and the service is gracious and attentive.

✉ Petit Hotel Ca'n Simó, Carrer d'En Serra 22, 07400 Alcúdia ☎ 971 529178 🕐 May–end Oct Tue–Sat 12–3, 7–11 🖐 L €25, D €30, Wine €10

CA'N COSTA

This family-run restaurant is located in a handsome old town house in the old town of Alcúdia. It serves traditional Mallorcan dishes from *tumbet* to *frit mallorquí* (here prepared with diced liver, potato, peppers and fresh herbs). You'll also find plenty of fish on the menu, from *bacallà* (cod) prepared Mallorcan style to a substantial paella. Finish up with home-made *gato*—local almond cake, served with a dusting of icing sugar. In summer, you can dine out in the courtyard.

✉ Carrer Sant Vicens 14, 07400 Alcúdia ☎ 971 545394 🕐 Tue–Sun 1–3, 7–11. Closed mid-Jan to mid-Mar 🖐 L €20, D €25, Wine €9

GENESTAR

www.genestarestaurant.com
Genestar is a fashionable new restaurant in Alcúdia, owned by gifted young chef Joan Josep Genestar Amengual. The space is chic, sleek and minimalist, decorated in shades of grey and white. Bamboo and spiky grasses in ceramic pots give it an Oriental feel. The cuisine is equally contemporary, and is prepared daily from the freshest seasonal ingredients. Choose from the five-course menu (€22) or the seven-course menu (€32–€35), which might include dishes like fresh fish of the day served with black rice risotto, or a lobster salad tossed with fresh herb dressing. Other themed menus are available according to what's in season.

✉ Plaça Porta de Mallorca 1, 07400 Alcúdia ☎ 971 549157 🕐 Thu–Tue 1–3.30, 7.30–11. Closed three weeks in Jan 🖐 L and D €30, Wine €10

SA PLAÇA

This elegant restaurant on the main square of Alcúdia offers a menu of Mallorcan, Mediterranean and Italian cuisine, making full use of local ingredients. The starters might include *trempó*, a Mallorcan summer salad served with apple and almonds, or courgettes stuffed with cabbage, raisins, pine nuts, sausage and Mallorcan cheese. Main courses vary from hake with purée of herbs and clams to grilled steak topped with goat's cheese, almonds and honey. For dessert, try almond cake with almond ice cream or *crema catalan*. A meal here can work out a little on the expensive side but it is worth it for a special occasion. There is a good-value lunchtime menu, with three courses plus wine and coffee for €12.

✉ Plaça Constitució 1, 07400 Alcúdia ☎ 971 546278 🕓 Thu–Tue 12–12. Closed Wed in winter ✋ *Menú del día* €15, L €24, D €30, Wine €10

SATYRICON

This exciting new restaurant opened in 2009 and has added another dimension to Alcúdia's dining scene, with a cordon bleu menu. It has an extraordinary setting, in the former art deco cinema which has been restored in faux Roman style, with Italian mosaic flooring (more than 700,000 mosaics), ceiling frescoes and replica Roman busts. It may sound kitsch, but somehow it works. The menu includes seafood soup scented with Armagnac (€10.25), followed by mains like duck *magret* filled with wild berries with a muscatel sauce (€16.25). Sweet treats include mango-glazed ice cream bisque with a cinnamon crisp and chocolate sauce (€5.25). There are seats outside for al-fresco dining, as well as occasional live music, including opera.

✉ Plaça Constitucio 4, 07400 Alcúdia ☎ 971 544997 🕓 Mar–end Oct daily 1–3, 7–10 ✋ L €22, D €28, Wine €8

ARTÀ

CAFÈ PARISIEN

There are several cafe-bar-restaurants on Artà's main street, but this is the most attractive and the most welcoming. You'll find the square-shaped bar in a high-ceilinged, Z-shaped room. The wicker chairs are comfortable, the music is inoffensively low and jazzy and the restaurant hosts regular art exhibitions. Large portions of pasta—*parpadelle a la genovesa, penne al salmón*—cost from €8 to €12. A salad starter costs €4.75. They're all prepared from fresh ingredients. Café Parisien also makes a good place for a break,

serving coffee and pastries to shoppers and sightseers.

✉ Carrer Ciutat 18, 07570 Artà ☎ 971 835440 🕓 Daily 9am–midnight. Closed Sun in winter ✋ L from €13, D from €17, Wine from €10

BADIA D'ALCÚDIA

MESÓN LOS PATOS

www.mesonlospatos.com
A great option for families, this large, friendly restaurant has plenty of room for kids to run around, plus a playground and private parking. The restaurant overlooks a lake, part of the wetlands of Alcúdia Bay, which are famous for locally caught eels (*anguiles*). You can try the special eel menu on Thursdays throughout the year. (These tiny creatures are a local delicacy, but may be an acquired taste for visitors.) There's an extensive menu offering traditional Mallorcan and Mediterranean home cooking including paella and other rice dishes, a range of fresh seafood (much of it caught in Alcúdia Bay), and roasted or grilled meats including duck (the house speciality) as well as lamb and kid. The wine list features plenty of local Mallorcan wines, along with some from the Spanish mainland. Prices are very reasonable.

✉ Cami de Ca'n Blau 42, Badia d'Alcúdia, ☎ 971 890265 🕓 Wed–Mon 1–3.30, 7–11.30 ✋ *Menú del día* €9, L €15, D €25, Wine €10

CALA SANT VICENÇ

CAVALL BERNAT

www.hotelcala.com
The menu at Cavall Bernat, the main trattoria at the Cala Sant Vicenç (hotel ▷ 156), changes every three months to ensure that the ingredients remain seasonal. Head chef Dominique L'Honoré gives a modern twist to Mediterranean classics. A lobster salad starter arrives with asparagus and a grapefruit sorbet, while a Binissalem red wine sauce adds a Mallorcan touch to a main course of fillet of beef with seasonal mushrooms. Try the *menú de degustació* (tasting menu), which offers five courses

for €70 and includes dishes like sea bass with spinach and pistachios for €23. An excellent wine list is dominated by Spanish wines, but there is still space for worthy New World wines such as California's Russian River Valley chardonnay. Cavall Bernat is one of the island's finest hotel-restaurants, with a well-drilled team of waiters.

✉ Carrer Maressers 2, Cala Sant Vicenç, 07469 Pollença ☎ 971 530250 🕓 Apr–end Sep daily 7.30–10.30; Feb, Mar, Oct, Nov, closed Sun. Closed Dec, Jan ✋ L €40, D €50, Wine €16.50

POLLENÇA

CLIVIA

Perhaps the most popular restaurant in Pollença, Clivia has built up a loyal clientele by serving simple but skilfully prepared meals in a smart 100-year-old town house in the town centre. Go for the fish dishes—seafood is fresh and available according to season. The house speciality is roasted sea bass and the seafood platter is also recommended. Mains cost from €12, while starters cost from €6 up to an extravagant €12 for *gambas al ajillo*. Although there are two dining rooms and a terrace, reservations are recommended. Clivia is less casual than the other exceptional restaurant in Pollença, La Fonda (▷ 154).

✉ Avinguda Pollentia 9, 07460 Pollença ☎ 971 533635 🕓 Daily 1–3, 7–10. Closed Wed 15 Nov–20 Dec ✋ L €17.50, D €22, Wine €11.50

EU CENTRO

This restaurant has a lot going for it: an excellent location in a quiet side street near the cathedral, an attractive interior design of bare stone walls and tasteful art, and, not least, keen prices. The cuisine is Mallorcan, with popular regional dishes like *canelones*. Starters are priced from €5.50 and mains from €6.60, while the specials board offers seasonal dishes such as baked cod on potatoes with *aïoli*. Mallorcan favourites such as paella, *tumbet* and roast kid are not forgotten.

Quality is about right for the prices: reasonable, but rarely rising above average. A children's menu makes it a better bet for families.

✉ Carrer Temple 3, 07460 Pollença ☎ 971 535082 ◷ Thu–Tue 11–3.30, 7–11 ✋ Menú del día €8, L €12, D €15, Wine €8

LA FONDA

Tuck into large portions of traditional seasonal Mallorcan cooking at this welcoming, rustic restaurant. You can find it on the left side of Plaça Major, as you face the church, and it offers better value than some of the restaurants on the actual square itself. The staff are friendly and the place is popular with locals. Most Mallorcan favourites, from *tumbet* to roast pork, are available. The paella comes with rice dyed black with squid ink (€20 for two persons), while more elaborate dishes, such as gilt head bream stuffed with prawns, cost up to €20. The *menú del día* is a good choice at less than €10.

✉ Carrer Antoni Maura 32, 07460 Pollença ☎ 971 534751 ◷ Daily 1–3.30, 7.30–11. Closed Mon Dec and Jan ✋ L €20, D €35, Wine €10

L'ILLA CAFÉ

This handsome cafe on Pollença's main square has a wood-panelled floor, stone walls, brown leather and chrome furniture, and some rather curious lightboxes of pictures of American singer and song-writer Bob Dylan. It opens for breakfast at 8am, with good coffee for €1, and is a good, central venue for a daytime snack while sightseeing, serving *tapas* (€2.50–€6), sandwiches (from €2.50) and *pa amb olí* (from €5.20, with ham). A slice of apple cake costs €2.90. If the weather is fine, get an outside table.

✉ Plaça Major 7, 07460 Pollença ☎ 971 531621 ◷ Wed–Mon 8am–9pm ✋ L €12, D €18

PORT DE POLLENÇA

BRISAS

One of a long row of mid-range restaurants along Port de Pollença's seafront, Brisas is a bright and breezy place close to the marina. The restaurant specializes in paella, fish and Mallorcan dishes, but you'll also find the usual tourist staples such a pasta and pizza on the menu, at a wallet-friendly €6.40. Expect to spend a little more on a main course such as fillet of salmon in cava (€18.50).

✉ Avinguda Anglada Camarasa 27, 07470 Port de Pollença ☎ 971 867000 ◷ Daily 12–4, 7–11 ✋ L €13, D €17, Wine €12

GRAN CAFÉ 1919

This cafe, located on the promenade opposite the marina, is one of the few places open in Port de Pollença in winter. In summer, visitors soak up the sunshine around the many outside tables, watching the sailing activity across the road. The cafe, styled as belle époque meets Modernism, serves sandwiches, salads, cakes and drinks, including beer, sangria and watery orange juice. Prompt service from the black-suited waiters make this a useful venue for a quick snack.

✉ Passeig Marítim, 07470 Port de Pollença ☎ 971 867535 ◷ Daily 8–11 ✋ L €12, D €19, Wine €7.75

STAY

www.stayrestaurant.com

Out on a jetty next to the marina and facing Port de Pollença's harbour front, Stay has a superb location with huge windows and a terrace from which to appreciate the view. The restaurant, popular with British expats, specializes in fresh, seasonal seafood, although it is just as respected for meat dishes such as pork escalopes with apples and calvados. Starters range from a light shrimp soup with Riesling for €7.30 to a platter of fish tartare with caviar for €67.80. Fishy main courses start from salmon supreme in white wine for €14.80 to the extravagant Menorcan lobster *calderette* at €30. The high prices are justified by the restaurant's location and liveliness rather than the food. You can eat inexpensively on snacks here; a cheese and tomato sandwich with salad costs just €3.30.

✉ Moll Nou, 07470 Port de Pollença ☎ 971 864013 ◷ Daily 12–4, 7.30–10.30 ✋ Menú del día €30.20, L €25, D €30, Wine €14

LOS ZARZALES

If you have grown weary of all-day English breakfasts, German sausages and, yes, even Mallorquín cuisine, Los Zarzales offers something a little different. Located just back from the beachfront with a sprawl of outside tables on this pedestrian street, the menu includes vegetarian starter options like fried vegetables with bio-seitan and seaweed (€7.90), battered brie salad with poppy seeds and seasonal fruits berry coulis (€9.80) and mains such as baked monkfish with king prawns with essence of almond blossom (€18.20).

✉ Carrer Jafuda Cresques 11, 07470 Port de Pollença ☎ 971 865137 ◷ Apr–end Dec daily 1–4, 7–11 ✋ L €18, D €25, Wine €7.50

SANT LLORENÇ DES CARDASSAR

ES MOLÍ D'EN BOU

A handsomely refurbished windmill surrounded by orange and almond groves makes a striking setting for this fine restaurant, which has won a Michelin star along with many other accolades. Mallorcan chef Tomeu Caldentey reinvents traditional regional cuisine, taking time-honoured recipes and preparing them using contemporary techniques. House specialities include *canelones* (a humble country dish elevated here to the heights of haute cuisine with the addition of fresh crabmeat and apple), and succulent lamb roasted with plump dates. Four different menus are offered, including the *petit* for €68 and the *grand* for €88. The wine list is equally starry, featuring all the major Mallorcan producers along with a good selection of other fine Spanish wines.

✉ Carrer Lilas s/n, 07560 Sant Llorenç des Cardassar ☎ 971 569663 ◷ Wed–Sat 1.30–3.30, 8–11, Sun 8–11 ✋ Menú del día €22, L €45, D €65, Wine €20

PRICES AND SYMBOLS

Prices are the lowest and highest for a double room for one night. Breakfast is included unless noted otherwise. All the hotels listed accept credit cards unless otherwise stated. Note that rates vary widely throughout the year.

For a key to the symbols, ▷ 2.

ALCÚDIA
CAN TEM

www.hotelcantem.com

Behind the medieval walls, Alcúdia is an appealing town of Gothic and Renaissance mansions sheltering in narrow streets. In recent years several of these houses have become stylish town-house hotels. Magdalena and Toni Reus have converted their family home, in a quiet lane off the main street, into just such a place, combining antique furniture with bright modern paintings. From the spacious entrance hall with its stone arch, a curving staircase leads upstairs to the bedrooms, which have televisions and central heating. The shady garden makes a peaceful spot to relax or have breakfast.

✉ Carrer de l'Església 14, 07400 Alcúdia
☎ 971 243537 🅖 All year ✋ €85–€90
🛈 4 🅢

CAS FERRER NOU HOTELET

www.nouhotelet.com

Tucked away in Alcúdia's lovely old town, this smart boutique hotel is located in a former blacksmith's. It has just six elegant rooms, with varying colour schemes ranging from lemon yellow to red. The petals scattered on the bedcovers are a lovely touch. For romance, book the Safo, with a gauze-draped four-poster bed and large private terrace with lounge bed, cushions and superb mountain views. DVDs are available to borrow and there is a small coffee corner with a library of books. WiFi available.

✉ Carrer Pou Nou 1, 07400 Alcúdia
☎ 971 897542 🅖 Feb to mid-Dec
✋ €110–€125 🛈 6 🅢

POLLENTIA CLUB RESORT (PORT DE POLLENÇA)

www.clubpollentia.com

Set back from the main road between Port de Pollença and Alcúdia, this is an unobtrusive, low-rise resort. There are two classes of accommodation, the cheaper Maris rooms and the larger Village rooms. Both are clean and are organized in small clusters in the landscaped grounds, each with its own buffet restaurant. All bedrooms have a bathroom, telephone, television, fridge, fan, central heating and a safe—the Village rooms also have sunbeds. On-site activities are free for guests. Facilities include three swimming pools, jacuzzis, tennis courts, squash courts, minigolf, an archery range, bicycle hire, a scuba centre, a health and beauty centre and a children's club. The hotel is good value for families wanting resort-style accommodation. Note that car-less guests have to take the bus to Port de Pollença and you have to cross a road to get to the beach, which is better suited to water sports than sunbathing. The resort is a popular base for cyclists in the off-peak seasons.

✉ Carretera Port de Pollença–Alcúdia, km 2, 07400 Alcúdia ☎ 971 546996
🅖 Mar–end Oct ✋ Maris rooms €58–€150, Village rooms €66–€170 🛈 292
🅢 ⛱ 🍴

SANT JAUME

www.hotelsantjaume.com

This 18th-century family house has been lovingly restored. Wherever possible, original features have been restored and retained, including the evocative hand-painted floor

Above *Son Brull, Pollença (see page 157)*

tiles where replacements were handmade to exactly copy the originals to superb effect. The rooms vary, but all combine old and new, with aesthetic attention to detail. They have luxurious canopy beds, high ceilings and good views, particularly room 6, which overlooks the rooftops of the historic centre. WiFi is available and all the rooms have refrigerators.

✉ Carrer Sant Jaume 6, 07400 Alcúdia ☎ 971 549419 🕓 Feb–end Nov ✋ €110 all year 🚪 6 🛇

ARTÀ
CA'N MORAGUES
www.canmoragues.com
This elegant, 18th-century town house hotel in Artà's old town offers guests a heated pool, solarium and sauna. Bedroom design is a mix of stylish, modern furnishings and rustic Mallorcan touches such as bare stone walls and wooden furniture. All rooms have telephone, television and central heating. There's an attractive courtyard, complete with orange trees, in which to enjoy breakfast. Four golf courses (▷ 149) are within a short drive of Artà.

✉ Carrer Pou Nou 12, 07570 Artà ☎ 971 829509 🕓 All year ✋ €125–€135 🚪 8 🛇 ⛵

SANT SALVADOR
www.santsalvador.com
The hotel-restaurant Sant Salvador is in a grand old palace in the

centre of Artà close to the Gothic church and the castle. The German owners have created a colourful, vibrant interior with warm lighting and a smattering of antiques. The bedrooms are individually furnished and decorated and all have central heating, telephone, television and fridge. Health and beauty treatments can be arranged. There are two restaurants; the Gaudí offers light mediterranean cuisine while Zezo is more creative and upmarket. There are four golf courses (▷ 149) close to Artà and beaches are a short drive away. Pets are welcome.

✉ Carrer Castellet 7, 07570 Artà ☎ 971 829555 🕓 All year ✋ €111–€150 🚪 8 🛇 ⛵

CALA RATJADA
SES ROTGES
www.sesrotges.com
Best known for its French restaurant, Ses Rotges' hotel accommodation is on the second and third floor of this handsome corner building. The French-owned hotel is in a quiet area of town, a brief walk from the seafront. Don't expect modern minimalism in the bedrooms; decor is on the chintzy side, but the rooms are a good size and have telephone, television and central heating. Dinner at Ses Rotges can be an extravagant experience, but there are plenty of cheaper options in Cala Ratjada's main street, two blocks away. In summer the patio outside is prepared for moonlit dining.

Excellent breakfasts are cooked to order.

✉ Carrer Rafael Blanes 21, 07590 Cala Ratjada ☎ 971 563108 🕓 Apr–end Oct ✋ €80–€120 🚪 24 🛇

CALA SANT VICENÇ
CALA SANT VICENÇ
www.hotelcala.com
Trapped between the tail end of the Serra de Tramuntana and the Mediterranean, the Cala Sant Vicenç is in a perfect location at the northeast corner of the island. It's the original hotel in the Suau empire and the family has developed one of Mallorca's top restaurants here, Cavall Bernat (▷ 153), which offers a finely crafted, seasonally adjusted, modern Mallorquín menu. There's also a less expensive grill (by the poolside) for lunchtimes and a trattoria. Bedrooms are as pretty as the hotel's dusky-pink exterior, and have television, WiFi, minibar and central heating. The grounds are spectacular, with landscaped gardens and a swimming pool, which is heated in winter.

✉ Carrer Maressers 2, 07469 Cala Sant Vicenç ☎ 971 530250 🕓 Apr–end Nov ✋ €164–€247 🚪 38 ⛵ 🛇

CAMPANET
MONNABER NOU
www.monnaber.com
On the western edge of the northeast and bordering the Serra de Tramuntana, Campanet is a quiet base for touring the northern end of

the mountains. Monnaber Nou is an imposing manor house just outside the village. In the grounds there are three swimming pools (two outdoor, one heated indoor) and tennis courts. Inside guests can use a gym and jacuzzi or have a massage. Among the treatments offered in the small spa is 'chocolate therapy'. Rooms have telephone, television and central heating, but make sure you get a room facing out; those looking into the interior courtyard can be gloomy. Apartments are also available.

✉ Possessió de Monnaber Nou, 07310 Campanet ☎ 971 877176 🕐 All year ✋ €121–€149 🚪 25 🐾 🏊

POLLENÇA
DES BRULL
www.desbrull.com

This boutique hotel on the edge of Pollença's centre opened in August 2003. It's in a converted 18th-century honey-coloured building, but the design is very modern and chic. Rooms have television and attractively plain bathrooms. The decor is a combination of metal fittings, stone walls and dark wood furniture. The continental breakfast is served in the downstairs bar area with its black marble tiles, gilt mirrors and more interesting artwork. There are a few outdoor tables for enjoying your morning *café con leche* or evening cocktail. WiFi available.

✉ Marquès Desbrull 7, 07460 Pollença ☎ 971 535055 🕐 Mid-Dec to mid-Nov ✋ €70–€90 🚪 6 🐾

HOTEL JUMA
www.hoteljuma.com

Overlooking this lovely square shaded by plane trees, this historic hotel has retained a sense of the traditional, its large rooms furnished with dark wood furniture and locally produced rugs. Cream linen, tasteful artwork and sparkling white-tiled bathrooms add to the appeal. The rooms looking towards the mountains at the back of the building

Opposite *Hotel Sant Salvador in Artà*

are quieter, while the downstairs restaurant is popular with locals and reliably good, particularly the reasonably priced tapas.

✉ Plaça Major 9, 07460 Pollença ☎ 971 535002 🕐 Feb–end Nov ✋ €102–€120 🚪 7 🐾

POSADA DE LLUC
www.posadalluc.com

The monastery at Lluc owned this small town house in Pollença's medieval core from the 15th to the 19th century. It is now a stylish hotel, with antique furniture and a pleasant garden. Rooms are cosy, and fitted with WiFi and television. Note that Pollença's summer music festival takes place close by.

✉ Carrer Roser Vell 11, 07460 Pollença ☎ 971 535220 🕐 Feb–end Nov ✋ €129–€158 🚪 8 🐾 🏊

SON BRULL
www.sonbrull.com

Not to be confused with Des Brull (▷ left), Son Brull is an ultra-chic hotel situated on the main Inca–Pollença road, just outside Pollença. The bedrooms are large, with the sort of tasteful, minimal furnishings you'd expect for around €300 per night. They have en-suite bathrooms, television and DVD and WiFi. The spacious bathrooms even have baths with hydro-massage jets and a hi-fi. The hotel has a spa and views of olive grove-clad hills.

✉ Carretera Palma–Pollença PM 220, km 49.8, 07460 Pollença ☎ 971 535353 🕐 Feb–end Nov ✋ €236–€380 🚪 23 🐾 🏊

SON SANT JORDI
www.hotelsonsantjordi.com

The best feature of this smart town house hotel is the fantastic interior design. Old elements of the manor house have been incorporated into the modern, minimalist bedrooms, so you'll find ancient tiling next to stylish bathroom fittings. The lights are movement-sensitive, another smart feature, and bedrooms have luxurious canopy beds and exquisitely tiled bathrooms. Two rooms have hydro massage baths,

which are particularly welcome if you have spent the day hiking. Other perks include an exotic garden, a pool and a sauna. Breakfast is a buffet. There is also a restaurant serving reasonable Mediterranean and international fare.

✉ Carrer Sant Jordi 29, 07460 Pollença ☎ 971 530389 🕐 All year ✋ €80–€186 🚪 8 🐾 🏊

PORT DE POLLENÇA
ILLA D'OR
www.hotelillador.com

The Illa d'Or opened in 1929, when tourism in Mallorca was in its infancy, and has retained a great deal of its original charm. Part of the attraction is the setting, a short stroll from the centre of the resort at the end of the 'Pine Walk' from the harbour. The clientele here is overwhelmingly British and many visitors have been coming since they were children. The hotel has a beauty centre with a sauna, jacuzzi and gym, indoor and outdoor pools and a tennis court, but it still has the feel of an old-style, family-run hotel. In summer, meals are served out of doors on a seafront terrace. The hotel has its own jetty and there are several small beaches nearby. WiFi available.

✉ Passeig de Colón 265, 07470 Port de Pollença ☎ 971 865100 🕐 Mar–end Oct ✋ €110–€200 🚪 120 🐾 🏊 🍴

SON SERVERA
EL ENCINAR
www.elencinardearta.com

On a hill 5km (3 miles) from Artà, this stone-clad 18th-century country house has been restored to offer nine bedrooms, a lounge with an open fireplace, a bar, a library and a wine cellar. And in sunny weather guests can use the barbecue outside. The medium-size bedrooms have WiFi and central heating. Decor is low-key, with plain furnishings and tiled floors. The hotel is ideally located for the east coast's beaches and four golf courses nearby.

✉ Cami des Rafal des Sants, 07550 Son Servera ☎ 971 183860 🕐 All year ✋ €130–€160 🚪 9 🐾

SIGHTS 161
WALK, DRIVE AND BICYCLE RIDE 170
WHAT TO DO 176
EATING 180
STAYING 184

THE SOUTH

This is the area of Mallorca that many visitors unwittingly overlook, particularly the inland rural region where picturesque small towns like Petra have a timeless simplicity and charm. This is coupled with excellent *agroturismos* and restaurant options, often in traditional stone buildings which have retained their integrity, despite catering for modern demands. Having your own wheels will help you explore off the beaten track, particularly inland, although the larger towns are easily accessed by public transport.

Dominated by the fertile Pla I Llevant and the manufacturing centres of Inca, Manacor and Algaida, the area also has some of the island's finest unsung beaches, which are often hard to access, but well worth the effort. These include long sweeps of pristine white sand backed by dense pine woods and natural protected parks. This region of the island is also famed for its vibrant viniculture, centred in Binissalem and Felanitx, where you can visit wineries and taste the tipple. But, above all, this is where you will find Mallorca's most dramatic attraction, the network of caves along the wind-whipped east coast which possess a wild and melancholic beauty.

BINISSALEM

www.ajbinissalem.net

This small town on the plain is best known for its wine. As you drive past Binissalem on the old road from Palma to Inca you will see the island's largest producer, Vinos Ferrer (tel 971 511050; www.vinosferrer.com; tours Mon–Fri 11am and 4.30pm, Sat 11am; €6; book in advance, minimum 5 people). There are also a couple of smaller *bodegas* in town—Vins Nadal (Carrer Ramón Llull 2, tel 971 511058; www.vinsnadal.net), who make the excellent Albaflor range, and Vins Ripoll (Carrer Pere Estruch 25, tel 971 511028), where you can buy wine straight from the barrel. The best time to be here is in the final week of September, when wine flows freely during the annual harvest festival (▷ 179).

Rather surprisingly, Mallorca's best-preserved ensemble of 17th- and 18th-century manor houses is to be found in the streets around the church square, Plaça de l'Església. There are particularly good examples in Passeig des Born, an attractive cobbled lane behind the church.

Can Sabater (Carrer de Bonaire 25, Mon–Sat 10–2, also Tue and Thu 4–8) was the home of the writer Llorenç Villalonga (1897–1980), who wrote novels—including *Bearn* (*The Dolls' Room*)—about the moral decline of the Mallorcan nobility. The house is now preserved as a museum, with Villalonga's original desk and library on display upstairs. ✚ 223 F5 🛈 Ajuntament, Carrer Concepció 7 ☎ 971 511043 🚍 From Palma and Inca ❓ Market Fri

CABRERA

www.excursionsacabrera.com

In 1991, after many years of military occupation, the island of Cabrera, 10km (6 miles) south of Mallorca, was declared a national park. Among the species protected here is the Balearic lizard (including endemic subspecies not found elsewhere), and now 80 per cent of its world population live on the island. Ospreys, peregrines and Eleanora's falcons build their nests on the cliffs; there are colonies of Balearic shearwaters and Audouin's gulls; and dolphins can sometimes be seen in the coastal waters.

The easiest way of visiting Cabrera is to take one of the excursion boats that leave Colònia de Sant Jordi. On arrival on the island, you can pick up leaflets in various languages from the small information office on the harbour, or take the short walk from the quayside to the beach at S'Espalmador, where you can swim or snorkel in crystal-clear waters.

You can't wander freely on Cabrera, but the park rangers offer two guided walks. The first walk, leaving at 11.30am daily, takes you up to the castle overlooking the harbour. Built in 1410, it became most famous as a prison for French soldiers defeated in the Battle of Bailén in 1809 (▷ 31). Unable to escape, and without regular supplies, the prisoners survived on a diet of lizards and rats. You can still see graffiti etched into the castle walls by some of the prisoners. On the second walk, departing at 1pm, you will see a monument to the French soldiers who died on Cabrera; it was placed here some 30 years later by a French prince. Nearby is Can Feliu, an old wine cellar now housing a small museum on the history of the island.

On the way back to Mallorca the boats usually stop off in Sa Cova Blava (Blue Grotto), where you can swim inside a natural cave with a depth of 40m (131ft). ✚ 226 G11 🛈 Excursions A Cabrera, Colònia de Sant Jordi ☎ 971 649034 🕙 Apr–end Oct, daily departure at 9.30 (reservation essential) 💷 Mon–Fri €28, Sat €32, Sun €34 child (3–10) half price 🍴 On boat

THE CALAS

▷ 162.

CA'N GORDIOLA

www.gordiola.com

The Gordiola family has been making glass in Mallorca since 1719 and this mock castle on the Palma to Manacor road near Algaida is the best place to see the glassmaking craftsmen in action. In the workshop, which resembles a medieval church, you can watch the workers blowing glass and fashioning it with tongs before placing it in ovens reaching temperatures of over 1,000°C (1,832°F). From the courtyard beyond, steps lead up to the museum, where there is an extraordinary collection of glass objects dating back to Egyptian and Roman times, together with more recent examples from Venice, China and elsewhere. Look into the library to see family portraits of the Gordiolas dating from the 18th century to the present day. If you want to take home a souvenir, the gift shop stocks an extensive range of Gordiola glass.

✚ 223 F6 ✉ Carretera Palma–Manacor, 19km (12 miles) ☎ 971 665046 🕙 Shop and museum: Mon–Sat 9–7, Sun 9–1.30. Glassworks: Mon–Sat 9–1.30, 3–6, Sun 9–12 💷 Free 📖 €6.60 🏧 💻

Opposite *Vineyard near Binissalem*
Below *View towards the island of Cabrera*

TIPS

›› Calas de Mallorca, north of Cala d'Or, means 'coves of Mallorca', but it is actually an uninspiring holiday resort set around a shopping centre.

›› An attractive cove closer to Palma is Cala Pi, south of Llucmajor, where steps lead down to a small beach framed by cliffs on the edge of a wooded gorge. A clifftop path from here leads to Cap Blanc, with fine views of Cabrera (▷ 161) out to sea.

›› Santanyí, the main town of the southeast, is a charming place built in the mellow local sandstone that was used in the construction of Palma Cathedral (▷ 70–73). One of the original town gates has survived, together with sections of the medieval walls. Cafes and bars line the pedestrianized main square, Plaça Major, in front of the church.

THE CALAS

Unlike the built-up coastlines of the Bay of Palma and the northeast, the southeast has few long beaches and few major holiday resorts. Instead, from Cala d'Or to Colònia de Sant Jordi, and especially around Santanyí, unspoiled beaches and creeks punctuate the shoreline. Sometimes access to the *calas* is only possible via narrow (sometimes steep) dirt tracks, which means a refreshing lack of concrete and commercialism.

CALA D'OR

Cala d'Or (Golden Cove) is the most southerly resort on the east coast. There are actually several rocky coves here, together with one decent-sized beach, Cala Gran. The whitewashed, flat-roofed houses around the harbour were designed in Ibizan style, and the harbour itself is now a glitzy marina. In summer a miniature road train connects the various parts of the resort as well as the fishing village of Porto Petro, whose harbour is now mostly filled with pleasure boats.

✚ 227 J8 ☒ Avinguda Perico Pomar,10 ☎ 971 657463 ◉ Mar–end Oct Mon–Fri 8.30–2, Sat 9–1 ☐ Buses from Palma via Santanyí

CALA FIGUERA

Sheltering at the end of a long, narrow inlet, Cala Figuera is the archetypal Mediterranean fishing village; white-painted, green-shuttered cottages line the waterfront, and fishermen sit on the slipways mending their nets. The lack of a real beach can often lead to the mildly incongruous sight of sunbathers on the quay as well. Although this is a working port, fish restaurants above the harbour do good business from the crowds of daytrippers. A path leads to the cliffs for views over the harbour. The nearest beaches are found to the south and west, at Cala Santanyí and Cala Llombards.

✚ 227 J9

CALA MONDRAGÓ

A clifftop path links the twin beaches at Cala Mondragó. There are hotels and restaurants beside the northern beach but development has been restricted since the area became a nature reserve in 1990. The information centre by the car park issues maps of walking routes through dunes, marshland, pine woods and wild olive groves.

✚ 227 J8 ☒ Parc Natural de Mondragó, 5km (3 miles) east of Santanyí ☎ 971 181022 ◉ Daily 8–1

Above *The beach of the Hotel Cala d'Or, which dates from 1932 and overlooks the bay of Cala d'Or*

CAPOCORB VELL

Along with Ses Païsses at Artà (▷ 135), the ruins of Capocorb Vell, 12km (7 miles) south of Llucmajor, are the most significant remains of Mallorca's Talaiotic era (▷ 27). The village was built around 1000BC and inhabited until Roman times. Like other Talaiotic settlements, it was surrounded by walls and dominated by *talaiots*—conical or pyramid-shaped structures that acted both as burial chambers and defensive fortresses, and which are found on both Mallorca and Menorca, but oddly not on Ibiza. At Capocorb Vell you can see the remains of five *talaiots* (three conical and two pyramidal), as well as 28 dwellings and animal enclosures arranged along a prehistoric street.

TALAIOTIC FINDS

An account of archaeological findings is available at the cafe, but you will need to use your imagination if you are to conjure up an image of Talaiotic life among the crumbling stone passageways and lanes. The most interesting feature is the large square *talaiot* on the left as you enter the village. You can climb to the top to see the upper room, whose central pillar consists of huge blocks of stone piled one on top of each other. A hole in the floor gives way to a narrow spiral staircase, which leads to an underground chamber roofed with wild olive trunks. This room was almost certainly used for some sort of religious or funerary ritual.

The settlement was surrounded by high walls over 3.6m (12ft) high in places. These days the local population consist mainly of goat herds, although the site is on a popular cyle route: Cicloturistica de Llucmajor (▷ 174). But there is a refreshing lack of commercialism about the place with not one Capocorb T-shirt on sale and just a simple outside bar for refreshments.

INFORMATION

⊕ 226 F8 ✉ Carretera Llucmajor–Cap Blanc, km23 ☎ 971 180155 🕓 Fri–Wed 10–5 ✋ Adult €2 📖 Can be borrowed 🔲

Below *The ruins of a Talaiotic settlement at Capocorb Vell*

COVES DEL DRAC AND DELS HAMS

INFORMATION

www.cuevasdeldrac.com

✛ 225 K6 ✉ 1km (0.6 miles) south of Porto Cristo overlooking Cala Murta ☎ 971 820753 ☉ Tours: Apr–end Oct daily 10, 11, 12, 2, 3, 4, 5; Nov–end Mar 10.45, 12, 2, 3.30 ✋ Adult €10, child (under 8) free 📷 €1.50 ♿ Disabled WC but no wheelchair access to caves
🍴 🎁

INTRODUCTION

The Coves del Drac (Dragon Caves) are high on the must-see list of every traveller to Mallorca. They attract large crowds of visitors, and because of the sheer number of people around you, it can be difficult to appreciate the caves' splendour. You may also have to wait for your tour, especially in the height of season. At least you can do so in beautiful surroundings. The landscaping is lovely, with lush tropical gardens surrounding the entrance to the caves. Olive and fig trees, as well as colourful hibiscus and bougainvillea contrast dramatically with the soft tonnes of the naturally sculptured sandstone. Several strutting peacocks add an appropriate exotic flourish to the scene, and there is a small snack bar on-site sells sandwiches, snacks and drinks.

The hour-long tour begins with a walk along 700m (765 yards) of underground paths, with stalactites and stalagmites all around you. Once inside the caves there is no easy way out, so think twice about going in if you are claustrophobic or have young children who may get scared. The installation of lighting has had a dramatic effect on the overall enjoyment of these caves. The climax is a magical concert on Lago Martel (Lake Martel), Europe's largest underground lake. The water has a temperature of 17°C (63°F) and is slightly salty, which proves a subterranean connection to the Mediterranean.

Located around 150m (165yds) from the exit of the caves is a small but reasonably good aquarium. The lower floor specializes on more exotic species, while the upper floor is devoted to Mediterranean marine life.

WHAT TO SEE

THE ROCK FORMATIONS

There are hundreds of caves like this throughout Mallorca, but few have been explored. All were formed by the erosive action of water, which carved out

Above *The weird and wonderful Coves del Drac are illuminated to great effect*

caverns in the limestone and produced extraordinary formations. Many of these have been given names (Ruined Castle, Fairies' Theatre, Pagoda), and if you look carefully you can usually make these images out, but it is just as much fun to make up your own. The guides point out Diana's Bath, where thousands of crystal-white stalactites hang from the roof of the cave, like an intricately carved ivory triptych suspended over a pool. Facing this is the Enchanted City, a forest of stalagmites and pillars. Alongside the path are pools of clear water up to 5m (16.5ft) deep, whose dramatic reflections only increase the sense of walking through a fantasy world.

THE ILLUMINATIONS
Carles Buïgas (1898–1979), an engineer famous for his illuminated fountains for the 1929 World Fair in Barcelona, designed the electric lighting inside the caves in 1935. He returned to the caves in 1950 to update his work, increasing the power supply to 100,000 watts and adding 630m (2,066ft) of cable. In some ways the lighting detracts from the caves' natural beauty, but most people think this is a work of genius, reaching its climax in the artificial sunrise over Lake Martel.

THE CONCERT
The walk ends at an underground amphitheatre beside Lake Martel. An illuminated boat appears out of the darkness and you hear the strains of classical music. On another boat, a quartet is playing *Alborada (Dawn Song)* by Caballero. The musicians continue to play as the boats are rowed across the lake, their lights reflecting thousands of stalactites in the clear water. Concert highlights include Albinoni's *Adagio*, Pachelbel's *Canon de Pachelbel* and serene works by Bach, Handel, Chopin, Boccherini and others. The experience is rounded off with Offenbach's *La Bararola (The Gondolier's Song)* as a finale.

THE LAKE
After the concert you can cross the lake by walking over the footbridge to your right. But if you have time to queue, it is worth taking the boat. There are eight passengers to each boat and they are skilfully steered in an elegant figure-of-eight rowing style. French speleologist Édouard Martel discovered the lake while studying these caves in 1896 under the sponsorship of Archduke Ludwig Salvator (▷ 32). After paddling across the lake in a canoe, he recorded in his journal that it was 177m (581ft) long, 30m (98ft) wide and up to 9m (29.5ft) deep, with coral-like islands growing out of the lakebed to meet stalactites from the ceiling, forming columns 'whose beauty had not been touched by any light before ours'.

MORE TO SEE
COVES DELS HAMS
www.cuevas-hams.com
If you want to avoid the crowds, these caverns on the edge of Porto Cristo make a good alternative. Pedro Caldentey, whose son provided the illumination, discovered them in 1905. The name of the caves means 'fish hooks'—and you can see why in the chamber known as Dream of an Angel, where thousands of fish-hook stalactites hang from the ceiling. The largest cave is known as Milton's Paradise Lost (Paraiso Perdido de Milton). Although there is no theatre here, the guided tour does include a brief concert on the Sea of Venice, and there is an underground lake filled with sea water. It is also possible to see a multimedia spectacle within the caves. Programmes can be found at www.digithams.com.

➕ 225 K6/J5 ✉ Carretera Porto Cristo–Manacor ☎ 971 820988 🕐 Apr–end Oct daily 10–5.30; Nov–end Mar 11–4.30 🖐 Adult €16, child (under 12) free 🈶 ▯

TIPS
>> Photography is not allowed inside the caves.
>> The paths can be wet and slippery, so wear sensible shoes.
>> If the thought of crowds puts you off, consider going on the last tour of the day after most of the tour groups have left.

Below *Reflections in the water pools of the Coves del Drac*

Above *Mallorca's Planetarium at Costitx*
Left *St. Michael standing on the Devil, the church of Sant Miquel, Felanitx*

COLÒNIA DE SANT JORDI

Beyond the Bay of Palma, this small-scale fishing port and holiday town is the only sizeable settlement along the south coast and the departure point for trips to Cabrera (▷ 161). From the harbour a promenade leads to the main beach, Platja d'es Port; from here you can walk east to a second beach, Es Dolç. Passing remote beaches, the path continues to Cap de Ses Salines, Mallorca's southernmost point. The main draw, however, is Es Trenc, a 3km (2-mile) stretch of fine sand to the west of Colònia de Sant Jordi. Although well known—the beach is popular with nudists and families—it is one of the least developed beaches in Mallorca. To get there, take the road from Colònia de Sant Jordi to Campos and turn left following the signs. You'll pass through the Salines de Llevant, where mountains of rock salt among the marshes make an impressive sight. The road ends at a car park behind Es Trenc (fee payable in summer).

✚ 226 G9 ℹ Carrer Doctor Barraquer 5 ☎ 971 656073 🚌 Buses from Palma

COSTITX

This small village is surrounded by countryside typical of Es Pla (The Plain); explore it on the drive (▷ 170–71). In the village itself, Casa de la Fauna Ibero-Balear (Tue–Fri 9–1.30, also 2nd and 4th Sat and

Sun of each month; closed Aug) is a natural history museum in the Casal de Cultura. It is based on the work of a taxidermist who has collected birds, butterflies, mammals, fish and reptiles representing more than 90 per cent of Mallorca's fauna. On a hill above Costitx is Mallorca's astronomical observatory and planetarium (▷ 177).

✚ 224 G5

COVES DEL DRAC AND DELS HAMS

▷ 164–165.

ELS CALDERERS

www.todoesp.es/els-calderers
This ivy-covered manor house on the edge of Sant Joan has been restored as an example of 18th-century aristocratic Mallorcan life. The first records of Els Calderers go back to 1285, when the manor belonged to the Calderers family, but the present building dates from 1750. You enter via a small staircase flanked by stone lions. The ground-floor rooms are arranged around a courtyard, beginning with the reception rooms, a private chapel and a wine cellar to the right. The master's sitting room, with armchairs in front of the fire, is where the owner of the estate would make conversation with his gentleman friends; the ladies, by contrast, were expected to indulge in music and sewing in the

mistress's room. On the first floor are the bedrooms and servants' quarters, along with a large pillared granary where produce from the farm is still kept. The shop sells wine and jam, and offers tastings of *sobrassada* sausage (▷ 210).

✚ 224 H6 ✉ Signposted from Carretera Palma–Manacor, 37km (23 miles) ☎ 971 526069 🕐 Apr–end Oct daily 10–6; Nov–end Mar 10–5 💰 Adult €8, child (3–12) €4 🛒 🎫

FELANITX

Felanitx, the main town of southeast Mallorca, is easily overlooked but fully rewards a short visit—particularly on a Sunday morning, when local pottery is displayed on the church steps during the lively weekly market. The 17th-century church of Sant Miquel, reached by a monumental baroque stairway, dominates the town. Felanitx's coat of arms is carved on the tympanum above the door, and farther up, beneath the rose window, is a sculptural relief of St. Michael trampling the Devil underfoot. Devils are also in evidence at the town's big festival, held on or around 28 August, when children dressed as hobby-horses are chased through the streets by *dimonis* (devils) and *capgrossos* (bigheads) to the accompaniment of bagpipes and flutes. Just outside Felanitx is the Santuari de Sant Salvador (▷ 167).

✚ 227 J7 🚌 From Palma ❓ Market Sun

INCA

Many people visit the leather factories on the outskirts of Inca (▷ 177), but few make it to the centre of Mallorca's third-largest town. If you arrive by train, walk down Avinguda Bisbe Llompart, opposite the station, and continue to the town hall on Plaça d'Espanya. On your right is Café Mercantil, which opened in 1936 as a meeting place for merchants and shoemakers. At one stage it had a ballroom, a string quartet and piano concerts, and it is still a good place to sink into a leather armchair and read the papers over a coffee. Near here are several good pastry shops, including Ca'n Delante at Carrer Major 27. The main street, Carrer Major, continues to the 18th-century parish church of Santa Maria La Mayor, with its distinctive separate belltower from an earlier church. On Thursday mornings Mallorca's biggest weekly market takes place in the streets around the church.

➕ 224 G4 🚆 From Palma ❓ Market Thu

MANACOR

Mallorca's second-largest town—at first sight a sprawl of ring roads and industrial estates—is known for its artificial pearl factories. The best known of these, Majorica (▷ 177–178), offers intriguing tours of the production process (Mon–Fri 9–7, Sat–Sun 10–1).

The town centre is based around the parish church of Nostra Senyora dels Dolors (Our Lady of Sorrows), whose minaret-like tower is a reminder that it was built on the site of a mosque.

About 1km (0.6 miles) out of town on the road to Calas de Mallorca is Torre dels Enagistes, a 14th-century fortified tower now housing a small archaeological museum (mid-Jun to end Sep Mon, Wed–Sat 9.30–2, 6–8.30; Oct to mid-Jun Mon, Wed–Sat 10–2, 5–7.30).

➕ 224 J6 🚆 From Palma and Inca ❓ Market Mon

PETRA

▷ 168.

SANTUARI DE CURA

▷ 169.

SANTUARI DE SANT SALVADOR

Founded in 1348 and rebuilt in the 17th century, the monastery is perched on the highest summit of the Serra de Llevant (509m/1,679ft). The road to the peak passes a cave chapel where a statue of the Virgin (now in the church) is said to have been discovered in the 15th century. The approach to the monastery is marked by two huge monuments, a 14m-high (46ft) stone cross and a 35m-high (115ft) statue of Christ. The gatehouse's walls are hung with jerseys of seven-times world cycling champion Guillem Timoner, while a chapel to the left has mementoes left behind by pilgrims. From a terrace below the statue of Christ you can see the ruins of Castell de Santueri, a 14th-century castle on the site of an Arab fortress some 4km (2.5 miles) to the south; you can walk to the castle from here.

➕ 227 J7 ✉ Puig de Sant Salvador, 5km (3 miles) southeast of Felanitx ☎ 971 827282 🖥

SINEU

With a royal heritage dating back to the 14th century, Sineu is one of Mallorca's oldest towns, yet its buzzy galleries and cafes give it a modern feel. On Wednesdays the only country market at which livestock is sold comes to town. Watch farmers haggling over pigs, chickens and sheep before heading for the *celler* restaurants (▷ 183) to eat *frit de porcella* (fried suckling pig). Notice the winged lion of St. Mark, Sineu's patron saint, at the top of the steps of the church of Santa Maria. The old railway station houses the S'Estació art gallery (Mon–Fri 9.30–2.30, 4–7).

➕ 224 G5 🚆 From Palma and Inca ❓ Market Wed

Below *Sineu's colourful market is one of the best on the island*

INFORMATION
⊞ 224 H5 From Palma From Palma and Inca Market Wed

TIPS

>> Follow the signs in the town centre to Es Celler (▷ 181–182), an excellent cellar restaurant.

>> Signs also point the way to Bodegues Miquel Oliver, Carrer Font 26 (☎ 971 561117, Sep–end Jun Mon–Fri 10–1.45, 3.30–6; Jul, Aug Mon–Fri 10–3), which sells good local wines.

PETRA

Apart from a few modern cafes on the shady main square, Petra is much the same sleepy little village in which Junípero Serra (▷ 31) grew up in the 18th century. A statue of Serra, one of the greatest Mallorcans of all times, stands on Plaça Junípero Serra and a plaque on the parish church pays tribute to this 'explorer, missionary, hero, civilizer born in the light of Spain'.

THE HOUSE AND MUSEUM

Junípero Serra was born in 1713 in a small house on Carrer Barracar Alt 6. To visit the house and the neighbouring museum (tel 971 561028 or 971 561149), go to the caretaker's house around the corner at Carrer Barracar Baix 2. He will let you in and ask for a small donation. The house, with its arched doorway and whitewashed walls, is a typical 18th-century rural home. In 1932 it was bought by the Rotary Club of Mallorca and given to the city of San Francisco, who returned it to Petra in 1981.

THE CONVENT

A street of baked-earth houses, clad with bougainvillea, runs from the museum to the San Bernardino convent, where Serra went to school. Along here majolica panels depict the missions founded by Serra, including San Diego and San Francisco. Ring the bell to be let into the convent (tel 971 561267, daily 10–12.30, 4–5.30). Here, a series of tableaux tells Serra's life story—working on the farm in Petra, preaching at Ermita de Bonany, his first mission at San Diego and his first baptism of a Native American, whom he named Bernardino after this convent.

ERMITA DE BONANY

Serra preached his last sermon in Mallorca at this hilltop hermitage some 4km (2.5 miles) from Petra, reached by a snaking lane. It takes its name from the *bon any* (good year) of 1609, when the villagers made a pilgrimage here during a drought: their desperate prayers were answered by rain. The sunset views from the terrace are magical. Stay the night in one of the basic cells (▷ 213).
⊞ 224 H6

Below *Junípero Serra's family home—his parents were farmers*

SANTUARI DE CURA

Puig de Randa rises 540m (1,771ft) out of the plain above the pretty village of Randa. The table mountain has been a place of pilgrimage ever since Ramón Llull (▷ 29) founded Mallorca's first hermitage on the summit in 1275, following the Catalan's conversion from a dissolute, agnostic life to devout Catholicism. On the lower slopes of the mountain are two other sanctuaries, Nostra Senyora de Gràcia (clinging precariously to the cliff face) and the Ermita de Sant Honorat, which has been aesthetically restored. Beyond here you can't miss the dramatic modern contrast of the giant ball of communications centre, which means that you are nearing the top of the 5km (3-mile) ascent.

INSIDE THE SANCTUARY

Passing through a 17th-century doorway, you enter the Santuari de Cura, on the site of Llull's original hermitage. Nothing remains from that time and most of the monastery was rebuilt in the 20th century after the arrival of Franciscan monks, who have been living here since 1913. The chapel on the right dates mostly from the 17th century; a crib is kept here throughout the year, according to Franciscan tradition, and there is a small statue of the Virgin carved out of Santanyí stone.

The Sala Gramàtica (Mon–Sat 10–1, 4–6, Sun 4–6), the former grammar school hall, is one of the oldest parts of the complex. It now houses a museum devoted to Ramón Llull, with copies of his manuscripts and various religious paintings. Outside there are peaceful gardens but most people head straight for the belvederes, which offer some of the best views in Mallorca. To the west you can see Palma and occasionally Ibiza beyond; to the south there are views of Cabrera (▷ 161). From the viewpoint behind the monastery you can see almost the whole island, from the Serra de Tramuntana, Cap de Formentor and the Bay of Pollença to the hills around Artà in the east. Look carefully and you can spy various towns and villages, such as Inca and Petra.

INFORMATION

www.santuaridecura.org
⊕ 224 G6 ✉ Puig de Randa, 9km
(6 miles) south of Algaida ☎ 971
660994 ⊙ Daily 10.30–1.30, 2.30–6
✋ Free ❓ Mass Sat 7.30pm, Sun noon
🍴 Closed Mon 🖥 Closed Mon 📅

Above *Santuari de Cura, site of Mallorca's first hermitage, founded by Ramón Llull*

ACROSS THE PLAIN

Experience a completely different side to Mallorca on a drive across Es Pla, the agricultural heartland of the island with timeless villages and solid rural towns.

THE DRIVE

Distance: 99km (61 miles)
Time: At least 2 hours
Start/end at: Algaida

HOW TO GET THERE

Take the Ma-15 from Palma, heading east

★For many people, the soul of Mallorca is to be found on the fertile plain known as Es Pla, an area of almond and apricot groves, sleepy villages and busy market towns. The population has declined, but many rural traditions live on. Farming has always been important here; as you drive across the plain you will see evidence of the area's agricultural history in the form of abandoned windmills, waterwheels and wells.

Begin in Algaida on the Ma-15, the main road from Palma to Manacor, heading east from the Ca'n Gordiola glass factory (▷ 161). Very shortly you will see another mock castle, this one housing the Alorda factory

shop, which produces leather goods. Turn left here and follow the road to Santa Eugènia, with views of the peaks of Alaró in the distance. After 6km (4 miles) you reach the Palma to Sineu road.

❶ A short detour left along this road leads to Natura Parc, where you can follow a walking trail to see farm animals and Mallorcan wildlife.

Turn left to stay on the main route and in 100m (110 yards) turn right, following signs to Santa Eugènia.

❷ Santa Eugènia huddles beneath Puig de Santa Eugènia on the left and the windmills of Es Putxet on the right. An easy path leads up from the church square to a stone cross at the summit of Es Puig (246m/807ft). Despite its modest height, there are great views from the peak stretching across the low plain to the Serra de Tramuntana. Santa Eugènia contains the only Jewish cemetery in Mallorca.

Pass through the centre of the village and continue in the direction of the serra. After around 3km (2 miles) turn right towards Sencelles. The road travels through vineyards and passes the pretty hamlet of Biniali.

❸ Sencelles is a typical country village set in farmland growing vines, almonds and figs. It is known for its *xeremies*, a Mallorcan version of bagpipes that used to be played to summon farmers home from the fields.

Follow the signs for the centre of the village. When you reach the main square turn right beside the town hall and the parish church of Sant Pere. Turn right again on the outskirts of the village (signposted Costitx). Note the stone crucifix at the junction of the Costitx road. This is one of several built in the 18th century to define village limits. Stay on this road for 4km (2.5 miles) to reach Costitx (▷ 166).

❹ Costitx is a good place for a break, with cafes around the two main squares. The Casal de Cultura, just off the main street, contains the Museu de Ciències Naturals, a small natural history museum. The walk on pages 172–73 starts from near here.

Keep straight ahead through the village. On reaching a junction turn right onto the main road to Sineu (▷ 167).

To visit Sineu, an old-fashioned market town with a strong sense of identity, turn right at the first signpost for it, passing the cemetery on your way to the town centre. Leave by following signs to Manacor. This will bring you back to the main road at Molí d'en Pau, an old windmill converted into a restaurant. If you do not wish to visit Sineu, stay on the main road and keep straight ahead at the roundabout by the windmill. Turn right at the next roundabout, signposted to Petra **❺** (▷ 168). When you see the village ahead of you, turn right to arrive near the church. You can park here to look around the village.

Continue around the church and follow signs for Felanitx through the centre of the village. On your way out of Petra, you pass the road up to Ermita de Bonany (▷ 168). Turn right at the next junction towards Felanitx. When you reach the Ma-15 Palma to Manacor road keep straight ahead at the roundabout. The rural road is lined with fields of fruit trees, with views of the Santuari de Sant Salvador (▷ 167) on a hill in front of you. Turn left at a junction, still following signs for Felanitx (▷ 166). Just before you reach the town take a sharp right turn (signposted Porreres) and continue for 12km (7 miles) across open fields to arrive in the centre of Porreres.

❻ Porreres is notable for its 17th-century church, known as 'the cathedral of the plain' due to its size. The street leading from the church to the main square is named after

Bishop Campins, a former Porreres priest who became bishop of Palma and was responsible for Antoni Gaudí's work on Palma Cathedral (▷ 72).

Leave Porreres following signs for Llucmajor. At the first roundabout keep straight ahead. A left turn leads to the Santuari de Monti-Sion, an attractive 15th-century oratory with a five-sided cloister. Villagers still make the pilgrimage up here once a year for a communal picnic on the Sunday after Easter. Follow this road for 12km (7 miles) through open countryside, which gives way to pine woods.

On reaching Llucmajor, turn left towards Palma to drive around the ring road. At the far end of town turn right to Algaida on a section of dual carriageway. At the next roundabout turn left. Stay on this road as it undulates around Puig de Randa (▷ 169) before returning to Algaida.

PLACES TO VISIT
NATURA PARC
✉ Carretera de Sineu, Santa Eugènia ☎ 971 144078 🕑 Daily 10–5 🎫 Adult €9, child (3–12) €6

MUSEU DE CIÈNCIES NATURALS
www.museuciencies.com
✉ Casal de Cultura, Costitx ☎ 971 876070 🕑 Tue–Fri 9–1.30; also 2nd and 4th Sat and Sun of each month; closed Aug 🎫 Adult €3, child (under 6) free

WHERE TO EAT
Many restaurants on this route specialize in Mallorcan cuisine, including Molí d'en Pau (tel 971 855116; closed Mon) at Sineu and Sa Plaça (▷ 182) in Petra. Centro (tel 971 168372; closed Sat lunch, Sun evening), in Porreres, serves lunches, or wait until the end and eat at Algaida's Cal Dimoni (▷ 180).

Opposite *The vineyards around the village of Sencelles, which is renowned for its vines, almonds, figs and bagpipes*

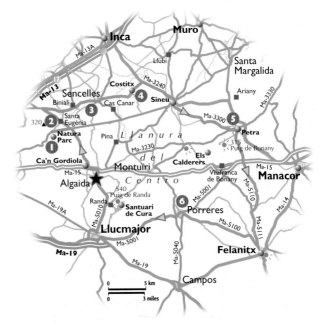

COSTITX—THE HEART OF MALLORCA

Take an easy walk on paved roads through the wide, open countryside around Costitx, with panoramic views of the mountains across the plain.

THE WALK

Distance: 6km (4 miles)
Time: 1.5–2 hours
Start/end at: Plaça des Jardí, Costitx
(✚ 224 G5)
Parking: Plaça de la Mare de Déu, Costitx

HOW TO GET THERE

Costitx is close to Sencelles

★Costitx (▷ 166) is one of those places that has managed to survive the huge changes that Mallorca has undergone over the past 50 years. It is set almost exactly in the centre of the island, on a quiet road between Sineu and Sencelles. This area is overlooked by the majority of visitors. Fields of almond trees and cereal crops surround cream-coloured cottages, and a bakery and a cluster of cafes are set around two neighbouring squares at the heart of the village. In prehistoric times Costitx was a significant centre of population, as evidenced by the remains of the Talaiotic culture

discovered here (▷ 27). Following the Catalan conquest of Mallorca, it became part of Sencelles, only gaining its independence in 1855. After a long period of decline Costitx is starting to recover; the population now stands at around 1,000 and a cultural centre contains a museum, library and swimming pool. The astronomical observatory, opened in 1991, draws visitors and school children from across the island.

The walk starts in Plaça des Jardí, outside the parish church.

This was one of the first churches in Mallorca to be dedicated to the Virgin Mary. It was begun in 1696, though there were earlier churches on this site. The otherwise plain facade has a rose window and a statue of the Virgin in a niche above the door.

Leave the church behind you and carry on walking straight ahead

along Carrer Major, the main street in Costitx.

After around 300m (330 yards), on your left you will pass S'Aljub, the village cistern. Originally built to provide drinking water for livestock, the granite and stone construction is a good example of Mallorcan rural architecture.

Continue to the end of this street on the way out of the village towards Sencelles.

A turn-off to the left leads to the Casal de Cultura, home to the natural history museum. To the right down a lane you will see an old windmill with an inscription above the doorway dated 1718. Also on the right, at a road junction, is a small shrine to Our Lady of Costitx, built in 1913. According to tradition, soon after the Catalan invasion of Mallorca a group of boys discovered a statue of the Virgin on this spot. Each year, on the Sunday after Easter, the Virgin is carried in procession from the church to the shrine and back.

Leave the village and continue along the road to Sencelles. Most of this walk is along quiet country lanes, though there may be some traffic on this first section. After 600m (660 yards) take the left fork onto the small lane Camí des Horts (signposted Planetarium/Observatori).

The road to your left leads up to the observatory, which can be visited by prior arrangement (▷ 177).

Pass the observatory road and continue for 1.6km (1 mile) past a well until you reach a large house with a swimming pool in the garden. Turn left onto the surfaced road directly opposite this house. Stay on this road across open fields with good views of Puig de Randa ahead. When you reach a crossroads, turn left along a rough track. This soon deteriorates further but remains wide enough for vehicles. Turn left at a T-junction onto a shady lane, which shortly becomes a paved road.

The road passes through the hamlet of Can Quiam, home to two of the most important *possessiós* (agricultural estates) in Costitx.

Stay on this road past orchards and citrus groves until you reach the access road to the observatory. Turn left here and right at the end of the road to climb the hill back into Costitx.

Alternatively, if you want to visit the estate of Son Corró, take the road out of Costitx to Sencelles and look for a sign to your right after about 1.5km (1 mile). Of the original horseshoe-shaped building, all that remains are six stone columns and some sections of wall.

The estate of Son Corró was the site of an important archaeological excavation in 1894 when a sanctuary from the post-Talaiotic era was discovered here. Among the finds were three bronze bulls' heads, together with their horns, probably dating from around the second century BC. These were especially interesting because they seemed to confirm the existence of bull worship in prehistoric Mallorca. The owner of the land put the bulls' heads up for sale, and they were bought by the National Archaeological Museum in Madrid, where they are now on display. Following a recent excavation, further bronze figures of a warrior and a Roman household god were discovered, suggesting that the sanctuary was still in use in Roman times. These are now on display at the Museu de Mallorca (▷ 64) in Palma.

PLACE TO VISIT
MUSEU DE CIÈNCIES NATURALS
www.museuciencies.com

✉ Casal de Cultura, Costitx ☎ 971 876070 🕒 Tue–Fri 9–1.30; also 2nd and 4th Sat and Sun of each month; closed Aug 💶 Adult €3, child (under 6) free

WHERE TO EAT
Bar Central (tel 971 513003), in Plaça des Jardí opposite the church, sells sandwiches and offers a lunchtime *menú del día* (closed Sun). There are other bars nearby, plus the Ca'n Font restaurant inside the Casal de Cultura.

Opposite *The countryside of Es Pla (The Plain) which surrounds Costitx*
Below *Exterior of the parish church of Costitx, dedicated to the Virgin Mary*

LLUCMAJOR TO CAP BLANC

This officially designated bicycle route follows largely flat and little-used country lanes through orchards, taking in the breezy headland of Cap Blanc.

THE BICYCLE RIDE

Distance: 45km (28 miles)
Time: 3–4 hours
Start/end at: junction of Camí de S'Aguila and the ring road (PM-602) to the south of Llucmajor

HOW TO GET THERE

Take the Ma-19 from Palma. From the roundabout at the western entrance to Llucmajor, follow signs to Santanyí. Camí de S'Aguila is the third road on the right

★ The bicycle route is signposted 'Ruta Cicloturistica de Llucmajor Camí des Cap Blanc'.
Also look for the signpost to the police station, which is at the start point.

From the police station cycle south, away from Llucmajor. Follow the road for 1km (0.6 miles), until it forks. Take the right lane, signposted Camí de S'Aguila. Continue on this road as it winds through meadows and almond tree orchards. You'll soon start passing kilometre

markers for the Camí de S'Aguila; the smoothly paved road will narrow after the 4km (2.5-mile) marker, but it should still be very quiet.

Continue along the Camí de S'Aguila, ignoring the right-hand turning for Camí de Sa Caseta after the 8km (5-mile) mark. The road, signposted Cap Blanc, bears left, with a wall on the left side and a fence on the right. It gets twistier. You'll arrive at a junction: the road bears left but take the right-hand turn (straight on), signposted Camí de Betlem.

Taking the left-hand lane brings you to restaurant Cas Busso, where you can refuel with a snack and a cold drink. You can then retrace your path back to the junction and continue to Betlem. At the next junction turn right towards Cap Blanc. On your immediate left is Capocorb Vell (▷ 163).

❶ The village of Capocorb Vell, the most important Talaiotic site in Mallorca, was inhabited until

the arrival of the Romans. All that remains now are five defensive structures (*talaiots*) made from stone, and 28 dwellings along a prehistoric street, but look out for more megaliths in the surrounding fields and orchards.

Follow the Carretera Militar (military road) to the right (not to Cala Pi).

As you reach the coast, there's a left turn and a short ride to the lighthouse on the rocky headland of Cap Blanc ❷ for views towards the island of Cabrera (▷ 161).

If you don't make a detour to the lighthouse, your first view of the sea will be as you round the right-hand bend, passing through a scrubby, wind-blasted landscape.

This main road heading north is straight so traffic will be travelling quickly, but it's wide enough for drivers to give bicyclists a safe berth and the surface is very good. The road also starts to undulate for long but gradual inclines and downhill stretches. As you reach the built-up area of Badia Gran, take a small road on the right signposted to Llucmajor and Sa Torre.

❸ You'll be able to see the church tower of Sa Torre for some time before you reach it. Sa Torre's second landmark is a derelict watchtower.

After passing Sa Torre, and the watchtower on your left, take a sharp right turn at the corner. You're now on the Camí de Sa Caseta and the road is once more narrow, well-paved and little-used by vehicles. After 3km (2 miles) you'll come to the junction with Camí de S'Aguila that you reached earlier. Turn left to retrace your tyre tracks back to Llucmajor.

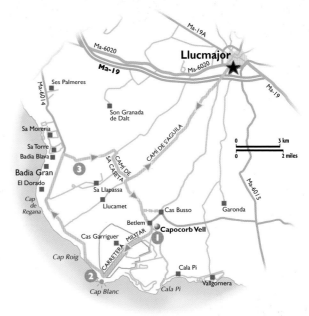

TIPS
>> Bicycling in summer's hottest temperatures can be a foolhardy enterprise. The best seasons for bicycling are spring and autumn; even then it is essential to avoid dehydration by drinking water regularly.
>> Keen cyclists should bring their own pedals and shoes because it is possible to hire high-performance racing bikes on the island.
>> Wearing a helmet is not required by law but is highly recommended; they can be hired easily.

OTHER BICYCLE RIDES
>> The terrific Bunyola–Orient–Alaró–Santa Maria del Camí–Bunyola circuit is very popular with fit cyclists; a section of it is covered in the Eastern Tramuntana drive (▷ 116–117). There's some shade, the hills are moderate by the vertiginous standards of the Serra de Tramuntana, and the roads are dominated by bicyclists rather than drivers, who should stick to the 40kmh (25mph) speed limit. There are plenty of places to eat in villages on the route.
>> Another beautiful, undulating route is Alaró–Lloseta–Selva–

Campanet but you'll need to arrange a lift back to the start before setting out if you don't want to make the return journey.
>> For experienced bicyclists, one of the most rewarding rides is the Pollença–Lluc–Selva–Campanet–Pollença circuit. Turn left at Lluc for a hair-raising run downhill to Selva where you take another left for Campanet and then make your way back to Pollença via the quiet lane (beyond the Coves de Campanet) that links the north side of Campanet to the Ma-2200 road to Pollença.

WHERE TO EAT
You can refuel at Cas Busso (Carretera Cabo Blanco 24, Llucmajor; tel 971 123002; closed Tue), a popular roadside cafe. There's also a supermarket 200m (220 yards) before the start point for stocking up on snacks and water for the ride.

Right *Cyclists taking a break at Cas Busso in Llucmajor*
Opposite *All along the watchtower: bicyclists passing Sa Torre's lookout post*

ALGAIDA
VIDRIERÍAS GORDIOLA
www.gordiola.com
The gift shop at Ca'n Gordiola
(▷ 199) displays a colourful selection
of the factory's handblown glass,
from ornate bottles with glass
stoppers and blood-red goblets to
plain glass jugs and vases.
✉ Carretera Palma–Manacor, km 19,
07210 Algaida ☎ 971 665046 🕐 Shop
and museum: Mon–Sat 9–7, Sun 9–1.30.
Glassworks: Mon–Sat 9–1.30, 3–6, Sun
9–12

BINISSALEM
JOSÉ L. FERRER
www.vinosferrer.com
José L. Ferrer is one of the
founding fathers of Mallorcan wine
production. His sizeable *bodega*
is impossible to miss, on the right
side of the C-713 as you enter
Binissalem from the south. It's a
worthwhile stop, with a large shop,
knowledgeable staff and guided
tours (tours must be arranged in
advance—minimum of 5 people;
€6). Try the substantial Franja Roja
Crianza.

✉ Carrer Conquistador 103, 07350
Binissalem ☎ 971 511050 🕐 Mon–Fri
11 and 4.30

CALAS DE MALLORCA
CALA MONDRAGÓ BAR-CAFETERÍA
Few undeveloped beaches remain
on the east coast, but beautiful Cala
Mondragó, protected as a nature
reserve, is a definite find. The open-
air beach bar services three white-
sand coves, each surrounded by pine
trees, rocky promontories and calm,
turquoise inlets. Park in the public
car park at the top of the hill.
✉ Cala Mondragó, Santanyí ☎ 971
657457 🕐 Apr–end Oct daily 10–9

CLUB ALBATROS
www.albatroscalafiguera.com
Daily diving trips to some of
the most beautiful diving areas
in Mallorca, departing from the
harbour at 9.30am, with free pick-up
from your hotel if necessary. Also
bubblemaker classes for children
aged 8 to 12 (€30), as well as
Divemaster and Rescue Dive PADI-
approved courses for adults.

✉ Harbour, 07659 Cala Figuera ☎ 608
534745 ✋ Divemaster course from €685

CLUB NÁUTICO PORTOCOLOM
www.cnportocolom.com
Portocolom's sailing school operates
during the summer, with dinghies
available for young sailors. The
marina has 252 berths for yachts,
as well as lifting gear. Fishing
expeditions are run from the club.
✉ Carrer Pescadors 23, 07670 Portocolom
☎ 971 824658 🕐 Apr–end Oct

JUMAICA
This children's zoo, with ponies,
llamas, rabbits and a variety of exotic
birds, has a tropical backdrop of a
banana plantation. There is also a
good restaurant in the grounds.
✉ Carretera Porto Cristo–Portocolom, km
4.5, 07689 S'Espinaganar ☎ 971 833979
🕐 Apr–end Oct daily 9–7; Nov–end Mar
daily 10–4.30 ✋ Adult €7, child (4–12) €4
🍴 🖻

MALLORQUIN BIKES
www.mallorquin-bikes.de
Mountain bikes, racing bikes and
tourers are available from this large

Opposite Portocolom's waterfront

shop in Cala d'Or. Mallorquin Bikes also offers guided bicycling tours of Mallorca for groups (from €35 per person for a four- to five-hour ride), tailored according to ability.

✉ Avinguda Fernando Tarrago 19, 07660 Cala d'Or ☎ 609 237637 🕐 Mon–Sat 9–2, 4–8, Sun 9–2 🚲 Adult from €10 per day, ~~ ~~lmet €1

~~OR~~ GOLF

~~www.~~orgolf.com

~~~~he easier courses in ~~~~, this 18-hole, par-71 opened ~~in 1~~ as a nine-hole course. Most greens are surrounded by pine trees but there are views out to Cala d'Or.

✉ Carretera Cala d'Or–Portocolom, km 7.7, 07669 S'Horta ☎ 971 837001 🚲 Green fee €98 🍴 💻 🏊

COSTITX
OBSERVATORIO ASTRONÓMICO MALLORCA

www.oam.es
www.mallorcaplanetarium.com

Mallorca's principal observatory has nine telescopes and eleven cameras. Although a scientific institution, it offers courses and activities. A planetarium projects remote images from space in real time. Visits are aimed at local schoolchildren but there are general sessions on Monday and Tuesday at 6pm. Book in advance (tel 971 513344, 9.30–1.30).

✉ Camí de l'Observatori, 07144 Costitx ☎ 971 876019 🕐 Mon–Fri 10–12, 4–8 🚲 €10 💻

FELANITX
CERÁMICAS MALLORCA

www.ceramicasmallorca.com

There's a colourful range of Mallorcan pottery at this display room in the industrial side of town. Most collections have been created by local artists and there are often some attractive designs. Expect to spend €10 to €30 for items such as plates, vases, cups and bowls.

✉ Carrer Sant Agustín 50–58, 07200 Felanitx ☎ 971 580201 🕐 Mon–Fri 9–1, 3.30–7.30, Sat 10.30–1

FORN PUNT DOLÇ

This well-known local bakery sells a mouthwatering selection of cakes, including fluffy *empanadas*—their speciality.

✉ Plaça Espanya 5, 07208 Felanitx ☎ 971 580910 🕐 Mon–Fri 9–1, 3.30–7.30, Sat 10.30–1

SON MENUT RIDING SCHOOL

www.sonmenut.com

This smart riding school, in countryside southeast of Felanitx, offers tuition (including Spanish dressage) and guided excursions on horseback from one hour to a full day. Riders can go as far as the coast or explore the surrounding farmland. Guides and instructors are multilingual. There's also tidy accommodation, a restaurant, and tennis courts and a swimming pool for guests.

✉ 3rd Volta 3040, Camí de Son Negre, 07208 Felanitx ☎ 971 582920 🕐 All year 🚲 Group class €16.50 per person, guided trail rides €16.50 per hour or €105 per person for a full day 🅿 Follow signs from the junction on the PM-512 outside Felanitx

INCA
CAMPER FACTORY SHOP

www.camper.com

Camper is perhaps the most famous Mallorcan brand of footwear. The shoes are certainly distinctive (for men's styles think bowling shoes made fashionable; for women, expect anything from chic sandals to knee-high boots) and this factory outlet sells a moderately sized selection from current and previous ranges in most sizes. Prices are keener in Spain than in Camper shops in the rest of Europe.

✉ Polígono Industrial Estate, 07300 Inca ☎ 902 364598 🕐 Mon–Sat 10–8.30

FESTIVAL PARK

www.festivalparks.es

Festival Park is a colossal, modern leisure centre complex. Shops figure significantly, with factory outlets and plenty of clothes shops, but there are also bars, restaurants, cinemas, a bowling alley, a nightclub (cube) and bungee jumping.

✉ Carretera Palma–Inca, km 7, 07141 Marratxí ☎ 971 140925 🕐 Mon–Sat 10–10, Fri–Sun 12–10

MUNPER CREACIONES

www.munper.com

The centre of leather production in Mallorca, Inca has several factory shops selling leather shoes, bags and clothing, including men's leather fashions, but you're no more likely to find a bargain here than in Palma. Munper is one of the easiest shops to find (on the left heading north out of Inca).

✉ Carretera Palma–Alcúdia, km 36, 07300 Inca ☎ 971 881000 🕐 Mon–Fri 9.30–7.30, Sat 9.30–7

LLUCMAJOR
CAN ORDINAS

The traditional Mallorcan bread knife is a vicious-looking, hook-bladed tool. This hardware shop still makes hand-made examples, as well as selling other useful articles.

✉ Carrer S'Avall 128, 07620 Llucmajor ☎ 971 660580 🕐 Mon–Fri 9–1, 4–7, Sat 9–1

MARRIOTT SON ANTEM

There are two 18-hole courses at Marriott's Son Antem golf resort, both of par 72. The East course is better suited to beginners, with wide fairways and fast greens, while the newer West course is more of a challenge, with narrow fairways and elevated greens.

✉ Ma-19, Salida 20, 07620 Llucmajor ☎ 971 129100 🚲 Green fee €72–€84 🍴 💻

MANACOR
HIPÓDROMO MANACOR

Manacor has a small racecourse, where trotting remains the main attraction (see Hipódromo Son Pardo, ▷ 82).

✉ Carretera Palma–Artà, km 50, 07500 Manacor ☎ 971 550023 🕐 Winter, Sat 4pm

MAJORICA

www.majorica.com

Mallorca's largest producer of artificial pearls has a factory shop

in Manacor. An hourly tour doesn't reveal the secret of how the artificial pearls are formed, but does show you jewellery (which you can later buy) being made.

✉ Avinguda Majorica 48, 07500 Manacor ☎ 971 550200 🕐 Mon–Fri 9–6, Sat–Sun 9.30–12.30

OLIV-ART
This warehouse-style shop on the main road out of Manacor sells every olive-wood product imaginable at good prices (bowls €11 to €22, salad servers from €12, smaller items €3 to €5). Kitchen utensils are a good purchase—olive wood is attractive and durable but needs to be washed carefully. There's an outdoor children's play area with life-size, if rather tatty, dinosaurs and bears.

✉ Carretera Palma–Manacor, km 47, 07500 Manacor ☎ 971 847232 🕐 Summer Mon–Fri 9–8, Sat 9–7.30, Sun 9.30–7.30; winter Mon–Fri 9–7, Sat–Sun 9–6.30

PERE SEDA BODEGAS
www.pereseda.com
Although Mallorca's most famous wines come from Binissalem, the central plains, the Pla I Llevant, have their own Denominación de Origen. Pla I Llevant wine production is based at Felanitx and Manacor; Pere Seda is one of the largest producers in the area, cultivating indigenous and foreign grape varieties. You can

buy direct from the *bodega* or place an order via the internet.

✉ Carrer Cid Campeador 22, 07500 Manacor ☎ 971 550219 🕐 Mon–Fri 10–7, Sat 10–2

MONTUÏRI
ORQUIDEA
www.perlasorquidea.com
This large factory shop sells artificial pearls; prices are similar to those of its main competitor, Majorica in Manacor. There's also a brief guided tour.

✉ Carretera Palma–Artà, km 30, Montuïri ☎ 971 644144 🕐 Mon–Fri 10–7, Sat–Sun 9–1

SANTA EUGÈNIA
NATURA PARK
With winged creatures from ugly marabou storks and black vultures to 500 varieties of butterfly, and lots of mammals and reptiles, there is a lot for children to see at Natura Park.

✉ Carretera de Sineu, km 15.5, 07412 Santa Eugènia ☎ 971 144078 🕐 Apr–end Oct daily 10–7; Nov–end Mar 10–6 🍴 🖫

SA RÀPITA
CLUB NÁUTICO SA RÀPITA
www.cnrapita.com
Sa Ràpita's sailing school has Optimist dinghies for children. This stretch of water also offers the island's best windsurfing; equipment and tuition are available in the summer.

✉ Esplanada del Puerto, 07639 Campos ☎ 971 640001 🕐 All year 🖐 Rental equipment from €30

SINEU
S'ESTACIÓ
This German-owned, quality contemporary art gallery showcases local and international artists over three well-lit, airy floors of exhibition space. The top floor has a delightful pitched beam ceiling.

✉ Carrer de S'Estació 2, 07510 Sineu ☎ 971 520750 🕐 Mon–Fri 9.30–1.30, 4–7, Sat 9.30–1

S'INDIC
This cafe-bar is adjacent to the marketplace, Sineu's centre of activity, with bars, cafes and restaurants. It stays open until the last person leaves at night and it's a good place for a coffee after the town's market on Wednesday mornings.

✉ Plaça Es Fossar 12, 07510 Sineu ☎ 971 520191 🕐 9am–late

SA MOLA
If you're in Sineu at a weekend, you might find live music at this dimly lit Irish pub-cafe-disco close to the train station. It's open for long hours and serves Guinness. There are several more bars beside the train station.

✉ Carretera Santa Margalida 1, 07510 Sineu ☎ 971 855273 🕐 Mon 8–3pm, Tue–Thu 8am–midnight, Fri–Sat 8am–6am

FIRA DES FANG
March
The *siurell*-producing town of
Marratxi holds an annual clay craft
festival, with no shortage of the
traditional white, green and red
figurines (▷ 23). Expect lots of
whistling.
✉ Marratxí

SETMANA SANTA (HOLY WEEK)
Easter
▷ 85, Palma

SANT BARTOMEU
24 August
Good versus evil is the theme of
one of Mallorca's most exciting
festivals. Villagers dress up as
women and devils and to the sound
of bagpipes, flutes and drums,
perform a dance which dates back
400 years.
✉ Montuïri

SANT AGUSTÍ
28 August
More make-believe dances, this
time with children dressed as
hobby-horses being chased by
giants (▷ 166 for details).
✉ Felanitx

FESTA DES MELÓ
September
On the last Sunday in September
the residents of this small village
celebrate the end of the harvest
with a melon festival.
✉ Vilafranca de Bonany

FESTA DE VERMAR
September
Wine buffs shouldn't miss this
annual festival of wine in Mallorca's
top wine-producing area. There's
no shortage of wines to taste, and
you won't go hungry either; the
traditional cuisine served during the
festival is goat meat.
✉ Binissalem

FESTA D'ES BOTIFARRÓ
October
Blood sausages are the object
of the celebrations at this quirky
autumnal festival, which revolves
around singing, dancing and
sausage consumption. Festivities
start at midday with the lighting of
bonfires to cook the sausages and
continue late into the evening.
✉ Sant Joan

DIJOUS BO
November
www.dijousbo.es
The last of Inca's annual autumn
fairs, Dijous Bo is the single
largest market in Mallorca, selling
everything from fruit, vegetables
and livestock to leather goods and
even cars. Fairground attractions
keep children entertained and
there are traditional parades, street
concerts and the *corre foc* (dragon-
running).
✉ Inca

Below *Traditional folkloric dancing*

EATING

PRICES AND SYMBOLS

The prices given are the average for a two-course lunch (L) and a three-course dinner (D) for one person, without drinks. The wine price is for the least expensive bottle.

For a key to the symbols, ▷ 2.

ALGAIDA
CAL DIMONI

Located next to Es 4 Vents (see right), this restaurant calls itself 'the house of the devil'. Why? Because it specializes in flame-grilling meat and blood sausages. Prices are keen, with salads costing €5–€6, roast pork or kid €14 and ice cream €4. If you like barbecues, you'll enjoy Cal Dimoni.

✉ Antigua Carretera Manacor–Palma, km 21, 07120 Algaida ☎ 971 665035 ◉ Daily 12–12 ✋ L €20, D €25, Wine €16

CA'N MATEU

Just around the corner from Cal Dimoni, you'll find Ca'n Mateu in a 400-year-old inn. The restaurant serves traditional Mallorcan meals, such as roast suckling pig, and is good value for money. It has a children's play area outside.

✉ Carretera Manacor–Palma, km 21, 07120 Algaida ☎ 971 665036 ◉ Wed–Mon 12.30–4, 7–12 ✋ L €17, D €25, Wine €9.25

ES 4 VENTS

The best of the cluster of restaurants at this crossroads outside Algaida is Es 4 Vents. It specializes in Mallorcan and Spanish cuisine but adds a layer of sophistication to the rustic classics. Starters, such as *frito mallorqin caracoles*, typically cost €11–€12. *Esgarraet* is a large plate of smoked salmon and cod with *pa amb oli*. The strips of salmon and cod, alternating with ribbons of roasted red pepper, are fanned out on a chilled tomato pulp. It's a delicious combination: the fresh, tart tomatoes offsetting the rich, smoky flavour of the fish and the sweet red pepper. Main meals are just as tasty, with dishes such as chicken breasts stuffed with prawns and mushrooms, and roast pork costing a reasonable €11. Fish options include cod with prawns and clam sauce and prawn and avocado salad. As with many Mallorcan restaurants, desserts are not such a priority, but the hazelnut

biscuit ice cream is worth trying. Es 4 Vents is popular with families from Palma and other nearby towns, who dress up in their best clothes for Sunday lunch. Despite the large dining room, it's wise to book ahead at weekends.

✉ Carretera Manacor–Palma, km 21.7, 07120 Algaida ☎ 971 665173 ◉ Daily 12.30–4, 7.30–11. Closed mid-Jun to mid-Jul ✋ L and D €25, Wine €9

CALA FIGUERA
ES PORT

Filled with a predominantly German clientele, the attractive dining room here is decorated with historic black-and-white photos of the Cala (it hasn't changed that much). Expect cheerful, swift service and an extensive menu with plenty of Italian options, including *tagliatelle al funghi y tartufo* (mushrooms and truffles) for €8, *focaccia* with tomatoes, onion and garlic (€8.50) and *calzone verde* with spinach and mushrooms (€8). The sprawling outside terrace is just across from the water.

✉ Carrer de la Verge del Carme s/n, 07650 Cala Figuera ☎ 971 165140 ◉ Mon–Sat 12–3.30, 7.30–11. Closed Nov–end Mar ✋ L €15, D €29, Wine €7

Opposite *Sa Plaça, Petra (see page 182)*

MISTRAL

A more upmarket choice on this energetic strip of restaurants across from the estuary, Mistral is the long-time favourite here for seafood and fish dishes, including stuffed squid, sea bass steamed in white wine and grilled sole. This stylish restaurant, with a few outside tables, is the place to come if you want to push the boat out for your seafood supper. After dinner you can enjoy a stroll up the hill beside the estuary.

✉ Carrer de la Verge del Carme 42, 07650 Cala Figuera ☎ 971 645118 ⊕ Mon–Sat 12–4. 7.30–11. Closed Nov–end Mar ✋ L €24, D €28, Wine €9

CALA D'OR

FERNANDO CAFÉ

Kick back under the white umbrellas at this tempting restaurant overlooking the bay. The menu includes some interesting twists on traditional fare, including tasty salmon, prawn and pineapple kebabs. There is also plenty for other tastes, like pizzas, pastas and seafood dishes.

✉ Plaça Ibiza 31, 07660 Cala d'Or ☎ 971 657011 ⊕ Daily 12–4, 7–11. Closed Nov–end Apr ✋ L and D €18, Wine €8

PORT PETIT

www.portpetit.com

Chef Gérard Deymier has been creating modern Mediterranean dishes at this exclusive restaurant since 1988. His repertoire is based around fresh, seasonal food and typically includes fish dishes such as cod fillet with sautéed fennel, crisp Iberian ham and bouillabaisse. The emphasis is on light and healthy, if slightly unadventurous, cooking. There are no surprises on the dessert menu either, with chocolate profiteroles and apple tart the most substantial options. The restaurant overlooks Cala d'Or's harbour, a well-to-do haven for yachties, which explains the high prices. But you do get to enjoy the views from the open-air terrace while eating.

✉ Avenida Cala Llonga, 07660 Cala d'Or ☎ 971 643039 ⊕ Daily 1–3.30, 7–11. Closed Jan–end Mar ✋ D €40. Two tasting menus at €39.50 and €55, Wine €18

CALONGE

LA CASCINA

This smart Italian restaurant is set in a 200-year-old monastery in the old centre of Calonge. The menu is constantly updated according to what is in season, and features an elegant fusion of classic and contemporary Italian cuisine. Gluten-free and vegetarian dishes are available. There's a pretty garden and terrace.

✉ Carretera Cala Llonga 22, 07669 Calonge ☎ 971 167152 ⊕ Daily 7–11pm. Closed Nov–Feb ✋ D €35, Wine €14

CAMPOS

CA'N CALENT

www.cancalent.com

Two brothers, Miquel and Joan Vicens, run this sleek restaurant, complete with water features, on the outskirts of Campos. The fusion cuisine is fresh and innovative, with unusual dishes such as bass with ginger and mango, or tender oven-roasted lamb with a red berry sauce. The gourmet menu costs €24.80. If you like the artwork, the restaurant features paintings by local artists which are for sale.

✉ Ronda Estació 44, 07630 Campos ☎ 971 651445 ⊕ Tue–Sun 1–4, 8.30–11. Closed Feb ✋ L €25, D €35, Wine €12

SA CANOVA

This friendly, family-run restaurant serves traditional Mallorcan cuisine. Chef Jerónima Pons prepares local specialities such as *tumbet, trampó* (Mallorcan salad), *llomo amb col* and hearty Mallorcan soups; finish up with *greixonera*, a delicious cake made with local soft cheese. Many dishes are prepared with vegetables grown in the family garden. Dine in the rustically decorated dining room—complete with well and traditional farming utensils—or eat out on the pretty terrace in summer. There are several set menus available, which cost from €17 to €25

per person. The wine list features a good range of local wines, with special monthly recommendations.

✉ Avenida Ronda Estació 35, 07630 Campos ☎ 971 650210 ⊕ Tue–Sat 1–4, 8–11, Sun 1–4 ✋ L €17, D €23, Wine €9

CA'N PASTILLA

EL RANCHO PICADERO

Not far from the Playa de Palma, this spacious Mallorquí restaurant specializes in roasted and grilled meats; dishes of the day might include mouthwatering T-bone steak or roast rabbit. Fresh fish and seafood are also available. There is an attractive terrace with a barbecue, and the size of the restaurant means it is a popular venue for larger parties (reserve ahead). They also have a 100-year-old *bodega* offering a large selection of wines.

✉ Ca'n Pastilla, Camino de Ca'n Alegria ☎ 971 261002 ⊕ Daily 1pm–1am ✋ *Menú del día* €10, D €20, Wine €8

MONTUÏRI

PUIG DE SANT MIQUEL

With wonderful views across the Pla, this restaurant is a fixture on the coach-tour circuit. But thanks to a large outdoor terrace there's enough space to accommodate most visitors, who come to sample the roast kid and other Mallorcan specialities. Expect to spend from €5 for a starter and from €12 for the house special, *cabrital al forn* (oven-baked kid). The restaurant can be found next to the hermitage at the top of a hill just off the main Manacor–Algaida road (on the north side).

✉ Carretera de Manacor, km 31, 07230 Montuïri ☎ 971 646314 ⊕ Jul, Aug daily 12–4, 7–11; Sep–Jun Tue–Sat 12–4, 7–11, Sun 12–4 ✋ *Menú del día* €9, D €20. Two tasting menus at €13 and €18.50, Wine €10

PETRA

ES CELLER

This typical *celler* restaurant is a two-minute walk from Plaça Ramón Llull in Petra. Venture beyond the unprepossessing exterior, down a stairway, and you'll enter a large, arched cellar with wooden tables and chairs, a long bar, an open log-fired oven for grilling meat and an olive press. The rustic Mallorcan cuisine is tasty and the prices are invitingly low. Seasonal mains might include stuffed aubergines, chops, roast rabbit or roast kid. Don't miss out on almond cake for dessert for the full gamut of Mallorcan specialities. Local wines are available.

✉ Carrer de l'Hospital 46, 07520 Petra ☎ 971 561056 ⏱ Tue–Sun 12–4, 6–12 ✋ L €12, D €15, Wine €5

SA PLAÇA

Lunch outside—in a secluded but busy square with palm trees and a fountain—is extremely enjoyable here. The house dates back to 1860, when it was built by an affluent local who made his money with sugar cane plantations in Puerto Rico. Today Sa Plaça is a Mallorcan restaurant that has succeeded in bringing sophisticated, inventive dining to the island's sleepy interior, far away from the hotspots of the coast and mountains. The chef is passionate about fresh ingredients and offers modern Mediterranean cuisine a notch above what you would expect for the prices. A €7.50 salad arrives with orange segments, a frothy orange dressing and five fleshy prawns. Mains start from €12.50 and the house speciality, langostinos con chocolate, costs around €17. At €12, the menú del día is excellent value. Sa Plaça is also a small hotel with 3 rooms (▷ 185).

✉ Plaça Ramón Llull 4, 07520 Petra ☎ 971 561646 ⏱ Daily 12–3.30, 7.30–11 ✋ Menú del día €12 (Mon, Wed–Fri), L €20, D €45, Wine €9.61

PINA
ES MOLÍ DE PINA

Some of the places in which you're most likely to find the best Mallorcan cooking are small towns in the island's interior—towns like Pina. Es Molí de Pina is a windmill restaurant, with an excellent

seasonal menu. If you visit in the winter you might catch a dish called escaldums de matances, which is served after a matança—the slaughter and preparation of the family pig, a tradition that continues in rural areas of Mallorca. Escaldums de matances is a rich casserole of chicken, pork meatballs and whole heads of garlic. If you miss out on this seasonal treat, console yourself with the almond cake and home-made almond ice cream.

✉ Carrer Sant Plácid 3, 07210 Pina ☎ 971 125303 ⏱ Wed–Sat 1–4, 8–11 ✋ Menú del día €8 (Wed–Fri), L €17, D €20

PORTOCOLOM
CELLER SA SÍNIA

At this appropriately located fish restaurant the day's fresh seafood is displayed at the door so you can see what catches your eye. The restaurant looks out across the port, although you can't see much from inside. The menu is weighted towards fish dishes such as cod with aïoli or sea bass with fennel, but you'll find a few traditional Mallorcan dishes. Expect to pay about €8 for a starter and €14–€18 for a main course, which is better value than many other restaurants in Portocolom.

✉ Carrer Pescadores, 07670 Portocolom ☎ 971 824323 ⏱ Feb–end Oct Tue–Sun 1.30–3.30, 7.30–10.30; Jul, Aug 8–11. Closed Nov–end Jan ✋ L €22, D €29, Wine €8

COLÓN

www.restaurante-colon.com
This large, smart restaurant is in the middle of a row of restaurants on the seafront at Portocolom, a pretty fishing village on the east coast. There's a roadside terrace overlooking the port and a spacious, low-lit interior. The cuisine is modern Mediterranean with an Austrian twist. Prices are high, with starters costing about €14, fish main courses €23 and dessert another €10.

✉ Carrer Cristobal Colón 7, 07670 Portocolom ☎ 971 824783 ⏱ Thu–Tue 2–3.30, 7–11.30 ✋ L €40, D €45, Wine €17

FLORIAN BAR RESTAURANT

Owned by German brother and sister team Florian and Katharina, this is one of the most attractive places to enjoy a drink or light meal in this laid-back resort. The wood-coffered ceiling, bench seating and gentle jazz music in the background make this a popular spot with hikers seeking a little sustenance and down-time in informal surroundings. There is a daily menu (€15) with typical dishes, including tomato and mozzarella salad and escalope with chips, as well as a long list of tasty innovative tapas, including vegetable spring rolls (€4.50) and date kebabs with bacon (€5). The shady outside terrace has superb views of the bay and boats. The restaurant also provides a backdrop for new Mallorcan artists with regular exhibitions.

✉ Carrer Cristobal Colón 11, 07670 Portocolom ☎ 971 824171 ⏱ Tue–Sun 1.30–4, 7–11. Closed Nov ✋ L €15, D €20, Wine €7

RANDA
ES RECÓ DE RANDA

www.esrecoderanda.com
Randa is a small, quiet village about 10km (6 miles) north of Llucmajor. It's dominated by the Puig de Randa, a hill which has three sanctuaries around it. The restaurant inside the hotel Es Recó de Randa produces highly regarded Mallorcan and Spanish cooking, with cod and pork featuring prominently. There are views from the restaurant over the Pla and a secluded terrace in the garden.

✉ Carrer Fuente 21, 07629 Randa ☎ 971 660997 ⏱ Daily 12.30–4.30, 7.30–11.30 ✋ Menú del día €24, D €30, Wine €12

SENCELLES
SA CUINA DE N'AINA

This restaurant offers good Mallorcan cuisine in a pleasant rural environment. Chef Aina Carbonell, a winner of the Mallorquin Cookery Competition (for turkey with almonds), produces traditional, meaty favourites such as roast suckling pig (€16.10) and lamb (€19.75) from the wood-burning oven. If weather permits, head for the outside terrace, shaded by palms, ferns and a dazzle of bougainvillaea.

✉ Carrer Rafel 31, 07140 Sencelles ☎ 971 872992 🕐 Wed–Mon 12.30–3.30, 8–11 🍴 Menú del día €22, D from €25, Wine from €12

SA PARRILLA

This Argentinean-style steak house has a large wood-burning oven and a warm inviting atmosphere, with ochre walls, terracotta tiles and dark wood furniture. The menu includes the predictable Argentinean steaks (€12.60), pollo a la brasa (€7.80) and, for a lightweight dessert, paper-thin crêpes with a variety of fillings.

✉ Carrer Rafel 1, 07140 Sencelles ☎ 971 874423 🕐 Tue–Sun 12.30–3.30, 8–11 🍴 L €18, D €24, Wine €7.50

SINEU
HOTEL CELLER DE CA'N FONT
www.canfont.com

On the main square in Sineu, Ca'n Font is a celler restaurant—with huge wine barrels lining the walls and an arched ceiling to prove it. The food served is traditional Mallorcan, with frit mallorquín costing €7, calamar a la plancha (grilled squid) €12.50 and gambas a la plancha (grilled prawns) €10. The restaurant is very busy on market day (Wednesday), when you need to be assertive to get served. There are also seven comfortable hotel rooms.

✉ Sa Plaça 18, 07510 Sineu ☎ 971 520313 🕐 Daily 11.30–4, 7.30–11 🍴 L and D €15, Wine €6 🛏 7 (double from €45)

MOLÍ D'EN PAU

Although it's not the only restaurant housed inside a converted windmill, it certainly makes Molí d'en Pau, just outside Sineu on the Llubi road, easier to find. The menu is dominated by traditional Mallorcan favourites, such as llom de porc (loin of pork) and calamar a la plancha (grilled squid), but you'll also find more unusual dishes, such as sautéed calves' brains. The food is excellent value, with a filling arròs brut the cheapest option. If the dark interior is a bit overwhelming (windmills were designed without many windows), you can sit outside on the terrace, which is set back from the main road and has thatched parasols, wooden tables, a well and an aviary.

✉ Carretera Santa Margalida 25, 07510 Sineu ☎ 971 855116 🕐 Tue–Sun 1–3.30, 7.30–10.30 🍴 L €18, D €20, Wine €9

Below Es Recó de Randa's sunny terrace for al-fresco dining

PRICES AND SYMBOLS

Prices are the lowest and highest for a double room for one night. Breakfast is included unless noted otherwise. All the hotels listed accept credit cards unless otherwise stated. Note that rates vary widely throughout the year.

For a key to the symbols, ▷ 2.

ALGAIDA
POSSESSIÓ BINICOMPRAT

www.fincabinicomprat.com
An ancient stone *finca*, which has remained in the same family for six centuries, has been transformed into a tranquil country hotel surrounded with vines and fragrant pine woods. Choose from a room or suite in the main building, or self-contained apartments in the grounds. All are elegantly furnished with pale fabrics and original details.
✉ Finca Binicomprat s/n, Algaida ☎ 971 125028 🕐 Feb–end Dec 💶 Double €130 all year, apartment €245 all year ⓘ 8 🏊 🚗 Take the Manacor road from Palma, and follow signs for Algaida after 20km (12 miles)

RAÏMS

www.finca-raims.com
This 17th-century manor house with its own private chapel is situated on the edge of the village, so it feels like both a town house in the country and a country house in the town. There is one room in the house plus four apartments in the various outbuildings, each with its own terrace. The owner of the house is a winemaker; Raïms means 'grapes' and each of the apartments is named after a different grape variety. The cellar, one of the oldest in Mallorca, is always open for guests to help themselves to wine. The apartments give onto the garden, a shady retreat with palm and orange trees and a swimming pool. Dinner is served once a week, and there are three excellent restaurants within walking distance. The minimum stay is three nights.
✉ Carrer Ribera 24, 07120 Algaida ☎ 971 665157 🕐 Feb–end Nov 💶 Double €133–€139, apartment €149 all year ⓘ 5 🏊 🚗

BINISSALEM
SCOTT'S

www.scottshotel.com
No room service, no reception—just an ambition to be 'the best, most elegant, most comfortable not-quite-a-hotel in the Mediterranean'. Scott's is co-owned by American crime writer George Scott and the place reflects his personality. Huge handmade beds, cotton percale sheets, goosedown pillows, country-house furnishings and a breakfast buffet served until noon make this a popular romantic getaway and a bolthole for celebrities in need of rest. There is a small indoor pool, a help-yourself bar, WiFi and a sunny terrace with views of the church. Scott's Café and Grill Salamandra has opened just up the street. No children under 12.
✉ Plaça de l'Església 12, 07350 Binissalem ☎ 971 870100 🕐 All year 💶 €175–€205 ⓘ 2 singles, 10 doubles and 6 suites 🏊 🚗

CALA D'OR
HOTEL CALA D'OR

www.hotelcalador.com
The Cala d'Or, which dates from 1932, is surrounded by pine trees and overlooks the bay of Cala d'Or; rooms on the eastern side of the hotel get a splendid sea view. Cala d'Or, the resort, is close to several pretty coves and sandy beaches, and a trip to the nature reserve at nearby Cala Mondragó (▷ 162) is recommended. Bedrooms have telephone, television and central heating. The hotel's facilities include an outdoor swimming pool and

a children's play area. There is a minimum stay requirement of two, four or seven nights depending on the season. WiFi available.

✉ Avinguda de Bélgica 33, 07660 Cala d'Or ☎ 971 657249 🕙 Apr–end Oct ✋ €110–€180 🛏 95 🔣 ≋

CAMPOS
SANT BLAI
www.santblai.com

The special feature of this large, family-friendly *agroturismo* in the southeast of the island is its small astronomical observatory with both a refracting and a reflecting telescope, so that guests can marvel at the starry skies in this quiet region. But that's not its only advantage: there's a swimming pool, self-service bar, barbecue and activities such as pony riding, which can be arranged at a stables nearby. And it's not far from the beach at Es Trenc (▷ 166). The three bedrooms and three cottages are decorated with wooden furniture and have telephone, television, central heating and WiFi. They used to be the farm's cowshed, timber shed, stable, barn and granary.

✉ Carretera Campos–Colònia Sant Jordi, km 2, 07630 Campos ☎ 971 650567 🕙 All year ✋ Double €130 all year, cottage €170 all year 🛏 3 🔣 ≋

CAS CONCOS
SA GALERA
www.hotelsagalera.com

A short drive from Cas Concos, Sa Galera offers guests complete rural seclusion. The converted 13th-century manor house has spacious rooms, each individually decorated in neutral linens. Watch out for the low doorways. Each bedroom has telephone, television and central heating. Outside there is an attractive patio, and, farther away from the main house, a large swimming pool with sunbeds. There are bicycles for hire, and some beautiful lanes leading out of Cas Concos to explore. Some of Mallorca's best-known beaches,

including Cala Mondragó (▷ 162) and Es Trenc (▷ 166), are nearby. There are good restaurants at Portocolom (▷ 182), 16km (10 miles) away—although Sa Galera does offer an à la carte menu in its restaurant, S'Espigó, in the evenings. WiFi available.

✉ Carretera Santanyí–Cas Concos, 07208 Cas Concos ☎ 971 842079 🕙 Jan to mid-Nov ✋ €128–€160 🛏 20 🔣 ≋

LLUCMAJOR
MARRIOTT'S SON ANTEM GOLF RESORT AND SPA
www.marriott.com/pmigs

Golfers can double their enjoyment at Son Antem; the resort has two top-class 18-hole, 72-par golf courses, both designed by Francisco López Segales. Beginners will prefer the East course, while the West course is championship standard. The resort itself is what you'd expect from the international chain: a very high level of comfort and service but a little short on character. The food, too, is decidely average. Bedroom facilities include a work desk and WiFi. For non-golfers, there are two swimming pools, a spa and health club and tennis courts. A vast range of excursions and activities, from water-skiing to day trips to Valldemossa, can be arranged, and there is a playground for younger guests.

✉ Marriott Son Antem Golf Resort and Spa ✉ Carretera Llucmajor, km 3.4, 07620 Llucmajor ☎ 971 129100 🕙 All year ✋ €160–€200 🛏 150 🔣 ≋ ▽

MANACOR
SON AMOIXA VELL
www.sonamoixa.com

Lying between Porto Cristo and Manacor, this grand 16th-century country house hotel is conveniently located for the east coast's two main attractions: caves and beaches. Bedrooms are fitted with modern comforts and are centrally heated. The dining room is relatively formal, but cosy, and there is also a bar, lounge and library. Tennis courts, a gym, sauna and a beauty salon are also available.

✉ Carretera Cales de Mallorca–Manacor, km 3.4, 07500 Manacor ☎ 971 846292 🕙 All year ✋ Double €198 all year, suite €320 all year 🛏 14 doubles and 1 suite 🔣 ≋

PETRA
SA PLAÇA
www.saplacapetra.com

Staying at this tiny hotel in Petra's main square is a bit of a treat. Not only are the rooms comfortably furnished, but the restaurant downstairs (▷ 182) is a cut above the average hotel restaurant. The three bedrooms are large, with antiques, oriental rugs, interesting artwork and exquisite hand-embroidered linen. They all have terraces. Petra isn't the sort of place you'd remain in for long—it's a pleasant village but there's little to do—but Sa Plaça is the perfect base for a visit to Fray Junípero Serra's birthplace and the hilltop hermitage, Ermita de Bonany (▷ 168), where he preached his final sermon in Mallorca before leaving for the Americas.

✉ Plaça Ramón Llull 4, 07520 Petra ☎ 971 561646 🕙 Dec–end Oct ✋ €109 all year 🛏 3 🔣

SON TORRAT
www.lavila.org/playamonte

Located 3km (2 miles) from Petra, this 15th-century farmhouse has been aesthetically restored and offers six comfortable apartments with all the necessary facilities, including private terraces. The setting is sublime, surrounded by orchards of almond and carob trees, backed by pine forests. There is a pool and jacuzzi, the latter situated atmospherically in a cave, as well as barbecue facilities.

✉ Cami de Bonany, km 2, 07520 Petra ☎ 630 017858 🕙 All year ✋ €90–€115 🛏 6 apartments

PORRERES
SA BASSA ROTJA
www.sabassarotja.com

One of the more opulent country-manor conversions on Mallorca, Sa Bassa Rotja boasts two swimming

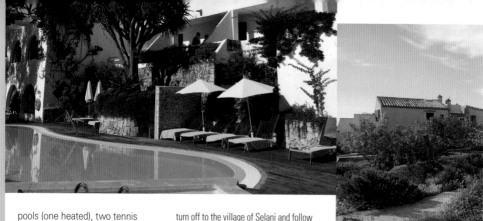

pools (one heated), two tennis courts, a gym, an Ayurvedic health spa and a children's play area. The owners have retained the rustic character of the 13th-century mansion, but bedrooms are richly furnished and there is even a pillow menu, to fine-tune nocturnal comfort. One suite has been specially designed for disabled guests. The hotel is west of Felanitx and about 19km (12 miles) from the closest beach.

✉ Finca Son Orell–Camino Sa Pedrera, 07260 Porreres ☎ 971 168225 🕐 All year 🍽 €140–€165 🛏 25 🔌 🏊 📺

PORTO CRISTO AND ENVIRONS

SA VALL

www.savalldesonmacia.com

Just 15 minutes by car from the beach and 10km (6 miles) inland from the family-friendly resort of Porto Cristo and its nearby caves (▷ 164–165), this charming *agroturismo* lies in an expanse of almond groves. The beautifully restored 16th-century farmhouse has three apartments and two double rooms. Both apartments and rooms have a terrace, television, minibar and central heating, and are furnished with antique Mallorcan furniture. The rural location makes Sa Vall a good choice for hikers and bicyclists.

✉ Sa Vall 205, Son Macià de Manacor, 07509 Son Macià ☎ 971 554279 🕐 All year 🍽 Double €80–€90, apartment €130–€145 🛏 1 apartment (4 people), 2 apartments (2 people), 2 doubles 🏊 🚍 From the Palma–Manacor road

turn off to the village of Selani and follow signs to Sa Vall

SON MAS

www.sonmas.com

Close to the Coves del Drac (▷ 164–165) and the beaches of the east coast, Son Mas is a luxurious country hotel. Two swimming pools (one heated), a sauna and a jacuzzi have been added to the renovated 17th-century property. All the bedrooms are spacious, with a terrace or a balcony, a living area and antique furniture, as well as telephone, television and internet connection. The hotel's setting, in extensive grounds, is superb; bicycles are provided so guests can explore the orchards or bicycle to the beach 4km (2.5 miles) away. Breakfast is buffet-style, and Mediterranean cuisine (prepared with the hotel's own produce where possible) is served at dinner. WiFi available.

✉ Carretera Porto Cristo–Porto Colom, 07680 Porto Cristo ☎ 971 558755 🕐 Feb–end Nov 🍽 €244–€286 🛏 16 🔌 🏊

SES SALINES

SA CARROTJA

www.sacarrotja.com

The friendly Mallorcan family that runs this small 17th-century farmhouse hotel has furnished its bedrooms with antique furniture as well as the modern features you'd expect to find: telephone, television and fridge. Five of the six rooms have their own terraces and there are two more communal terraces.

Above *Sa Carrotja, Ses Salines*
Above left *Hotel Cala d'Or (see page 184)*

The open-air swimming pool is heated and organic vegetables from the garden are served in the restaurant. Bicycles are available for guests' use, and there is plenty of countryside to explore. The hotel is not suitable for children under 15 years.

✉ Cami de Carrotja 7, 07640 Ses Salines ☎ 971 649053 🕐 All year 🍽 €115–€175 🛏 6 🔌 🏊

S'HORT DES TURÓ

www.hortdesturo.com

This small hotel, with five apartments, is perched on the southern tip of the island, close to Colònia de Sant Jordi, making it a good base for a day trip to the island of Cabrera (▷ 161). Each centrally heated apartment sleeps between two or four people and is kitted out with household equipment including a fridge, oven, dishwasher and kettle; there's also a shared washing machine. The apartments have also been fitted with WiFi. The decor is plain, with terracotta tiles and modern fittings. Pets are welcome.

✉ Carretera Ses Salines–Colònia de Sant Jordi, km 2.5, 07640 Ses Salines ☎ 647 967056 🕐 All year 🍽 €77–€120 🛏 5 🔌 🏊

PRACTICALITIES

Practicalities gives you all the important practical information you will need during your visit from money matters to emergency phone numbers.

Essential Information   188
    Weather   188
    Documents   189
    Money   189
    Health   191
    Basics   192
    Finding Help   193
    Communication   194
    Tourist Information   196
    Books, Maps and Media   197

What to Do   198
    Shopping   198
    Entertainment and Nightlife   200
    Sports and Activities   202
    Health and Beauty   205
    For Children   206
    Festivals and Events   207

Eating   208

Staying   212

Walking in Mallorca   214

Words and Phrases   215

WEATHER

Mallorca's island climate is surprisingly variable. Islanders like to boast of 300 days of sunshine annually and summers are typically very hot and sunny, but spring, autumn and winter can bring spells of wind, rain and cold temperatures at short notice. The surrounding sea moderates Mallorca's climate so there are no dramatic seasonal extremes, but temperatures will be lower in the mountainous Serra de Tramuntana the higher you travel.

WHEN TO GO

➤ The summer months of June, July and August make up Mallorca's high season. Accommodation will be booked to capacity as holidaymakers fly in to enjoy average high temperatures of around 30°C (86°F) by day and sea water that is almost as warm. During these months the sun shines for an average of 11 hours per day and beaches are tightly packed with people; the sea temperature goes as high as 26°C (79°F). For many it is too hot to do anything active, which is why many of the visitors who come to Mallorca

for golf, bicycling or other activities arrive in the cooler months of April, May, September and October.
➤ These shoulder months are perhaps the best time to see Mallorca. Attractions are open, prices slightly lower, queues shorter and there is space to move freely on the beaches and roads. Bring a waterproof jacket and warm clothing: you're as likely to experience a week of wet, overcast days as a sunny heatwave. Typically 40 per cent of the island's annual rain will fall in the autumn (September–end November), 25 per cent in winter (December–end February) and a further 25 per cent in spring (March–end May).
➤ Temperatures in the winter can reach as high as 15°C (59°F) but heavy snow may fall in the Serra de Tramuntana during some winters. Sea temperatures will remain relatively warm, at about 14°C (57°F). However, only doughty dog walkers will frequent the beaches during the winter and the island's resorts close for the season and don't reopen until April. Most of the urban attractions remain

open—Christmas is a busy period for Palma—but many of the visitors to Mallorca during the winter are walkers.

WEATHER WARNINGS

Although the mountain regions of the Serra de Tramuntana are not especially high, because they are exposed on the west coast to weather fronts coming in off the Mediterranean they can experience unpredictable weather conditions. The west side of the range is often cloudy and foggy while the inland side is clear, and conditions can quickly change from warmth and good visibility to cold and windy weather with low visibility. For this reason, take a waterproof jacket and some food and drink when walking in the mountains.

In summer, temperatures sometimes reach 40°C (104°F); consequently the risk of heat stroke and dehydration also rises. During such extreme temperatures it is

TIME ZONES

Mallorca is on CET (Central European Time), one hour ahead of GMT (Greenwich Mean Time).

CITY	TIME DIFFERENCE	TIME AT 12 NOON PALMA
Amsterdam	0	noon
Berlin	0	noon
Brussels	0	noon
Chicago	-7	5am
Dublin	-1	11am
Johannesburg*	+1	1pm
London	-1	11am
Montréal	-6	6am
New York	-6	6am
Perth*	+7	7pm
Rome	0	noon
San Francisco	-9	3am
Sydney*	+9	9pm
Tokyo*	+8	8pm

Summer Time begins on the last Sunday in March and ends on the last Sunday in October. For starred cities, which do not have daylight saving, take off one hour during Summer Time.

PALMA
TEMPERATURE

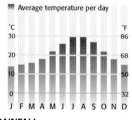

POLLENÇA
TEMPERATURE

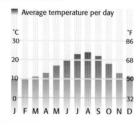

RAINFALL

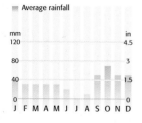

RAINFALL

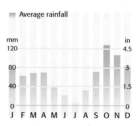

advisable not to do anything too energetic.

WEATHER REPORTS

Spain's Instituto Nacional de Meteorología posts basic daily weather forecasts on its website (www.inm.es), but the BBC (www.bbc.co.uk/weather) offers a five-day forecast for Palma in English. Detailed forecasts follow the regular Spanish news programmes on television.

WHAT TO TAKE

» Outside the summer months (June–August) it is advisable to take a waterproof jacket, and from late autumn to spring some warm clothing is necessary; the evenings can be quite chilly.

» It's a good idea to bring your own equipment for specific activities, such as hiking boots or cycling kit, although most items can be purchased on the island.

DOCUMENTS
PASSPORTS AND VISAS

» All visitors must have a valid passport (a national ID card can be used by EU nationals instead). You are required by Spanish law to keep one of these documents with you at all times, but it is extremely rare to be stopped and asked.

» EU visitors do not require a visa for entry. Visitors from the US, Canada, Japan, Australia and New Zealand require a visa for stays exceeding 90 days.

» Always check with your consul about visa requirements and entry regulations as they may change, often at short notice.

MONEY

As a region of Spain, Mallorca has had the euro as its official currency since January 2002, when the peseta was replaced by euro notes and coins.

BEFORE YOU GO

» It is advisable to use a combination of cash and credit cards rather than relying on any one

DUTY-FREE AND DUTY-PAID GUIDELINES

GOODS YOU BUY IN THE EU

These are in line with other EU countries. There is no limit on the amount of foreign currency or euros that you can bring into Spain. Tax-paid goods for personal use (such as notebook computers) can be brought in from other EU countries without customs charges being incurred. Guidance levels for tax-paid goods bought in the EU are as follows:

• 3,200 cigarettes; or	• 110 litres of beer
• 400 cigarillos; or	• 10 litres of spirits
• 200 cigars; or	• 90 litres of wine
• 1kg of smoking tobacco	(of which only 60 litres can be sparkling wine)
	• 20 litres of fortified wine (such as port or sherry)

VISITING SPAIN FROM OUTSIDE THE EU

You are entitled to the allowances shown below only if you travel with the goods and do not plan to sell them.

• 200 cigarettes; or	• 1 litre of spirits or strong liqueurs
• 100 cigarillos; or	• 2 litres of still table wine
• 50 cigars; or	• 2 litres of fortified wine, sparkling wine
• 250g of smoking tobacco	or other liqueurs
	• 50g of perfume
	• 250cc/ml of eau de toilette

means of payment. Avoid carrying all your money in one place.

» Note that it is very difficult to change a 200 euro note and virtually impossible to change a 500 euro note, apart from at a bank.

CHANGING MONEY

» You can change money at some hotels, bureaux de change and banks. Since the switch to the euro there are far fewer bureaux de change in Mallorca, with banks taking over much of their business.

» You can withdraw money from cashpoints (ATMs) using a credit or debit card. It is a good idea to inform your bank of your travel plans if you plan to use a credit card.

ATMS

» These are known as *telebancos* and are widespread throughout Mallorca. On-screen instructions are available in a choice of languages.

» If your card is a Maestro or Cirrus you can use it to pay for goods and services as well as withdraw cash.

» Your bank may charge you for withdrawing money from another bank's cash machine.

CREDIT CARDS

» Most larger restaurants, hotels and shops accept credit cards but some may need a minimum spend.

» Smaller shops and cafes generally prefer cash.

>> When paying with a credit card, you must show ID (a passport or driving licence).

BANKS

>> Spanish banks in Mallorca have foreign exchange desks (*cambio*) where you can draw out money using a credit or debit card. Remember to bring your passport for ID.

>> Banking hours tend to be Monday to Friday 8.30–2 and Saturday 8.30–1.

WIRING MONEY

>> In an emergency you can have money wired from your home country using international agents such as Western Union (tel 0800 833833, www. ukmoneytransfer. com), but this can be time-consuming and expensive.

TAXES

>> Sales tax, at 7 per cent and known as IVA, is added to some goods sold in Mallorca, and even services such as hotel accommodation and meals in restaurants. Note that hotels frequently don't include this sales tax when quoting their prices. This tax is non-refundable.

>> For all other goods and services 16 per cent tax is added.

>> Visitors from non-EU countries are entitled to a reimbursement of the 16 per cent tax paid on purchases to the value of more than €90.15, which must have been spent in the same store.

>> The store should provide an invoice itemizing all the goods, the price paid for them and the tax charged, as well as full address details of both the vendor and the purchaser, a form for the sales tax refund, and a tax-free receipt of purchase. The goods must then be taken out of the EU within three months.

>> When leaving Mallorca, take the goods and the invoices to the booth provided at Spanish customs, prior to checking in your baggage. This is where your claim will be processed.

Above Cashpoint machines accept most types of credit card

TIPPING

Locals rarely tip—it is not a Spanish custom. There are different expectations of tourists. As a general guide, the following applies:

Restaurants	5–10 per cent*
Bar service	change*
Cafés	5 per cent*
Tour guides	optional
Hairdressers	change–5 per cent
Taxis	3–5 per cent, more if carried luggage
Chambermaids	€1–€2
Porters	€1–€2
Toilet attendants	€1

*Or more if you are impressed with the level of service

LOST/STOLEN CREDIT CARDS

Phone one of the following contact numbers in case of loss or theft:

American Express / cards
tel 902 375637

American Express / traveller's cheques
tel 900 994426

Diners Club
tel 902 401112

MasterCard
tel 900 971231

Visa
tel 900 991124 / 91 519 21 00

10 EVERYDAY ITEMS AND HOW MUCH THEY COST

Takeaway sandwich		€2.50–€3.50
Bottle of mineral water	(from a shop, half a litre)	€0.65–€0.80
Cup of coffee	(from a café, espresso)	€1–€1.85
Beer	(half a litre)	€1.85–€2.50
Glass of house wine		€1.85–€2.50
Spanish national newspaper		€1.10–€1.25
International newspaper		€2.50–€5.50
Litre of petrol	(98 unleaded)	€1.19
	(diesel)	€1.05
Bus ticket	(single)	€1.10
Cocktail		€5–€8

HEALTH

Spain's national health service works alongside the private sector, and its hospitals are generally of a high standard.

BEFORE YOU GO

» No inoculations are required, but if you last had a tetanus jab more than 10 years ago, have a booster before you travel.

» Spain has a reciprocal agreement with other EU states entitling EU citizens to a certain amount of free health care. You must complete all the necessary paperwork before you travel. The old E111 form has been replaced by the European Health Insurance Card (EHIC). In the UK, you can apply online at www.dh.gov.uk or call 0845 606 2030. Cards should be delivered in 7–10 days.

» EU citizens requiring treatment for a pre-existing condition while they are away should apply to their department of health for an E112 form.

USEFUL NUMBERS

Emergencies	112
Ambulances	971 204111
Red Cross	971 295000
Balearic Institute of Health	971 175600

24-HOUR PHARMACIES

Avinguda Joan Miró 188, Palma	971 402133
Carrer Balanguera 3, Palma	971 458788
Pharmacies on duty	11888

» If you think you will need to renew a prescription while you are away, ensure you know the chemical name of the drug before you travel; it may be sold under another name in Mallorca.

» Taking out health insurance is strongly advised, despite the reciprocal health care. For non-EU visitors it is essential.

IF YOU NEED TREATMENT

» To use your EHIC, you will need to confirm that the doctor you visit works within the Spanish Health Service. Make it clear that you want to be treated under this system.

» In some clinics there are separate surgery times for private patients and those treated under the health service. Make sure that you are treated at the appropriate surgery. If you are treated as a private patient or go to a private clinic you will not be entitled to your money back.

FINDING A DOCTOR

» A doctor *(médico)* can be found by asking at a pharmacy *(farmacia)*, at your hotel, at a hospital or by looking in the phone book *(Páginas Amarillas)*.

PHARMACIES

» Most towns in Mallorca have a pharmacy *(farmacia)*, identified by a flashing green cross outside. Call 11888 for information about late-opening duty pharmacies.

» Staff normally provide good over-the-counter advice, often in English. For minor ailments it is worth consulting a pharmacist before finding a doctor.

» Drugs that are obtained on prescription in other countries may be available without one in Spain. Check with a pharmacist.

DENTISTS

» Dental treatment is not covered by reciprocal health agreements. For emergency treatment look under *Clíniques dentals* or *Dentistas* in the phone book.

OPTICIANS

» Pack a spare pair of glasses or contact lenses. If you bring your prescription, an optician *(Ópticos* in the phone book) can make another pair of glasses speedily, if needed.

HEALTH CONCERNS

» It is generally safe to drink tap water (unless marked *no potable*) but recurring water shortages in the summer mean that bottled water can be a more reliable option.

» The summer sun can be very powerful; prevent heatstroke and sunburn by avoiding the sun during the middle of the day, drinking water regularly and wearing a high-factor sunscreen.

» According to UN statistics, Spain has the highest number of AIDS cases and deaths in Europe. The majority are the result of drug users using infected needles, as opposed to sexual contact, and most of the cases are on mainland Spain, rather than on the Balearics. However, appropriate precautions should always be taken. The Spanish national AIDS helpline can provide advice and more information in English on 900 111000.

HOSPITALS ON MALLORCA

	ADDRESS	TELEPHONE
Hospital de la Cruz Roja Española	Pons i Gallarça 90, Palma	971 751445
Hospital General de Mallorca	Plaça de l'Hospital 3, Palma	971 212100
Hospital Universitario Son Dureta	Andrea Doria 55, Palma	971 175000
Hospital d'Alcúdia	Formentera 5, Alcúdia	971 547373
Hospital Joan March	Carretera Palma–Sóller km 12, Bunyola	971 212200
Fundación Hospital de Manacor	Carretera Manacor–Alcúdia, Manacor	971 847000
Hospital General de Muro	Carrer Veler, Urbanización Las Gaviotas, Muro	971 891900

BASICS

ELECTRICITY

>> Mallorca's power supply is 220 volts. Plugs have two round pins and an adaptor is required.

LAUNDRY

>> Most resorts and villa complexes have a self-service laundry.

>> Your hotel's laundry service is the most convenient way to have your clothes cleaned. Alternatively, there are laundries *(lavanderías)* in Alcúdia, Palma, Pollença, Felanitx, Sóller and other large towns.

>> There are several dry cleaners *(tintorerías)* in Palma, but they are not easily found outside the city.

PUBLIC LAVATORIES

>> Public lavatories *(serveis)* are free but are hard to find or non-existent outside Palma and the main towns and resorts.

>> Use the washrooms in large department stores, museums, galleries, cafes, restaurants or bars, even if you end up having to buy something.

MEASUREMENTS

>> Mallorca uses the metric system. Distances are measured in metres and kilometres, fuel is sold by the litre and food is weighed in grams and kilograms.

SMOKING

>> Smoking is not permitted in public spaces such as museums, galleries, theatres and cinemas, and, increasingly, in bars and restaurants. A total ban is anticipated in line with EU regulations.

LOCAL CUSTOMS

>> The typical greeting between friends is a kiss on both cheeks. Shake hands when you meet people, even if it's not the first time.

>> Outside the beach resorts, Mallorca retains many traditional values. Dress respectfully when visiting religious sites and avoid arriving at smart restaurants in beach wear.

>> Although English and German are widely understood, locals may speak in Spanish, Catalan and Mallorquín.

CONVERSION CHART		
FROM	**TO**	**MULTIPLY BY**
Inches	Centimetres	2.54
Centimetres	Inches	0.3937
Feet	Metres	0.3048
Metres	Feet	3.2810
Yards	Metres	0.9144
Metres	Yards	1.0940
Miles	Kilometres	1.6090
Kilometres	Miles	0.6214
Acres	Hectares	0.4047
Hectares	Acres	2.4710
Gallons	Litres	4.5460
Litres	Gallons	0.2200
Ounces	Grams	28.35
Grams	Ounces	0.0353
Pounds	Grams	453.6
Grams	Pounds	0.0022
Pounds	Kilograms	0.4536
Kilograms	Pounds	2.205
Tons	Tonnes	1.0160
Tonnes	Tons	0.9842

Visitors making an effort to speak Catalan or even Mallorquín are genuinely appreciated by residents.

Below *Palma's Plaça Major*

FINDING HELP

PERSONAL SAFETY

Crime rates in Mallorca are low and Palma is a relatively safe place when compared with other major Spanish cities. Pickpockets operate in the city and in some larger resorts. Sensible precautions include:
>> Never carrying more cash than you need.
>> Keeping belongings close by in crowded areas.
>> Being aware of ploys to distract your attention by thieves working in pairs.
>> Wearing bags slung diagonally across your chest rather than hanging from a shoulder. If you use a waist pack don't assume that it is safe since thieves will know that you're keeping valuables in it. Back pockets are also vulnerable to pickpockets.
>> Sticking to brightly lit, main thoroughfares at night.
>> Never leaving valuables on display in your car or unattended on the beach.
>> Keeping valuables in your hotel safe.
>> Taking a photocopy of your passport (kept separately) and ensuring you have the necessary telephone numbers to report credit card loss in the event of theft.

>> Keeping a (separate) record of all bank and credit card details in case of robbery.

POLICE

There are several types of police force in Mallorca, each responsible for a different aspect of public order.
>> Policía Municipal, the local police, are largely responsible for traffic and wear blue uniforms.
>> Guardia Civil has a small presence in Mallorca, monitoring rural areas.
>> Mallorcan police are generally approachable and, if asked, will give information and directions. The Guardia Civil is a quasi-military department and perhaps the least forthcoming force.
>> Report crimes to the police within 24 hours by calling 902 112122. You will be required to sign the report at a local police station. This is the fastest and most efficient way of reporting crimes—you can spend hours queuing in police stations. You will need a police report to claim through your insurance company.

INSURANCE

>> As well as health insurance, it is advisable to have travel insurance (often part of the same policy). This will cover you in the event of the loss or theft of property.

LOST PROPERTY

>> There are lost baggage facilities at Palma airport. If you lose something significant report its l oss at a police station.
>> If your passport is lost or stolen your consul can organize an emergency passport for returning to your home country for a fee. A photocopy of your passport, or its serial number, will speed the process up. Consuls in Mallorca do not issue visas.

IF YOU ARE ARRESTED

>> Ask for your consul to be informed. Your consul can give you the contact details of local multilingual solicitors but they can't give you legal advice or pay any bills.
>> Drink-driving penalties are severe and can result in large fines or even imprisonment. If you are detained by the police behave respectfully; your behaviour will have a bearing on how you are treated, even if you know a mistake has been made.

EMERGENCY NUMBERS

General	112
Municipal police	092
National police	091
Fire service	080 and 085
Maritime emergencies	900 202202

EMBASSIES AND CONSULATES IN PALMA

COUNTRY	ADDRESS	TELEPHONE
France	Carrer Mateu Enric Lladó 1, 2nd floor, 07002 Palma	971 730301
Germany	Carrer Portopí 8, 3rd floor, 07015 Palma	971 707737
Ireland	Carrer Sant Miguel 68A, 07002 Palma	971 719244
United Kingdom	Carrer del Convent dels Caputxins 4, 07002 Palma, www.fco.gov.uk	971 712445
United States	Carrer Portopí 8, 9th floor, 07015 Palma	971 403707

SPANISH EMBASSIES ABROAD

COUNTRY	ADDRESS	TELEPHONE
Australia and New Zealand	15 Arkana Street, Yarralumla, ACT 2600, Canberra	06 273 3555
Canada	74 Stanley Avenue, Ottawa, Ontario K1M 1P4	613/747-2252
The Netherlands	Lange Voorhout 50, NL – 2514 EG The Hague	70/302 4999
Republic of Ireland	17a Merlyn Park, Ballsbridge, Dublin 4	(01) 269 1640
UK	20 Draycott Place, London SW3 2RZ	020 7589 8989
	visa information	0906 550 8970
	Suite 1a, Brook House, 70 Spring Gardens, Manchester, M2 2BQ	0161 236 1233
	63 North Castle Street, Edinburgh, EH2 3LJ	0131 220 1843
USA	2375 Pennsylvania Avenue NW, 20037 Washington Dc	202 452 0100

COMMUNICATION

In the age of the internet and the mobile phone it's easy to stay in touch with friends, family and even the workplace, and Mallorca presents very few technological problems to the traveller.

TELEPHONES

➤➤ All telephone numbers in Spain have a nine-digit number, which includes the area code. All area codes start with 9; the Balearic Islands' code is 971 and covers Mallorca, Menorca and Ibiza. You must include the area code even when making a local call. Areas can have two- or three-digit area codes.

• To call Spain from outside the country you will need to dial your country's international access code (usually 00 in Europe and 011 in North America) followed by Spain's country code, which is 34, then the area code and telephone number. To call the UK from Spain dial 00 44 then drop the first 0 from the area code.

➤➤ The Spanish phone book, *Páginas Amarillas* (Yellow Pages; www.paginasamarillas.es), contains the telephone numbers for the emergency services as well as Mallorca's telephone directory.

PUBLIC TELEPHONES

➤➤ Public telephone booths are blue and you won't have to go far to find one. Look for the *teléfono* signs.

➤➤ They operate with coins, phone cards (*tarjeta telefónica* or *credifone*), available from newsagents, post offices and other shops, and, increasingly, credit cards.

➤➤ Phones will accept 5, 10, 20 and 50 cent coins or phone cards of 5, 10, 15 and 20 euros.

➤➤ The international operator number is 1008 for Europe, 1005 for the rest of the world. For national directory enquiries dial 11818.

➤➤ Call charges are cheaper after 10pm on weekdays, after 2pm on Saturdays and throughout Sundays.

➤➤ Using the telephone in your hotel room is considerably more expensive than using a public phone outside, whatever time you call.

MOBILE TELEPHONES

➤➤ Check with your mobile phone operator before departure that you will be able to use your mobile phone in Mallorca. Most single, dual and tri-band phones will work abroad, but your contract with the operator may impose limitations.

➤➤ You will be charged a higher rate for calls made from your mobile phone when not in your home country and you will also be charged for receiving calls and picking up messages.

➤➤ For extended stays buying a Spanish SIM card for your mobile phone lets you use a local network, which is cheaper.

THE INTERNET

➤➤ Internet cafes, where you can access web-based email accounts such as Hotmail, are gradually becoming more widespread in Mallorca. There are several in Palma and you are likely to find others in resort areas.

➤➤ Charges vary but should be around €1.50–€2 per hour.

POSTAGE RATES FOR LETTERS UP TO 20G

Within Spain	€0.34
To Western Europe	€0.68
To Eastern Europe	€0.68
To America	€0.72
To Africa	€0.72
To Asia	€0.72
To Australia	€0.72

AREA CODES WITHIN SPAIN

Madrid	91
Barcelona	93
Seville	95
Bilbao, Vizcaya	94
Valencia	96
Santander	942
Navarra	948
Granada	958

CALL CHARGES FROM PUBLIC PAY PHONES (PER MINUTE)

	PEAK RATE	REDUCED RATE
Local	€0.08	€0.06
National	€0.12	€0.08
Western Europe	€0.20	€0.20
Eastern Europe	€0.42	€0.42
USA	€0.20	€0.20
North Africa	€0.42	€0.42
Australia	€0.98	€0.98
India	€0.98	€0.98
Japan	€0.98	€0.98
China	€0.98	€0.98

INTERNATIONAL DIALLING CODES

Australia	00 61
Belgium	00 32
Canada	00 1
France	00 33
Germany	00 49
Greece	00 30
Ireland	00 353
Italy	00 39
Netherlands	00 31
New Zealand	00 64
Spain	00 34
Sweden	00 46
UK	00 44
USA	00 1

USING A LAPTOP

» To use your laptop in Mallorca remember to bring a power converter to recharge it and a plug adaptor. A surge protector is also a good idea. To connect to the internet you may need a phone socket adaptor (available from www. teleadapt.com). Many hotels now offer WiFi internet access. WiFi areas are also increasingly common in town centres, cafes and other public areas.

» If you use an international service provider, such as Compuserve or

INTERNET CAFES

Babaloo
Carrer de la Barrera de Baix 2, Palma
Tel 871 957725

Café 1550
Avinguda de l'Argentina 1,
Pollença
Tel 971 531330

Portality–Blue
Carrer Andratx 32,
Portals Nous
Tel 971 677513

Highlander Bar
Carrer Mariscos 12,
Port d'Alcúdia
Tel 971 549831

AOL, it is cheaper to dial up a local node rather than the dial-up number in your home country. Otherwise, sign up with a free local service provider.

» Dial tone frequencies vary from country to country so set your modem to ignore dial tones.

SENDING A LETTER

» Post boxes in Mallorca are bright yellow and are widespread in towns and resorts.

» Stamps (*segells*) are widely available from tobacconists and

newsagents, as well as post offices. Some hotels sell stamps and have a post box.

» The Spanish postal service has improved enormously in recent years and you can expect a letter to take an average of two to three days to reach its destination within the EU and five days to the USA, Asia and Australia.

» Use the Postal Exprés system to send an urgent parcel within Spain: it guarantees next-day delivery to main cities or within 48 hours to the rest of the country.

ADDRESSES

» The abbreviation s/n stands for *sin número* and signifies a building that has no street number. It may also, for example, be on a junction or street corner. This is predominantly used by businesses, shops and museums. The word for street, *carrer*, is often abbreviated to c/.

POST OFFICES

» Post offices are usually open Monday to Friday 9–2 but larger branches open during the afternoon and Saturday mornings.

» Palma's central post office is at Carrer de Consitució 5.

TOURIST INFORMATION

Holidays in Mallorca can be researched through Spanish tourist offices worldwide. The official website of the country's tourist office (www.spain.info) is a good starting point. When you are in Mallorca, most towns have a source of tourist information, whether it is a kiosk or a staffed centre. These local tourist information offices will provide details on public transport, local events, places of interest and activities. Some may operate a last-minute accommodation-booking service. The Mallorca Tourist Board, the world's first tourist board (▷ 33), is also an excellent source of advice and suggestions.

OPENING TIMES

>> The early afternoon siesta persists in Mallorca, with many shops closing from 1 to 4.30pm and opening until 8pm on weekdays. The general rule is that the busier the area is with tourists, the more likely it is that places will stay open throughout the day.

>> Banks, pharmacies and shops often close on Saturday afternoons.

>> Opening times for individual attractions are given in the relevant sections: The Sights and What to do. Most places are closed on Sundays and on public holidays.

GREEN CARD (TARGETA VERDA)

The Green Card was brought in to replace the unpopular eco-tax. It costs 910 and offers discounts on museums, shops and restaurants. Proceeds go towards environmental projects in Mallorca. More information is available from www.targetaverda.com or by dialling 902 929998.

PUBLIC HOLIDAYS

1 January	(New Year's Day)
6 January	(Epiphany)
Maundy Thursday	(March/April)
Easter Monday	(March/April)
1 May	(Labour Day)
15 August	(Assumption of the Virgin)
12 October	(National Day)
1 November	(All Saints' Day)
6 December	(Constitution Day)
8 December	(Immaculate Conception)
25 December	(Christmas Day)
26 December	(St. Stephen's Day)

SPANISH TOURIST OFFICES

Great Britain
79 New Cavendish Street,
London W1W 6XB
Tel 020 7486 8077
www.tourspain.co.uk

Germany
Kurfürstendamm 63, 0707 Berlin
Tel +49 308 826 543

Italy
Via del Mortaro 19, 00187 Rome
Tel +39 066 783 106
www.turismospagnolo.it

The Netherlands
8a Laan Van Meerdevoort, 2517
The Hague
Tel +31 703 465 900
www.spaansverkeersbureau.nl

Mallorca Tourist Board
Fomento del Turismo de Mallorca, Consitució 1, 07001 Palma
Tel 971 725396
www.newsmallorca.com

TOURIST INFORMATION OFFICES IN MALLORCA

Palma
Plaça de la Reina 2, 07012 Palma
Tel 971 712216; www.infomallorca.net

Aeropuerto, 07611 Palma Tel 971 789556

Passeig des Born 27, 07001 Palma
Tel 971 724090
www.palmavirtual.es

Port d'Alcúdia
Passeig Marítim, 07410 Alcúdia
Tel 971 547257; www.alcudia.net

Cala d'Or
Avinguda de Cala Llonga s/n, 07660 Cala d'Or
Tel 971 826084

Cala Millor
Passeig Marítim, 07560 Son Servera
Tel 971 585864

Cala Rajada
Plaça dels Pins, 07590 Capdepera
Tel 971 563033

Cala Sant Vicenç
Plaça Cala Sant Vicenç, 07469 Pollença
Tel 971 533264

Colònia Sant Jordi
Carrer Doctor Barraquer, 5, 07638 Ses Salines
Tel 971 656073

Magaluf
Pere Vaquer Ramis 1, 07182 Calvia
Tel 971 131126; www.palmanova-magaluf.com

Manacor
Plaça Ramón Llul, 07500 Manacor
Tel 971 847241

Palma Nova
Passeig de la Mar 13, 07181 Calvia
Tel 971 682365

Pollença
Sant Domingo 2, 07460 Pollença
Tel 971 535077; www.pollensa.com

Port de Pollença
Passeig Saralegui, 07470 Pollença
Tel 971 865467

Port de Sóller
Canonge Oliver 10, 07108 Sóller
Tel 971 633042

S'Arenal
Plaça Reina M. Cristina, 07600 Llucmajor
Tel 971 440414

Sóller
Plaça Espanya, 07100 Sóller
Tel 971 638008

Valldemossa
07170 Valldemossa
Tel 971 612019

BOOKS, MAPS AND MEDIA

BOOKS

Vicky Bennison: *The Taste of a Place: Mallorca* (2003)
If you want to learn more about Mallorcan food, wine and restaurants, *The Taste of a Place: Mallorca* (£12.99, Chakula Press) is a well-informed gastronomic guidebook with restaurant reviews, recipes and accessible explanations of Mallorcan cuisine. Updated restaurant reviews are featured on www.thetasteofaplace.com.

Valerie Crespí-Green: *Landscapes of Mallorca* (revised edition, 2006)
Landscapes of Mallorca lives up to its billing as the original and best walking guide to Mallorca. Written by a long-term resident, it describes 10 car tours, 60 walks of varying distances and degrees of difficulty and no fewer than 27 picnic locations.

Agatha Christie (1890–1976): *Problem at Pollença Bay*
The doyenne of murder-mystery writers stayed at the Illa D'Or hotel in Port de Pollença between 1931 and 1934. Agatha Christie was sufficiently inspired to write this short story and use it in a Parker Pyne story.

Robert Graves (1895–1985): Collected Poems (1975); *The White Goddess: A historical grammar of poetic myth* (1948)
Robert Graves is responsible for the most prominent body of written work to come from a resident of Mallorca. His first visit to the island was with his first wife, Laura Riding, an American poet and critic, before World War II. In 1946 he settled permanently in Deià (▷ 98).

Poetry, for Graves, took precedence over everything, but he also wrote literary criticism, successful novels such as *I, Claudius* (1934) and a resonant autobiography, *Goodbye to All That* (1929). The most recent edition of his *Collected Poems* draws on more than 20 volumes of poetry. His best poems

tend to be love poems; unsurprising from a man who explained his belief that a powerful, female muse inspired real poetry in *The White Goddess*.

His son, William Graves, has written an account of 40 years of living in Deià called *Wild Olives*.

George Sand (1804–76): *A Winter in Majorca* (1841)
If your name was Amandine-Aurore Lucille Dupin, Baronne Dudevant, you too might be tempted to change it to George Sand, for simplicity's sake. George Sand made her reputation as a French novelist with an early series of romantic novels and later accounts of rural life in France. She spent the winter of 1838 to 1839 in Valldemossa with her lover Frédéric Chopin (1810–49). Her account of their Mallorcan sojourn has, oddly, been a foundation of Valldemossa's tourism industry ever since. It's odd because Sand and Valldemossa's locals patently loathed each other (▷ 110) and she bemoaned the miserable weather and primitive living conditions. In one respect, selling the book so persistently is the islanders' final act of defiance.

MAPS

▷▷ This book has a map of central Palma (▷ 52–53) and an atlas of the island (▷ 220–227). *The AA Island Map of Mallorca* (sold separately) has a 1:75,000 scale and is marked with walking and cycling routes, attractions and other points of interest.

▷▷ The Balearic government and local councils have planned walks and bicycle rides in Mallorca and

produced maps of the routes for tourists. These maps are usually available from local tourist offices free of charge. Look out for the *Landscapes of Calvià* booklet by Valerie Crespí-Green and the *A Stroll Through History* series of walks through Palma.

▷▷ The tourist office also publishes an excellent booklet outlining 12 walking excursions of varying difficulty and an interesting booklet called *The Other Mallorca*, which details cultural itineraries around the island. For a good online map check out www.mallorca-map.de.

MEDIA

▷▷ The *Majorca Daily Bulletin* (www.majorcadailybulletin.es) is a daily English-language newspaper serving the Balearics' English-speaking communities. Other local papers include *Última Hora* and *Diario de Mallorca*; all include information about what's on locally.

▷▷ Most mainstream Spanish newspapers, including *El País* (www.elpais.es) and *El Mundo* (www.elmundo.es), are available on the island. Larger newsagents sell same-day editons of major national newspapers from Britain, Germany and other EU countries.

TELEVISION AND RADIO

▷▷ Most hotels have televisions with news channels in English, as well as the main Spanish television channels TVE1 and TVE2. TV3 is a Catalan channel.

▷▷ You can get the BBC World Service on 15485, 12095, 9410 and 6195 short wave, depending on the time of day, and 648kHz medium wave or 98.5FM.

SHOPPING

Whether it's an early-morning visit to the local bakery for freshly baked pastries or a search for shoes on Palma's Avinguda Jaume III, shopping in Mallorca tends to be an enjoyable experience. Although there are chain stores and supermarkets everywhere, it pays to seek out the independent local shops and boutiques.

LEATHER

Spain has a reputation for well-made, competitively priced leather goods, including bags, footwear and clothing, and much of it once came from Mallorca. Footwear, notably Camper shoes, is still made on the island, but not to the same extent. The town of Inca is regarded as the island's leather capital, with numerous factory outlets, but you can buy leather goods all over the island at similar prices; Palma is just as good a place to browse. Hip footwear from Camper is also ubiquitous, and there are several Camper-only shops, such as the factory outlet in Inca (▷ 177). The Sóller-based cobbler Ben Calçat (▷ 122) is one of the few craftsmen still creating traditional Mallorcan sandals, which are very stylish and make interesting reminders of your holiday.

PEARLS

One of Mallorca's few surviving traditional industries is the manufacture of artificial pearls. It centres on Manacor and is dominated by Majorica (▷ 177). You can see jewellery being crafted in the factories but not the actual process of making the pearls. Manmade pearls are more durable than the real thing, but don't expect them to be cheap—a pair of earrings will cost at least €20.

FOOD AND DRINK

A few of the Mallorcan specialities detailed on pages 210–211 travel well enough to make the trip home. Bottles of good Mallorcan wine (▷ 210) from Binissalem or the Mallorcan aperitif *herbes* are the obvious examples. Expect to spend about €10 on a respectable wine in the wine shops of Palma.

In the *bodegas* of Binissalem and the Pla I Llevant you can try before you buy. Some foods also make good souvenirs: the spicy sausage *sobrassada*, for example, or jars of preserved fruits. If you do intend to take food home with you, be sure to check your country's customs regulations.

SOUVENIRS

You'll find all the usual things in the souvenir shops in the resorts: towels, T-shirts, leather goods and the like. But the most authentically Mallorcan souvenir is the *siurell*, a small clay whistle typically painted white with dabs of red and green. They've been made in Mallorca since Moors occupied the island in the 10th century. A variety of shapes, such as a figure of a man riding a horse or playing a guitar, are produced.

CERAMICS

Marratxí, in central Mallorca, is the heart of Mallorca's pottery industry. It is here that the cheap and cheerful *siurells* are produced, but other ceramics are also made in the area's factories, including crockery, tiles and garden ornaments. These are sold in numerous outlets across the island, ranging from unmissable roadside emporiums to designer boutiques in towns such as Artà. An annual craft fair, Baleart, is held in Palma in December (▷ 85).

GLASS

Algaida's Gordiola glassworks (▷ 176) and the Lafiore shop near Valldemossa (▷ 123) are the best sources of Mallorca's famous glassware. Their collections include pots and vases, ornaments and tableware. Quality is high and you can see glassblowers at work at both places. Designs range from the traditional to the avant-garde; there is something for all tastes.

OLIVE WOOD

It's hard to equate the relatively small olive tree plantations in Mallorca with the enormous quantity of olive wood products sold in the island. Plates, bowls, utensils and carvings—all are piled high and sold reasonably cheaply across Mallorca. The biggest shops are on the outskirts of Manacor. Olive wood makes for a durable and good-looking souvenir, but there are varying degrees of finishing quality. It's worth paying a little more for products that display some form of craftsmanship, rather than buying the rougher, mass-produced items.

WHERE TO SHOP

Palma offers the most diverse shopping opportunities in Mallorca. Indeed, its assortment of shops rivals other major Spanish cities such as Barcelona and Madrid. Designer boutiques, antiques shops, souvenir shops and tempting delicatessens: Palma has them all in a relatively compact area. The capital's principal shopping areas border Avinguda Jaume III and extend throughout the pedestrianized zones just east of the city centre. Other Mallorcan towns may offer a less glossy shopping experience, but a brief exploration often yields some rewarding results: the Finca Gourmet delicatessen in Sóller, or the art galleries of Artà, for example. Only in the biggest resorts is there a degree of mundanity.

MARKETS

Business starts early in the morning at Mallorca's weekly markets and most deals are are concluded in time for lunch. If you're self-catering they're a good way of buying fresh, local produce.
Monday: Caimari, Calvià, Manacor, Montuïri
Tuesday: Alcúdia, Artà, Campanet, Llubi, Porreres
Wednesday: Andratx, Capdepera, Llucmajor, Petra, Port de Pollença, Santanyí, Selva, Sineu
Thursday: Campos, Deià, Inca, Sant Llorenç
Friday: Algaida, Binissalem, Can Picafort, Son Servera
Saturday: Bunyola, Cala Rajada, Lloseta, Palma, Sóller
Sunday: Alcúdia, Felanitx, Muro, Pollença, Sa Pobla, Valldemossa

DEPARTMENT AND CHAIN STORES

Spain's leading department store, El Corte Inglés, can be found in Palma, along with other top Spanish chain stores: Zara for clothing and Camper for shoes. Outside the city centre large supermarkets, such as Carrefour, sell everything from bicycles to cheese. These, and the department stores, tend to be open all day, every day.

SHOPPING MALLS AND FACTORY OUTLETS

Shopping malls have yet to colonize Mallorca—the only major out-of-town mall is the modern Festival Park complex north of Palma. Factory outlets are more common, selling leather in Inca and pearls in Manacor, among other items. They are not necessarily a guarantee of the lowest prices and not all goods are made in Mallorca, but they are accessible and can offer good value.

HOURS AND PAYMENT

Typical opening hours are 10–1 and 4.30–8, Monday to Friday, but many of the larger stores in the busier shopping areas (such as central Palma) forego the mid-afternoon siesta and open from 10am to 8pm or even later. Many shops only open for the morning on Saturdays and most remain closed on Sundays. For all-night pharmacies see page 191.

Most larger shops accept credit cards but it is wise to have euros available for smaller stores. Most smaller shops and boutiques, not to mention market traders, prefer cash.

Below *Colourful, locally produced glassware is a Mallorcan speciality*

Sa Màniga in Cala Millor and Auditori d'Alcúdia demonstrate the fact that Mallorca is serious about widening its cultural horizons. Both venues, together with the large Auditorium de Palma, offer live music, theatre, ballet and opera, plus children's activities, films and workshops. The island's nightlife is most notorious for the raucous all-night hedonism of resorts such as S'Arenal and Magaluf.

WHERE

Palma is home to a thriving (and imported) tapas bar culture centred in La Llotja. After grazing at a few haunts, people often move on to a bar for drinks or one of Palma's celebrated nightclubs. Thanks to the compact city centre, the geography of a night out is simple and most of the time you can walk from one area to another. As well as the concentration of tapas bars in La Llotja, Santa Catalina to the west is an up-and-coming neighbourhood of bars, clubs and restaurants. Palma's biggest clubs are on the Passeig Marítim to the south of La Llotja and Santa Catalina.

On the western side of Palma's bay, Magaluf, home to one of Europe's biggest nightclubs, has a well-deserved reputation for a beer-fuelled nightlife for the under 30s. In Mallorca it is matched only by S'Arenal on the opposite side of the bay. S'Arenal is as German as Magaluf is British.

Nightlife in the heights of the Serra de Tramuntana and the central plains is quiet, consisting mainly of village bars. There's more going on in the coastal towns, such as Port de Sóller and Port d'Alcúdia, and things pick up in the resorts of the Cala d'Or and Cala Millor, along the east coast.

We've recommended specific bars in Palma and well-established bars elsewhere, but in the main resorts bars change name and ownership with such frequency that recommendations would be meaningless—the best tactic is to try a few venues before settling on a favourite. In the resorts, bars often have a similar ambience; most have a television on and a selection of imported and Spanish beers.

WHEN

In Mallorca nightlife really means nightlife. A typical night out won't begin earlier than 9pm, starting with a visit to a tapas bar or restaurant.

Serious bar-hopping begins at 11pm. Nightclubs open their doors by 12am, but clubbers won't start arriving until 1am and the party will peak at 3–4am. Doors close at 5–6am but some clubbers see in the new day with a *xocolata* (hot chocolate) and a pastry at a café before heading to bed. Most resort bars open from April to the end of October, with only bars and clubs in Palma remaining open during the winter.

WHAT'S ON

Most clubs advertise specific events with flyers and posters. Sometimes presenting a flyer on entry will gain clubbers a reduced entry fee or a free drink. Events with famous acts may be listed in the *Majorca Daily Bulletin* newspaper (www.majorcadailybulletin.es), on the website of the Balearic Islands' tourist board (www.visitbalears.com) or Palma city council's website (www.palmademallorca.es).

Entry to bars and tapas bars is typically free, but nightclubs usually charge, as much as €10–€20 at weekends. Many places offer special discounts, from free drinks to free admittance for women—these vary according to the night of the week, or the time of evening. Bars with live music may make a small cover charge. The minimum legal drinking age is 16, but most clubs are for over-18s.

GAY MALLORCA
The centre of Palma's gay and lesbian scene is Plaça Gomila, west of the city centre. There are several gay venues on Avinguda Joan Miró. Ben Amics, the Gay and Lesbian Association of the Balearics, has an information service on Thursdays (6–9): tel 971 715670 or visit www.benamics.com. Outside Palma, there are few gay beaches.

CINEMA
Cinema is not a significant part of Mallorcan culture. Modern screens at the Festival Park complex (▷ 177) show the latest blockbusters, and the three main auditoriums often screen films (usually art-house and Spanish films), but you won't find a cinema in every town.

LIVE MUSIC
For all Mallorca's reputation as a clubbing mecca, there's enough live music to satisfy the most demanding and eclectic ears. The island's three auditoriums stage operas and classical concerts by visiting orchestras and groups throughout the year. Palma's own Balearic Symphony Orchestra (www.simfonica-de-balears.com) performs an annual season in the city and tours the island. The biggest dates in the classical calendar are the series of performances during the annual festival Noches Mediterráneas at Costa Nord (▷ 113). But folk music is the traditional sound of Mallorca. Costa Nord, Son Marroig (▷ 101) and La Granja (▷ 99) periodically hold folk concerts and you may hear local musicians in village bars.

After-dinner shows have caught on in recent years. Many resorts offer some sort of entertainment but the most famous shows are the Pirates spectacle and the cabaret of Son Amar, during the summer months. Prices often include meals, but may still be relatively high. Troupes of acrobats and magicians are not to everyone's taste.

Those who prefer jazz or blues will find a couple of good venues in Palma. Live music performances in bars and clubs generally start late; at Bluesville in Palma acts arrive at midnight.

THEATRE
Several of the theatres in Mallorca have interesting programmes throughout the year. Artà's theatre is noted for contemporary drama, while Palma's theatres offer a wide range of drama productions, with the Teatre Principal veering towards more traditional material.

Mallorca's theatres and arts centres also organize a large number of activities for children, particularly during the summer when demand for watching plays indoors dwindles. Smoking is not allowed in the auditoriums, but most venues have bars that permit smoking.

Above *Folk musicians at La Granja*
Opposite *Live music is staged in many bars, clubs and theatres*

WHAT'S ON
Major cultural events, such as Palma's ballet season and Castell de Bellver's music festival (▷ 85), are listed in *On Anar*, a quarterly booklet produced by the tourist board, available from any tourist information office. Check the English language *Majorca Daily Bulletin* newspaper (www.majorca dailybulletin.es), the website of the Balearic Islands' tourist board (www.visitbalears.com) and Palma's city council (www.palmademallorca.es), all of which have detailed calendars of events. Rock, blues and jazz events, and much more, are advertized in the free *Youthing Guía de Mallorca* magazine, available from bars, cafes and venues.

TICKETS
Buying tickets from the venue's box office is the simplest way. Credit cards are widely accepted, although a booking fee may be added. Prices vary according to the show and other factors. The upper price limit is generally €50, with most theatre and concert tickets being much cheaper.

SPORTS AND ACTIVITIES

One of Mallorca's greatest strengths is the choice of outdoor activities available to visitors. Resorts offer a number of activities to holidaymakers, from tennis and beach volleyball to water-skiing. Spectator sports are rather more limited. Mallorca has a Primera Liga football team with a stadium north of Palma and two racecourses. Several glitzy yachting events are held during the summer and the Tour of Mallorca is a winter bicycling event.

BEACHES

There are more than 80 beaches along the Mallorcan coastline. They vary considerably; many are jam-packed with tourists during the summer and intensively developed but it is still possible to find relatively quiet and secluded beaches even in busy areas, such as Cala Mondragó or Cala d'Or (▷ 162). Many of the busier beaches offer a number of activities—anything from volleyball contests to paragliding behind a motorboat or water-skiing. During the summer, when they are rigorously maintained, Mallorca's beaches are known for their high quality of hygiene, with over 40 receiving the European Union's Blue Flag Award as of 2010

Note that the following beaches are nudist: Dique del Oeste and Cala Portals Vells in the southwest; S'Agulló in the northeast; Punta de n'Amer in the east; and Es Trenc, Cala Blava, El Bosque and Es Carnatge in the south and southeast. You can download a booklet with all Mallorca's beaches and a list of their facilities from www.infomallorca.net

BICYCLING

Bicycling, with golf and sailing, is one of Mallorca's three most popular sports. Every winter and spring thousands of keen bicyclists arrive on the island for pre-season training. The island's long bicycling history started with the first winter Tour of Mallorca in 1913, an annual five-day event taking place in February. Bicyclists come to Mallorca for the diversity of terrain. In the morning you can inch up the long mountain roads of the Serra de Tramuntana and in the afternoon you can speed through the flat landscape of Es Pla.

The local government has extended a network of bicycle routes across the island. The signposted routes take riders past sites of interest on quiet roads or bicycle paths. With Mallorcan villages less than 10km (6 miles) apart, there is always a place to stop for refreshments. A local tourist information office will provide route maps of bicycle rides in the region. To hire a bicycle ask in a tourist information office for a local hire firm. Some of the larger operators, who can supply bicycles across the island, are included in the listings, but most towns and many hotels have bicycles available for hire. Serious riders fly out their own bicycles to Mallorca. Ensure the bicycle is properly boxed or bagged for transit and note that some airlines will charge a fee for carrying it. Palma airport is good at dealing with oversized luggage. Federació de Ciclisme de les Illes Balears, Francesc Fiol I Juan 2, 07010 Palma, tel 971 757628; www.webfcib.org

BULLFIGHTING

Bullfighting is not followed as avidly in Mallorca as it is on the mainland, but there are several bullrings on the island. The format of the fights remains the same: after a horseback procession (*corrida*) into the ring, the bull is softened up by picadors before the matador moves to the centre of the stage. Palma's bullring (▷ 82) is the island's principal arena, but you'll also find a Plaça de Toros in Alcúdia, Felanitx, Inca and Muro.

FISHING

Mallorca is not renowned for its fishing and although towns such as Port de Sóller and even Palma remain active ports, few people visit Mallorca specifically to go fishing. However, day trips can be organized in the ports; for local operators ask in a tourist information office. Federación Balear de Pesca y Casting, Avinguda Joan Miró 327, 07015 Palma, tel 971 702088

FOOTBALL

Mallorca's football team (▷ 24) is one of the best in Spain; the team plays at the Son Moix stadium (▷ 82), to the north of Palma. It's the only option for watching first-class football on the island. The Spanish football season runs between September and the end of May. Tickets are generally available on the day for all but the biggest matches.

GOLF

There are 20 golf courses on the island—a remarkably high number for such a small place. For a comprehensive list, check out www.mallorcagolfclubs.com. Most are of average difficulty, but the chief attraction is the variety: there are courses in the mountains, courses by the beach, courses in the city and courses on the plains. Another advantage is the mild climate—golfers, like cyclists, avoid the scorching summer months and arrive chiefly during spring and autumn. The courses themselves are invariably attractive, often with pine, almond and olive tree woodland, white-sand bunkers and water hazards. Clubs accredited by the Balearic Islands' government have a minimum of 25 buggies and trolleys and ensure players start with a gap of at least eight minutes between each group. Such clubs also have practice areas and P.G.A.-qualified instructors.

Federación Balear de Golf, Avinguda Jaume III 17, 07012 Palma, tel 971 722753; www.fbgolf.com

HANG-GLIDING

Areas suitable for hang-gliding include Alcúdia, Artà, Bunyola, Inca, Pollença, Petra and Sa Calobra. It is recommended that pilots contact the Club de Vuelo Libre Mallorca for advice before setting off.
Club de Vuelo Libre Mallorca, tel 655 766443; 871 950859; www.cvlmallorca.com

HIKING

Year on year, through autumn, winter and spring, Mallorca has attracted

ever-increasing numbers of hikers. They come to explore the Serra de Tramuntana and the beautiful trails that thread through the mountains and gorges. The government-funded Dry Stone Route (Ruta de Pedra en Sec) project will see seven renovated lodges offer overnight accommodation to walkers. There are currently six lodges (▷ 120). Specialist tour operators, such as Inntravel (▷ 214) in the UK, offer walking holidays.

Even if you're interested only in going for a day walk it pays to be prepared. Remember that the Serra de Tramuntana can be difficult mountain terrain. Always wear

supportive footwear and carry a waterproof jacket and some food and water. The tourist information offices in Pollença (tel 971 535077) and Sóller (tel 971 638008) can offer advice on safe and accessible routes.

HORSE RIDING

Horse riding is popular. Several riding schools and ranches, such as Son Menut (▷ 177) in Felanitx, take visitors on hacks or offer tuition in jumping and dressage, and are happy to look after inexperienced riders. The centres provide all the equipment and sometimes food and accommodation for multi-day rides.

You can watch trotting races at Mallorca's two race courses in Palma and Manacor.
Federación Balear de Hípica, Carrer Metge Camps, 07740 Es Mercadal (Menorca); mallorca@hipicabaleares.com; www.hipicabaleares.com

KAYAKING
Sea-kayaking is a relaxing way of exploring Mallorca's hidden bays and, in calm conditions, it is easy to master. Several yacht clubs around the island offer kayaks for hire, with or without a guide or tuition.
Federación Balear de Piragüismo, Avinguda Joan Miró 327, 07015 Palma, tel 971 702019; www.fibp.org

ROCK CLIMBING
Mallorca's varied crags and cliffs attract rock climbers from across Europe. The local climbing scene is undeveloped, but a little research before departure will reveal hotspots, such as Fraguel near Bunyola. Other good areas include Alaró, Caimari, Valldemossa, Santanyí and some sea cliffs. Climbing is possible all year round, but March, April, October and November are the most suitable months.
Federación Balear de Montañismo, Carrer Francesc Sitjar 1, 07010

Palma, tel 971 291374; www.fbmweb.com

SAILING AND WINDSURFING
Yacht charter is an increasingly widespread way of holidaying and many sailors use Mallorca as a base. Palma, after all, is the yachting capital of the Mediterranean. You can charter a yacht or motorboat with or without a skipper. Prices vary according to the boat, the season and several other factors. Alternatively, there are more than 40 marinas and 30 sailing clubs and many have operators who take visitors on day-long sailing trips, an excellent way to get a taste of yachting and see the island from another perspective. The Asociación Provincial de Empresarios de Actividades Marítimas de Baleares (www.apeam.com) is the trade association for larger yacht charter firms, with listings of many that operate from Mallorca.

Sailing is the island's most prestigious sport, with events such as the Copa del Rey regatta attracting royal participants and some of the world's top sailors. But there's more to sailing here than money and mega-yachts. Many of the resorts, such as Port de Pollença, have dinghies and small catamarans on the beach available for hire and the sheltered bays are perfect for learning the basics.

Windsurfing is also widely available at the larger sailing clubs, although the wind is not strong or consistent enough to attract expert windsurfers. The best stretch of coast is around Sa Ràpita on the south coast.
Federación Balear de Vela, Avinguda Joan Miró 327, 07015 Palma, tel 971 402412; www.federacionbalearvela.org

SCUBA DIVING AND SNORKELLING
With water temperatures ranging from 10°C (50°F) in the winter to 25°C (77°F) in the summer, Mallorca is a justifiably popular destination for scuba divers. It's great for

beginners too, because conditions are generally forgiving and visibility good. Most of the coastal resorts have a scuba dive outfit. Equipment and tuition by qualified instructors are usually available but note that dive insurance is compulsory in Spain. It may be covered by membership of an association such as BSAC (British Sub Aqua Club). Due to the competition between the dive outfits standards are generally high, with experienced guides and well-maintained equipment. Divers can expect to see several varieties of fish, including conger, but there is not the profusion of fish you find at reefs. For experienced divers several operators offer wreck diving, night diving and cave diving. Don't forget to bring your diving certification.

Snorkelling is an alternative to scuba diving, requiring just a mask, snorkel and perhaps fins. Mallorca's warm, shallow waters are perfect for snorkelling but remember to apply a high-factor waterproof sunscreen regularly.
Federación Balear de Actividades Subacuáticas, Polideportivo Son Moix, Camí La Vileta 40, 07011 Palma, tel 971 288442; www.fbdas.com

SWIMMING
There are 30 public swimming pools, most in sports centres. Some are outdoor pools that may not be heated.
Federación Balear de Natación, Piscinas Son Hugo, Carrer Teniente Oyaga, 07004 Palma, tel 971 764624; www.fbnatacion.org

TENNIS
Rafael Nadal has inspired many Mallorquíns to take up the sport, and these days most towns have tennis courts, usually as part of their sports centre and available for a fee.
Federación Balear de Tenis, Avinguda Alemanya 11, 07003 Palma, tel 971 720956; www.ftib.net

Left *Having a round at the Son Vida Golf Club in Palma*

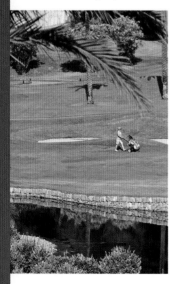

HEALTH AND BEAUTY

Until recently, Mallorca was not an obvious choice for a pampering break. But the spa trend has reached the island and it is now possible to check into a chic spa for a couple of days of self-indulgent health and beauty treatments. Many of the top hotels offer some sort of spa experience.

The rise in the number of spas mirrors the number of new golf courses on the island; most of the major golf resorts have a spa for golf widows to enjoy while their partners are out on the course. Some of the luxury hotels with spas are listed below; most will have day passes available to visitors. Good-value deals, including accommodation and spa short breaks, are likely to be advertised on the hotels' websites in the low season (from October to the end of April).

So far there are few dedicated spas outside the hotels but as Mallorca moves upmarket you can be sure that more will appear. Thalassotherapy is tipped to be an increasingly popular treatment, with several spas, such as Altira Spa at the Mardavall hotel, already offering Mediterranean seawater and seaweed therapies.

Few people go to Mallorca and head straight into a gym but those that are so inclined will find a municipal sports centre in most medium-sized towns. There are also a number of smart private health and fitness centres, such as Nord Esport in Pollença, which are listed in the regional sections.

Palma is the best place to get a stylish haircut, with several chains of Spanish hair salons. But most resorts will have hair and beauty salons.

SPA HOTELS
Arabella Son Vida, Palma
Tel 971 787100 (▷ 90)
Balneari Sant Joan de sa Font
Santa, Campos
Tel 971 655016
Hotel Dorint, Camp de Mar
Tel 971 136565
Illa D'Or, Port de Pollença
Tel 971 865100 (▷ 157)
La Residencia, Deià
Tel 971 639011 (▷ 128)
Mardavall, Son Caliu
Tel 971 629400 (▷ 91)
Marriot Son Antem, Llucmajor
Tel 971 129100 (▷ 185)
Gran Hotel Sóller, Sóller
Tel 971 638686

FOR CHILDREN

Many of Mallorca's beaches are gently shelving, with shallows for children to play in. During the summer high season the beaches are regularly cleaned. Resorts usually have a programme of supervised activities and areas, including swimming pools, for children of all ages.

Most interests are catered for. Sporty children (and their parents) will enjoy the island's outstanding mini-golf courses and the go-karting tracks in Magaluf and Arenal. Two water parks—Aqualand El Arenal and Aqualand Magaluf—and the Western Park theme park offer high-octane excitement with water slides and rides, and will be packed with families in July and August.

Animals are central to several attractions: there are performing dolphins at Marineland (▷ 84), llamas and boar at Jumaica (▷ 176), wild animals at Auto-Safari (▷ 149) and fish at Aquari de Mallorca (▷ 151). You'll see more fish on the Nemo submarine trip (▷ 84), but this is a particularly expensive excursion.

Most children's attractions are found in the Bay of Palma and in a few of the resorts along the coast. Aquapark, Aquacity (one of the world's largest water parks), Marineland and Western Park are on the Bay of Palma. A smaller water park can be found in Port d'Alcúdia

(▷ 148) and several wildlife parks are on the east coast.

There's less for children in the central plains and Serra de Tramuntana, but children will enjoy the shows at La Granja (▷ 121) in the mountains. The light shows in the caves on the east coast (Coves del Drac and Coves dels Hams, ▷ 164–165) are always popular.

Economical alternatives to the theme parks' rides include taking the rickety train from Palma to Sóller, or seeing Palma from a horse-drawn carriage, which you can meet at the top of Costa de la Seu, beside the cathedral and Palau de l'Almudaina. In the summer, make a note of the children's shows that many resorts stage, such as the afternoon performances of Pirates Adventure (▷ 81).

WATCH OUT FOR...

Wherever you go, children always get a warm welcome, but although Mallorca is an exceptionally child-friendly destination, there are certain

hazards. The most dangerous is the strong summer sun. Apply a high-factor sunblock regularly to youngsters, especially after swimming: it's wise to follow the example of the Mallorcans and seek shade during the middle of the day.

Families staying in high-rise hotels should check that any balcony railings are secure. When hiring a car, specify the number of child seats you require when booking.

Note that some of the rides in the theme parks and water parks may have age or height restrictions, although there are rides available in each park for all ages and sizes. Most parks are closed out of season, as are many children's attractions.

Prices are the final peril for families. The principal theme and water parks are some of Mallorca's most expensive attractions and most do not offer a discounted family ticket. This means that a family of two adults and two children should expect to spend up to €60 on tickets alone.

Left *Mallorca has a wealth of water parks*
Below *Motorcycling for the kids*

MUSIC AND CULTURE

Summer brings a crop of cultural festivals, timed to coincide with the arrival of the bulk of the island's visitors. Classical music is well represented, with several headline events such as the Festival de Pollença. But folk, world and pop music all take their own place centre- stage during the summer.

In autumn, thanksgiving harvest festivals, celebrating anything from melons in Vilafranca de Bonany to wine in Binissalem, are a reminder of Mallorca's agrarian roots. These festivals take over towns and villages for a day or more and are a great opportunity to try local produce.

Another vestige of rural Mallorca can be witnessed in winter: *matances*. These are neighbourhood parties based around the slaughter and preparation of the family pig for future eating. The slaughterman (*matancer*) turns up on the designated morning and despatches the animal.

Family members then roll up their shirt sleeves and turn the pig into sausages, hams, lard and cuts of meat. The day ends with a well-deserved party and a pile of preserved pork. As fewer families own livestock and younger generations move into cities, this traditional way of preparing food for the larder is gradually dying out.

SPORT

As well as events of largely local appeal, such as bullfights, Mallorca hosts several internationally important sporting events. Top of the list are the glitzy Palma-based yachting regattas that attract royalty, celebrities and huge numbers of wealthy sailors. You can see the yachts when they are moored in Palma's marinas.

Football, and the prospects of the Real Mallorca team, is keenly followed by islanders, who look forward to visits from Spain's top teams at the Estadio Son Moix (▷ 82).

Bicycling fans can catch professional teams racing in the five-day Tour of Mallorca every February. You won't see the biggest names in the sport in action, but it's still an exciting spectacle, which, like the sailing, you can watch for free.

FAIRS AND MARKETS

If you're more interested in souvenir hunting, visit one of Mallorca's craft fairs and markets. These are held at regular intervals during the year and include Baleart, Fira del Fang and Dijous Bo. Additionally, most Mallorcan towns have a weekly market selling fresh food, local produce and traditional handicrafts (▷ 199).

Top *Garlands and streamers can be seen everywhere during festivals*
Above *Muro's bullring, Plaça de Toros*

Mallorcan cuisine has its roots in rustic, peasant traditions. It focuses on seasonal food designed to sustain farmers and fishermen, but scratch the surface and you'll find rich flavour combinations, deliciously fresh produce and truly interesting dishes.

WHERE TO EAT

You can judge how seriously Mallorcans take their food by how many places serve it: bars, cafes, restaurants, pubs and *cellers* are everywhere. Choosing a favourite is a matter of trial and error. In general, avoiding anywhere that lists burgers and chips on a laminated menu and looking for places frequented by locals are sound tips for success. For good Mallorcan cuisine try exploring Gènova, on the western outskirts of Palma, where people from the capital go to eat out. You can also find excellent restaurants at out-of-town crossroads and roadsides. These places are where travellers have traditionally stopped to refuel; you can find one such concentration of Mallorcan restaurants just outside Algaida.

Another source of traditional Mallorcan food is a *celler*, an old wine cellar converted into a restaurant. These often have redundant wine vats in the dining room to prove the point. Towns in which you'll find good *cellers* include Petra and Sineu.

If you don't want a full meal, tapas bars (▷ 209) and cafes provide filling snacks. Cafes will often be open at all hours of the day, while tapas bars do most of their business in the evening. To blur the distinction, some cafés serve tapas dishes as well as sandwiches and pastries.

Because of numerous previous invasions and a regular stream of international visitors and settlers, Mallorca has perhaps a greater range of cuisines than you'd typically find on the Spanish mainland. French, Italian, Indian, Thai: Mallorca has them all, and in Palma you can even eat Argentinian, Ethiopian or Japanese food. In the resorts, however, the dominant cuisines are British and German, with lots of British-owned pubs and restaurants serving all-day English breakfasts or bratwurst.

Outside these areas, more Mallorcan restaurants, serving traditional dishes, have opened in recent years. See pages 210–211 for a guide to Mallorcan specialities.

BREAKFAST

Breakfast is not the most important meal of the day for Mallorcans: They'll simply kick-start the morning with a strong, black *café solo* or a *café amb llet* (coffee with milk) and a pastry. Most hotels offer a buffet breakfast for larger northern European appetites, with bread, cold meats, cheese, cereals and fruit.

LUNCH
Restaurants typically serve lunch from 1pm to 3pm. Mallorcans prefer to eat a late lunch but in tourist areas most restaurants will be open from 1pm. The *menú del día* is an economical way of having lunch. For a set price you'll get three courses and even a drink.

DINNER
If you arrive for dinner before 9pm, you're likely to be dining in an empty restaurant—Mallorcans don't go out to eat until late in the evening, typically from 9pm to midnight.

CHILDREN
Children are welcomed at the majority of restaurants, but we have indicated in the listings those places where they are not.

VEGETARIAN FOOD
Seasonal vegetables play a large part in Mallorcan cooking and it is not difficult to find vegetarian dishes, including such tasty Mallorcan staples as *tumbet*.

RESERVATIONS
Booking ahead is advised for restaurants in the middle to upper price range in the high season. Tables for dinner at the very best restaurants, such as Read's (▷ 125–126), may be booked up some time in advance, but lunch can be a less busy time. Popular local restaurants will often be full on Sunday lunchtimes.

DRESS CODE
In only a handful of exclusive restaurants, usually attached to expensive hotels, will you feel uncomfortable in casual clothing. While few restaurants ban customers from wearing T-shirts and shorts, most require that men wear something on top. While dressing up for dinner is not strictly

necessary, except perhaps in the smartest hotel restaurants, such as Read's in Santa Maria del Camí (▷ 125–126), Mallorcans manage to appear casually smart when they go out.

SMOKING
Smoking is banned in public spaces larger than 100sq m (1,075sq ft). Observance of this law can seem lax, although indications are that a stricter anti-smoking ban will be enforced in line with EU regulations.

WHEELCHAIR USERS
Some restaurants, bars and cafés in Mallorca have limited access for wheelchair users. Many of the tapas bars in La Llotja, for example, are up or down flights of steps. Places that have an outdoor terrace are probably the most accessible. It's a good idea to check in advance whether there will be problems.

MONEY
Locals don't tend to tip 10 per cent, but it is expected of tourists. Restaurants will state on the menu whether a 7 per cent tax (▷ 190) will be added to the bill—this tax is often applied in more expensive restaurants. Virtually all restaurants will take credit cards. We have indicated in the listings those restaurants in which they are not accepted.

PRICES
The restaurant prices given are for the least expensive à la carte two-course lunch (L) and three-course dinner (D) per person and the least expensive bottle of wine. Where relevant, the price of the *menú del día* or the price of tapas has been included.

TAPAS IN MALLORCA
Tapas, snack-size portions of food once served free with a drink, are central to Spanish cuisine. But they're not a Mallorcan tradition; the idea was imported to meet tourists' expectations of eating out in Spain. It has caught on, however, and

most towns in Mallorca will have a choice of places—bars, restaurants and cafes—serving tapas. Because it is not a local custom, you won't find the specially crafted dishes that you might find in Andalucía. Many Mallorcan tapas specialities are simply miniaturized versions of main dishes, such as meatballs or spicy sausages. But, as well as the basic choices such as olives and slices of ham, there are some more interesting variations that regularly appear on Mallorcan menus: battered calamari rings and small octopi, deep-fried vegetables such as aubergine and cauliflower, *pimientos de padrón* (deep-fried hot green peppers), ham croquettes and dates wrapped in bacon. You'll also find cured meats and pickled fish.

FIVE OF THE BEST TAPAS BARS IN PALMA
La Bodeguilla (▷ 87)
La Bóveda (▷ 87)
La Cueva (▷ 88)
El Pilón (▷ 88)
Florian Bar Restaurant (▷ 182)

Opposite *Dining al fresco is a pleasure*
Below *Mallorca has many acclaimed chefs*

The menu reader (below) describes some of the Mallorcan specialities you're most likely to find on restaurant menus, from savoury dishes to local wines. The glossary of Spanish food (right) arms you with general words and phrases to help you decipher a menu. Each is given in Catalan, followed by the Castilian in brackets.

LOCAL DISHES

Pa amb oli
Bread, preferably crusty and brown, is rubbed with garlic and tomato then served with olive oil and sea salt; snacks don't get much better than this cheap Mallorcan favourite.

Tumbet
A ratatouille-like vegetable stew of onions, tomatoes and aubergines, or other vegetables such as courgettes and peppers, depending on the season.

Sobrassada
Large, cured sausages, the best being made from Mallorca's small, indigenous black pigs. Central to Mallorcan cuisine, they're flavoured with a combination of paprika, salt and spices and can be eaten in any number of ways, including raw as a pâté on toast or cooked with honey. Sausages flavoured with hot cayenne pepper will be strung with red string; those with white strings are flavoured with milder paprika. A sobrassada should have a rich red colour and feel soft to the touch; those made from the black pigs boast a black wrapper. Botifarrons are smaller Mallorcan sausages, which are strung together.

Cordero lechal
Suckling lamb, commonly served in the form of palatillas (shoulders) and piernas (whole legs) gently roasted over rosemary sticks and garlic cloves until tender. A full-bodied Mallorcan red wine is the perfect accompaniment to this dish.

Sopas mallorquínas
A robust winter dish made from stale bread and braised vegetables. Soup is a slightly misleading name because any liquid will have been absorbed by the bread.

Frit mallorquí
Another unusual dish, often served in tapas bars. Potatoes and vegetables are fried with chopped lamb or pork offal and flavoured with garlic and bay leaf.

Arròs brut
'Dirty rice', a filling meal of meat, game, vegetables and rice, flavoured with sobrassada.

Triqueros
Wild asparagus, which grows all over the island and is much sought after by locals.

Cargols
Snails, mostly served in local restaurants with a garlicky mayonnaise called aïoli.

Llom amb col
Pork wrapped in cabbage leaves, often flavoured with sobrassada.

SEAFOOD
Catches off Mallorca's shores include cap roig (scorpion fish), antós (grouper), moll (red mullet) and dorada (sea bream), and all find their way to local markets and restaurants. Sóller is famous for big, red Mediterranean prawns. Have them grilled with garlic and parsley. Llagosta (crayfish) are used in calderetas (fish soups and stews). A favourite Mallorcan dish is peix a la mallorquina, a fillet of fish topped with a light vinaigrette made from toasted pine nuts, sultanas, diced tomatoes and parsley. Don't leave without trying sea bass (llobarro) baked in rock salt, another delicious speciality.

SWEETS

Ensaïmada
Mallorca's answer to the croissant—light, spiral-shaped pastries, dusted with sugar and usually served with coffee or hot chocolate. Fillings can be savoury (such as sobrassada) or sweet (such as pumpkin or apricots). Vegetarians beware: the texture is achieved by using lard. Poorly made ensaïmadas are not uncommon.

Bunyols
Potato fritters dipped in sugar and served with pumpkin or apricot jam.

Gato d'ametlla
A light almond sponge cake that you'll find in every bakery.

DRINKS

Herbes
This aniseed-flavoured digestif comes in sweet or dry variations. The arresting flavour is created by 30 aromatic plants, including orange, camomile and mint.

Beer
Most beer (cerveza) will be from mainland Spain. If you want a draught beer ask for una caña.

Wines
Binissalem and Vi des Pla i Llevant wines are labelled as Protected Designations of Origin (PDO) and are the best wines on the island. Two Mallorcan grape varieties to look out for are Callet and Manto Negro. The most renowned vineyards are in Binissalem. Wine houses Anima Negra and Macia Batle produce some of Mallorca's best wines. For comprehensive coverage of Mallorca's wines, check the www.vinosdemallorca.es website (in Spanish).

GLOSSARY OF SPANISH FOOD

CARN (CARNE) MEAT
ànec (pato) duck
anyell (cordero) lamb
bistec (bistec) steak
botifarra negra (butifarra negra) blood sausage
carn (carne) beef
conill (conejo) rabbit
fetge (hígado) liver
Gall d'Indi (pavo) turkey
perdiu (perdiz) partridge
pernil (jamón serrano) cured ham
pernil dolç (jamón cocido) cooked ham
peus (pies) trotters
pollastre (pollo) chicken
porc (cerdo) pork
salsitxa (salchicha) sausage
vedella (ternera) veal
xoriço (chorizo) spicy sausage

PEIX (PESCADO) FISH
anxoves (anchoas) anchovies
bacallà (bacalao) salt cod
llenguado (lenguado) sole
llobarro (lubina) sea bass
lluç (merluza) hake
moll (salmonete) red mullet
rap (rape) monkfish
salmó (salmón) salmon
tonyina (atún) tuna
truita (trucha) trout

MARISC (MARISCOS) SEAFOOD
anguila (anguila) eel
calamars (calamares) squid
cranc (cangrejo) crab
gambes (gambas) prawns (shrimps)
llagosta (langosta) lobster
musclos (mejillones) mussels
ostres (ostras) oysters
pop (pulpo) octopus

VEDURES (VERDURAS) VEGETABLES
albergínia (berenjena) aubergine
bròquil (brécol) broccoli
carabassó (calabacín) courgette
ceba (cebolla) onion
cogombre (pepino) cucumber
col (berza) cabbage
enciam (lechuga) lettuce
espàrrecs (espárragos) asparagus
faves (habas) broad beans
mongetes tendres (judías verdes) green beans
pastanagues (zanahorias) carrots
patates (patatas) potatoes
pebrots (pimientos) peppers
pèsols (guisantes) peas
xampinyons (champiñones) mushrooms

FRUITA (FRUTA) FRUIT
albercoc (albaricoque) apricot
cirera (cereza) cherry
gerd (frambuesa) raspberry
llimona (limón) lemon
maduixa (fresa) strawberry
meló (melón) melon
pera (pera) pear
pinya (piña) pineapple
plàtan (plátano) banana
poma (manzana) apple
préssec (melocotón) peach
raïm (uva) grape
taronja (naranja) orange

COOKING METHODS
a la brasa (a la brasa) flame-grilled
a la planxa (a la plancha) grilled
al forn (al horno) baked, roasted
cru (crudo) raw
escumat (poché) poached
farcit (relleno) stuffed
fregit (frito) fried
rostit (asado) roast

STAYING

Wherever you stay, most sights and beaches will be within a short drive. Accommodation ranges from large resort hotels to rural farmhouses, but we've focused on the more interesting hotels. Some are notable for their location, others for their food.

HOTELS

Today, the number of hotel beds in Mallorca is close to 300,000, the majority being in the beach resorts (▷ 213). But, as Mallorca aims upmarket, an increasing proportion of these beds is in four- or five-star hotels. Facilities at most of the hotels we have selected include air-conditioning, essential in July and August, as well as television, telephone, minibar and sometimes tea- or coffee-making facilities. Many have swimming pools or even a spa centre, and some offer specialist sport facilities—particularly golf.

Most hotels include breakfast (usually a buffet) in the basic cost of accommodation. Full-board and half-board options can save money,

but don't miss out on sampling Mallorca's excellent restaurants.

In the high season (May to the end of September) prices can be double those in winter months. Deals, such as four nights for the price of three, are common in the low season and are good value for walkers and bicyclists enjoying the mild winter weather.

Hostals are cheap hotels (mostly located in Palma) and are not connected to a youth hostel scheme. Even in the capital's cheaper establishments, expect to spend €65 to €80 on a double room. By spending €105 to €150 per night you can get a characterful room in a town-house hotel, but prices escalate for the city's most luxurious hotels. A smattering of

luxury hotels across Mallorca charge rates from €150 to €450 per night, but even these will offer deals to get customers in the quieter months. Note that a significant proportion of hotels close in winter; the coastal resorts are more or less empty from November to the end of April.

FINCAS AND AGROTURISMOS

A *finca* is a rural property that has been converted to provide guest accommodation. Typically, *fincas* fall into three categories: *hoteles rurales*, which are larger, manor house-style hotels; *agroturismos* (▷ 15)—often smaller, simpler farmhouses; and *turismo de interior*—smart hotels in towns and villages. Accommodation varies widely: some *agroturismos* offer just one or two self-catering apartments, others a dozen bedrooms. Prices too are variable, depending on location, season and facilities. *Agroturismos* offer some of the most enjoyable accommodation on the island and the cooking at many is outstanding, but in rural areas alternative choices for an evening meal will be limited, and may require driving into a town. Check out www.agroturismo-balear. com for a good choice of options.

CASAS RURALES
These are self-catering properties, often in charming historic buildings, which usually enjoy a rural setting. Prices and amenities vary considerably.

RESORTS
The large beach-resort hotels provide the cheapest accommodation on the island, but you'll get the best prices at these by booking rooms as part of a package holiday through a travel agent, rather than independently. Most resorts are block-booked by major tour operators during the summer and are closed during the winter. They typically operate on an all-inclusive basis, and provide bars, swimming pools and entertainment.

FULL AND HALF-BOARD ACCOMMODATION
A particular strength of many Mallorcan *fincas* and hotels is the high standard of cuisine in their restaurants. This applies especially to rural hotels and the upmarket establishments, which are worth visiting even if you're not a guest.

SELF-CATERING ACCOMMODATION
With many expats renting out their properties for the summer, there is a large stock of self-catering accommodation on the island. Note that prices can more than double in the high season. Firms such as the long-established Mallorca specialists Try Holidays (tel 0870 7544545;

www.tryholidays.com) provide a wide choice of apartments and villas.

SMOKING
Almost all the hotels in Mallorca will have rooms for smokers. We have stated where smoking is banned completely by a hotel.

PRICES
Prices given are for a double room for one night in the low and high seasons and include breakfast and the 7 per cent IVA tax (▷ 190), unless stated otherwise. Prices can double during the summer and will vary widely throughout the year; always check rates carefully. All the hotels listed accept credit cards unless stated otherwise.

MONASTERIES
For a different experience stay at one of the island's hilltop sanctuaries and hermitages. Few are working monasteries, but they are quiet places of refuge, with simple accommodation, a spiritual atmosphere and unforgettable views. Most visitors are walkers rather than pilgrims, or people looking for somewhere cheap and characterful to stay. The two biggest sanctuaries, at Lluc (▷ 102–105) and Santuari de Cura (▷ 169), still have active religious communities. They both offer comfortable accommodation; the pilgrim rooms at Lluc all have their own private showers and there are a number of restaurants on site.

More basic are monasteries where you sleep in a former monk's cell, making your own bed and

sharing simple shower facilities, as at Ermita de Bonany (▷ 168), near Petra, Puig de Maria (▷ 142–143), near Pollença, and Santuari de Sant Salvador (▷ 135), near Felanitx. All are run by caretakers rather than monks, and, except for Ermita de Bonany, evening meals are available. For the authentic pilgrim experience head for Puig de Maria or Nostra Senyora del Refugió above Castell d'Alaró (▷ 97), as both can only be reached on foot. Nostra Senyora del Refugió offers the most basic accommodation of all, with bunk beds in a dormitory building and no showers—though the sunset views from the terrace and the excitement of watching your dinner being carefully brought up the mountainside by mule more than make up for the lack of creature comforts. *A Stay in Mallorcan Monasteries*, by Nick and Jill Carter, is available from Amazon (www. amazon.com) and bookshops.

Lluc
☎ 971 871525 ✋ €25

Santuari de Cura
☎ 971 120260 ✋ €55 double

Ermita de Bonany
☎ 971 826568 ✋ €15 per person

Puig de Maria
☎ 971 184132 ✋ €25

Santuari de Sant Salvador
☎ 971 827282 ✋ €30

Nostra Senyora del Refugió
☎ 971 182112 ✋ €12

PRACTICALITIES STAYING

Mallorca offers a great variety of walking, from the high peaks of the Tramuntana to scenic coastal paths and quiet country lanes.

WHEN TO GO

The best months for walking are May, June, September and October, though winter can also be a pleasant time. The countryside of southern Mallorca is especially beautiful in February, when almond blossom covers the ground like a fresh fall of snow.

WHAT TO TAKE

>> Walking boots or shoes
>> Waterproof clothing
>> Sunhat and suncream
>> Insect repellent
>> Water bottle
>> Compass, torch and whistle in case of emergency

RIGHTS OF WAY

Many of the most popular walks in Mallorca cross private land and in recent years there has been a tendency for landowners to deny or limit access, even to traditional mule paths or pilgrim trails which may have been used for centuries. In part, this is because walking has become a victim of its own success, with growing numbers of hikers causing increasing problems of litter and erosion. It is not always clear whether you have a right of way, and signs indicating private property do not mean that you cannot walk. You can help future generations of walkers by observing a few simple rules (see below). Although signed footpaths in Mallorca are rare, the island's government has recently laid out more than 250km (155 miles) of waymarked hiking routes where access is permitted. These include the Camí Vell de Lluc, an old pilgrim trail from Caimari to Lluc, and the Ruta de Pedra en Sec (Dry Stone Route) over the sierra from Andratx to Pollença (▷ 21).

COUNTRY CODE

>> Leave all gates as you find them.
>> Do not disturb livestock.
>> Do not drop litter.
>> Do not pick wild flowers.

BOOKS

Landscapes of Mallorca by Valerie Crespi-Green (Sunflower Books, www. sunflowerbooks.co.uk): the first and the best walking guide to Mallorca, by an author who lives in Santa Eugènia. It includes maps and bus timetables to help you plan your walks. Updates are available on the website.

Walk! Mallorca (North and Mountains) and *Walk! Mallorca (West)* by Charles Davis (Discovery Walking Guides, www.walking. demon. co.uk): published in their 5th edition in 2009, and accompanied by durable maps. The first book features walks around Alcúdia, Pollença and Sóller, while the second concentrates on Andratx and Palma Bay.

Walking in Mallorca by June Parker (Cicerone Press, www.cicerone. co.uk): first published in 1986, a comprehensive walking guide. Includes background sections on flora, fauna, agriculture and rural industries, and also features two walks on the islet of Sa Dragonera.

Holiday Walks in Mallorca by Graham Beech (Sigma Press, www.sigmapress.co.uk): this book features town trails as well as mountain and countryside walks. Updates are available on the website.

MAPS

The most useful maps for walkers are the IGN 1:25000 series. These are available at La Casa del Mapa (▷ 78) in Palma, which also sells individual leaflets on some of Mallorca's most popular walks.

ACCOMMODATION

The island's government maintains six refuges for walkers in the Serra de Tramuntana, with at least one more now under restoration. To book, visit the Departament de Medi Ambient i Natura, c/General Piera 11, or call 971 173700. These offer dormitory beds, meals and showers in basic but comfortable accommodation. Bed linen is also available for hire or you can take your own sleeping bag. Refugi Tossals Verds (to book, ▷ above), in the heart of the sierra, can only be reached on foot; Refugi Muleta (to book, ▷ above) stands beside the Cap Gros lighthouse above Port de Sóller. The refuges may be closed in winter or at weekends, so it is essential to book in advance. Another good option for walkers is to stay in one of Mallorca's monasteries, such as Lluc (▷ 102–105) or Castell d'Alaró (▷ 97).

GUIDED WALKS

The Palma tourist office organizes a number of guided walks. For details and bookings, tel 971 177715.
   Mallorcan Walking Tours (▷ 151) offers a number of day walks of between 10km (6 miles) and 16km (10 miles) during spring (March–end May) and autumn (September–end November). These are ideal for holidaymakers who are already in Mallorca. If you want to plan your entire trip around walking, the company also has a one-week walking holiday based at San Telmo, and a week-long trek across the Serra de Tramuntana from Valldemossa to Pollença.

WALKING ORGANIZATIONS

Tour operators such as Inntravel (tel 01653 617788, www.inntravel. co.uk) in Britain can organize walking holidays in the Serra de Tramuntana. The website for the Ruta de Pedra en Sec is www.conselldemallorca. net/mediambient/pedra

Catalan is the dominant language in Mallorca and its pronunciation differs from that of Castilian (Spanish). It is more closed and less staccato than Castilian, but is likewise nearly always phonetic, with a few rules. When a word ends in a vowel, an n or an s, the stress is usually on the penultimate syllable; otherwise, it falls on the last syllable. If a word has an accent, this is where the stress falls. You may also hear Mallorquí, a version of Catalan.

Catalan

au	ow as in wow
c	ss or k (never th)
ç	ss
eu	ay-oo
g	g or j (never h)
gu	(sometimes) w
h	silent
j	j (never h)
ig	ch at the end of a word: *vaig* sounds like batch
ll	lli as in million
l.l	ll as in silly
ny	as in canyon
r/rr	heavily rolled
s	z or ss
tg/tj	dge as in lodge
tx	ch as in cheque
v	b (*vi*, wine, sounds like 'bee')
x	sh as in shake

Spanish

a	as in pat
e	as in set
i	as **e** in be
o	as in hot
u	as in flute
ai, ay	as **i** in side
au	as **ou** in out
ei, ey	as **ey** in they
oi, oy	as **oy** in boy

Consonants as in English except:

c	before **i** and **e** as **th**
ch	as **ch** in church
d	at the end of a word becomes **th**

g	before **i** or **e** becomes **ch** as in loch
h	is silent
j	as **ch** in loch
ll	as **lli** in million
ñ	as **ny** in canyon
qu	is hard like a k
r	usually rolled
v	is a **b**
z	is a **th**

Each of the words and phrases is given in English, **Catalan** and then *Spanish*.

NUMBERS

1	**u (un, una)**	*uno*
2	**dos**	*dos*
3	**tres**	*tres*
4	**quatre**	*cuatro*
5	**cinc**	*cinco*
6	**sis**	*seis*
7	**set**	*siete*
8	**vuit**	*ocho*
9	**nou**	*nueve*
10	**deu**	*diez*
11	**onze**	*once*
12	**dotze**	*doce*
13	**tretze**	*trece*
14	**catorze**	*catorce*
15	**quinze**	*quince*
16	**setze**	*dieciséis*
17	**disset**	*diecisiete*
18	**divuit**	*dieciocho*
19	**dinou**	*diecinueve*
20	**vint**	*veinte*
21	**vint-i-u**	*veintiuno*
30	**trenta**	*treinta*
40	**quaranta**	*cuarenta*
50	**cinquanta**	*cincuenta*
60	**seixanta**	*sesenta*
70	**setanta**	*setenta*
80	**vuitanta**	*ochenta*
90	**noranta**	*noventa*
100	**cent**	*cien*
200	**dos-cents**	*doscientos*
1,000	**mil/mil**	*million milió/millón*

USEFUL WORDS

yes/no	**sí/no**	*sí/no*
please	**si us plau**	*por favor*

thank you	**gràcies**	*gracias*
there	**allà**	*allí*
where	**on**	*dónde*
here	**aquí**	*aquí*
when	**quan**	*cuándo*
why	**per què**	*por qué*
how	**com**	*cómo*
who	**qui**	*quién*
I'm sorry	**Em sap greu**	*Lo siento*
excuse me	**perdoni**	*perdone*
large	**gran**	*grande*
small	**petit**	*pequeño*
good	**bo**	*bueno*
bad	**dolent**	*malo*
open	**obert**	*abierto*
closed	**tancat**	*cerrado*

SHOPPING

When does the shop open/ close?
A quina hora obre/tanca la botiga?
¿A qué hora abre/cierra la tienda?

Could you help me, please?
Que em pot atendre, si us plau?
¿Me atiende, por favor?

How much is this?
Quant costa això?
¿Cuánto cuesta esto?

I'm looking for…
Busco…
Busco…

I'm just looking
Només miro
Sólo estoy mirando

I'd like…
Voldria…
Quisiera…

I'll take this
M'enduc això
Me llevo esto

Do you have anything smaller/larger?
Té alguna cosa més petita/gran?
¿Tiene algo más pequeño/grande?

Please can I have a receipt?
Em dóna un rebut, si us plau?
¿Me da un recibo, por favor?

Do you accept credit cards?
Accepten targetes de crèdit?
¿Aceptan tarjetas de crédito?

HOTELS

Do you have a room?
Té una habitació?
¿Tiene una habitación?

I have a reservation for … nights
Tinc una reserva per a … nits
Tengo una reserva para … noches

How much per night?
Quant és per nit?
¿Cuánto es por noche?

Single room
Habitació individual
Habitación individual

Twin room
Habitació doble amb dos llits
Habitación doble con dos camas

Double room
Habitació doble amb llit de matrmoni
Habitación doble con cama de matrimonio

With bath/shower/lavatory
Amb banyera/dutxa/vàter
Con bañera/ducha/váter

Is breakfast/lunch/dinner included in the price?
S'inclou el desdejuni/el dinar/el sopar en el preu?
¿Está el desayuno/la comida/la cena incluido/-a en el precio?

Is the room air-conditioned/ heated?
Té aire condicionat/calefacció l'habitació?
¿Tiene aire acondicionado/ calefacción la habitación?

non smoking
no fumeu
se prohibe fumar

I'll take this room
Em quedo l'habitació
Me quedo con la habitación

Please can I pay my bill?
El compte, si us plau
La cuenta, por favor

EMERGENCIES

I don't feel well
No em trobo bé
No me encuentro bien

Could you call a doctor?
Pot cridar un metge?
¿Puede llamar a un médico?

Where is the hospital?
On hi ha l'hospital?
¿Dónde está el hospital?

Call the fire brigade/police/ ambulance
Truqui als bombers/la policia/una ambulància
Llame a los bomberos/la policía/una ambulancia

I have had an accident
He tingut un accident
He tenido un accidente

I have been robbed
M'han robat
Me han robado

Where is the police station?
On hi ha la comissaria?
¿Dónde está la comisaría?

I have lost my passport/ wallet/ purse/handbag
He perdut el passaport/la cartera/ el moneder/la bossa
He perdido el pasaporte/ la cartera/el monedero/el bolso

Is there a lost property office?
Que hi ha una oficina d'objectes perduts?
¿Hay una oficina de objetos perdidos?

Help!
Auxili
Socorro

Stop thief!
Al lladre
Al ladrón

IN THE TOWN

castle
el castell
el castillo

cathedral
la catedral
la catedral

church
l'església
la iglesia

lavatories
els lavabos
los aseos

museum
el museu
el museo

palace
el palau
el palacio

town
la ciutat
la ciudad

no parking
prohibit aparcar
prohibido aparcar

entrance
entrada
entrada

exit
sortida
salida

town hall
l'ajuntament
el ayuntamiento

RESTAURANTS
What time does the restaurant open?
A quina hora obre el restaurant?
¿A qué hora abre el restaurante?

I'd like to reserve a table for … people at …
Voldria reservar una taula per a … persones per a les …
Quiero reservar una mesa para … personas para las…

A table for …, please
Una taula per a …, si us plau
Una mesa para …, por favor

Is this table free?
Està lliure aquesta taula?
¿Está libre esta mesa?

Could we see the menu?
Podem veure la carta?
¿Podemos ver la carta?

Could we see the wine list?
Podem veure la cartade vins?
¿Podemos ver la carta de vinos?

What do you recommend?
Què ens recomana?
¿Qué nos recomienda?

Is there a dish of the day?
Té un plat del dia?
¿Tiene un plato del día?

How much is this dish?
Què costa aquest plat?
¿Cuánto cuesta este plato?

I am a vegetarian
Sóc vegetarià
Soy vegetariano/-a

I ordered …
He demanat …
Yo pedí …

Can I have the bill, please?
Em duu el compte, si us plau?
¿Me trae la cuenta, por favor?

The bill is not right
El compte no està bé
La cuenta no está bien

GETTING AROUND
Where is the information desk?
On hi ha el taulell d'informació?
¿Dónde está el mostrador de información?

Is this the way to…?
Aquest és el camí per a anar a…?
¿Es éste el camino para ir a…?

Please take me to…
A…, si us plau
A…, por favor

Go straight on
Continuï recte
Siga recto

Turn left
Tombi a l'esquerra
Gire a la izquierda

Turn right
Tombi a la dreta
Gire a la derecha

TIMES/DAYS/MONTHS/HOLIDAYS
morning	**el matí**	*la mañana*
afternoon	**la tarda**	*la tarde*
evening	**el vespre**	*la tarde*
day	**el dia**	*el día*
night	**la nit**	*la noche*
today	**avui**	*hoy*
yesterday	**ahir**	*ayer*
tomorrow	**demà**	*mañana*
now	**ara**	*ahora*
later	**més tard**	*más tarde*
week	**la setmana**	*la semana*
spring	**primavera**	*primavera*
summer	**estiu**	*verano*
autumn	**tardor**	*otoño*
winter	**hivern**	*invierno*
Monday	**dilluns**	*lunes*
Tuesday	**dimarts**	*martes*
Wednesday	**dimecres**	*miércoles*
Thursday	**dijous**	*jueves*
Friday	**divendres**	*viernes*
Saturday	**dissabte**	*sábado*
Sunday	**diumenge**	*domingo*
January	**gener**	*enero*
February	**febrer**	*febrero*

March	**març**	*marzo*
April	**abril**	*abril*
May	**maig**	*mayo*
June	**juny**	*junio*
July	**juliol**	*julio*
August	**agost**	*agosto*
September	**setembre**	*septiembre*
October	**octubre**	*octubre*
November	**novembre**	*noviembre*
December	**desembre**	*diciembre*

CONVERSATION
What is your name?
Co es diu?
¿Como se llama usted?

What is the time?
Quina hora és?
¿Qué hora es?

I don't speak Catalan/Spanish
No parlo català/espanyol
No hablo catalán/español

Do you speak English?
Parla anglès?
¿Habla inglés?

I don't understand
No ho entenc
No entiendo

I don't like
No m'agrada
No me gusto

Please repeat that
Si us plau, repeteixi això
Por favor, repita eso

Please speak more slowly
Si us plau, parli més a poc a poc
Por favor, hable más despacio

Can you say that in Spanish, please?
M'ho pot dir en castellà, si us plau?
¿Se puede decir en español, por favor?

Good morning/afternoon
Bon dia/Bona tarda
Buenos días/Buenas tardes

Goodbye
Adéu-siau
Adiós

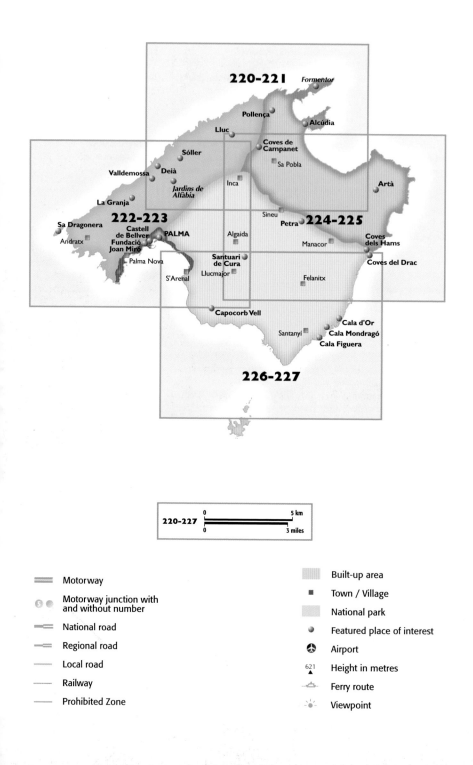

220-221

Formentor

Pollença

Alcúdia

Lluc

Coves de Campanet

Sóller

Sa Pobla

Valldemossa

Deià

Jardins de Alfàbia

Inca

Artà

La Granja

Sineu

Petra **224-225**

Sa Dragonera

Castell de Bellver

PALMA

Algaida

Coves dels Hams

Andratx

Fundació Joan Miró

Manacor

Palma Nova

Santuari de Cura

Coves del Drac

S'Arenal

Llucmajor

Felanitx

222-223

Capocorb Vell

Cala d'Or

Santanyí

Cala Mondragó

Cala Figuera

226-227

| 220-227 | 0 ———————————— 5 km |
| | 0 ———————————— 3 miles |

Motorway		Built-up area
Motorway junction with and without number		Town / Village
National road		National park
Regional road		Featured place of interest
Local road		Airport
Railway	621	Height in metres
Prohibited Zone		Ferry route
		Viewpoint

MAPS

Map references for the sights refer to the atlas pages within this section or to the Palma city map on pages 52–53. For example, Valldemossa has the reference ✚ 223 D4, indicating the page on which the map is found (223) and the grid square in which Valldemossa sits (D4).

Maps   220

Atlas index   228

D   E   F   G

I

2

Punta Beca

3

Platja de
Torrent de
Pareis

*Cala
Tuent*

462
▲ Torre de
Can Palou

Sa Calobra

921
▲ Puig Caragoler

1002
● Puig Roig

1103
● Puig Tomir

Serra de

Escorca

Ma-10

Lluc

Es Guix

Ma-2130

S'Illeta

579
▲ Puig de Balitx

1447
● Puig Major

*Embassament
des Gorg Blau*

1367
● Puig de Massanella

**Port de
Sóller**

Cap Gros

Muleta

Es Travès

Ma-11A

Pont d'en Barona

Fornalutx

Biniaraix

Ma-10

*Embassament
de Cúber*

1115
▲ Puig des
Tossals Verds

Campanet

1084
▲ Puig de
sa Rateta

Caimari

Moscari

*Cala
Deià*

Llucalcari

Sóller

Serra de Tramuntana

1091
● Puig de
l'Ofre

Comasema

Can Xalet

Biniarroi

Selva

4

Ma-10

Deià

1067
Alfàbia

501
Coll de
Sóller

825
▲ Puig d'Alaró

Castell d'Alaró

813
▲ Puig de
S'Alcadena

Orient

Mancor
de la Vall

Biniamar

287
● Puig de
Inca

Ma-2130

Ma-13

874
● Puig de Teix

1062
● Puig de Teix

Ses Fontanelles

Valldemossa

*Jardines
de Alfàbia*

Ma-2100

223

Lloseta

Ma-2110

Inca

Ma-3440

Es Nogueral

Ma-111

Alaró

Ma-2100

Ma-2110

Ma-13A

Jornets

Bunyola

671
● Puig de
N'Aimeric

Binissalem

Ma-13

Ma-3240

Ma-3120

5

Palmanyola

Son Amar

Ma-1140

Ma-2030

Baix des Puig
Ma-2020

Consell

Biniagual

Costitx

Ses Rogetes

S'Esglieta

Son Serra
Nou

Ma-2040

**Santa María
del Camí**

Ma-13A

Ma-13

Ma-3020

Sencelles

PM-111

E

F

G

220

2

Cap de
Catalunya
Cala
Figuera   Cap de Formentor

Es Colomer

Formentor   334
Es Fumat

**Cala
Bòquer**   Cala Pí
de la
Posada

Cala Sant
Vicenç   *Serra de
Cavall Bernat*   350
El Morral   *Illa de Formentor*

Port de Pollença

839
Puig Gros
de Ternelles   Las Palmeras   Siller
La Font   El Vilar
Can Tirana   Gotmar   Menorca
Ma-2200

Pollença   Llenaire   *Badia de Pollença*   Cap des Pinar

Ma-10   *Platja des
Coll Baix*
333   *Reserva
Naturel
de S'Albufereta*   Es Barcares   Bon Aire   445   Cap de Menorca
T r a m u n t a n a   Puig de
Maria   **Es Mal Pas**   *Península de la Victòria*   Talaia
d'Alcúdia
So n'Ali
Ma-2200   **Alcúdia**   Sa Bassa Blanca

3

Ma-13   Mar del Plata   **Port d'Alcúdia**
339   Poblado
Puig de   268   *Es Llac*   G E S A
Son Vila   Puig de   *Gran*   *Port d'Alcúdia*   *Illa d'Alcanada*
Ma-2220   Son Fé   **Lago Esperanza**
327   Crestatx   Ses Fotges   *Platja de Alcúdia*
Puig des Fangar

**Coves de
Campanet**   *Parc Natural*   Playas de Mallorca   *Badia d'Alcúdia*
Ma-13   *de S'Albufera*
Ullaró

*Salines
de s'Illot*
Sa Pobla
Búger   **Can Picafort**   *Cala*
Son Bauló   *Illa dels Porros*   Caló des
Corb Marí

4

Son Serra   **Colònia
de Marina   de Sant Pere**
Muro   *Estany del*   **Ermita de
Bisbe*   Betlem**
Sa Colonia   S'Es
Ma-3450   **224**   **225**   522
Ma-3410   Puig de Ferrutx
Ma-3400   Son Fortesa Vell
Ma-3500   Ma-3430
Ma-3440   Ma-12

Llubí   Ma-12   Carrossa
487
Santa Margalida   Puig d'Alpare   Ses Full
Ma-3520
Ma-3240   Ma-3340   Ma-3330   5

Maria de la Salut
Ma-3510
Ariany   473
Sineu   Ma-3301   Muntanya   **221**

4

Sa Marin
Port de Valldemoss

Cala
Gata

George
Sand

Son Coll

Cala Banyalbufar

561
Claret ▲ Nov

Ma-10 **Banyalbufar**

Esporles

Planícia

934
▲ Planícia

La Granja

5

Cala Cas
Xeremier

Estellencs

893
▲ Puntals de
Son Fortesa

Es Farallons

Ma-10

Serra

de

Tramuntana

1027
▲
Puig de Galatzó

La Reserva

Puigpunyent

928
▲
Sa Mola
de S'Esclop

Galilea

Son Serralta

Es Rafal

614
▲
Puig de na Baucà

Ma-1016

Cap de
Tramuntana

Cala en
Basset

Sa Dragonera

349
▲ Far Vell

483
▲
Puig de sa Grua

361
▲
Font

Parc Natural
de Sa Dragonera

Sant Elm

Illa Es
Pantaleu

Ma-1030

S'Arracó

Ma-10

Es Capdellà

Calvià

Cap des
Llebeig

Cala es
Conills

312
▲
Puig d'en Ric

Sa Coma

Andratx

486
▲
Puig
Gros de Berdinat

6

Cap des Falcons

Mont Port

Ses
Egos

Ma-1

Costa d'en
Blanes

Cala
Moragues

Port d'Andratx

Peguera

Ma-1

Ma-1C

Cap de sa Mola

Ses Moles

Es Camp
de Mar

Aldea Cala
Fornells

Costa de la Calma

Ma-1

Puerto
Portals

Portal
Nous

Sa Mola

Cala
Llamp

Cala en
Cranc

Costa de
Andratx

Port de
Mar

Cala
Fornells

Galatzó

Palma Nova

Cap des Llamp

Cap
Andritxol

Ses Rotes Velles

Son Maties

Torre Nova

Ensenada de
Santa Ponca

Costa de
la Luz

188
▲
Puig d'en
Saragossa

Santa Ponça

Magaluf

Illa de sa Porrassa

Illa des Conills

Son Ferrer

Badia de
Palma

Illa Malgrats

Cap
Negret

Palville

Pista de
Ultraligeros

Cap des Falcó

7

Sol de
Mallorca

Illot del Sec

El Toro

Portals Vells

Ses Barbines

Castell
de Sant Carles

Illa del Toretó

Cap de Cala Figuera

Illot de sa Galera

Cabrera
Menorca

Palma

Platja de Palma
Palma Aquarium
Ses Meravelles
Montemar
Ses Cadenes

S'Arenal
El Arenal

Bellavista

Son Verí Nou

Bella Vista   Cala Blava
                Ses Palme   **223**

Cap Enderrocat

Cap Negret

Son Granada
de Dalt

Sa Morería

Cap de Paret
des Puig de Ros

Sa Torre

Badia Gran

Badia Blava

El Dorado

Sa Llapassa

Cap de Regana

Betlem

Capocorb Vell

Cas Garriguer

Cap Roig

Cala Pi

Cap Blanc

Cala Pi   Vallgornera

Garonda

Son Bieló   Sa Ràpita

Punta Plana   Ses Covetes

*Salobrar
de Campos*

*Salines des
Llevant*

Ensenada de sa Ràpita

Platja des Trenc
Illa Gavina
Illot de sa Llova
Illot Gros
Sa Llarga

Colònia de Sant Jordi

Illot des Cabots
Sa Corberana
Sa Guardis
Platja des Carbó
Sa Moltona
Sa Pelada

Son Mandivia
de Dalt

Puig de
Randa

Randa

**Santuari
de Cura**

Son Sastre

Llucmajor

Ma-19A

Ma-6020

Ma-6020

Ma-19

Ma-5010

Ma-5020

Ma-5020

Ma-19

Ma-19

Ma-6030

Ma-6014

Ma-6015

Ma-6030

Ma-6040

Ma-6014

7

8

Cap Enderrocat

9

S'Illot Foradat

Na Pobre   S'Illot Plá

Illot Esponja   Illa Plana

Punta Escaleta

Punta Cala Estreta

I Conillera

Palma
Colònia de Sant Jordi

Cap de Llebeitx

Cap d'es
Moro Botí

Cala
Ganduf

Es Port

Illa Redona

Cap Ventós

Cala Mal Entredo

Punta de
Picamosques   172
                Cabrera

Cabrera

Cala
Olja

Cap de sa Carabassa

Illot de ses Bledes

Illa de Cabrera

Punta de Anciola

Estels
Xapats

Cap Falcó

Estels de Fora

Cabrera

10

S'Illot Foradat

Na Pobre   S'Illot Plá

Illot Esponja   Illa Plana

Punta Escaleta

Punta Cala Estreta

I Conillera

Illa Redona

Porreres

H

J

Coves del Drac

Cala Murta

Portocristo Novo

K

Cala Anguila

Son Macià

334 ▲
Puig de
sa Bandera

Cala Romàntica

S'Estany d'en Mas

Can Frasquet

Ma-500

Ma-5100

Ma-5040

Ma-5111

Ma-14

Ma-5100

224

225

319
▲
Mola des
Fangar

7

Felanitx

Ma-4010

Calas de
Mallorca

Son Rosselló

Ma-5120

**Santuari de
Sant Salvador**

Ma-4014

494 ▲
Puig de
Sant Salvador

Platja Tropicana

Ma-5040

Ma-14

Cala Murada

272
▲ Puig de
Mamelles

Ma-4010

Port
de sa Capella

Son Negre

Es Carritxó

Portocolom

Campos

Punta de s'Homonet

Cova de la Mare de Déu

Cas Concos

S'Horta

Ma-14

Calonge

Ma-6040

Ma-J9

272
▲
Puig Gross

Alqueria
Blanca

Ma-4012

Cala Fe

Cala Ferrera

Son Alegre

Serra del Levante

Ma-J9

Cala Serena

Cala d'Or

Es Palmer

Es Fortí

Punta de sa Galera

Parque
de Mar

Santanyí

Parc Natural de
Mondragó

Portopetro

8

Es Rafal Llinàs

Ma-6100

Cala Mondragó

Caló d'en
Burgit

Llombards

Son Mòger

Es Savinar

Ses Salines

Sa Covassa

Cabrera

Ma-6100

Cala Santanyí

Cala Figuera

Sa Vall

Cala Llombards

Cala Santanyí

Caló des Moro

Sa Vallet

Ma-5110

9

Illot d'en
Curt

Platja des
Caragol

Cap de ses Salines

Freu de Cabrera

10

H

J

K

Alaró	223	F5	Costa de la Calma	222	C6	Muleta	220	E4	Santanyí	227	H8
Alcúdia	221	H3	Costa de la Luz	222	C7	Muro	221	H4	S'Aranjassa	223	E6
Aldea Cala Fornells	222	C6	Costa en Blanes	222	D6				S'Arenal el Arenal	223	E7
Algaida	223	F6	Costa des Pins	225	L5	Nova Valldemossa	222	D5	S'Arracó	222	B6
Alqueria Blanca	227	J8	Costitx	224	G5				Selva	220	G4
Andratx	222	C6	Crestatx	221	H3	Orient	220	E4	Sencelles	224	G5
Ariany	224	H5				Palma	223	D6	Ses Alqueries	223	F5
Artà	225	K5	Deià	220	D4	Palma Nova	222	D6	Ses Cadenes	223	E7
						Palmanyola	223	E5	Ses Coves	223	F5
Badia Blava	226	E7	El Dorado	226	E8	Palville	222	C7	Ses Covetes	226	G8
Badia de Palma	222	C7	El Terreno	223	D6	Parque de Mar	227	J8	Ses Egos	222	B6
Badia Gran	226	E7	El Toro	222	C7	Peguera	222	C6	Ses Fotges	221	H3
Baix des Puig	223	E5	El Vilar	221	H2	Petra	224	H5	Ses Fulles	225	K5
Banyalbufar	222	C5	Es Barcares	221	H3	Pina	224	G6	Ses Llegitimes	223	E5
Base Aèria de Son			Es Camp de Mar	222	C6	Planícia	222	C5	Ses Meravelles	223	E6
Sant Joan	223	E6	Es Capdellà	222	C6	Platja Tropicana	227	K7	Ses Moles	222	B6
Bella Vista	223	E7	Es Carritxó	227	J7	Playas de Mallorca	221	H4	Ses Palmeres	223	E7
Bellavista	223	E7	Es Fortí	227	J8	Poblado G E S A	221	J3	Ses Rogetes	223	D5
Betlem	221	K4	Es Garrovers	223	E5	Polígon de Son Castelló	223	E6	Ses Rotes Velles	222	C6
Betlem	226	F8	Es Guix	220	F3	Pollença	221	G3	Ses Salines	227	H8
Biniagual	223	F5	Es Mal Pas	221	H3	Pont d'en Barona	220	E4	S'Esgleieta	223	D5
Biniali	223	F5	Es Molinar	223	E6	Pont d'Inca	223	E6	S'Estanyol	221	J4
Biniamar	220	F4	Es Nogueral	223	D5	Porreres	224	H6	S'Horta	227	J8
Biniaraix	220	E4	Es Palmer	227	H8	Port d'Alcúdia	221	H3	Síller	221	H2
Biniarroi	220	F4	Es Pont d'Inca Nou	223	E6	Port d'Andratx	222	B6	S'Indioteria	223	E6
Binissalem	223	F5	Es Port	226	G11	Port de Mar	222	C6	Sineu	224	G5
Bon Aire	221	J3	Es Rafal	222	C6	Port de Pollença	221	H2	So n'Ali	221	G3
Búger	221	G4	Es Rafal Llinàs	227	H8	Port de sa Capella	227	K7	Sol de Mallorca	222	C7
Bunyola	223	E5	Es Rafal Vell	223	E6	Port de Sóller	220	E4	Sóller	220	E4
			Es Savinar	227	J8	Port Nou	223	D6	Son Alegre	223	E6
Cabrera	226	G11	Es Secar de la Real	223	D6	Port Verd	225	L5	Son Alegre	227	G8
Caimari	220	G4	Es Través	220	E4	Portals Nous	222	D6	Son Amar	223	E5
Cala Blava	223	E7	Es Vivero	223	E6	Portals Vells	222	D7	Son Ametler	223	E6
Cala Bona	225	L5	Escorca	220	F3	Portitxol	223	E6	Son Anglada	223	D6
Cala d'Or	227	J8	Esporles	222	D5	Porto Cristo	225	K6	Son Bauló	221	J4
Cala Fe	227	J8	Establiments	223	D5	Portocolom	227	J8	Son Bieló	226	G8
Cala Ferrera	227	J8	Establiments Nous	223	D5	Portocristo Novo	225	K6	Son Blanc	223	E5
Cala Figuera	227	J9	Establiments Vell	223	D5	Pòrtol	223	E5	Son Buit	223	D6
Cala Lliteres	225	L4	Estellencs	222	C5	Portopetro	227	J8	Son Carrió	225	K6
Cala Llombards	227	H9				Puerto Portals	222	D6	Son Coll	222	D5
Cala Major	223	D6	Felanitx	227	J7	Puigpunyent	222	C5	Son Espanyol	223	D5
Cala Mesquida	225	L4	Font de Sa Cala						Son Ferrandell	223	D5
Cala Millor	225	K6	Provença	225	L5	Randa	224	G6	Son Ferrer	222	C7
Cala Moragues	222	B6	Fornalutx	220	E4	Ruberts	224	G5	Son Ferriol	223	E6
Cala Moreia	225	K6							Son Fortesa Vell	225	K5
Cala Morlanda	225	K6	Galatzó	222	C6	Sa Bassa Blanca	221	J3	Son Granada de Dalt	226	F7
Cala Murada	227	K7	Galilea	222	C5	Sa Cabana	223	E6	Son Gual	223	F6
Cala Pi	226	F8	Garonda	226	F8	Sa Cabana Nova	223	E5	Son Macià	224	J7
Cala Ratjada	225	L4	Génova	223	D6	Sa Cabaneta	223	E5	Son Mandivia de Dalt	223	F6
Cala Romàntica	225	K6	George Sand	222	D5	Sa Calobra	220	F3	Son Mas	225	J6
Cala Santanyí	227	J8	Gotmar	221	H2	Sa Casa Blanca	223	E6	Son Maties	222	D7
Cala Serena	227	J8				Sa Colonia	221	J4	Son Mòger	227	H8
Cales de Mallorca	227	K7	Illetes	223	D6	Sa Coma	222	C6	Son Moro	225	K6
Calonge	227	J8	Inca	224	G4	Sa Covassa	227	J8	Son Moro Buenavista	225	K6
Calvià	222	C6				Sa Creu Vermella	223	E6	Son Negre	227	H7
Campanet	220	G4	Jornets	224	G5	Sa Garriga	223	E5	Son n'Olésa	223	D4
Campos	227	H7				Sa Llapassa	226	F8	Son Ramonell	223	E5
Can Farineta	223	E5	La Font	221	G2	Sa Marina Port			Son Roca-Son Ximelis	223	D6
Can Frasquet	225	K7	Lago Esperanza	221	H3	de Valldemossa	223	D4	Son Rosselló	227	H7
Can Maniu	224	J6	Las Palmeras	221	H2	Sa Mola	222	B6	Son Sardina	223	E5
Can Pastilla	223	E6	Llenaire	221	H3	Sa Morería	223	E7	Son Sastre	224	G6
Can Picafort	221	J4	Llombards	227	H8	Sa Pla de na Tesa	223	E6	Son Serra de Marina	221	J4
Can Tirana	221	H2	Lloret de Vista			Sa Pobla	221	H4	Son Serra Nou	223	E5
Can Xalet	220	F4	Alegre (Llorito)	224	G5	Sa Ràpita	226	G8	Son Serralta	222	D5
Canyamel	225	L5	Lloseta	223	F4	Sa Torre	226	E7	Son Servera	225	K5
Capdepera	225	L5	Llubí	224	G5	Sa Vall	227	H9	Son Verí Nou	223	E7
Carrossa	225	K5	Lluc	220	F3	Sa Vileta	223	D6	Son Vida	223	D6
Cas Canar	224	G5	Llucalcari	220	E4	Sant Agustí	223	D6			
Cas Concos	227	H8	Llucmajor	223	F7	Sant Elm	222	B6	Torre Nova	222	D7
Cas Garriguer	226	F8				Sant Joan	224	H6	Trempes de Son Daviu	223	E5
Ciutat Jardí	223	E6	Magaluf	222	D7	Sant Jordi	223	F6			
Coll d'en Rebassa	223	E6	Manacor	224	J6	Sant Llorenç			Ullaró	221	G4
Colònia de Sant Jordi	226	G9	Mancor de la Vall	220	F4	des Cardassar	225	K5			
Colònia de Sant Pere	221	K4	Mar del Plata	221	H3	Santa Eugènia	223	F5	Valldemossa	223	D4
Comasema	220	F4	Maria de la Salut	224	H5	Santa Margalida	221	H5	Vallgornera	226	F8
Consell	223	F5	Mont Port	222	B6	Santa María del Camí	223	E5	Vilafranca de Bonany	224	H6
Costa de Andratx	222	B6	Montemar	223	E7	Santa Ponça	222	C7			
Costa de Berdinat	223	D6	Montuïri	224	G6						
Costa de Canyamel	225	L5	Moscari	220	G4						

A

accidents 45
accommodation 212–213
   agroturismo 15, 212–213
   casas rurales 213
   fincas 212–213
   full and half-board 213
   hostals 212
   hotels *see* hotels
   monastery accommodation 12, 103, 213
   refuges 120, 214
   self-catering 213
addresses 195
agriculture 7, 14, 21, 170
agroturismo 15, 212–213
AIDS 191
air travel 38–39
airport 38
Albarca Valley 104
Alcúdia 132–134, 144
   accommodation 155–156
   Can Torró 134
   market 134
   Museu Monogràfic de Pollentia 134
   Museu de Sant Jaume 134
   Oratori de Santa Anna 134
   Pollentia 133
   Port d'Alcúdia 133, 134, 144
   restaurants 152–153
   Teatre Romà 134
   town walls 134
   what to do 148–149
Alfàbia 100
Alfonso III 28, 29
Algaida 170, 176, 180, 184
almond farming 21
Amis, Kingsley 18, 98
Andratx 97, 114
   Castell Son Mas 97, 114
   Centro Cultural Andratx 97
   Port d'Andratx 97
   Santa Maria 97
   what to do 120–121
Angel Sunday 85
animal attractions
   Auto-Safari 149
   bird of prey flying displays 101
   Jumaica 176
   Marineland 84
   Natura Parc 170, 171, 178
   see also aquariums; wildlife
Antich, Francesc 7, 36
Aqualand El Arenal 58, 84
Aqualand Magaluf 84
aquariums
   Palma 68
   Porto Cristo 151
Arab Baths 59, 66
Arc de la Drassana 66
archery 122
architecture 16, 17
   Gothic 59, 63
   neoclassical 111
   Romanesque 66
   see also Modernista
arrest by police 193
Arroyo, Eduardo 63
art collections *see* museums and galleries
art galleries, commercial 150, 167, 178
Artà 135
   hotels 156
   restaurants 153
   Santuari de Sant Salvador 135
   Ses Païsses 135
   Transfiguració del Senyor 135
   what to do 149
arts 16–17
arts festival 19
ATMs 189
Auditori d'Alcùdia 148
Auto-Safari 149

B

Badia d'Alcúdia 153
Badia de Palma 56–58
   Castell de Sant Carles 57
   Ciutat Jardí 57
   Illetes 10, 58
   Magaluf 58
   Palma Nova 58
   Platja de Palma 58
   Portals Vells 58
   Portitxol 57
   Puerto Portals 15, 58
Balearic Islands 6, 35
Balearic lizard 106, 161
Baleart Craft Fair 85
ballet and modern dance 85, 149
Banco de Sóller 108
Banderas, Antonio 18
banks 190
Banyalbufar 97, 121, 124, 127
Banys Àrabs 59
Barbarossa (Redbeard) 106
Barcarès 144
Barceló, Miquel 17, 63, 72–73
Bardolet, Josep Coll 104, 112
bars and clubs 200–201
   Palma 79–80, 81, 200
Basílica de Sant Francesc 59
Battle of Bailén 31, 161
Bay of Palma 56–58
Bayeu, Manuel 111, 136
BCM 58, 80
beaches 202
   Blue Flag status 202
   nudist beaches 166, 202
Beaker culture 26
beauty salons 83
Becker, Boris 35
Bellver Castle 10, 60–61
Bennàssar, Dionís 143
best of Mallorca 10–12
Bestard walking boots 121
bicycling 20, 21, 46, 81–82, 120, 202
   bike rental 151, 176–177
   cycle routes 46, 174–175, 202
   guided cycling tours 176–177
   mountain biking 123, 148
   own bicycle 202
   safety 46, 175
   Tour of Mallorca 123, 207
Biniali 170
Biniaraix 109
Binifaldó 119
Binissalem 161, 176, 184
bird of prey flying displays 101
birdwatching 12, 20, 106, 117, 139, 161
black vulture 20
Blessing of the Animals 85
Blue Grotto 161
boat trips 43
   catamaran trips 122, 123
   glass-bottomed boats 43, 149
   schooner charter 150
   submarine excursions 84
   see also sailing; yacht charter
books
   about Mallorca 197
   bookshops 78, 79
   walking guides 214
Botanical Garden, Lluc 104
Botanical Garden, Sóller 109
Boveri, Atilio 142
Branson, Richard 18
Buïgas, Carles 165
bullfighting 23, 82, 202
Bunyola 117, 121, 123, 127
Burgess, Anthony 98
buses 39, 40–41

C

Ca N'Alluny 10, 19, 98
Ca S'Amitager 104
cabaret 121
Cabrera 6, 31, 43, 161
Caimari 116, 121, 127–128
Cala Agulla 136
Cala Bona 136
Cala Bóquer 138, 143
Cala Deià 98
Cala Estreta 135
Cala Figuera, northeast Mallorca 138
Cala Figuera, southern Mallorca 162, 180–181
Cala Gat 136
Cala Lladó 106
Cala Llombards 162
Cala Millor 136, 149
Cala Mitjana 135
Cala Molins 143
Cala Mondragó 11, 162, 176
Cala d'Or 162, 181, 184–185
Cala Pi 162
Cala Ratjada 136, 149, 156
Cala Sant Vicenç 143, 153, 156
Cala Santanyí 162
Cala Torta 135
calas 162
Calas de Mallorca 162, 176–177
Calonge 181
Calvià 115
Camarasa, Hermen Anglada 63, 141
Camel Rock 119
Camp de Mar 19
Campanet 156–157
Camper Factory Shop 177
Campos 181, 185
Can Aguila 74
Can Barceló 77

Can Bateman 139
Can Casasayas 75
Can Corbella 74
Can Forteza Rey 74
Ca'n Gordiola 161
Can Marquès 17, 59
Ca'n Pastilla 181
Can Picafort 144–145
Can Planes 11, 139
Can Prunera 108
Can Quiam 173
Can Solleric 69
Can Torró 134
canoeing 121, 150
canyoning 123
Cap Blanc 162, 174–175
Cap de Cala Figuera 58
Cap de Formentor 12
Cap des Llebeig 106
Cap des Pinar 146
Cap de Ses Salines 166
Cap de Tramuntana 106
Cap Vermell 136
Capdepera 149–150
Capocorb Vell 163, 174
car hire 38–39
Casa de la Fauna Ibero-
  Balear 166
Casa Museu Dionís
  Bennàssar 143
Casa Museu J Torrents
  Lladó 59
Casa Natal de Santa
  Catalina Thomàs 113
Casa Olesa 59
casas rurales 213
Cas Concos 185
cashpoints 189
Casino Mallorca 58, 80
Castaldo, Lluís 69
Castell d'Alaró 97, 116
Castell de Bellver 10, 60–61
Castell de Capdepera 136
Castell de Sant Carles 57
Castell de Santueri 167
Castell Son Mas 97, 114,
  115
Catalan 7, 24, 35, 215
Catalina Thomàs, Santa
  31, 113
catamaran trips 122, 123
Catholic Church 6, 22, 34,
  104
Cavalcada de Reis 85
cave complexes
  Coves d'Artà 136
  Coves de Campanet 137

Coves del Drac 164–165
Coves dels Hams 165
  Sa Cometa des Morts 119
  Sa Cova Blava 161
celebrities 18–19
Cementeri, Sóller 109
Centro Cultural Andratx 97
ceramics 177, 199
Chaplin, Charlie 18, 33
charcoal burning 118–119
children
  children's activities 84,
  206
  eating out with 209
  hazards 206
Chillida, Eduardo 63
Chopin, Frédéric 18, 110,
  112, 123
Christie, Agatha 18, 33, 197
churches and chapels
  Basílica de Sant Francesc
  59
  El Calvari 142
  Monti-Sion 77
  Nostra Senyora dels
  Àngels 141
  Nostra Senyora dels
  Dolors 167
  Nostra Senyora de la
  Esperança 136
  Nostra Senyora de Gracia
  77
  Nostra Senyora del
  Refugió 97
  Nostra Senyora dels
  Socors 77
  Oratori de Santa Anna 134
  Sant Bartomeu 108
  Sant Jeroni 76
  Sant Joan Baptista,
  Calvià 115
  Sant Joan Baptista, Deià
  98
  Sant Miquel 166
  Santa Maria, Andratx 97
  Santuari de Sant Salvador
  135
  La Seu (Palma cathedral)
  70–73
  Transfiguració del Senyor
  135
  see also hermitages;
  monasteries
Churchill, Winston 33, 138
cinema 201
City History Museum, Palma
  61

Ciutat Jardí 57
climate and seasons
  188–189
coach trips 41
Coll Baix 147
Colom, Joan 31
Colònia de Sant Jordi 166
Colònia de Sant Pere 136
Columbus, Christopher 30
Consolat de la Mar 69
Contemporary Spanish Art,
  Museum of 63
conversion chart 192
Copa del Rey 19, 21, 24, 85
Corr, Caroline 19
cossiers dance 22
Costa Nord 19, 113
Costitx 166, 170, 171,
  172–173, 177
  Museu de Ciències
  Naturals 166, 171, 172,
  173
  Observatorio Astronómico
  Mallorca 166, 173, 177
country code 214
Cove de la Mare de Déu
  58
Coves d'Artà 136
Coves de Campanet 137
Coves del Drac 164–165
Coves dels Hams 165
craft fairs and markets 85,
  207
credit cards 189–190, 199
  lost/stolen 190
Cresques, Abraham and
  Jafuda 30, 76
crime 193
Cúber reservoir 12, 117
cultural centres
  Centro Cultural Andratx
  97
  Costa Nord 19, 113
  Fundacío La Caixa 63,
  80–81
  Sa Taronja 120–121
  Teatro de Lloseta 121
currency exchange 189
customs regulations 189
cycling see bicycling

D

dance, traditional 22, 99,
  179
Deià 10, 98
  Ca N'Alluny 10, 19, 98
  Cala Deià 98

hotels 128
  restaurants 124–125
  Sant Joan Baptista 98
  what to do 121
Deià International Festival
  123
dentists 191
department and chain stores
  199
Despuig Collection 61
Dijous Bo 179
dinner shows 80, 81, 121,
  201
Diocesan Museum 73
disabilities, visitors with
  48
  eating out 209
  transport 48
Diumenge del Angel 85
doctors 191
Domènech i Montaner, Lluís
  17, 63
Don Pedro of Portugal 29
Douglas, Michael 18, 19,
  110, 113
Dragon Caves 164–165
dress codes 192, 209
drinking water 191
drives
  Eastern Tramuntana
  116–117
  Es Pla 170–171
  Pollença and Alcúdia
  Bays 144–145
  Western Tramuntana
  114–115
driving 44–45
  accidents 45
  car crime 39, 45
  car ferries 39
  car hire 38–39
  distances and journey
  times 45
  drink-driving 44, 193
  fuel 44
  motorways 44
  own car 44
  parking 45
  regulations 44
  road network (map) 44
  security 45
  speed limits 44
  tolls 44
drugs and medicines 191
Dry Stone Route 21, 120
duty-free and duty-paid
  guidelines 189

E

eating out 208–211
  with children 209
  dress code 209
  meals and mealtimes
    208–209
  menu reader 210–211
  reservations 209
  smoking etiquette 209
  tapas 200, 209
  tipping 209
  vegetarian food 209
  wheelchair users 209
  where to eat 208
  see also restaurants
eco-tax 14, 15
economy 7
Edward VIII of England 33
El Calvari 142
El Davallament 143
El Pi de Formentor 138
electricity 192
Els Blauets 103
Els Calderers 166
embassies and consulates
  abroad 193
  Palma 193
emergencies 193
emergency telephone
  numbers 193
  words and phrases 216
entertainment and nightlife
  200–201
  bars and clubs 200–201
  cinema 201
  dinner shows 80, 81, 121,
    201
  gay and lesbian scene 80,
    201
  listings 200, 201
  Palma 79–81
  tickets 201
  see also music; theatre
Ermita de Betlem 136
Ermita de Bonany 145, 168
Ermita de Sant Honorat 169
Ermita de la Trinitat 113
Ermita de la Victòria 146,
  147
Es Capdellà 115
Es Colomer 138
Es Dolç 166
Es Molinar 57
Es Pantaleu 106
Es Pla 6, 166, 170–171
Es Portitxolet 57
Es Puig 170

Es Trenc 11, 166
Escolania (choir) 103
Esporles 121
Estellencs 114
etiquette
  dress codes 192, 209
  local etiquette 192
  smoking 192, 201, 209,
    213
European Health Insurance
  Card (EHIC) 191

F

Felanitx 166, 177
ferry services 39, 43
Festa d'es Botifarró 179
Festa de l'Estendard 85
Festa des Meló 179
Festa de Vermar 179
Festival Bunyola 123
Festival Chopin 123
Festival de Música Castell
  de Bellver 85
Festival de Pollença 141,
  151
festivals and events 22, 207
  food festivals 179, 207
  music festivals 85, 123,
    141, 151, 207
  northeast Mallorca 151
  Palma 85
  religious festivals 22, 85,
    143
  Serra de Tramuntana 123
  the south 179
  sporting events 207
fincas 212–213
Fira des Fang 179
fish auction, Palma 69
fishing 123, 150, 176, 202
Flynn, Errol 18
folk music 99, 123, 201
foners 23
Font Cuberta 104
food and drink
  drinking water 191
  festivals 179, 207
  food shopping 78–79,
    122–123, 149, 198
  tapas 200, 209
  wines 24, 79, 115, 161,
    176
  see also eating out
football 24, 82, 202
foreign population 6, 19, 35
Formentera 6
Formentor 11, 138

Forn des Teatre 12, 75, 78
Fornalutx 11, 109, 125, 128
Forteza Rey, Lluís 74
Franco, General Francisco 34
Friel, Anna 19
Fundació Joan Miró 10, 62
Fundació La Caixa (Gran
  Hotel) 63, 80–81

G

Galilea 115
gardens
  Jardí Botànic, Lluc 104
  Jardí Botànic, Sóller 109
  Jardines de Alfàbia 14,
    100
  Jardins de la Faixina 75
  S'Hort del Rei 66
Gardner, Ava 18, 98
Garrido, Carlos 35
Gaudí, Antoni 17, 33, 72,
  74, 104
gay and lesbian scene 80,
  201
geography 6
German residents 19, 35
gifts and souvenirs 198
Glass Museum 161
glassmaking 11, 123, 161,
  176, 199
go-karting 84
Golden Cove 162
golf 11, 82, 83, 120, 121,
  148, 149–150, 177,
  202–203
Gorg Blau reservoir 117
La Granja 12, 99, 121
Graves, Robert 12, 18, 19,
  59, 98, 197
Green Card 15, 196
Griffiths, Melanie 18
Grup Ornitològic Balear
  (GOB) 35
Guasp printing press 112
Guerrero, Joan 23
Guinness, Alec 18
gyms and fitness centres 83,
  151, 205

H

hairdressing 83, 205
hang-gliding 82, 148, 203
Hannibal 27
health 191
  AIDS 191
  dentists 191
  doctors 191

drinking water 191
drugs and medicines 191
European Health
  Insurance Card (EHIC) 191
  health insurance 191
  hospitals 191
  inoculations 191
  medical treatment 191
  opticians 191
  pharmacies 191
  sun safety 191, 206
health and beauty 205
health insurance 191
hermitages
  Ermita de Betlem 136
  Ermita de Bonany 168
  Ermita de Sant Honorat
    169
  Ermita de la Trinitat 113
  Ermita de la Victòria 146,
    147
  see also monasteries
Hidropark 148
hiking see walking and
  hiking
historic mansions
  Alfàbia 100
  Can Marquès 17, 59
  Can Torró 134
  Casa Olesa 59
  Els Calderers 166
  La Granja 99
  Miramar 101
  Son Marroig 101, 121
history 25–36
  Carnival Revolt 31
  Catalonian outpost 30
  Franco dictatorship 34
  Golden Age 28–29
  Jaume I of Aragón 28, 29
  Jewish communities 30
  Modernist era 32–33
  Moorish rule 27
  prehistory 26–27
  Roman occupation 27,
    133
  Statute of Autonomy 35
  Talaiotic era 27
  twenty-first century 36
horse-riding 101, 121, 122,
  148–149, 151, 177,
  203–204
hospitals 191
Hostal Cuba 75
hostals 212
hot-air ballooning 149
Hotel Formentor 33, 138

hotels 212
  northeast Mallorca
  155–157
  Palma 90–93
  resort hotels 213
  Serra de Tramuntana
  127–129
  smoking etiquette 213
  the south 184–186
  spa hotels 205
  words and phrases 216

I

Ibiza 6, 43
Illa Mitjana 106
Illes Balears 6
Illetes 10, 58
immigrants 35
Inca 6, 167, 177, 179
inoculations 191
insurance
  health insurance 191
  travel insurance 193
International Boat Show 85
Internet cafés 194, 195

J

Jardí Botànic, Lluc 104
Jardí Botànic, Sóller 109
Jardines de Alfàbia 14, 100
Jardins de la Faixina 75
Jaume I of Aragón 28–29, 66
Jaume II 28, 29, 60, 73, 113
Jaume III 28, 60, 73
Jaume IV 60
jazz and blues 80, 81, 123,
  201
jewellery 78, 123, 150
Jewish communities 30,
  76–77
Jovellanos, Gaspar Melchor
  de 60
Juan Carlos, King 19, 21,
  23, 65, 66
Jumaica 176

K

kayaking 82, 120, 121, 123,
  204
Kelly, Grace 18
King's Cup 85
King's Garden 66
kite-surfing 149

L

Lacy, Luis de 60
Lake Martel 164, 165

language 6–7, 192
  Catalan 7, 24, 35, 215
  Mallorquí 6, 24, 215
  menu reader 210–211
  words and phrases
  215–217
laptops 195
laundry and dry cleaning 192
lavatories 192
leather goods 79, 116, 122,
  167, 177, 198
Leek Island 145
Lennox, Annie 18
livestock market 167
Lloseta 116, 121
La Llotja 63
Lloyd Webber, Andrew 19
Lluc Monastery 12, 102–105,
  118
  Basilica 102–103
  Ca S'Amitager 104
  Escolania (choir) 103
  Font Cuberta 104
  Jardí Botànic 104
  La Moreneta 103, 105
  Museu de Lluc 103–104
  pilgrimage 23, 102
  Way of the Rosary 104
Llucmajor 174, 177, 185
Llull, Ramón 29, 101, 169
  museum of 169
  tomb of 59
lost property 193

M

McGough, Roger 19
Magaluf 58, 200
Mallorquí 6, 24
Manacor 6, 167, 177–178,
  185
maps 197
  for walkers 214
  map shop 78
March, Joan 17, 67
Marès, Frederic 73
Maria de la Salut 145
marinas 15
Marineland 84
markets 199
  Alcúdia 134
  Felanitx 166
  Inca 167, 179
  Plaça Major, Palma 69
  Pollença 12, 142
  Santa Catalina, Palma 10
  Sineu 167
  Sóller 109

Marquez, Gabriel García 18
Marratxí 179
Martel, Édouard 165
matances 207
Matas, Jaume 35
measurements 192
medical treatment 191
Mediterranean Nights
  festival 19, 123
melon festival 179
Menorca 6, 43
menu reader 210–211
midwife toad 15, 104
mineral water springs 119
mini-golf 84, 148
Mirador des Colomer 138
Mirador des Pixarells 119
Mirador de Ricardo Roca 114
Miramar 101
Miró, Joan 16, 63, 66, 104,
  113
  Fundació Joan Miró 10,
  62
mobile telephones 194
Modernista 12, 16, 17, 32
  Can Aguila 74
  Can Barceló 77
  Can Casasayas 75
  Can Corbella 74
  Can Forteza Rey 74
  Can Marquès 59
  Forn des Teatre 75, 78
  Fundació La Caixa (Gran
  Hotel) 63
  Hostal Cuba 75
  Modernist Palma (walk)
  74–75
  La Seu (cathedral), Palma
  33, 70
  Sóller 108
monasteries
  Lluc 12, 102–105, 118
  Puig de Maria 142, 143
  Reial Cartoixa 111–113
  Santuari de Cura 169
  Santuari de Sant Salvador
  167
  see also hermitages
monastery accommodation
  12, 103, 213
money 189–190
  banks 190
  cashpoints 189
  credit cards 189–190, 199
  currency exchange 189
  everyday items and prices
  190

sales tax 190
  tipping 190, 209
  wiring money 190
Monti-Sion 77
Montuïri 178, 181
La Moreneta 103, 105
Moros i Cristianos 123,
  143
mosques
  Palma 77
  Sa Pobla 139
motorboat rental 121
motorcycles 46
motorways 44
mountain biking 123, 148
mountain ranges 6
multiculturalism 35
Muñoz, Gil Sánchez 73
Muro 150
  bullfighting 23
  Museu Etnològic de Muro
  139
museums and galleries
  Ca N'Alluny 98
  Can Bateman 139
  Can Planes 11, 139
  Can Sabater 161
  Casa de la Fauna Ibero-
  Balear 166
  Casa Museu Dionís
  Bennàssar 143
  Casa Museu J Torrents
  Lladó 59
  Castell de Sant Carles 57
  Cathedral Museum 73
  City History Museum,
  Palma 61
  Contemporary Spanish
  Art, Museum of 63
  Despuig Collection 61
  Diocesan Museum 73
  Fundació Joan Miró 10,
  62
  Glass Museum 161
  Junípero Serra museum
  168
  Miramar 101
  Museu d'Art Espanyol
  Contemporani 63
  Museu Balear de Ciències
  Naturals 109
  Museu de Ciències
  Naturals 166, 171, 172,
  173
  Museu Diocesà 73
  Museu Es Baluard 10, 12,
  63

Museu Etnològic de Muro 139, 145
Museu del Fang 23
Museu de Lluc 103–104
Museu de Mallorca 64
Museu Martí Vicenç 142
Museu dels Molins 75
Museu Monogràfic de Pollentia 134
Museu Municipal 112–113
Museu de Pollença 11, 142
Museu de Sant Jaume 134
Museu de Sóller 109
Natural History Museum 166, 171, 172, 173
Palau March 17, 67
Pottery Museum 23
Ramón Llull museum 169
Torre dels Enagistes 167
Toy Museum 139
music
    classical music 10, 80, 121, 165, 201
    folk music 99, 123, 201
    jazz and blues 80, 81, 123, 201
music festivals 85, 123, 141, 151, 207
Myotragus balearicus 26, 64, 109

N

Na Foradada 101
Nadal, Rafael 19, 24
national holidays 196
Natura Parc 170, 171, 178
Natural History Museum 166, 171, 172, 173
nature reserves
    Cabrera 161
    Parc Natural de Mondragó 11, 162, 176
    Parc Natural de S'Albufera 139, 144
    Península de Llevant 145
    Peninsula de la Victòria 134, 146–147
    Punta de n'Amer 136
    La Reserva 101
    Reserva Puig de Galatzó 101, 122
    Sa Dragonera 6, 35, 106–107
Nemo submarine 84

Newman, Philip 141
newspapers 197
Nicholson, Jack 18
nightlife and entertainment and nightlife
Nin, Anaïs 98
Nordic walking tours 148
northeast Mallorca 9, 130–157
    festivals and events 151
    hotels 155–157
    map 131
    restaurants 152–154
    sights 11, 132–143
    walks and drives 144–147
    what to do 148–151
Nostra Senyora dels Àngels 141
Nostra Senyora dels Dolors 167
Nostra Senyora de la Esperança 136
Nostra Senyora de Gracìa, Palma 77
Nostra Senyora de Gràcia, Puig de Randa 169
Nostra Senyora del Refugió 97
Nostra Senyora dels Socors 77
nudist beaches 166, 202

O

Observatorio Astronómico Mallorca 166, 173, 177
olive oil production 116, 121
olive wood products 122, 178, 199
opening times 196
opticians 191
Oratori de Santa Anna 134
Orient 11, 101, 117, 125, 129
orienteering 122

P

packing tips 189
Palau de l'Almudaina 65–66
Palau March 17, 67
Palau Marivent 19
Palau del Rei Sanç 113
Palma 8, 10, 17, 36, 50–93
    accommodation 90–93
    airport 38
    Arab Baths 59, 66
    Avinguda Jaume III 75
    Badia de Palma 56–58
    Banys Àrabs 59

Basílica de Sant Francesc 59
buses 40–41
Can Aguila 74
Can Barceló 77
Can Casasayas 75
Can Corbella 75
Can Forteza Rey 74
Can Marquès 17, 59
Can Solleric 69
Casa Museu J Torrents Lladó 59
Casa Olesa 59
Castell de Bellver 10, 60–61
children's activities 84
City History Museum 61
Consolat de la Mar 69
Despuig Collection 61
entertainment and nightlife 79–81, 200, 201
festivals and events 85
Forn des Teatre 75, 78
Fundació Joan Miró 10, 62
Fundació La Caixa (Gran Hotel) 63, 80–81
health and beauty 83
Jardins de la Faixina 75
Jewish Quarter 76–77
La Llotja 63
Mercat de Santa Catalina 75
Modernism 74–75
Monti-Sion 77
Museu d'Art Espanyol Contemporani 63
Museu Diocesà 73
Museu Es Baluard 10, 12, 63
Museu de Mallorca 64
Museu dels Molins 75
Nostra Senyora de Gracìa 77
Palau de l'Almudaina 65–66
Palau March 17, 67
Palau Marivent 19
Palma Aquarium 12, 68
Parc de la Mar 16, 69
parking 45
Passeig des Born 69
Passeig Marítim 12, 69
Plaça Major 69
Plaça Mercat 75
restaurants 86–89
Sa Calatrava 76

Sant Jeroni 76
Santa Catalina 10, 75
Ses Voltes 69
La Seu (cathedral) 33, 70–73
shopping 78–79, 199
S'Hort del Rei 66
sights 10, 56–73
sightseeing bus 40–41, 82
sports and activities 81–83
street map 52–55
taxis 47
walks 74–77
what to do 78–85
Palma Nova 58
Palmanyola 121
Parc de la Mar 69
Parc Natural de Mondragó 11, 162, 176
Parc Natural de S'Albufera 139, 144
Parc Natural de Sa Dragonera 6, 35, 106–107
parking 45
passeig 7
Passeig des Born 69
Passeig Marítim 12, 69
passports 189
    lost/stolen 193
pearls 79, 167, 198
pearl factory tours 167, 177–178
Peninsula de Llevant 145
Peninsula de la Victòria 134, 146–147
Penya des Migdia 146
personal safety 193
    bicycling 46, 175
    driving 45
Petra 168, 181–182, 185
petrol stations 44
pharmacies 191
Picasso, Pablo 63, 113
pilgrimage 22, 23, 102, 147, 169, 171
Pina 182
Platja El Mago 58
Platja de Palma 58
Platja d'es Port 166
police 193
politics and government 7, 35, 36
Pollença 140–143
    Cala Sant Vicenç 143
    Casa Museu Dionís Bennàssar 143

El Calvari 142
hotels 157
market 12, 142
Museu Martí Vicenç 142
Museu de Pollença 11, 142
Nostra Senyora dels Angels 141
Plaça Major 141–142
Pont Romà 143
Port de Pollença 141, 143, 144, 154, 157
Puig de Maria 142–143
restaurants 153–154
what to do 150–151
Pollença Festival 141, 151
Pollentia 133
Pont Romà 143
population 6
Porreres 171, 185–186
Port d'Alcúdia 133, 134, 144, 148
Port d'Andratx 97
Port de Pollença 141, 143, 144, 150–151, 54, 157
Port de Sóller 109, 121, 125
Port de Valldemossa 111
Portals Nous 15, 54
Portals Vells 58
Portitxol 57
Porto Cristo 151, 186
Porto Petro 162
Porto Pí 57
Portocolom 182
Pòrtol 23
post offices and postal services 194, 195
Pottery Museum 23
Princess Sofia Trophy 85
Procession of the Three Kings 85
public holidays 196
public transport
buses 40–41
disabilities, visitors with 48
taxis 47
trains 42
Puerto Portals 15, 58, 82
Puig d'es Teix 110
Puig d'Alaró 101, 116–117
Puig des Boc 147
Puig de Galatzó 101
Puig Major 6, 109, 117
Puig de Maria 142–143
Puig de Massanella 117, 118
Puig de Na Pòpia 106

Puig de Randa 169
Puig Roig 104
Puig de S'Alcadena 101, 116–117
Puig de Sant Salvador 167
Puig de Santa Eugènia 170
Puig Tomir 119
Puigpunyent 115, 122, 129
Pujada dels Misteris 104
Punta de Capdepera 136
Punta de n'Amer 136

R
radio 197
rainfall 188
Real Club Náutico 19, 21, 83
Ramis, Juli 113
Randa 182
refuges 120, 214
Refugi Muleta 120
Refugi Tossals Verd 120
Reial Cartoixa 111–113
religion 6, 104
religious festivals 22, 85, 143
see also pilgrimage
Renaixença 32
Reserva Puig de Galatzó 101, 122
restaurants
northeast Mallorca 152–154
Palma 86–89
Serra de Tramuntana 124–126
the south 180–183
words and phrases 217
Reüll, Bernat 112
rights of way 214
roba de llengües 142
rock climbing 101, 122, 204
romería see pilgrimage
royal family, Spanish 18, 19, 21, 58
Rubió, Joan 17, 33, 108
Rusinyol, Santiago 104
La Ruta de Pedra en Sec 21, 120

S
Sa Cabaneta 23
Museu del Fang 23
Sa Calobra 101
Sa Coma 97
Sa Cometa des Morts 103, 119
Sa Cova Blava 161

Sa Dragonera 6, 35, 43, 106–107
Cala Lladó 106
Cap des Llebeig 106
Cap de Tramuntana 106
Puig de Na Pòpia 106
Sá Mostra International Folklore Festival 123
Sa Pobla 139, 145
Can Planes 11, 139
Sa Ràpita 178
Sa Roca 139
Sa Rúa 85
Sa Taronja 120–121
Sa Torre 175
safari park 149
Sagrera, Guillem 63
sailing 11, 20, 21, 82, 120, 204
regattas 21, 85, 207
tuition 11, 82, 83, 121, 149, 150, 176, 178
sales tax 190
Salines de Llevant 166
Salvator, Archduke Ludwig 19, 32, 101
Sand, George 18, 110, 112, 197
sandals, Mallorcan 79, 122
Sant Agustí 179
Sant Antoni Abat 85
Sant Bartomeu 108
Sant Bartomeu Festival 179
Sant Elm 106
Sant Joan Baptista, Calvià 115
Sant Joan Baptista, Deià 98
Sant Miquel 166
Sant Sebastià 85
Santa Catalina 74, 75
Santa Catalina Thomàs 31, 113
Santa Eugènia 170, 178
Santa Margalida 145
Santa Maria del Camí 126, 129
Santanyí 162
Santuari de Cura 169
Santuari de Monti-Sion 171
Santuari de Sant Salvador, Artà 135
Santuari de Sant Salvador, Puig de Sant Salvador 167
Schiffer, Claudia 19, 35
schooner charter 150
Schumacher, Michael 19, 35

scooters 46
scuba diving and snorkelling 121, 123, 151, 176, 204
sea kayaking 121, 123, 204
segway tours 83
self-catering 213
Sencelles 170, 182–183
Serra de Llevant 6, 167
Serra de Tramuntana 6, 8–9, 15, 94–129
festivals and events 123
hotels 127–129
map 95
restaurants 124–126
sights 10–11, 96–113
walks and drives 114–119
what to do 120–123
Serra, Juniípero 31, 168
Sert, Josep Lluís 62, 67
Ses Païsses 135
Ses Salines 186
Ses Voltes 69
S'Esgleieta 123
S'Estaca 19, 32
Setmana Santa (Holy Week) 85, 151, 179
La Seu (Palma cathedral) 70–73
shopping 198–199
department and chain stores 199
markets see markets
opening hours 196, 199
Palma 78–79, 199
payment 199
sales tax 190
shopping malls and factory outlets 199
words and phrases 215–216
S'Hort del Rei 66
siesta 196
S'Illot des Porros 145
Simpson, Wallis 33
Sineu 167, 171, 178, 183
siurells 23, 139, 179
slingshot 23, 27
smoking etiquette 192, 201, 209, 213
Sóller 108–109
Banco de Sóller 108
Can Prunera 108
Cementeri 109
hotels and restaurants 126, 129
Jardí Botànic 109
Mercat Municipal 109

Modernism 108
Museu Balear de Ciències Naturals 109
Museu de Sóller 109
Plaça Constitució 108
Port de Sóller 109, 121, 125
railway station 108
Sant Bartomeu 108
trams 42, 109
vintage train 42
what to do 122–123
Sóller Pass 117
Sóller Tunnel 117
Son Boter 62
Son Corró 173
Son Marroig 101, 121
Son Real necropolis 144–145
Son Sant Joan airport 38
Son Servera 157
the south 9, 158–186
drive, walk and bicycle ride 170–175
festivals and events 179
hotels 184–186
map 159
restaurants 180–183
sights 11, 160–169
what to do 176–179
Spanish Civil War 34, 60
spas 205
speed limits 44
sports and activities 20–21, 202–204
archery 122
beaches 202
bicycling see bicycling
birdwatching 12, 20, 106, 117, 139
bullfighting 23, 82, 202
canyoning 123
fishing 123, 150, 176, 202
football 24, 82, 202
go-karting 84
golf 82, 83, 120, 121, 148, 149–150, 177, 202–203
hang-gliding 82, 148, 203
horse-riding 101, 121, 122, 148–149, 151, 177, 203–204
hot-air ballooning 149
kayaking 82, 120, 121, 123, 204
orienteering 122
rock climbing 101, 122, 204

sailing see sailing
scuba diving and snorkelling 121, 123, 151, 176, 204
swimming pools 204
tennis 24, 204
trotting races 82, 177, 204
walking and hiking see walking and hiking
water-skiing 83, 121
windsurfing 149, 150, 178, 204
zip-wire rides 101, 122
stamps 195
Stewart, Rod 18
submarine excursions 84
sun safety 191, 206
swimming pools 204

T
Talaia d'Albercutx 138
Talaia d'Alcúdia 146
Talaiotic people 27, 64
Talaiotic settlements
Capocorb Vell 163, 174
Ses Païsses 135
talaiots 27, 135, 163, 174
tap water 191
tapas 200, 201, 209
taxis 39, 47
Taylor, Elizabeth 138
Teatre Municipal 81
Teatre Principal 81
Teatre Romà 134
Teatro de Lloseta 121
telephones 194, 195
television 197
Temporada de Ballet de Mallorca 85
tennis 24, 204
tetanus 191
thalassotherapy 205
theatre 201
Artà Teatre 149
Auditori d'Alcúdia 148
Auditòrium Sa Màniga 149
Ses Voltes 69
Teatre Municipal 81
Teatre Principal 81
theme parks 84
time zones 188
Timoner, Guillem 167
tipping 190, 209
toilets 192
tolls 44

Torre dels Enagistes 167
Torre de Ses Animes 97, 114
Torrent de Lluc 118
Torrent de Pareis 101, 117
Torrent de Sant Jordi 143
Torrents Lladó, Joaquín 59
Torres, Salvador 135
tourism 7, 14–15, 33, 34
tourist information 196
Toy Museum 139
traditions 22–23
trains 42
Palma–Inca train 42
Sóller train 12, 42
Transfiguració del Senyor 135
travel
around Mallorca 40–47
to/from Mallorca 38–39
travel insurance 193
trotting races 82, 177, 204

U
Ustinov, Peter 18

V
Vall d'Orient 101
Valldemossa 31, 110–113
Casa Natal de Santa Catalina Thomàs 113
Chopin's cells 112
Costa Nord 19, 113
Ermita de la Trinitat 113
Guasp printing press 112
hotels 129
Museu Municipal 112–113
Palau del Rei Sanç 113
pharmacy 111
Reial Cartoixa 111–113
restaurants 126
what to do 123
vegetarian food 209
Vicenç, Martí 142
Villalonga, Llorenç 161
Vintage Car Rally 123
visas 189

W
walking and hiking 11, 12, 21, 203, 214
accommodation 120, 214
books and maps 214
country code 214
Dry Stone Route 21, 120
guided walks 151, 214
Nordic walking tours 148

rights of way 214
walking holidays 123, 214
see also walks
walks
Camel Rock 118–119
Costitx 172–173
Jewish Quarter, Palma 76–77
Modernist Palma 74–75
Peninsula de la Victòria 146–147
watchtowers 138, 146
water parks 58, 84, 148, 206
water-skiing 83, 121
Way of the Rosary 104
weather reports and warnings 188–189
Western Park 84
what to do
children's entertainment 206
entertainment and nightlife 200–201
festivals and events 207
health and beauty 205
northeast Mallorca 148–151
Palma 78–85
Serra de Tramuntana 120–123
shopping 198–199
the south 176–179
sports and activities 20–21, 202–204
wildlife 15, 101, 106, 161
see also birdwatching; nature reserves
windmills 75, 145
windsurfing 149, 150, 178, 204
wine festival 179
wine tours and tastings 115, 161, 176
wines 12, 24, 79
Winter in Majorca (George Sand) 18, 110, 112, 197

X
xeremies 170

Y
yacht charter 82, 149, 204
yachting see sailing

Z
zip-wire rides 101, 122

PICTURES

The Automobile Association wishes to thank the following photographers and organizations for their assistance in the preparation of this book.

Abbreviations for the picture credits are as follows – (t) top; (b) bottom; (l) left; (r) right; (c) centre; (AA) AA World Travel Library.

2 AA/T Carter;
3t AA/T Carter;
3c AA/K Paterson;
3b AA/T Carter;
4 AA/T Carter;
5 AA/T Carter;
6 AA/T Carter;
8t AA/T Carter;
8b AA/P Baker;
9 AA/T Carter;
10 AA/T Carter;
11l AA/T Carter;
11r AA/T Carter;
12l AA/K Paterson;
12r Photodisc;
13 AA/T Carter;
14 AA/T Carter;
15l AA/T Carter;
15r AA/T Carter;
16 AA/K Paterson;
17l AA/T Carter;
17r AA/T Carter;
18 J Reina/AFP/Getty Images;
19l AA/T Carter;
19r AA/T Carter;
20 AA/T Carter;
21l AA/J Cowham;
21r AFP/Getty Images;
22 IBATUR/M Munoz;
23l B Amengual/Alamy;
23r AA/T Carter;
24 AA/T Carter;
25 AA/T Carter;
26 AA/K Paterson;
27l AA/T Carter;
27r AA/T Carter;
28 AA/K Paterson;
29l Bridgeman Art Library;
29r Mary Evans;
30 The Stapleton Collection/ Bridgeman Art Library;
31l AA;
31r AA/T Carter;
32 AA/P Baker;
33l AA/T Carter;
33r Bettmann/Corbis;
34 AA/T Carter;
35l AA/T Carter;

35r AA/K Paterson;
36 AA/C Sawyer;
37 AA/T Carter;
38 AA/T Carter;
39 AA/T Carter;
40 AA/T Carter;
41 AA/P Baker;
42 AA/T Carter;
43 AA/C Sawyer;
46l AA/C Sawyer;
46r AA/T Carter;
47 AA/C Sawyer;
48 D Crausby/Alamy;
49 AA/T Carter;
50 AA/J Cowham;
56 AA/T Carter;
57 AA/T Carter;
59 AA/C Sawyer;
60 AA/T Carter;
61 AA/K Paterson;
62 AA/T Carter/Succession Miro/ ADAGP, Paris and DACS, London 2010;
63 AA/T Carter;
64 AA/K Paterson;
65 AA/T Carter;
66 AA/T Carter;
67 AA/C Sawyer;
68 D Kilpatrick/Alamy;
69 AA/T Carter;
70 AA/T Carter;
71 AA/T Carter;
73l AA/T Carter;
73r AA/T Carter;
74 AA/C Sawyer;
76 AA/T Carter;
78 AA/T Carter;
79 AA/T Carter;
80 LOOK Die Bildagentur der Fotografen GmbH/Alamy;
81 AA/T Carter;
82 AA/P Baker;
83 AA/K Paterson;
84 Travel Division Images/Alamy;
85 J Parker/Alamy;
86 AA/C Sawyer;
89 AA/C Sawyer;
90 AA/C Sawyer;

92 AA/C Sawyer;
93 AA/T Carter;
95 AA/T Carter;
96 AA/T Carter;
97 AA/T Carter;
98 AA/T Carter;
99 AA/K Paterson;
100 AA/T Carter;
101 AA/T Carter;
102 AA/K Paterson;
103l AA/T Carter;
103r AA/T Carter;
104 AA/J Cowham;
105 AA/K Paterson;
106 AA/K Paterson;
107 Spanish Tourist Board;
108 AA/K Paterson;
109 AA/T Carter;
110 AA/K Paterson;
111 AA/T Carter;
112l AA/T Carter;
112r AA/K Paterson;
113 AA/T Carter;
114 AA/K Paterson;
115 AA/T Carter;
116 AA/T Carter;
117 AA/C Sawyer;
118 AA/P Baker;
119 AA/P Baker;
120 AA/T Carter;
122 AA/T Carter;
124 AA/T Carter;
127 AA/T Carter;
130 AA/K Paterson;
132 AA/T Carter;
133 AA/T Carter;
135 AA/T Carter;
136 AA/T Carter;
137 Courtesy of Coves de Campanet Agua;
138 AA/T Carter;
139 AA/T Carter;
140 AA/K Paterson;
141 AA/K Paterson;
142 AA/K Paterson;
144 AA/T Carter;
145 Travel Division Images/Alamy;
146 AA/T Carter;

147 AA/C Sawyer;
148 LOOK Die Bildagentur der
Fotografen GmbH/Alamy;
150 AA/T Carter;
152 AA/T Carter;
155 AA/T Carter;
156 AA/T Carter;
158 AA/T Carter;
160 AA/T Carter;
161 AA/T Carter;
162 AA/T Carter;
163 AA/T Carter;
164 AA/K Paterson;
165 AA/K Paterson;
166l AA/K Paterson;
166r AA/T Carter;
167 AA/T Carter;
168 AA/T Carter;
169 AA/T Carter;
170 AA/C Sawyer;
172 AA/T Carter;
173 AA/T Carter;
174 R Barton;
175 R Barton;
176 AA/T Carter;
178 AA/T Carter;
179 Expuesto - N Randall/Alamy;
180 AA/T Carter;
183 Travel Division Images/Alamy;
184 AA/C Sawyer;
186l AA/T Carter;
186r LOOK Die Bildagentur der
Fotografen GmbH/Alamy;
187 AA/T Carter;
189 K Britland/Alamy;
190 AA/C Sawyer;
192 AA/T Carter;

194 Photodisc;
195 mediacolor's/Alamy;
196 AA/C Sawyer;
197 AA/K Paterson;
198 AA/T Carter;
199 AA/K Paterson;
200 AA/K Paterson;
201 AA/T Carter;
203 R Barton;
204 AA/T Carter;
205 AA/A Mockford & N Bonetti;
206l Travel Division Images/Alamy;
206r AA/K Paterson;
207t AA/K Paterson;
207b AA/K Paterson;
208 Courtesy of Punta Negra;
209 Courtesy of Cavall Bernat;
211t AA/C Sawyer;
211b Courtesy of Reco de Randa;
212 AA/C Sawyer;
213 AA/T Carter;
219 AA/T Carter.

Every effort has been made to trace the copyright holders, and we apologize in advance for any accidental errors. We would be happy to apply any corrections in the following edition of this publication.

CREDITS

Managing editor
Sheila Hawkins

Project editor
Parkside Publishing

Design
Catherine Murray

Picture research
Michelle Aylott

Image retouching and repro
Neil Smith, Jackie Street

Mapping
Maps produced by the Mapping Services Department of
AA Publishing

Main contributors
Robin Barton, Tony Kelly, Josephine Quintero

Updater
Josephine Quintero

Indexer
Marie Lorimer

Production
Lorraine Taylor

Published by AA Publishing, a trading name of AA Media Limited, whose registered office is
Fanum House, Basing View, Basingstoke, RG21 4EA. Registered number 06112600.
A CIP catalogue record for this book is available from the British Library.

ISBN 978-0-7495-6758-3

KeyGuide is a registered trademark in Australia and is used under license.
Colour separation by AA Digital Department
Printed and bound by Leo Paper Products, China

We believe the contents of this book are correct at the time of printing. However, some details, particularly prices, opening times and
telephone numbers do change. We do not accept responsibility for any consequences arising from the use of this book.
This does not affect your statutory rights. We would be grateful if readers would advise us of any inaccuracies they may encounter, or any
suggestions they might like to make to improve the book. There is a form provided at the back of the book for this purpose, or you can email us
at travelguides@theaa.com

A04201
Maps in this title are produced from mapping © MAIRDUMONT/Falk Verlag 2011.
Weather chart statistics supplied by Weatherbase © Copyright (2004) Canty and Associates, LLC.

Find out more about AA Publishing and the wide range of travel publications and services the AA provides by visiting our website at
theAA.com/shop

Thank you for buying this KeyGuide. Your comments and opinions are very important to us, so please help us to improve our travel guides by taking a few minutes to complete this questionnaire.

You do not need a stamp (unless posted outside the UK). If you do not want to cut this page from your guide, then photocopy it or write your answers on a plain sheet of paper.

Send to: **KeyGuide Editor, AA World Travel Guides**
FREEPOST SCE 4598, Basingstoke RG21 4GY

Find out more about AA Publishing and the wide range of travel publications the AA provides by visiting our website at www.theAA.com/bookshop

ABOUT THIS GUIDE

Which KeyGuide did you buy? ....

Where did you buy it?..

When? ....month .... year

Why did you choose this AA KeyGuide?
☐ Price ☐ AA Publication
☐ Used this series before; title
☐ Cover ☐ Other (please state)

Please let us know how helpful the following features of the guide were to you by circling the appropriate category: very helpful (VH), helpful (H) or little help (LH)

Feature			
Size	VH	H	LH
Layout	VH	H	LH
Photos	VH	H	LH
Excursions	VH	H	LH
Entertainment	VH	H	LH
Hotels	VH	H	LH
Maps	VH	H	LH
Practical info	VH	H	LH
Restaurants	VH	H	LH
Shopping	VH	H	LH
Walks	VH	H	LH
Sights	VH	H	LH
Transport info	VH	H	LH

What was your favourite sight, attraction or feature listed in the guide?

Page.................Please give your reason ....
....

Which features in the guide could be changed or improved? Or are there any other comments you would like to make?

....

ABOUT YOU

Name (Mr/Mrs/Ms)...

Address ....

....

....

....

Postcode.. Daytime tel nos...

Email...

Please only give us your mobile phone number/email if you wish to hear from us about other products and services from the AA and partners by text or mms.

Which age group are you in?
Under 25 ☐   25–34 ☐   35–44 ☐   45–54 ☐   55+ ☐

How many trips do you make a year?
Less than1 ☐   1 ☐   2 ☐   3 or more ☐

ABOUT YOUR TRIP

Are you an AA member?   Yes ☐ No ☐

When did you book?............. month................. year

When did you travel?.............month................. year

Reason for your trip?   Business ☐   Leisure ☐

How many nights did you stay? ....

How did you travel?   Individual ☐   Couple ☐   Family ☐   Group ☐

Did you buy any other travel guides for your trip? ....

If yes, which ones?...

Thank you for taking the time to complete this questionnaire. Please send it to us as soon as possible, and remember, you do not need a stamp (unless posted outside the UK).
AA Travel Insurance call 0800 072 4168 or visit www.theaa.com

Titles in the KeyGuide series:
Australia, Barcelona, Berlin, Britain, Brittany, Canada, China, Costa Rica, Croatia, Florence and Tuscany, France, Germany, Ireland, Italy, London, Mallorca, Mexico, New York, New Zealand, Normandy, Paris, Portugal, Prague, Provence and the Côte d'Azur, Rome, Scotland, South Africa, Spain, Thailand, Venice, Vietnam, Western European Cities.

The information we hold about you will be used to provide the products and services requested and for identification, account administration, analysis, and fraud/loss prevention purposes. More details about how that information is used is in our privacy statement, which you'll find under the heading "Personal Information" in our terms and conditions and on our website: www.theAA.com. Copies are also available from us by post, by contacting the Data Protection Manager at AA, Fanum House, Basing View, Basingstoke, Hampshire RG21 4EA.

We may want to contact you about other products and services provided by us, or our partners (by mail, telephone, email) but please tick the box if you DO NOT wish to hear about such products and services from us. ☐

AA Travel Insurance call 0800 072 4168 or visit www.theaa.com